MW00808466

Voices Raised in Protest

For Mel,

There are always
dissenters.

Stephanie
Bangarth

Stephanie Bangarth

Voices Raised in Protest
Defending Citizens of Japanese
Ancestry in North America, 1942-49

UBC Press / Vancouver and Toronto
University of Washington Press / Seattle

© UBC Press 2008

All rights reserved. No part of this publication may be reproduced, stored in a retrieval system, or transmitted, in any form or by any means, without prior written permission of the publisher, or, in Canada, in the case of photocopying or other reprographic copying, a licence from Access Copyright (Canadian Copyright Licensing Agency), www.accesscopyright.ca.

16 15 14 13 12 11 10 09 08   5 4 3 2 1

Printed in Canada on ancient-forest-free paper (100% post-consumer recycled) that is processed chlorine- and acid-free, with vegetable-based inks.

Library and Archives Canada Cataloguing in Publication

Bangarth, Stephanie, 1972-
Voices raised in protest : defending citizens of Japanese ancestry in North America, 1942-49 / Stephanie Bangarth.

Includes bibliographical references and index.
ISBN 978-0-7748-1415-7 (bound); ISBN 978-0-7748-1416-4

1. Japanese Canadians – Civil rights – History. 2. Japanese Americans – Civil rights – History. 3. Japanese Canadians – Evacuation and relocation, 1942-1945. 4. Japanese Americans – Evacuation and relocation, 1942-1945. 5. Co-operative Committee on Japanese Canadians – History. 6. American Civil Liberties Union – History. 7. Human rights advocacy – Canada – History. 8. Human rights advocacy – United States – History. I. Title.

E29.J3B36 2007   323.1195'6071   C2007-905793-4

Canadä

UBC Press gratefully acknowledges the financial support for our publishing program of the Government of Canada through the Book Publishing Industry Development Program (BPIDP), and of the Canada Council for the Arts, and the British Columbia Arts Council.

This book has been published with the help of a grant from the Canadian Federation for the Humanities and Social Sciences, through the Aid to Scholarly Publications Programme, using funds provided by the Social Sciences and Humanities Research Council of Canada.

Printed and bound in Canada by Friesens
Set in Stone by Robert Kroeger
Copy editor: Deborah Kerr
Proofreader: Sharron Wood
Indexer: David Luljak, Third Floor Research

UBC Press
The University of British Columbia
2029 West Mall
Vancouver, BC V6T 1Z2
604-822-5959 / Fax: 604-822-6083
www.ubcpress.ca

University of Washington Press
PO Box 50096
Seattle, WA 98145-5096, USA
www.washington.edu/uwpress

The battle of liberty must be fought in marginal cases and for unpopular minorities. If a vigorous democracy does not react when these minorities are attacked, then democracy will lose its vigour.

> *– F. Andrew Brewin, Legal Counsel, Co-operative Committee on Japanese Canadians*
> *February 1945*

Contents

Illustrations

Acknowledgments

I can still recall when I first learned about the incarceration of persons of Japanese ancestry in Canada during the Second World War. A first-year student at King's College at the University of Western Ontario, I was taking HIST 025E, a Canadian history survey taught by Dr. George Warecki. I was shocked, fascinated, perplexed. Little did I know then where my interest in that particular event would lead me.

The decision to work on the subject began innocently enough at a party in January 1996, with a suggestion from my graduate supervisor, Dr. James W. St. G. Walker, one of Canada's most esteemed historians of "race." It was his idea that the story of the incarceration needed to be told with an eye to agency and a focus on human rights activism. My years under his supervision were marked by intellectual challenge, encouragement, and scholarly debate of the best sort. I am deeply indebted to him for both his scholarship and his mentorship. The advice of Dr. Mike Howard and Dr. Karin MacHardy added important methodological elements to the study. I also learned so much from my co-student and dear friend Dr. Karolyn Smardz Frost, whose enthusiasm for her own significant study was a constant source of inspiration for me. Dr. Sandra Burt, Dr. Patricia E. Roy, Dr. John English, and Dr. David Murray offered invaluable critiques of earlier drafts of my work.

This study was also made possible through the assistance of a number of archivists, particularly the staff members at Library and Archives Canada, the United Church of Canada archives, and the Anglican Church of Canada archives. I enjoyed my time at the Presbyterian Historical Society in Philadelphia, the Butler Library at Columbia University, the Multicultural History Society of Ontario, and the McMaster University Archives. But my gratitude extends especially to the staff at the Seeley G. Mudd Manuscript Library of Princeton University, whose suggestions throughout my eight-month stay (2000-1) greatly enhanced the depth and breadth of this work. Their collegiality and friendliness made my time researching there very pleasant. Thanks, Dan Linke and staff! My appreciation also goes to Gretchen Oberfranc of the *Princeton University Library Chronicle* for suggesting that I contribute some of my research results and for including such wonderful illustrations in the article.

I am certainly indebted to the many individuals who heard parts of this study at various conferences, especially at the biennial meetings of the Association for Canadian Studies in the United States (ACSUS), and who expressed an interest in it. Thanks also to the following journals for their permission to use these works to inform sections herein: Stephanie D. Bangarth, "The Co-operative Committee on Japanese Canadians and the American Civil Liberties Union: Engaging Debate, 1942-1949," *Princeton University Library Chronicle* 63, 3 (Spring 2002): 496-533, and Bangarth, "Religious Organizations and the 'Relocation' of Persons of Japanese Ancestry in North America: Evaluating Advocacy," *American Review of Canadian Studies* 34, 3 (Fall 2004): 511-40.

The generosity of organizations also made this book possible. I am grateful for financial support from the Canada-U.S. Fulbright Program Foundation in particular, as well as the Social Sciences and Humanities Research Council of Canada, the Friends of the Princeton University Library, the Ontario Graduate Scholarship Program, King's University College, and the University of Waterloo.

Along the way and throughout, I am thankful to those whose kindness and generosity helped in the completion of this book. Dr. Joseph Kellerstein kept me sitting comfortably in my chair. Thanks also to Ab Gould (posthumously, sadly) and Betty Simpson, of Glencoe, Ontario. Lodging in the Ottawa area was always graciously offered by Sarah Baxter, Reena Dar, and Bill and Sue Carey. My brother, Greg, was always there for me when I needed a place to stay in Toronto. Dr. Jason Churchill, Dr. P. Whitney Lackenbauer, Dr. Ross Lambertson, Dr. Ruth Compton Brouwer, Dr. Patricia E. Roy, and Belinda Huang shared their expertise and their suggestions for further research. I am so very indebted to the anonymous reviewers who provided a conscientious and thorough interrogation of this work. As they challenged me to face its inadequacies, they also trumpeted its strengths. My editor, Emily Andrew; production editor, Anna Eberhard Friedlander; copy editor, Deborah Kerr; and others with UBC Press who helped bring this project to fruition were similarly enthusiastic and encouraging.

Finally, and with my deepest affection and love, I must thank my parents, Daniel and Josephine Bangarth, for their support in all the years of my life. My great-aunt Maria and my great-uncle Imre are as proud of me as I am of them. Lastly, I must acknowledge my wonderful husband, Julius Olajos. It is not easy to live with someone writing a dissertation and then preparing a manuscript for publication. I owe him more than I can possibly say.

Acronyms

ACC	Anglican Church of Canada Archives
ACLU	American Civil Liberties Union
AFL	American Federation of Labor
AFSC	American Friends Service Committee
BCSC	British Columbia Security Commission
CBC	Canadian Broadcasting Corporation
CCF	Co-operative Commonwealth Federation
CCJC	Co-operative Committee on Japanese Canadians
CCJC-AT	Co-operative Committee on Japanese Canadian Arrivals to Toronto
CCJC-MAC	Co-operative Committee on Japanese Canadians Papers, McMaster University Archives
CCL	Canadian Congress of Labour
CIO	Congress of Industrial Organizations
CJA	Canadian Japanese Association
CJC	Canadian Jewish Congress
CLAT	Civil Liberties Association of Toronto
CLAW	Civil Liberties Association of Winnipeg
CLDL	Canadian Labour Defense League
CRCIA	Committee for the Repeal of the Chinese Immigration Act
DEA	Department of External Affairs
DOCR	Defence of Canada Regulations
DOJ	Department of Justice
FBI	Federal Bureau of Investigation
FCCC	Federal Council of the Churches of Christ
FCSO	Fellowship for a Christian Social Order
FOR	Fellowship of Reconciliation
IPR	Institute of Pacific Relations Papers
JACD	Japanese American Committee for Democracy
JACL	Japanese American Citizens League

JACL-ADC	Japanese American Citizens League – Anti-discrimination Committee
JCCA	Japanese Canadian Citizens Association
JCCC	Japanese Canadian Citizens Council
JCCD	Japanese Canadian Committee for Democracy
JCCL	Japanese Canadian Citizens League
LAC	Library and Archives Canada
MP	Member of Parliament
NAACP	National Association for the Advancement of Colored People
NC-ACLU	Northern California American Civil Liberties Union
NCCLU	Northern California Civil Liberties Union
NCJW	National Council of Jewish Women
NCW	National Council of Women
NIAC	National Interchurch Advisory Committee on the Resettlement of Japanese Canadians
NJCA	Naturalized Japanese Canadian Association
NJCCA	National Japanese Canadian Citizens Association
NMEG	Nisei Mass Evacuation Group
PHS	Presbyterian Historical Society
PJBD	Permanent Joint Board of Defense
RCMP	Royal Canadian Mounted Police
S-ACLU	Seattle American Civil Liberties Union
SC-ACLU	Southern California American Civil Liberties Union
SCM	Student Christian Movement
UCC	United Church of Canada Archives
UDHR	Universal Declaration of Human Rights
USW	United Steelworkers of America
UWO	University of Western Ontario
VCC	Vancouver Consultative Council
VCCLU	Vancouver Canadian Civil Liberties Union
WIB	Wartime Information Bureau
WILPF	Women's International League for Peace and Freedom
WMS	Women's Missionary Society
WRA	War Relocation Authority

Voices Raised in Protest

Introduction

In 1970, Herbert Marx, a legal expert and former minister of justice in the Quebec provincial government, observed that "Nothing has stirred the disquietude of Canadians on civil liberties more than the treatment of Japanese Canadians in World War II. It is the skeleton in the closet that stalks out to haunt all our discussions on civil liberties."[1] In 1976, on the thirty-fourth anniversary of Executive Order 9066, which authorized the incarceration of Japanese Americans, President Gerald R. Ford issued a proclamation revoking that order. In the process, he stated, "We now know what we should have known then – not only was evacuation wrong, but Japanese-Americans were and are loyal Americans."[2] This book is intended to engage "the skeleton in the closet" by examining both the incarceration and deportation/expatriation policies in Canada and the United States. Contrary to President Ford's assertion, there were individuals and groups in North America, long overlooked in any comparative format, that disagreed with the actions of the government of the day. *Voices Raised in Protest* examines the nature and meaning of the opposition to these policies, principally the responses to expatriation in Canada and incarceration in the United States.

It is important to highlight the comparative experience because both Canada and the United States initially followed similar paths when it came to the persecution of persons of Japanese ancestry resident in each nation. An examination of dissent regarding these policies is of intrinsic importance, both for an understanding of the Second World War and its impact on Canadian and American society and for a sense of the evolution of human rights on a global scale. For twenty-first-century readers, it has far-reaching implications with respect to current debates over ethnic and racial profiling, the confinement of "enemy combatants," and whether governments can effect the right balance between national security and civil liberties in counterterrorism laws.

Speaking on 10 December 1988, forty years after the adoption of the

Universal Declaration of Human Rights, John Humphrey, constitutional expert and principal architect of this historic document, noted that "the achievement of 1948 was much greater than anybody would have dared to imagine at the time."[3] The Second World War period was important on many levels and would herald significant global societal change. Canada was no exception to this trend: in particular, its post-war era witnessed some preliminary, yet fundamental, reconsiderations of the concepts of democracy and equality, which included efforts to recognize and secure human rights. Human rights agitation in Canada had its basis in the protests of white and Japanese organizations against the persecution of the country's own citizens during the Second World War, in which Japanese Canadians on the west coast were incarcerated, relocated elsewhere across the country, and, in some cases, deported/expatriated later to Japan.

Between 1943 and 1946, select individuals, usually English Canadians and minority group activists, cautiously initiated coordinated campaigns to address the problem of racial discrimination in Canada. That the movement for justice for Japanese Canadians was dominated by an "Anglo" focus is underscored by the fact that even in Quebec the organizations supporting Japanese Canadians were comprised mainly of non-Francophones. But by mid-1945, Japanese Canadians could claim organized support from Canadians in all provinces, with the exception of those in Atlantic Canada.

Recent scholarship points to the federal government's policies of incarceration and deportation as having an impact on the "surge of egalitarian idealism" that took place in post-war Canada.[4] Although there was almost no opposition to the relocation of Japanese Canadians in 1942, their disfranchisement and expatriation mobilized dissent. Indeed, the campaign to obtain justice for persons of Japanese ancestry, especially with respect to the deportation and expatriation, represents Canada's earliest significant involvement with the discourse on human rights. The attention of advocates and their lobbying strategies moved beyond civil liberties and the call to respect "traditional British liberties" to a rhetoric that included the newly articulated ideals of human rights as expressed in the Atlantic Charter and later in the Charter of the United Nations.[5] Canadians were not alone, however, in moving to secure justice for persons of Japanese ancestry: nearly parallel government policies were being followed in the United States. Americans would also recognize the prejudice and injustice inherent in the treatment of persons of Japanese ancestry resident in their country.

A basic accounting of the similarities and differences in the situation of American and Canadian Nikkei (persons of Japanese descent in North America) sets forth something like this: In North America in general, the Japanese were subjected to discriminatory treatment upon arrival; they negotiated this impediment by clustering in "ethnic enclaves" on the west coast and increasingly became objects of suspicion, fear, and envy over the course of the early twentieth century. Following the 7 December 1941 attack on Pearl Harbor, both countries "evacuated" Japanese aliens, Japanese nationals, and their North American–born children from their west coasts and "relocated" them to inland camps on the basis of "military necessity," a then politically expedient term for historic racist animus. Both the US and Canada also developed policies that were used to defraud the Nikkei of their property and to encourage a more even "dispersal" of the population throughout the country. The policies diverged when the Canadian government expatriated Canadian citizens of Japanese ancestry and deported Japanese aliens. The Americans also deported some, but only those who renounced their American citizenship. Japanese Canadians were disfranchised; by virtue of the Bill of Rights, those Japanese Americans who had been born in the US were not. In addition, they were permitted to enlist and did so proudly in the 100th Infantry Battalion and the 442nd Regimental Combat Team. Throughout much of the war, however, their Canadian counterparts were prohibited from serving in the armed forces and thereby demonstrating their loyalty.[6]

These differences aside (there are others, as the following pages will reveal), both countries experienced the development of significant organized dissent regarding aspects of the above-noted policies. The American Civil Liberties Union (ACLU), the Co-operative Committee on Japanese Canadians (CCJC), religious groups, the media, organized labour, women's groups, and various individuals were all active in resisting government injustice to the Nikkei. The court cases launched in Canada and the US represented manifestations of this dissent in the justice system of each country. Persons of Japanese ancestry were also active in defending their own rights, establishing their own organizations, and working very closely with the above-listed groups.

This comparative review of wartime policies and post-war developments concerning the Nikkei examines a number of elements common to both countries: government decision making, Nikkei resistance, key interest groups, the role of the press, and cross-border connections and cooperation. It traces the development of the advocacy movement and the associated discourse that provided the moral, political, and legal foundations for dissent. It suggests that the contextual differences of the two countries shaped the divergent responses of these organizations. These developments occurred over the course of the Second World War period, although the American ordeal had largely concluded by 1945, whereas the Canadian struggle was then in its middle course. This is not incongruous; cross-border cooperation and awareness were long in existence, and basic policies were enacted at similar points in early 1942. Whereas American advocates could call upon constitutional protections and language, Canadians could not. Instead, throughout the latter half of the 1940s, they turned increasingly to the belief that human rights were universally applicable. Eventually, the idea of human rights made its way into the discourse espoused by Canadian advocates for persons of Japanese ancestry, a discourse that was distinct from that of their American contemporaries. The lack of an American-style bill of rights compelled Canadian advocates to look to the Atlantic Charter and the Charter of the United Nations to give their arguments meaning and substance. This does not suggest, however, that the Canadian experience heralded something more laudable: indeed, Canadians made a virtue out of necessity.

Furthermore, while Canadians began to depart from a British civil liberties discourse to a human rights discourse, and while American advocates remained wedded to a civil liberties discourse, the reality was somewhat more complex. Canadian and American dissent over the wartime treatment of the Nikkei was, at times, alike in its appeals to anti-Nazi rhetoric, anti-racism language, and frequent use of the language of "fair play" (usually prefaced by the term "British" or "American," depending on context). The commonalities of rhetoric and approach helped to unite activists in Canada and the United States, although two different "dialects" arose from this commonality: the British liberties approach and the American civil rights approach. In Canada, while a terminological shift from British civil liberties to human rights took place over the course of the 1940s, so too did a normative shift from a focus on discrimination (treating people differently) to equality (treating people equally).

Methodological Orientations

There is a tendency in ethnic studies to view the immigrant as "victim." Interestingly, writers, playwrights, musicians, and others have approached the wartime injustice to the Nikkei from a variety of avenues that avoid victimization. In "Kiri's Piano," noted Canadian folksinger James Keelaghan tells the fictionalized story of Kiri Ito, a Japanese Canadian woman who threw her piano into the sea before being transported to an incarceration camp. His is an introspective tale, blending history with poetry and song. In David Guterson's mystery novel *Snow Falling on Cedars,* a mixed-race community on an island in the Pacific Northwest is the backdrop against which the politics of race relations and the wartime incarceration are played out. More recently, *The Gull,* a Noh ghost drama by Canadian poet Daphne Marlatt, places an emphasis on healing within the Japanese Canadian community of Steveston. These and other non-scholarly works evoke the raw emotional sentiments and the drama of social injustice.[7] Indeed, the same can be said for Japanese American and Japanese Canadian writers and the explosion of evocative fictional and non-fictional accounts of the removal.[8]

Historians and other scholars have held fast to victimization, however: the oppressed suffering at the hand of the oppressor, helpless against the demands of the powerful, whether they be in the form of capitalist exploitation, prejudice, and/or government actions. This is certainly the case with some of the literature detailing the incarceration, where Japanese Canadians/Americans are often presented as unfortunate victims of a prejudiced government bureaucracy. Although this type of literature does make a solid contribution in revealing that racism is a part of Canadian and American history, its weakness is that Japanese Canadians/Americans are shown not to be responsible for their own history. Instead, they are lost in a sea of policy discussions, mere bystanders in a particular historical account. The victimization thesis was once popular among ethnic historians, but recent studies have shown this approach to be extremely limiting. Indeed, many fields of ethnic studies now successfully employ the "subjects of history" methodology.[9] To this end, *Voices Raised in Protest* agrees with Roger Daniels' appeal in *Asian America: Chinese and Japanese in the United States since 1850* for scholars to focus on "what these people did rather than what was done to them."[10] Thus, although this study explains the role of Anglo-Canadians in the development of human rights rhetoric, it also demonstrates that Japanese Canadians can and should share equally in this recognition.

Increasingly, social historians have concentrated their attention on the wartime experiences of those Nikkei who bore the brunt of American and Canadian government policy. Historians have also examined the varied, and often contradictory, strategies that the incarerated developed in order to maintain their sense of dignity in the very undignified environment of the camps.[11] Additionally, the later movements for redress (1980s) and the revival of the Japanese American and Japanese Canadian communities have attracted scholars' consideration.[12] Nevertheless, these important spotlights on the struggles and the persecution of North America's people of Japanese ancestry should not induce historians and others to overlook those uncelebrated Canadians and Americans who supported them during the war. There were "cracks in the consensus [of racism]," as Robert Shaffer notes.[13]

Highlighting the groups and individuals who promoted the rights of Japanese Americans and Japanese Canadians should not be interpreted as an attempt to play down the nature of racism in North America at the time, or to minimize the meaning of the incarceration and expatriation. On the contrary, concentrating on this aspect of incarceration and expatriation serves only to underscore the failure of democracy in North America and of its political leadership and supporting populace. That there were public debates and individuals who were appalled at the policies of their respective countries weakens the excuse that the administrations of President Franklin Delano Roosevelt and Prime Minister William Lyon

Mackenzie King avoided moral conflict because they were not confronted with alternative views.[14] Indeed, opposition was voiced loudly and publicly in early 1942 in the United States. Opposition was certainly more muted in Canada, but those who voiced their criticisms of government policy should not be completely disregarded.

Although both Canadian and American historians have offered a variety of explanations for the causes of the incarceration, they show remarkable unity in their belief that few Americans or Canadians opposed the removal or sought to protect the rights of Nikkei citizens or non-citizens. Many textbook accounts of the incarceration stress this view, as does some of the literature on removal and incarceration.[15] When scholars have referred to supporters of Nikkei rights, they qualify their comments, noting these as exceptional cases or as compromised and uneasy support.[16] Richard Drinnon, for example, cites the American Civil Liberties Union (ACLU) and its leader, Roger Baldwin, in their concordance with Roosevelt's policy![17]

Of course, some concerned Canadians and Americans did oppose aspects of the policies enacted by their governments, if not by action, then at least in principle. The dissenters even included Jews and blacks, both historically disadvantaged groups in North America with respect to civil liberties. According to Robert Shaffer, socialists, left/liberals, academics, Protestant organizations, and African Americans opposed the incarceration to varying degrees, primarily because they believed that victory in the war would be seriously flawed if the US did not treat minority populations as equal allies in the fight against tyranny at home and abroad.[18] Cheryl Greenberg maintains that organizations representing both Jewish and African American groups realized that the rights of Japanese Americans could be closely linked with their own, but that a lapse of their "usual" sensitivity to discrimination was ironic at a crucial time for civil rights in the United States. Although Greenberg downplays Jewish and African American opposition to President Roosevelt's executive order, her work is nevertheless useful in outlining the pertinent debates on this issue by representatives from these two groups. The reaction of religious bodies to the removal policy, and the involvement of various religious organizations in this regard, has received only a modicum of scholarly attention.[19] Within the context of a local history framework, Ellen Eisenberg details the multi-levelled opposition to incarceration in Portland, San Francisco, and Seattle.[20] More sufficiently discussed has been the role of the ACLU in the removal question, especially in general histories of this group and in biographies and autobiographies of its members.[21]

Little popular awareness of wartime dissent and rights activism exists in Canada. In *The Politics of Racism*, Ann Gomer Sunahara devotes a single chapter to Canadian opposition to deportation, painting in a broad fashion both white and Japanese groups who were active in the campaign.

In *The Canadian Japanese in World War II*, Forrest LaViolette provides some references to wartime dissent and rights activism. For detailed information on the Co-operative Committee on Japanese Canadians (CCJC), the only sources are a chapter in a larger work by Ross Lambertson, a doctoral dissertation by Peter Nunoda, and a Master's thesis by Sidney Olyan. Only CCJC member Rabbi Abraham Feinberg left his autobiography for researchers; source material on other CCJC members such as Irving Himel and Andrew Brewin must be gleaned from primary and secondary works.[22]

Only recently have the efforts of Canada's early human rights community attracted the attention of scholars. Herbert Sohn and, later, John Bagnall and Brian Howe have explored the nature of human rights legislation in Ontario, in particular, and the evolution of the public philosophies that underlined the incremental changes in public policy on human rights in Canada generally.[23] Other scholars have concentrated on Canadian libertarian rights, with mention of various groups in the civil liberties community.[24] More promising directions have been taken by Ross Lambertson and James W. St. G. Walker, who, to varying degrees, highlight how certain human rights groups operated within the economic, ideological, and institutional context of their times. In his four case studies of legal challenges to race in Canadian law, Walker demonstrates how discriminatory policies directed towards African Canadians, Jews, Chinese, and South Asians encouraged activists to pressure government officials and institutional bodies for legislative reform.[25] In all four cases, constituent organizations rallied behind the challenger, and thus served symbolically as community causes. Lambertson's work is also useful in that he traces the interplay of various individuals, groups, and institutions as they affected human rights reform in the early post-war period. Lambertson suggests that on several occasions these broad-ranging coalitions had a major impact on government policy, even though the community itself was divided in ideological, geographical, class, and functional ways.[26] In the case of the Canadian removal and deportation, these explorations have yet to be the primary focus of a book.

Other scholars have added to the growing literature on the social origins of the campaigns for human rights in post-war Ontario by specifically highlighting the direct involvement of minority groups in the quest for legislation that would outlaw discrimination on the basis of race, religion, ancestry, and national origin in employment, housing, military service, and the sale of property. They make important observations concerning the similarity of human rights campaigns in post-war Ontario and those in the United States. The success of many of these campaigns was based on the application of American organizational and tactical methods, with Canadian adaptations, as Carmela Patrias and Ruth Frager note. This Intergroup Relations Movement, as it has been termed, received the attention of American scholars such as Stuart Svonkin and Philip Gleason.[27] This study will demonstrate that even as Canadian advocates looked to developments and groups in the United States for guidance, a "Canadian" solution was eventually adopted.

Comparative Orientations

An examination of some of the representative Canadian and American scholarly works on the Nikkei incarceration also reveals little comparison of the actions in Canada with those in the United States. Roger Daniels has managed to maintain near exclusivity in this respect, with the publication of *Concentration Camps: North America* and a few review articles.[28] This is astonishing, especially since both nations maintained, at least in principle, very similar policies. Following the bombing of Pearl Harbor, government policy made borders almost irrelevant as Canada, the US, and countries in South America all restricted the movements of their resident Japanese population. This was a continent-wide phenomenon that is rarely presented as such by scholars. Later in the war, as policies diverged, the border became relevant again.

The available sources also lend themselves to a comparative approach. Clear examples demonstrate that Canadians and Americans were aware, to varying degrees, of what was going on in the neighbouring nation. The significant amounts of north-south document and letter exchanges and cooperation are good examples of this. The ACLU files in the Mudd Manuscript Library at Princeton University contain several letters exchanged between Roger Baldwin, ACLU president, and Andrew Brewin, CCJC lawyer. Mike Masaoka of the Japanese American Citizens League and George Tanaka of the Japanese Canadian Citizens Association also exchanged letters throughout 1945 and 1947. Insofar as they could in the early days of 1942, the Canadian and American governments maintained policies that were as similar as possible and kept in touch on that basis. Even religious groups attempted transnational cooperation, with the Home Missions Council and the Foreign Missions Conference of the Presbyterian Church of North America holding an informal conference between Canadian and American representatives. Newspapers, especially those operated by and for the Nikkei themselves, were well aware of events as they unfolded on both sides of the border.

Terminological Orientations

This study recognizes and explores the issue of context in analyzing the discourse employed by the various groups and individuals in their campaigns. Throughout the period examined, a profound change occurred in the conceptualization of "rights." The evaluation of who had a right and how it should be fulfilled underwent a considerable degree of redefinition towards the end of the war and immediately following its conclusion. It seems prudent to clarify the conceptual morass of terms such as "civil liberties," "civil rights," "human rights," "egalitarian," and "libertarian rights."[29] For the purposes herein, the terms will be employed as the participants themselves used them.

Essential constitutional differences provide the foundation for understanding how advocates came to advance their arguments. The 1867 British North America Act, Canada's foundational document, makes no specific reference to human rights or fundamental liberties. The traditional British term "civil liberties" was the most widely used descriptor of all rights and liberties in Canada before 1945; it included such liberties as were guaranteed to the individual by law and custom, as well as such cherished notions as freedom of expression, voting rights, mobility rights, and legal rights.[30] The term "civil rights" requires defining, as it contains a great deal of conceptual baggage, largely due to its American usage. In the US, it pertains to the rights of a person by virtue of citizenship, or to rights assured by the Thirteenth and Fourteenth Amendments of the American Constitution. It is not interchangeable with the notion of "civil liberties." In the Canadian lexicon, the term "civil rights" has a particular constitutional meaning and is referred to only in connection with the property rights that are included in section 92(13) of the British North America Act, which lists provincial powers such as the right to enter freely into a contractual agreement, to own or lease property, and to sue for breach of duty owed. Additionally, a right is an advantage conferred and protected by law, granted to an individual; it often implies some form of corresponding duty on the part of another. A liberty is what one may do without legal impediment.[31]

In Canada, until the 1982 passage of the Charter of Rights and Freedoms, considerable disagreement occurred over which level of government was responsible for legislating in the matter of civil liberties. Much of that disagreement centred on the adoption of egalitarian rights. Libertarian rights and egalitarian rights are normally used as classifications of civil liberties. Libertarian rights refer to the rights to free speech, legal counsel, and property ownership, among others. Egalitarian rights, in a classical liberal interpretation, refer to the right to equal protection of the law. In the post-war period, the scope of egalitarian rights moved to encompass the right to state protection against discrimination by public and private individuals against persons because of race, colour, creed, religion, or national origin. The evolution of egalitarian civil liberties comprises what one scholar has referred to as the "modern" stage of this definition.[32] In the United States, however, civil liberties are protected by the Bill of Rights; these include freedom of speech, the right to privacy, freedom of and from religion, due process, and the right to vote, among others.[33]

The prevailing contemporary notion of human rights is derived from an acceptance of "natural rights" theory, as expounded by such liberal philosophers as John Locke. With the advent of the Universal Declaration of Human Rights (1948), the term "human rights" became the universal label for all manner of rights and freedoms, both individual and collective,[34] egalitarian and libertarian. These belong to all people by virtue of their membership in the human race and are generally defined as those rights that are inherent in our nature; that are inalienable, regardless of legal jurisdiction; and that are both legally and morally justifiable. Individual human rights encompass the claim to all that constitutes a desirable life. By contrast, collective human rights, such as the right of Aboriginal peoples to national self-determination, can be exercised only by a collectivity. Although human rights emphasize civil and political rights, today they have also come to highlight economic and social entitlements, such as the right to a living wage.[35] This study will focus on the development of individual human rights and civil liberties as they relate to the function and purpose of the involved advocacy groups within the context of the emerging human rights community in Canada and the United States.[36]

It should also be remembered that my use of the term "internment" does not suggest an equating of experiences with the Jewish internment and concentration camps that were established in Europe at this time by the Nazis. In fact, only about 750 Japanese Canadians and Japanese nationals were actually interned (in the exact sense of the word) at a camp near Angler, Ontario. In the United States, nearly eighteen thousand Japanese Americans were segregated at Tule Lake, a camp that began as a relocation centre in 1942 but became a segregation centre in 1943. Yet, as Roger Daniels has noted, "words do matter." Daniels has made an interesting case for the use of the term "incarceration" instead of "internment," arguing that the former is accurate whereas the latter is misleading and inappropriate. He notes that, while the wartime internment of enemy aliens followed the rules established in both American and international law, Japanese Americans were placed in army and War Relocation Authority camps by unlawful means.[37] The terms "evacuation" and "evacuees," though employed by some researchers, will rarely appear in this study because they do not accurately describe what was experienced by the 130,000 Japanese North Americans during the Second World War and because many persons of Japanese ancestry find them offensive and misleading. Instead, "incarceration" and "imprisonment," "relocation" and "removal," are employed, following the guidelines proffered by Daniels and Tetsuden Kashima. If this appears confusing, it is because no consensus yet exists on an acceptable vocabulary for the entire operation.[38] Additionally, I eschew the term "repatriation" in reference to Canadian and American citizens of Japanese ancestry, using the more accurate and appropriate "expatriation" whenever applicable. The deportation of disloyal aliens and the exile of unoffending citizens, as CCJC lawyer F. Andrew Brewin pointed out in a case before the Judicial Committee of the Privy Council, are two different issues. The former is recognized by international law, whereas the latter is beyond the constitutional power of the US Congress and, in the words of Brewin himself, was "never found necessary in the gravest emergency by the Parliament of Great Britain."[39] At the time, however, the government argued that it possessed the authority to "deport or exile or banish aliens or subjects or citizens of the state and to deprive them of citizenship."[40] Both the Supreme Court and the Judicial Committee of the Privy Council vindicated this position on the grounds that the government could do whatever it liked under the War Measures Act and Transitional Powers Act. This was due to the principle of parliamentary supremacy, as practiced in Canada, whereby a legislature is able to pass laws provided they do not violate the federal-provincial division of powers (although the 1982 Charter of Rights and Freedoms places some limitations on this matter). After the Second World War, common law precedents and constitutional traditions placed the responsibility of safeguarding fundamental freedoms within parliamentary jurisdiction, instead of within the courts or provincial legislatures. Although the courts in the United States served as a check on the powers of elected representatives, under the British system that Canada inherited, Parliament reigned supreme. It is interesting to note the nearly parallel Tokyo and Nuremberg trials, which dealt with the charges of deportation of civilians on racial grounds. The Charter of the United Nations, upon which these charges were based, refers to such deportation as a crime against humanity. Although the charter is politically binding on Canada, international law does not normally override the sovereignty of the state, including Canadian parliamentary supremacy. The significant degree of opposition to Canadian policies, however, indicates that international principles regarding human rights had secured a place of importance in the resolve of many activists. Thus, the wisdom of the Supreme Court of Canada must be scrutinized, even in light of the principle of parliamentary supremacy.

Lastly, some Japanese terms should also be clarified. First-generation Japanese Canadians and Japanese Americans are referred to as the Issei. The second generation is known as the Nisei; the third is called the Sansei. The Japanese refer to themselves collectively as Nikkei, and this term will be used in place of "citizens of Japanese ancestry in North America" or "Japanese Americans and Japanese Canadians." It applies to any person of Japanese ancestry in North America, and it includes both immigrant and successive generations.

Thematic Orientations

Five thematically based chapters comprise the essence of this book. Each chapter isolates the manner in which the lead groups, the associated groups, minorities, and the justice system in Canada and the United States approached the "Japanese problem" and advocacy. Consequently, the reader may experience periodic feelings of déjà vu as some events and issues are examined in relation to the specific actors mentioned previously in different contexts. Chapter 1 provides the necessary framework of the policies enacted by the Canadian and American governments in relation to Nikkei incarceration and deportation during the Second World War. It adds to the existing scholarly literature by exploring some of the similarities in policy choices pursued by the Canadian and American governments. Notably, this chapter also chronicles the nature of the cooperation among Canadian and American government policy makers in their attempts to pursue what they viewed as a practicable coincidence of policies, suggesting that interest was generally one-sided on the part of Canadian bureaucrats. In order to understand how and why advocates identified these government policies as problematic, this chapter examines how racial discrimination and human rights came to be useful concepts in their rhetoric.

Both Chapters 2 and 3 address the relative paucity of sources regarding the incarceration and expatriation of the Nikkei and the nature of the associated advocacy movement. Chapter 2 reviews the CCJC and the ACLU in terms of their organizational history, their membership, and their efforts on behalf of Japanese Canadians and Japanese Americans. The character of the CCJC and ACLU membership had a significant impact on how each group functioned in the interest of the Nikkei. In particular, this chapter places great emphasis on how the CCJC and the ACLU defined and articulated their opposition to government policies dealing with the "Japanese problem." It demonstrates that the discourse utilized by the CCJC differed significantly in terms of its focus from that of the ACLU.

Chapter 3 identifies other groups and individuals who expressed an interest in attaining justice for persons of Japanese ancestry. In both Canada and the United States, these were numerous and included many religious organizations, civil liberties groups, student and youth groups, and the media. This chapter also evaluates the interconnections between these groups and the ACLU and the CCJC, the main advocacy groups, as well as with the government. Having allies in the government bureaucracy, or, at the very least, obtaining the recognition of government officials, was as important to the ACLU and the CCJC as achieving the support of other interested organizations. In both chapters, the rhetoric used by Canadian advocates over the course of the 1940s is analyzed and compared with the American rhetoric to demonstrate how human rights principles gradually permeated the Canadian discourse.

Chapter 4 highlights the role of Japanese Americans and Japanese Canadians who were active in the campaign to secure justice for their own communities. In many respects, their struggles to achieve representation were very similar; however, the ways in which they acted as agents, whether individually or collectively, differed. Although Nikkei individuals eventually assumed advocacy roles, their cooperation with and support from organizations such as the CCJC and the ACLU, whose members came from largely "respectable" white, middle-class backgrounds, was a necessary means to an end. Nevertheless, persons of Japanese ancestry must claim partial credit for their contribution to human rights discourse in North America. Additionally, this chapter outlines the responses of other minority groups to the incarceration and dispersal and to the continuation of racially discriminatory policies against Japanese Americans and Japanese Canadians.

The actions of both white and Japanese advocates culminated in cases that were appealed to each nation's highest courts. Chapter 5 investigates the legal briefs submitted by the ACLU and the CCJC in an effort to determine the substance of their advocacy in relation to civil liberties and human rights. It also dissects the legal judgments rendered by the US Supreme Court, the Supreme Court of Canada, and the Judicial Committee of the Privy Council. The decisions delivered in the highest courts of Canada and the United States reveal much about the nature of civil liberties, human rights, and the divisions within each society over how to consider the treatment of persons of Japanese ancestry.

There were many different components to the broad mosaic of advocacy for the Nikkei. Religious groups, the media, intellectuals, liberals, and minority organizations combined to oppose the racially discriminatory policies enacted by Ottawa and Washington. Collectively in the United States, these voices loudly proclaimed the need to respect the Bill of Rights. This tradition of appealing to a constitutional document was not available to Canadian advocates; nor, in the early years of the war, was there any emerging consensus to which advocates could appeal in proclaiming their opposition. Drawing on the experiences of their American counterparts, but mainly creating their own path, some Canadians would appeal to a new concept dawning in international thought, that of "human rights." This important campaign would provide the basis for other quests encouraging the protection of individuals from religious and racial discrimination in Canada.

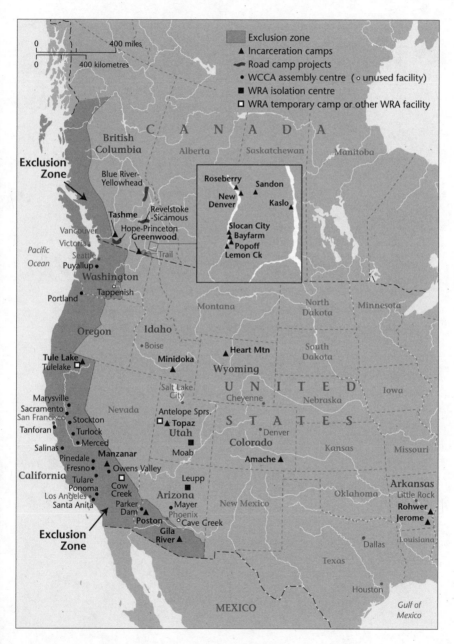

North American incarceration and exclusion zones.
Map by Eric Leinberger.

1

A Practicable Coincidence of Policies?

> Perhaps the most crucial problem of our time is the problem
> of race. With the emergence of the new nations of the
> under-developed world after the Second World War, with the
> rise of the civil rights movement in the US, and racial problems
> in our own country, we are forced to look at our basic attitudes
> and presuppositions.
>
> –Grace MacInnis, "Background Material re:
> Treatment of Japanese Canadians, 1941-47"

The contrasting implications of race and ethnicity and the Second World War were nowhere more clearly revealed than in a group that embodied the issues pointed out by Grace MacInnis: persons of Japanese ancestry resident in North America. Although various restrictions targeted many minority groups, it was the wartime plight of Japanese Canadians and Japanese Americans that piqued the interest of advocates in both nations. Canadians and Americans of Japanese ancestry, both native-born and naturalized, had suffered a multitude of injustices based on race since they arrived in North America in the late nineteenth century. The policies enacted during the Second World War, however, were extreme and seriously challenged many North Americans' views about their democratic institutions.

This chapter provides historical background for US and Canadian government policies as they pertain to the incarceration and deportation of the Nikkei. It also explores the level of coordination between the two governments as they attempted to pursue similar policies. In reality, Canadian bureaucrats paid much closer attention to the activities of the Americans, not unlike the Canadian advocates who took their cue from American rights organizations. This chapter also describes the ideas of "race" and rights as these terms underwent a meaningful reconsideration during the 1940s. This, too, provides context for the motivations of and rhetoric employed by Canadian and American activists, and for the generally approving attitude that most advocates harboured towards the assimilationist goals of relocation policy.

The Nikkei and the 49th Parallel

The history of the Nikkei in the United States is remarkably similar to that of their Canadian counterparts. In both countries, the first Japanese immigrants had arrived by the 1870s, quickly establishing communities on the Pacific coast. There they encountered a constant fear dating from the 1860s that an East Asian power – usually, but not always, Japan – would at some point invade and take over the continent.[1]

In both countries, the demographic impact of the Japanese followed a similar pattern: Japanese immigrants tended to cluster in the developing Pacific coast regions. From the 1870s to the 1950s, fewer than 350,000 Japanese emigrated to North America; of that number, some 275,000 went to the United States, whereas some 40,000 chose Canada. The numbers here are complicated by the nature of transnational movements between Canada, the US, and Japan. In the continental United States, the Japanese never exceeded more than 1.7 percent of the Pacific coast population. In Canada, the figure was slightly higher but no more than 3.2 percent of British Columbia's total population.[2] In actuality, the Japanese presence in North America was minimal.

Although population and settlement patterns were very similar in the United States and Canada, the legal status of Japanese immigrants and their children differed markedly in the two countries. In the United States, Asians were considered aliens; therefore, under the federal naturalization statute of 1870, which limited the right of naturalization to white persons and persons of African descent, they were ineligible for citizenship. Because voting in federal and state elections was contingent upon citizenship, Japanese immigrants – the Issei – were denied the vote. Several western states even prevented aliens from possessing, purchasing, or leasing land; these measures remained in place until they were extended to the Nisei, the American-born children of the Issei. The courts then moved to strike down these statutes, since the Fourteenth Amendment mandated that all persons born in the United States were citizens (and allowed to vote) and that no state could "deprive any person of life, liberty, or property, without due process of law." In striking down the infamous California Alien Land Law, the courts maintained that the Nisei had a right to own property, and, more significantly, that they had a natural right to have their parents as guardians of that property.[3]

The situation of the Nikkei in Canada with respect to citizenship, however, varied from that in the United States. The right of naturalization for Asian immigrants was subject to no federal constraint, and several thousand Japanese immigrants became naturalized Canadian citizens. However, neither they nor their Canadian-born children could vote in British Columbia, the province in which more than 90 percent of the Canadian Nikkei lived. Exclusion from the provincial voters' list barred them from voting federally as well. In 1895, the Provincial Voters Act had been amended such that "no Chinaman, Japanese or Indian shall have his name placed on the Register of Voters for any Electoral District."[4] In October

1900, Tomekichi Homma challenged the law when he applied to have his name added to the voters' list for Vancouver. When his application was refused, he filed a lawsuit disputing the decision and the offending clause of the act. He was supported, albeit variously, by members of the Japanese immigrant community in Vancouver but by no one else. The case would make its way to the Judicial Committee of the Privy Council, where the amendment to the Provincial Voters Act was upheld. There was a slight exception to the act. From 1931 to 1941, BC Nikkei veterans of the Canadian Expeditionary Force from the First World War could vote. Fewer than 100 individuals were so affected. The exclusion from the franchise rendered the Nikkei politically powerless, a fact that served to further isolate them from Canadian society.[5]

When Japan attacked Pearl Harbor on 7 December 1941, anti-Japanese forces in North America had the excuse they needed to rid the west coast of a loathed population. The very nature of the attack – its "treacherous" manner and "sneak" method of execution – seemed to underscore the long-standing charges against the resident Japanese that were entertained by many Canadians and Americans, especially on the west coast. Examples of newspaper incitement of racial violence appeared thereafter. Although distinctions were made between "good" and "bad" Germans, the media seldom differentiated between the Japanese. Tensions were high on the coast, and rumours abounded.

The media, however, were not alone in creating and promoting panic and confusion. Politicians, government officials, and some members of the military, particularly in the United States, also contributed to the charged atmosphere in the days and weeks immediately following Pearl Harbor. Prior to the attack, Culbert L. Olson, Democratic governor of California, asserted that, in the event of war with Japan, Japanese Americans were entitled to all rights and freedoms; he pointed out that equal protection under the law was a "basic tenet" of American government. After Pearl Harbor, Olson told the press that he was considering ordering all Japanese, whether aliens or citizens, to observe house arrest "to avoid riot and disturbance." So much for equal protection of the law. The Canadian Legion alleged that the Japanese in British Columbia held rejoicing parties when Hong Kong fell, and a Victoria MP capped his argument for relocation by referring to Pearl Harbor as evidence that citizenship meant nothing to the Nikkei: "blood is thicker than water."[6] The demand for incarceration arose from an artificially created and manipulated situation; it was a means to an end based on racial animosity and economic and political promotion. It was a racial action because, even after the entire Japanese population on the west coast had been uprooted and incarcerated, further repressive measures were taken, such as the sale of property, that had nothing to do with military security. Additionally, as this chapter will reveal, the fact that the majority of Hawaiian Nikkei were not incarcerated also belied the "military necessity" reasoning.

The decision to relocate all Japanese Canadians was not made overnight; nor was it reached without confusion, as one writer indicated in her memoir of the ordeal: "The federal government has been at a loss, not knowing exactly how to deal with us Japanese in Canada. Orders keep changing without any guiding principle."[7] In fact, the relocation unfolded incrementally, in a series of ad hoc steps taken by William Lyon Mackenzie King's Liberal government. It began with the registration of all Japanese non-citizens in British Columbia, followed by the arrest and internment of thirty-eight who were allegedly dangerous to national security. In the spring and summer of 1941, all Nikkei, whether citizens or not, were required to undergo the registration process and to carry their registration cards at all times. In December 1941, after the attack on Pearl Harbor, twelve hundred Japanese-owned fishing boats were impounded, and the movements of their owners were monitored and restricted by the RCMP. On 5 January 1942, the final step in this initial phase of the relocation policy began – a federal Standing Committee on Orientals called for the "internment" of all male Japanese Canadians of military age. Three days later, a conference of federal and provincial politicians, as well as military and police officials, met to discuss the situation on the west coast. On 14 January, Order-in-Council P.C. 365 announced that all male Japanese nationals between eighteen and forty-five were to be removed from the BC coast. On 24 February, when these partial measures were not enough to quell loud anti-Japanese voices in British Columbia and across Canada, King announced a policy, under Order-in-Council P.C. 1486, of total removal of all Nikkei, without distinction as to alien or citizen status, from the 100-mile protected zone of the west coast for conditions of military necessity.[8] Thus, the initial phase was completed. The relocation was not an original idea. Anti-Japanese elements on the west coast had been advocating some sort of similar measure for years. British Columbia, as one scholar noted, was "the Canadian problem child in so far as discriminatory legislation is concerned."[9]

Although the removal policy bore the unmistakable imprint of west coast opinion, the government of the day cannot be completely absolved from blame. King and the members of his government were products of their times and certainly believed in current racial ideology. Nevertheless, there was no military need for the removal, and Canadian military officials and the RCMP disagreed strongly with King's government that it was necessary. The Japanese population of British Columbia was a mere 2.7 percent of the provincial total, but the issue was with the heavy concentration patterns and the creation of "ethnic ghettos" in the urban centres. Not all the Japanese concentrations were in urban areas, however.

Significant clusters existed in the Lower Mainland fishing village of Steveston and in several locations in the Fraser Valley. In the end, the Canadian relocation policy involved over twenty-one thousand Nikkei, representing more than 90 percent of the entire Japanese population in Canada. Of those, almost four thousand would be "repatriated" to Japan, or, more accurately, in the case of Canadian citizens of Japanese ancestry, expatriated. Of the remaining seventeen thousand, only about four thousand returned to the west coast; the remainder resettled east of the Rockies.[10]

Many Japanese American businessmen were forced to close their stores in order to comply with the "evacuation." This store at the corner of 13th and Franklin Streets in Oakland, California, displays the owner's feelings on 8 December 1941, in the aftermath of Pearl Harbor.
Courtesy US National Archives and Records Administration, photo no. 210-G-C519

From September 1939 to 8 December 1941, the United States remained officially uninvolved in the war, although it was engaging in an "undeclared war" by participating in a "lend-lease" program with Britain, and later, with the Soviet Union. Thus, while the war was pursued in this manner, the American government applied the same rules to its Japanese citizens as it did to its other citizens. For example, Japanese Americans were subject to the draft, accepted for military service, and given reserve commissions. Additionally, all aliens, including Germans and Italians, who were in the United States as of 1940 were required to register and carry identification papers. Immediately after the war broke out, the Japanese American Citizens League (JACL) wired President Roosevelt pledging its support and affirming the loyalty of all Japanese Americans.[11] The 7 December 1941 attack on Pearl Harbor changed the rules for all persons of Japanese ancestry in the continental United States, including citizens.

On 29 January 1942, the US Department of Justice began to clear all Japanese aliens from a number of coastal areas deemed strategic by the Western Defense Command of the US Army. Thereafter, as in Canada, President Roosevelt used instruments available to the executive level of government to carry out the removal orders. Like its Canadian counterpart Order-in-Council P.C. 1486, Executive Order 9066 achieved the mass uprooting of almost the entire west coast population of Nikkei under its sweeping terms. Signed on 19 February 1942, it gave the military the authority to create military areas and to exclude people from them. Although the executive order did not mention the Japanese or evacuation by name, everyone involved understood that its purpose was to give the army the power to remove people of Japanese ancestry from the west coast. John L. DeWitt, commanding general of the Western Defense Command, issued Public Proclamation No. 1 on 2 March, which enabled the western half of California, Oregon, and Washington to be designated a "military area" – Military Area No. 1 (essentially the entire Pacific coast to 100 miles inland) – and permitted the movement of persons of Japanese ancestry "in the interest of military necessity." Later, all of California and southern Arizona became excluded areas as part of Military Area No. 2. Public Proclamation No. 2 of 16 March established four additional military areas covering the states of Idaho, Montana, Nevada, and Utah. The intention was to expel the Nikkei from these areas, but the War Department quashed this idea. Two more public proclamation orders in March facilitated more specific restrictions against persons of Japanese ancestry, such as curfew and travel regulations, that affected their daily lives on numerous levels. Under 108 "exclusion orders," they were directed to assembly centres and then to ten relocation centres. Criminal penalties would be imposed on anyone who attempted to leave the centres without permission. President

Roosevelt also enacted Public Law 503, which made refusing to obey any command issued under Executive Order 9066 a federal offence.[12]

Eventually, 113,000 Japanese living on the US Pacific coast were moved from their homes to incarceration camps in the inland states, such as Idaho, Arizona, New Mexico, and Texas. In Alaska, 190 Nikkei were incarcerated: most were sent to a camp in Minidoka, Idaho. Only those in Hawaii and on the east coast were exempt.[13] Japanese Americans were thus treated as if the Bill of Rights had been repealed. To justify these decisions, the War Department asserted that racial ties predisposed the Japanese to behave disloyally; Lieutenant General John DeWitt claimed that even fully Americanized second- and third-generation Japanese posed a threat because "the racial strains are undiluted" and "racial affinities are not severed by migration." Indeed, Roosevelt himself harboured deeply felt anti-Japanese prejudices and had considered the incarceration of Japanese Americans as early as 1936.[14]

Persons of Japanese ancestry arrive at the Santa Anita Assembly Center from San Pedro. Evacuees lived at this center at the former Santa Anita racetrack before being moved inland to relocation centers. Clem Albers, Arcadia, CA, 5 April 1942. Courtesy US National Archives and Records Administration, photo no. 210-G-3B-414

It seems prudent at this point to note the divergent wartime experiences of the Canadian, continental US, and Hawaiian Nikkei. Whereas in British Columbia the Nikkei represented less than 3 percent of the population, and in California less than 2 percent, they constituted more than a third of the population in Hawaii. Although there was a strong force in Congress and vigorous support from Roosevelt for the idea of incarcerating all Japanese Americans and Japanese immigrants in Hawaii, it was rejected. Only about 2,000 of Hawaii's 150,000 Japanese were ever incarcerated. Yet Hawaii was the most obvious theatre of war for the continent, a fact that calls into question the "military necessity" argument for the entire North American operation.

Since the early nineteen hundreds, the Hawaiian Nikkei had constituted what one scholar has termed "a numerically important portion" of Hawaii's population and were well represented in its social and economic history.[15] More specifically, Japanese workers dominated its plantation industry in sugarcane and pineapple. They were also merchants, service workers, and

In the spring of 1942, a young evacuee of Japanese ancestry waits with the family baggage before leaving by bus for an assembly centre. Clem Albers, California, April 1942.
Courtesy US National Archives and Records Administration, photo no. 210-G-2A-6

restaurant owners. In the aftermath of Pearl Harbor, Hawaiian Americans of Japanese descent were needed to rebuild the defences at the base. In other words, they were vital to the territory's economy and military position. Additionally, by 1943, Nisei in Hawaii, along with their mainland brethren, were accepted as volunteers to serve in segregated units. This represented a shift in policy from an earlier regulation passed by the Selective Service System on 14 September 1942 that classified eligible Nisei as 4-C, or "unsuitable for service because of nationality and ancestry."[16] The army formed the 100th Infantry Battalion with Nisei from Hawaii, who would ultimately spend much of the war on the Italian front, serving both heroically and as an important public relations example for the incarcerated Nisei and their detractors.[17]

Logistics also posed a problem for government officials who favoured incarceration in Hawaii. People of Japanese ancestry comprised some 35 percent of its population, which meant that about 100,000 potentially disloyal Japanese would have to be incarcerated, either on one of the Hawaiian islands or, as was suggested, on the mainland. By late 1941, the US was officially engaged in the war; thus, the diversion of manpower and resources required to achieve the first proposal was nearly untenable. The latter proposal would have meant the removal of a major part of the territory's necessary workforce. Additionally, some officials in Roosevelt's government recommended against removing the Hawaiian Nikkei to mainland US incarceration camps for two main reasons: it would place a strain on transport facilities needed for the war effort and would probably spark a hostile political reaction and inflame public opinion, especially in California. By January 1943, the idea of mass incarceration in Hawaii was undone. As Greg Robinson succinctly states, "Ironically, Hawaii's isolation and military importance – the very factors that led Roosevelt to press repeatedly for preventative custody of the local Japanese – represented the strongest deterrents to any mass evacuation in the islands."[18]

However, Hawaii's Nikkei did not entirely escape harsh treatment. A total of 2,092 Japanese Hawaiians were transported to mainland camps; throughout the war, approximately 1,500 remained imprisoned without trial in Hawaii; and 675 were transported to alien incarceration camps on the American mainland shortly after the attack on Pearl Harbor. Of those who were not incarcerated, many were victims of workplace discrimination and subjected to a period of repressive military rule under martial law declared in the immediate wake of Pearl Harbor.[19] The differential treatment of the ethnic Japanese in Hawaii would provide an important caveat in the arguments of advocates for Nikkei in the continental US. The policy pursued in Hawaii also provides an alternative to those policies, so markedly similar, that were followed elsewhere in the United States and Canada.

In both countries, special agencies were created early in 1942 to over-see the "evacuation" process. In Canada, the British Columbia Security Commission (BCSC) was established on 4 March. In the United States, the War Department's Wartime Civil Control Administration (WCCA), hastily created by the army, supervised the assembly centres and the civilian War Relocation Authority (WRA) – a civilian agency – which oversaw the incarceration camps. At the outset of the removal process in the United States, the proceedings were conducted by the US Army. In signing Executive Order 9102 on 18 March, Roosevelt created the WRA as the agency jointly responsible with the War Department for the relocation program. It would oversee the incarceration centres and would later assist Japanese Americans in returning to American life.[20] The Canadian operation was undertaken by the BCSC and the Department of Labour under the auspices of Minister of Justice Louis St. Laurent. The RCMP cooperated with the British Columbia Security Commission, but it was given primary responsibility for the removal and resettlement. Under Order-in-Council P.C. 1665, the commission was given wide and sweeping powers, limited only in that the minister of labour, then Humphrey Mitchell, had to approve its plans. Within its "duties and powers," the BCSC was authorized

> to require by order any person of the Japanese race, in any protected area in British Columbia, to remain at his place of residence or to leave his place of residence and to proceed to any place within or without the pro-tected area at such time and in such manner as the Commission may pre-scribe in any such order, or to order the detention of any such person, and by any such order may be enforced by any persons nominated by the Commission to do so.[21]

What was life like for the incarcerated? The great majority of them were sent to live in relatively isolated areas far from their homes. The whole experience involved dislocation, discomfort, anxiety, and boredom. The process itself could be chaotic: some were evacuated in the middle of the night by the RCMP; others received a few months' warning. Their prop-erty was seized and sold at bargain-basement prices: for example, nine-teen acres in the Fraser Valley with a two-storey house and livestock sold for $1,492.59. After deductions for taxes and commissions, the owner received a cheque for $39.32.[22] In the United States, the "evacuees" were given approximately six days in which to dispose of their property. Told that they would be allowed to take only what they could carry, many Jap-anese Americans had to sell most of their possessions. One man described his feeling of despair and humiliation during the process, "as we watched the Caucasians coming to look at our possessions and offering such nom-inal amounts knowing we had no recourse but to accept whatever they were offering because we did not know what the future held for us."[23] Newspaper ads detailed the contents of auctions conducted by the custodian of enemy property in Canada. The Nikkei cooperated because they wanted to demonstrate their loyalty. Many never expected events to progress so far; they were confident of the "tolerance" of their fellow Canadians and Americans. Historian Hugh Brogan has noted that the "only agreeable thing to record of this episode is that as a result of the abandonment and destruction of the Japanese farms and gardens the price of fresh fruit and vegetables soared on the West Coast, leading to bitter complaints from the white citizenry." In the words of Muriel Kitagawa, one of the incarcerated, "We are Israelites on the move."[24]

In each country, the places of relocation were similar in their isolation but different in the methods designed to confine the incarcerated. In Canada, the population was initially segregated. Approximately twelve thousand women, children, and the elderly were placed in camps in the interior valleys of British Columbia, most of which were renovated ghost towns. Able-bodied men were sent to various road work projects in northern British Columbia and northern Ontario, and to become farm labourers in southern Ontario. Approximately four thousand men and women and their families were dispatched to southern Alberta and Manitoba to assist on sugar beet farms.[25] In the United States, interned Japanese families were not separated; they were sent to ten isolated (mostly) desert sites in Idaho (Minidoka), Arizona (Poston and Gila River), eastern California (Manzanar and Tule Lake), Utah (Topaz), Colorado (Amache), Arkansas (Jerome and Rohwer), and Wyoming (Heart Mountain). They lived in flimsy barrack-like buildings, surrounded by barbed wire, watchtowers, and armed guards.[26]

US and Canadian post-war plans for the Nikkei were also similar. Both President Roosevelt and Prime Minister King wanted to discourage the pre-war concentration patterns of the ethnic Japanese. Speaking in the House of Commons in August 1944, King enunciated the basic policy of his government: "it would be unwise and undesirable ... to allow the Japanese population to be concentrated in [British Columbia] after the war." In that same year, Roosevelt emphasized the desirability of dispersing the Japanese Americans more evenly throughout the country and noted that the WRA's policy was to facilitate this objective.[27]

Canada's revised "Japanese policy," announced in August 1944, imposed a program of resettlement on the Japanese Canadians; it also included a plan to separate the loyal from the disloyal and to "repatriate" the latter to Japan.[28] Loyalty and disloyalty were to be determined according to two criteria: Nikkei who chose resettlement east of the Rockies were loyal; those who opted for "repatriation" to Japan were not. Eventually, 81 percent of people over age sixteen who were resident in Interior camps requested repatriation, but only 15 percent of those who were living east of the Rockies did so. But, as the war in the Pacific wound down in 1945, many Japanese nationals and Japanese Canadians asked for cancellation of their repatriation requests. In order to sift through this new problem, Ottawa decreed that cancellation requests made *before* September 2 (the date of Japan's surrender) would be accepted. Those made *after* that date suggested disloyalty, and would not be allowed. Recently, allegations have been made that some civil servants won "career brownie points" for persuading Canadian Nikkei to go to Japan, but collaborating evidence is missing to support this claim.[29]

The Canadian dispersal policy promoted the movement of Japanese – mostly young single men and family units – to points further east to work on sugar beet and vegetable farms in Alberta, Manitoba, and Ontario, as well as in mining and lumber camps in northern Ontario. The wages of the men were garnisheed and sent to their families in the BC evacuation centres to pay for their relocation. When those who had gone east relayed details of their hard work, exploitation as cheap labour, and being made to feel unwelcome, getting additional Japanese to move beyond the Rocky Mountains became difficult. But the people and the politicians of the west coast did not want the Japanese back: "No Japs from the Rockies to the sea" was then a familiar cry.[30]

The plans of the Roosevelt government to scatter persons of Japanese ancestry across the nation were eventually hindered by the 18 December 1944 *Endo* decision, a case heard by the US Supreme Court that made confinement for "loyal" citizens unconstitutional. Even as early as mid-1944, officials in the War and Justice Departments were communicating their misgivings about the constitutionality of excluding citizens from the west coast when military necessity no longer existed. On 2 January 1945, total exclusion of loyal Japanese American civilians from the west coast was terminated.[31] The official "policy of dispersal" continued in Canada for more than three and a half years *after* the end of the war in the Pacific. Not until 1 April 1949 were persons of "Japanese race" permitted to return to the "protected zone" in British Columbia.

Canadian and American policy also differed regarding the question of military service, an issue not lost on the Nikkei on both sides of the border, as evidenced by numerous articles and editorials published in the Nisei-run newspapers. As early as June 1942, Hawaiians of Japanese descent were already serving their country through enlistment in the 100th Infantry Battalion. Due to their valour on the Italian front, the US Army concluded in January 1943 that it needed Japanese American personnel; thus, it decided to recruit an all-Nisei combat team – the 442nd Regimental Combat Team – drawn from both the Hawaiian Islands and the incarceration camps on the mainland. By 20 January 1944, Secretary of War Henry Stimson announced that, due to the admirable record of the volunteers with the 442nd Regimental Combat Team and 100th Infantry Battalion, normal selective service procedures would be applied to Japanese Americans. This was much to the delight of WRA head Dillon Myer, a long-time proponent of drafting Japanese Americans as an expression of equality. President Roosevelt's public statement praising the decision was illustrative of this ideal, and perhaps, as Greg Robinson has stated, stemmed from a "combination of political expediency and ideological principle":[32]

> No loyal citizen of the United States should be denied the democratic right to exercise the responsibilities of citizenship, regardless of his ancestry. The principle upon which this country was founded and by which it has always been governed is that Americanism is a matter of the mind and the heart; Americanism is not, and never was, a matter of race and ancestry.[33]

As mentioned earlier, service in the armed forces provided Americans of Japanese ancestry with a public means by which they could demonstrate their loyalty. It was also useful in promoting acceptance of Nikkei resettlement elsewhere throughout the US. By comparison, only a few Japanese Canadians were allowed to perform military service in the war, and many began their assignments, primarily as members of an intelligence unit, too late to experience overseas duty. Even with that, a quota of 150 was instituted. Thus, Canadian Nisei, denied the opportunity for combat, would develop no impressive war record and evidence of loyalty that could be used to mellow racist sentiment against them. Recognition of these issues can be found in sharply worded editorials in the *New Canadian*, a Japanese Canadian newspaper, between 1943 and 1944. That their exclusion was based entirely on racial prejudice is borne out by the fact that Chinese Canadians, who shared ancestry with a wartime ally of Canada, also faced similar restrictions, as Patricia Roy has revealed.[34]

Further measures depriving the Japanese Canadian population of some very basic civil liberties provide a stark contrast with the American case. In July 1944, the House of Commons passed Bill 135, clause 5 of which barred "persons of the Japanese race" who had moved from British Columbia after Pearl Harbor from voting in federal elections. King made his philosophy of civil liberties clear to everyone when he said, "The intention was not to take away a right from any one who had the right but to see to it that rights were not given to persons who had not previously enjoyed them, particularly when they were of a race with whose country we are at war."[35] Where was the military necessity or national security in this measure? It actually disadvantaged those 4,300 persons of Japanese ancestry who had complied with government orders and had relocated east of the Rockies by that time. But this was precisely the intention of the King government. According to Joseph Noseworthy (CCF MP, York South) in a letter to the Rev. A.E. Armstrong of the United Church of Canada, the content of clause 5 had never been mentioned in the committee that drafted the bill; it had been slipped in at the time of printing. Noseworthy referred to this as "one of the most unfortunate episodes that has occurred in the House for many years."[36]

In September 1945, Ottawa introduced Bill 15, the National Emergency Transitional Powers Act, which extended the powers given under the War Measures Act until the end of the year. The War Measures Act endowed the federal government, and specifically the Cabinet, with sweeping emergency powers to administer the war effort without being accountable to Parliament, and without regard for existing legislation. Pursuant to governing by decree, the King administration forged ahead with further measures: on 15 December 1945, it tabled Orders-in-Council P.C. 7355, 7356, and 7357 to put through its deportation policy. The first measure stripped naturalized deportees of their citizenship; the second, which was never established, provided for a loyalty commission to determine who among naturalized citizens should be deported. The third authorized the government to deport those interned Japanese nationals, naturalized citizens, Japanese Canadians, *and* their dependants who requested "repatriation."[37]

These measures would not go unnoticed by Canadians; neither would the repatriation policy, as the ensuing chapters will demonstrate. In addition, many Americans expressed their horror and distaste for Ottawa's proposal to expatriate citizens. By late 1945, opposition to the government's flagrant misuse of power in wartime had begun to mobilize in Canada. The Canadian situation must be seen in light of the parallel American situation, which the Canadian government closely monitored. But, because the "evacuation" of Canada's west coast was a logical outcome of decades of public and political agitation, Canadians did not need an American precedent either to justify their own action or to claim that the American removal plans had influenced their own decision.[38]

The Canadian decision of 14 January 1942 to remove male Japanese nationals from the coast preceded the American order by four weeks. Nonetheless, evidence demonstrates that the two governments took at least a step towards preplanning and coordinating their policies. However, historian Roger Daniels suggests that the diplomatic and other consultations that took place cannot be causally linked with what both governments did to their resident Japanese populations in February 1942 and after. Thus, he asserts, the two nations arrived individually at noticeably similar decisions.[39] This is true, but only to a certain point. Canadian government officials, particularly those in the Department of External Affairs (DEA), kept a close watch on the policies enacted by the Americans, and advised accordingly. Conditions inherent to each country precluded following identical policies; nevertheless, Canadian officials seriously heeded a 1941 promise made between representatives of both nations to follow as similar a course as possible regarding their Nikkei populations.

However, as the war progressed, the desire to maintain similar policies regarding the Nikkei became increasingly restricted to the Canadians. Initially, the meetings of the Permanent Joint Board of Defense (PJBD)[40] discussed the desirability of similar policies. At a 10-11 November 1941 PJBD meeting held in Montreal, its members agreed that, in the event of hostilities with Japan, "it would be desirable that steps be taken to arrange for consultation between the appropriate officers of the two governments, with a view to bringing about a practicable coincidence of policies in this matter in Canada and in the continental United States."[41] There is no evidence to suggest that this consultation took place, although the US Department of State and the Department of External Affairs (DEA) exchanged correspondence in the weeks following Pearl Harbor. For example, in a 5 February 1942 letter, George A. Gordon of the Department of State reminded Hume Wrong, minister counsellor of Canada, of the agreement reached previously in Montreal.[42] On 14 January 1942, when the Canadian government issued the order that all male Japanese nationals in British Columbia be removed, American newspapers took little notice; nor is there any evidence, according to Greg Robinson, that the Canadian decision figured in any American administration discussions of relocation.[43] However, a 14 January 1942 document sent to the US State Department from the US Legation in Ottawa reported a series of pronouncements by Prime Minister King regarding Canada's cooperation with the British and US governments "with a view to the substantial coordination of their policies in relation to persons of Japanese racial origin." Although that document is evidence of at least some American awareness of Canada's position, it indicates little else. A memorandum prepared by the DEA observed that, thus far (January 1942), Canada had attempted to deviate as little as possible from the policy of the United States. Nevertheless, the department was aware of the differences inherent in the situations of each country, namely, that American Nikkei citizens were subject to the draft. It also remarked that the United States had "gone further than Canada in urging employers not to draw racial distinctions and in denouncing 'racial discrimination in any of its ugly forms.'" The DEA also knew that, unlike Canada, the US had not yet removed either its citizens of Japanese ancestry or Japanese nationals from the fishing fleet or the coastal areas.[44]

Although meetings were not conducted between Canadian and American bureaucrats, the available Canadian evidence suggests that, by 1943, Canadian government officials paid a great deal of attention to matters taking place in the United States. In a secret memo addressed to Prime Minister King, Acting Undersecretary of State for External Affairs Norman

Robertson noted that "the policy we have pursued since Pearl Harbor has been largely influenced by what we understood the policy of the US to be."[45] At about the same time that American policy was "softening," Canadian policy was taking a harsher turn. In September 1943, Roosevelt announced that loyal Japanese Americans would be allowed to leave the relocation centres and move to any area in the United States, with the exception of the evacuation zones; once the military situation made it possible, they could return to the evacuated areas of the Pacific coast.[46] At a meeting to discuss the position of the Japanese in Canada, which officials from External Affairs, the RCMP, and the Department of Labour attended, it was decided that, until some idea of American policy could be realized, "it would be unwise" to approach the Cabinet on a draft proposal regarding the segregation and repatriation of persons of Japanese ancestry. In its decision to delay action and to recommend further study of the American situation, the Cabinet acknowledged the influence of American policy and its "softening."[47] Late in 1943, US State Department officials took notice of Canada's proposal to deport "disloyal Japanese, or who may prove disloyal or who request repatriation," as a result of a letter sent by Canadian officials requesting details as to how the United States planned to address similar issues. The American evidence clearly suggests that, though both nations were interested in each other's policies, neither was greatly influenced by the other due to differing citizenship statutes and differing approaches to foreign and domestic policy.[48] It is evident that Ottawa did not want to appear out of step with the Americans on the Nikkei issue, yet the decision not to accept the enlistment of Japanese Canadians, in addition to the proposal to deport Canadian citizens of Japanese ancestry, greatly differed from American policy. Later, the decision to deport citizens, unlike the policy of dispersal and relocation, would result in a crisis of public condemnation of government actions.

Well into 1944, Canadian officials still maintained a close watch over developments in American policy with respect to the Japanese American population. CCJC members and others made some attempt to promote the enlistment of Japanese Canadians, pointing to the success of Japanese Americans in the US Army, but to no avail. In August, a detailed twenty-five-page study of American policy was circulated among DEA officials, as was a statement that compared the nature and timing of the various steps taken by Washington and Ottawa.[49] This coincided with King's formal statement in the House of Commons on 4 August about future Canadian policy regarding Nikkei residents. He underscored the approach of the past three years, in which Canadian bureaucrats and elected officers had attempted, insofar as it seemed "desirable," to "maintain a policy that ... can be considered as part of a continental policy."[50] King continued:

The situation in the United States in a great many essentials is the same as our own, and to the extent that it seems desirable we shall endeavour to ensure that our policy takes account of the policies which are being applied south of the border. There is no need for an identity of policy, but I believe there is merit in maintaining a substantial consistency of treatment in the two countries.[51]

Despite King's statement, Canadian and American policy regarding the Nikkei began to diverge dramatically in December 1944 when the US lifted its ban on Japanese returning to the Pacific coast. State Department and External Affairs officials continued their correspondence into 1945 on the subject of repatriation, as American officials were interested in Canadian decisions regarding cancelled requests for repatriation.[52]

The American government also promoted a repatriation program designed around a loyalty questionnaire. This proposal was favoured by Department of War officials and the WRA as a means to subject military-aged Japanese American men to the same selective service rules as other Americans. The confusing and inappropriate questionnaire was eventually used by the WRA as a basis for separating the "loyal" from the "disloyal" and transporting the latter to Tule Lake, California, which became a segregation centre for the "disloyal." Eventually, more than a third of the 18,000 internees at Tule Lake formally applied for repatriation to Japan after the war; of the 7,222 persons who did so, nearly 65 percent were American-born. Approximately eight thousand people of Japanese descent left for Japan immediately following the war. During the war, 5,766 American citizens of Japanese ancestry renounced their citizenship and for a time were legally regarded as stateless persons resident in the United States. The Nisei renunciants, legally considered "aliens ineligible to citizenship," faced legal and economic discrimination similar to that experienced by their Issei parents. In fact, the renunciation of citizenship, normally difficult to effect, was supported by the Justice Department, which hoped that three hundred to a thousand citizens might avail themselves of the provisions of an act of Congress, the Denaturalization Act of 1944. Furthermore, government officials hoped that the renunciation initiative would diffuse tensions among the more militant and active dissidents in places such as the Tule Lake Segregation Center.[53]

From the beginning, the only support that the renunciants received was from lawyers Wayne Collins, loosely affiliated with the Northern California branch of the ACLU, and Abraham Lincoln Wirin, of the Southern California ACLU (hereafter referred to as A.L. Wirin, as he disliked his full name and used only his initials). Both Collins and Wirin were convinced that many of the renunciants had been intimidated by the FBI into signing the forms that could consequently lead to their deportation. The JACL, however, rejected the former citizens as part of its pledge to support the United States government. The organization was also embarrassed by the apparent "disloyalty" within the Japanese community and disassociated itself from the renunciants. Similarly, the ACLU did not favour advocating for the renunciants, a decision based on a policy that limited assistance to persons accused or suspected of disloyalty. Agreeing to renounce American citizenship, whether as a reaction to wartime treatment or as a result of duress, clouded some of the renunciants with a great deal of suspicion, thus barring them from mainstream support.[54]

Although the policy of resettlement and assimilation would be anathema to today's multicultural common sense, it was strongly supported by many liberals. It should be pointed out that almost no Canadians publicly opposed the wartime relocation and forcible removal of the Japanese Canadians from the west coast. Assimilation, it was believed, would assist them in integrating into the Canadian fabric. As a result, few felt that the assimilationist goals of the resettlement program were unjustified. Although the policy of disfranchisement first aroused indignation, the announcement of the deportation policy made Canadians begin to realize the injustice of the policies directed against Japanese Canadians; Canadian advocates began to harness and cultivate such opposition to the federal government.[55]

For their part, few Americans initially protested Executive Order 9066, lest they demonstrate disunity and disapproval of President Roosevelt. Fewer still objected to the deportation of the renunciants. In the years that saw an extraordinary emphasis on the value of national unity and, to a remarkable degree, the achievement of that unity, "race" remained the source of deepest division in American life. On the whole, white liberals offered a confused response to the decision for dispersal. Few disapproved of its assimilationist goals; however, when the relocation policy did not appear to be achieving this goal and, in fact, seemed to represent something more insidious, liberals raised their level of protest. But the confusion of white liberals was nothing compared to that of Japanese American and Japanese Canadian leaders. Their only courses of action – resistance to relocation or compliance with it – were charged with risks. How to prove their loyalty was at the crux of the dilemma for the North American Japanese. In the end, the issue would prove highly divisive and costly for the entire community.

Nevertheless, Nikkei community leaders eventually recognized that racial disadvantage, as it was then understood, would have to be addressed. Although some of the initial momentum for reform came from the North American Japanese themselves, non-Japanese advocates in both countries led the offensive. Many of these white liberals were already well-seasoned participants from other battles; they included the members of the ACLU and such Canadian civil libertarians as B.K. Sandwell and F.R. Scott, who felt concern for the growing and brazen government interference in the traditional civil liberties of the citizenry. Not surprisingly, the continuing tragedy of the Nikkei helped to raise the public's awareness of the presence of racial discrimination in Canada and the US.

Negotiating "Race" and Rights during the 1940s

Prior to the Second World War, libertarian rights superseded egalitarian rights. It was during the Great Depression, however, that individuals interested in the protection of civil liberties began to organize clearly defined groups. Specifically, the 1937 passage of Quebec's infamous Padlock Law (Act Respecting Communistic Propaganda) marked the onset of coordinated resistance by individuals and, later, groups dedicated to the protection of civil liberties. Those on the political left increasingly became targets of police and were charged with a number of offences – vagrancy, unlawful assembly, and rioting – as the state took repressive measures to combat what was perceived as radicalism. Although communists in Canada – specifically in the form of the Canadian Labour Defense League (CLDL) – were on the forefront in organizing protests, non-communists would soon play a central role in opposing police excesses, deportations, and other strong-arm tactics sanctioned by the state.

Individuals such as F.R. Scott, Eugene Forsey, and others became involved in the Montreal branch of the Canadian Civil Liberties Union, formed in 1937. It was followed by the creation of the Toronto branch of the Civil Liberties Union. However, tensions between communist and non-communist members proved problematic for the effectiveness of civil liberties groups. Fault lines emerged over such issues as free speech, free association, and the right to due process. Once war with Germany was declared, civil libertarians turned their attention to the threats to traditional "British liberties" posed by the emergency powers allocated to the federal executive branch under the War Measures Act. The most reviled of these was the Defence of Canada Regulations (DOCR). While the War Measures Act gave the executive branch of the Canadian government powers that could not be exercised in peacetime, the DOCR broadened these powers to include, among other things, the waiving of habeas corpus and public trials, bans on political and religious groups, internment, restrictions on free speech, and the confiscation of property. The Cabinet, not Parliament, adopted these measures by way of order-in-counciil on 3 September 1939, one week before Canada declared war; the Order-in-Council included sixty-four regulations that led to the immediate roundup of a number of Germans and German Canadians on suspicion of their possible support for Nazi Germany.

Civil liberties groups generally opposed the DOCR, although they did allow that the nature of the times necessitated unusual policies. However, they were, for the most part, without allies. Enjoying only limited support of the media, lawyers, and politicians, civil libertarians were divided geographically and ideologically; as a result, their opposition to government authoritarianism was not effective. They were clearly a distinct minority in Canadian society, outsiders with a critical perspective that was out of step with that of the mainstream. Although civil libertarians scarcely spoke out against the incarceration policy, the proposed "repatriation" raised their ire. For a number of reasons, civil liberties groups would join with other organizations to protest racially discriminatory policies directed against the Nikkei, and thus would not be outsiders regarding that particular issue. They would address the latter three of the major issues surrounding the "Japanese problem" of the 1940s: relocation and incarceration, disfranchisement of those relocated outside of British Columbia, involuntary expatriation, and the elimination of discriminatory federal and provincial laws.[56]

By the mid-1940s, assumptions about race and racial discrimination had begun to change, provoking some Canadians and Americans to become active in the campaign for justice for the Nikkei. The war would herald an important attitudinal shift on the part of North Americans when it came to race. The reaction of Canadians and Americans to the Holocaust and to Adolf Hitler's doctrine of Aryan superiority compelled millions of white citizens to re-examine their views about race. If, during war, both nations expected minorities to risk their lives for the common good, how could society continue to treat them as second-class citizens? African American leaders in the United States, for example, pointed out the inconsistency between fighting for democracy abroad and ignoring it at home.[57]

Some definition of the word "race" is necessary at this point. The use of quotation marks around the term reflects long-standing acceptance of "race" as a social construction. Although the belief that "race" refers to a biologically significant characteristic of human beings that can be used to classify them into certain populations does remain common, the concept is a historically contingent phenomenon. At the time of the Second World War, Canadians and Americans were still conflating phenotypes – skin colour, facial features – with genotypes to indicate and support a system of inviolable racial identities: white, black, yellow, red. This was, and to some degree still is, "common sense."

In the early years of the war, race and racism lost their remaining shreds of intellectual respectability. For decades, anthropologists such as Franz Boas and Otto Kleinberg challenged the idea that some races were superior to others, but only during the war did a popular consensus began to form around their views. Works such as Ruth Benedict's *Race: Science and Politics* (1940), Gunnar Dahlberg's *Race, Reason and Rubbish* (1942), and Ashley Montagu's *Man's Most Dangerous Myth: The Fallacy of Race* (1942), addressed primarily to a mass audience, taught very similar lessons: all human beings had a tremendous amount in common.[58] All emphasized the adaptability, not the permanence, of human nature and that the rise of fascism demonstrated "where we end up if we think that the shape of the nose or the color of the skin has anything to do with human values and culture."[59]

That the idea of race was in a state of flux in Canada and the United States is nowhere more clearly emphasized than in the treatment of the Nikkei at the hands of their own governments, a treatment that was sanctioned by a portion of the populace. Although most Canadians and Americans were prepared to accept the policies of internment, incarceration, and relocation at the outset of 1942, far fewer were willing to do so later. In particular, the Canadian government's 1944 decision to disfranchise persons of Japanese ancestry who had moved from British Columbia to provinces where they were entitled to vote roused the ire of some Canadians, as later chapters will detail. In July 1944, Liberal MP Arthur Roebuck asserted in the House of Commons that, though racial equality was a main principle of liberalism, his own government's policy of disfranchisement smacked of "race discrimination"; he pointed out that if the policy and others like it were maintained, "it will not be long before Canada will be Hitlerized."[60] Racial discrimination was thus linked with the behaviour of the enemy. It was unacceptable and increasingly viewed as an aberration.

In general, it can be said that Canadian perceptions of some minority groups were changing, too. Over the course of the Second World War, the Chinese, for example, were progressively viewed through a new lens, so much so that, in discussing Vancouver's Chinatown, the *Vancouver Sun* could remark, "Time was when that foreign quarter ... had an aura of wickedness for the Vancouver consciousness ... How it has changed! Or perhaps, how we, under the impact of World War II have changed. China is now our ally, and visitors look at Chinatown through new eyes."[61] Still, in 1940s Canada and the United States, "race" was still race. However artificial the term was becoming to scholars who understood its invidious heritage, its importance to those calling for harsh treatment of the Nikkei, to government policy makers, and to officials was hardly diminished. Most North Americans still viewed the world in explicitly race-conscious terms, and so the lives of nearly 140,000 Nikkei were affected on the basis of racial assumptions.

As ideas regarding race changed in Canada during the war, the notion of "British liberties" was being supplanted by a new discourse on human rights. For most Canadians, the concept of British liberties meant a steadfast conviction in individual freedom protected by "the formal legal equality of the Rule of Law."[62] By war's end, however, some important reconsiderations of the British liberties ideal were already under way. In August 1941, American president F.D. Roosevelt and British prime minister Winston Churchill issued the Atlantic Charter, which they prefaced with a statement that victory over the Axis powers was "essential to decent life, liberty, independence and religious freedom, and to preserve human rights and justice."[63] Indeed, this shift in language was important in bringing focus to Canada's problems of racial discrimination. Anti-discrimination statements made by one contemporary civil liberties group attest to this shift: "It is not too much to say that wars and the terrible consequences of war have arisen as much from the refusal, whether through ignorance or wilfulness, to recognize basic human rights, as from any other cause."[64] In 1945, the United Nations Charter was formulated; its statements about human rights and non-discrimination gave support to the idea that people are entitled to certain basic rights because they are human beings, not simply because they are citizens of a particular nation. The charter formally declared its "faith in fundamental human rights, in the dignity and worth of the human person," and asserted that the newly formed United Nations organization would be dedicated to "promoting and encouraging respect for human rights and fundamental freedoms for all without distinction as to race, sex, language or religion."[65]

The above is not to suggest, however, that references to the idea of human rights were completely absent prior to the Second World War, and in particular prior to the creation of these documents and agreements on human rights. Although the instances are rare, they do exist and speak to the idea that the move from traditional British liberties towards human rights was gradual but hastened by developments in the early to mid-1940s. For example, in his capacity as Co-operative Commonwealth Federation (CCF) leader, J.S. Woodsworth wrote of human rights in reference to Nova Scotia miners and their relationship (or lack thereof) with Besco, the British Empire Steel Company; later, discussing the Winnipeg General Strike of 1919, he made the same observation. An earlier reference to human rights dates from the late nineteenth century: in response to discriminatory practices with regard to black porters on the railways, Reverend J. Francis Robinson, pastor of Cornwallis Street Baptist Church in Halifax, Nova Scotia, declared that "they are not only deprived of the privilege of their civil rights, but in many instances denied the human right to gain an honest livelihood for themselves and their families."[66]

How the concept of human rights gained recognition among Canadian advocates, and why both Canadian and American advocates came to reject the discriminatory policies pursued by the governments of the day, is the subject of the following chapter. In particular, the campaigns of the Co-operative Committee on Japanese Canadians and the American Civil Liberties Union were central in promoting the rights of Nikkei citizens to the rest of the population, and surely to elected and non-elected government officials. Interestingly, neither organization operated in isolation from the

This political cartoon was titled "Stretched around the World."
Richmond Times-Dispatch, 29 October 1942

other. The ACLU took an active interest in affairs north of the border; however, as was the case for the correspondence between Canadian and American bureaucrats and the desire to maintain a "practicable coincidence of policy," the Canadian advocacy groups focused more intently on the American situation than their US counterparts did on Canadian affairs.[67] This is very significant, as it highlights how the American example influenced the way in which Canadians would address their own situation. Still, to a certain extent, the CCJC-led Canadian response to government policies concerning the Nikkei resident in Canada had its own variations.

2
The CCJC and the ACLU: Engaging Debate, 1942-46

> Non-co-operation with the government is being used as grounds for deportation of the Japanese. May I ask when non-co-operation with the government became a ground for deportation?
>
> – Senator Arthur Roebuck (Liberal), addressing a CCJC-sponsored meeting, 1946

> I beg the Japanese Americans not to despair of democracy or of America. I ask it to be remembered that there are millions of other American citizens who believe in justice and fairness and equality, and that these are the true Americans.
>
> – Pearl Buck, speaking to a mass meeting held under the auspices of the Japanese American Committee for Democracy, 1942

Senator Arthur Roebuck, a labour lawyer and Canadian politician who ardently promoted the rights of Jews in the 1930s and later figured prominently in post-war Canadian civil liberties campaigns, and author Pearl Buck, Nobel and Pulitzer Prize winner and civil and women's rights activist, were among the many influential Canadians and Americans who lent their names, their support, and their efforts to the Co-operative Committee on Japanese Canadians (CCJC) and the American Civil Liberties Union (ACLU). The CCJC and the ACLU, however, relied and thrived on the support of ordinary individuals as much as on that from high-profile citizens. The risks and sacrifices made by CCJC and ACLU members during the Second World War, a time when dissent was sometimes unwelcome or unacceptable, were essential in making other ordinary Canadians and Americans take notice of the situation of the Nikkei.

The CCJC was a Toronto-based umbrella group composed of representatives of Canadian missionary organizations, influential Canadians from a wide spectrum of society, liberal-minded professionals, and other persons concerned with safeguarding the human rights and freedoms of Japanese Canadians during and after the war. For the ACLU, an established civil liberties group with a broader mandate, the relocation issue was but one of several rights causes that engaged its membership during the war years.

The harsh criticisms levelled by both groups at the government policies of removal and (in Canada) deportation reflected the growing concern with rights that had already begun to emerge at this time.

The process through which the CCJC and the ACLU assumed advocacy roles for persons of Japanese ancestry in Canada and the United States, respectively, was fraught with dissension in the latter and blessed with cooperation in the former. Both groups drew heavily upon social justice and religious organizations for their membership, the character of which significantly affected how they functioned in the interest of the Nikkei. Additionally, how each group defined the problem of the removal and deportation of citizens reveals much about the nature of rights advocacy in Canada and the United States. In particular, the CCJC's major efforts to oppose deportation and to coordinate the activities of other interested organizations represent the earliest evidence of a campaign for human rights in Canadian history. Although the CCJC's work fuelled concern for other campaigns defending human rights, the ACLU's tactics neither served as inspiration nor provided organizational momentum for the 1950s civil rights revival. That would be left for the Japanese American Citizens League (JACL) and other minority group organizations.

"A Humanitarian Solution of the Problem Is Necessary and Urgent"

Whereas the ACLU became involved in the removal issue due to a concern for the abrogation of civil rights, the CCJC, as an organization, initially confined its activities to the immediate welfare of Japanese Canadians newly arrived from relocation centres in British Columbia. Ross Lambertson has noted that the development and history of the CCJC falls into three stages. In its initial period (1943-45), the CCJC was largely apolitical, localized, and concerned only with resettlement issues. As it moved into the second stage (1945-47), it became much more politicized and sophisticated, expanding its mission to include the wholesale defence of Japanese Canadian civil liberties. In its later years (1947-1951), the CCJC scaled back in size, focusing on the issue of restitution for property losses.[1] It remained politically involved, however, albeit in a more muted manner. By the time the CCJC finally disbanded in early 1951, many of its members, and many of the organizations that lent it support, had graduated to other causes with wider appeal, namely, anti-discrimination legislation.

The initial phase of the CCJC evolved from a project established in 1943 to assist with the resettlement of single Japanese Canadian women. Integration and assimilation were the main goals of the early group, which was composed of members of the National Council of the YWCA, the Toronto YWCA, and the women's missionary societies of four large Protestant denominations. Indeed, this limited focus was evident in the group's original name: the Co-operative Committee on Japanese Canadian Arrivals to Toronto (CCJC-AT). The early CCJC also included members of the YWCA and missionary societies resident in Toronto. Shortly after its first meeting, the committee was broadened to include representatives from the YMCA, the Student Christian Movement, and the Fellowship of Reconciliation (FOR). For several committee members, concern for the Japanese Canadians grew from their earlier experiences and service at missions in Japan.[2]

On 8 June 1943, the CCJC-AT held its first meeting at the YWCA at 21 McGill Street in Toronto. The meeting was chaired by Mrs. Walter C. Rean, YWCA board president, and included, among others, Florence Bird, a representative of the United Church Women's Missionary Society, who was delegated to assist Japanese Canadians in Ontario. Mrs. H. Watts was similarly charged by the Church of England in Toronto. Also present at this inaugural meeting were Ernest Trueman, the placement officer for the Ontario Farm Service Force; Mrs. Brownell, assistant director of the Toronto branch of the National Selective Service, who was delegated to oversee Japanese Canadian employment; and Mrs. C.V. Booth, a representative of the British Columbia Security Commission (BCSC).[3]

The inclusion of the latter three individuals helps to explain the assimilationist focus of the CCJC-AT. As Ann Gomer Sunahara has observed, resettling the Japanese Canadians east of the Rocky Mountains appealed to the assimilationist social ideals of the committee members. Most Canadians at this time firmly believed that it was both desirable and necessary for immigrants to conform to the Anglo-Canadian ideal; according to liberal reasoning of the day, geographic dispersal was the most effective means to achieve assimilation. Moreover, geographic concentration was perceived to be the cause of racist reactions among many Canadians, who would not tolerate the perpetuation of immigrant cultures in ethnic enclaves. Thus, the early CCJC-AT was hardly articulating intolerance by promoting dispersal: it was, in fact, wholly in line with contemporary liberal thinking on the issue of preventing racism and discrimination. Indeed, the idea that relocation might be beneficial was also espoused by some Nisei, such as Thomas Shoyama, editor of the *New Canadian*.[4]

It should be remembered that the BCSC was established by the federal government on 4 March 1942 to "plan, supervise and direct" the removal process. In her presentation to the CCJC-AT, BCSC representative Mrs. C.V. Booth made it very clear that the BCSC policy was to encourage the dispersal of Japanese Canadians across the country but to avoid the formation of segregated communities of people in doing so. The BCSC "had no further interest in these people once they were moved out of Vancouver," Booth noted, and she stressed that it was up to organizations such as the churches, the YWCA, and the CCJC-AT to help prevent the establishment of segregated Japanese Canadian settlements in Toronto. In response, the committee resolved to identify all new Japanese Canadian arrivals in Toronto according to their respective religious affiliations, at which point the appropriate church would contact them, welcome them into its flock, and find them a home through the YWCA Rooms Registry.[5]

The overwhelmingly female nature of CCJC-AT membership would not last long. One of the committee's first acts was the resolution to invite male members of the churches and the YMCA to the next meeting. This decision was based on simple demographics: in Toronto, Japanese Canadian men outnumbered their female counterparts. Expecting their activities to extend to male Japanese Canadian newcomers, members of the fledgling CCJC-AT thought it best to have the appropriate gender representation on the committee.[6]

Similarly, the CCJC-AT recommended that Japanese Canadian men and women be invited to advise the committee on their needs. Accordingly, two subcommittees were formed, divided along gender lines. Among the initial participants were Roger Obata and George Tanaka, who would later form the Japanese Canadian Committee for Democracy (JCCD), a lobby group.[7] Thus, from its inception the committee worked cooperatively with the Japanese Canadians themselves, an approach that guided the CCJC's activities throughout its history.

The politicization of the CCJC-AT can be dated to a 15 June 1943 meeting during which it formed a subcommittee to redraft and promote throughout Ontario a petition drawn up by the Vancouver Consultative Council (VCC) that urged the government to "take some constructive action toward resettling the Japanese Canadians."[8] Over the next three months, the subcommittee studied the Orders-in-Council and the various government policy statements relating to Japanese Canadians. Basing its decision on the fact that those who had circulated the petition had encountered an uninformed public, the CCJC-AT undertook a program of public education concerning the treatment of Japanese Canadians in the incarceration centres and the hardships they faced because of resettlement throughout Canada. By September 1943, it had printed ten thousand copies of *A Challenge to Patriotism and Statesmanship*, a pamphlet by Dr. Norman F. Black of the Vancouver Consultative Council, and circulated them widely throughout the country, largely by way of the churches. The piece was a condensed version of a *Saturday Night* article in which Black detailed the background of the removal, the incarceration centres, and the government's resettlement policy. The VCC stance was not surprising, given its inception as a study group devoted to the "Japanese problem" and comprised of representatives of the United Church, other Christian organizations, and the Co-operative Commonwealth Federation (CCF).[9]

Throughout 1944, the CCJC-AT continued its localized efforts to arrange housing for Japanese Canadian men and women. Because Order-in-Council

P.C. 1457 of 24 February 1942 made it illegal for a person of Japanese ancestry or a Japanese company, except under special licence from the minister of justice, to acquire, lease, or hold land in any part of Canada,[10] many Nikkei had difficulty finding new homes. One solution, initiated by the Women's Missionary Society of the United Church in cooperation with the CCJC-AT, was to purchase a hostel for single men in Toronto. The committee also aided in finding recreational activities, in cooperation with the Toronto YMCA and YWCA, as well as the United Church. Emma Kaufman of the YWCA organized Sunday teas to enable youth from various churches to socialize with young Japanese Canadians. Some committee members visited Hamilton, London, Chatham, and other centres to meet with church and youth groups and to confer on assistance to Nikkei relocatees. Advisory councils, created in Hamilton, London, and Brantford to help in finding jobs, housing, and recreation for the Japanese Canadians, functioned like the CCJC-AT. Many of these initiatives were based on specific proposals submitted by the Japanese Canadian men and women's subcommittees of the CCJC-AT.[11]

At this early stage in CCJC-AT activities, the most immediate issue remained the problem of providing aid for individuals at the local level. Soon, however, the efforts of the CCJC-AT and the resettlement committees in other centres such as Hamilton, London, and Brantford were applied in a more coordinated fashion. In particular, they targeted municipal government opposition to Japanese Canadian settlement in select Ontario urban areas. For example, CCJC-AT members lobbied Toronto city council on behalf of Jimmie Hirai, who appealed eight times to obtain a restaurant licence for the building that the minister of justice had permitted him to purchase. The city council cited Hirai's race as the reason for his failed application attempts. Although Hirai's efforts would prove unsuccessful, the CCJC-AT eventually persuaded city council to relax racial restrictions on business permits. The cooperative committees in other parts of the province were also effective in exposing the discrimination inherent in their city councils' refusal to allow Japanese Canadians to settle in various locales. Public education campaigns were undertaken in concert with these efforts, with the result that public and municipal government opposition decreased, although it is worth noting that, in Toronto, Japanese Canadians required permits for residence until 1946.[12]

These early activities of the CCJC-AT and other interested groups provide the first demonstration of the tactics they would use in later campaigns, namely, articulating the problem of exclusion from cities as discriminatory and persuading government officials to agree with that assessment and to work cooperatively to remedy the situation. Still, its focus on individual resettlement represented the CCJC-AT's overall assumption that assimilation was the best course of action for the Nikkei. Indeed, in August

1944, when Prime Minister William Lyon Mackenzie King outlined a three-part approach to resolving the Japanese Canadian "problem" – halting immigration from Japan, deporting those found to be disloyal, and dispersing the remainder of the population across Canada – the CCJC-AT welcomed his statement as a clear-cut government policy and pledged its cooperation to aid resettlement to that end. The committee also fully endorsed King's intention to allow no further immigration from Japan. Until Canadians overcame their racial prejudice, the group felt, it would be prudent not to admit any more Japanese. The CCJC-AT's entreaties to municipal governments regarding the restrictive legislation against renting and buying property reflected its commitment to the principles of assimilation.[13]

In June 1944, members of the committee, now informally known as the Co-operative Committee on Japanese Canadians, took part in the campaign to amend Bill 135, clause 5, which, in its initial form, proposed to disfranchise all persons of Japanese "race" for the duration of the war. The CCJC did not organize effectively; only individual committee members wrote letters of protest to the secretary of state, N.A. McLarty. Other groups, such as the National Interchurch Advisory Committee on the Resettlement of Japanese Canadians, the official church body concerned with resettlement issues, and the Japanese Canadian Committee for Democracy (JCCD), which sent a brief to the government opposing the bill, were more active. The widespread public protests sparked by their efforts persuaded a Senate committee to reduce the scope of the measure. As passed in the House of Commons, it applied only where "such legislation is now operative." In effect, the new law applied only to Japanese Canadians who had previously resided in British Columbia.[14]

The involvement of CCJC members in this campaign indicates that the group was beginning to realize the ramifications of government policies regarding the Canadian Nikkei. Local efforts would have little impact if the broader issues were not addressed. Similarly, this case presented a good learning experience for the now year-old committee: to effect change, public opinion would have to be aroused and harnessed.

Early in 1945, Ottawa took measures to hasten the dispersal program. Instead of removing the restrictions on renting and buying property and securing business licences, as suggested by the CCJC, the JCCD, and many other groups, the government pursued a more ominous measure – repatriation – that was hinted at in King's 4 August 1944 policy statement. In February 1945, the King administration announced the details of a "voluntary repatriation" plan that offered all persons of Japanese ancestry a choice: make a "voluntary application to go to Japan after the war or sooner where this can be arranged," or move east of the Rockies and accept employment in accordance with the established dispersal program. Those who did not accept employment in provinces other than British Colum-bia·would be regarded as uncooperative and would be deported. By August 1945, 6,884 Japanese Canadians over the age of sixteen had signed up for "repatriation" to Japan, along with their 3,503 dependants, representing 43 percent of the Japanese population of Canada. According to the 1941 Dominion census, of the approximately twenty-four thousand Nikkei in Canada, almost fifteen thousand had been born there, and three thousand were naturalized citizens.[15]

Announcement of the "repatriation survey" greatly alarmed CCJC members, who recognized the threat to civil liberties posed by any deportation of Canadian citizens. Many realized the importance of organizing an immediate and intensive campaign to galvanize public opinion. A special meeting on 22 May, to which representatives from twenty organizations were invited, decided to oppose the government's policy, to meet again on 19 June, and to reorganize the Toronto committee into a formal federated body known as the Co-operative Committee on Japanese Canadians. Cooperative committees in other centres would continue to act as regional adjuncts to the main committee in the same fashion as the earlier resettlement committees had. All would work towards securing justice for Japanese Canadians. An executive was then appointed to direct activities and coordinate the various groups. The chair of the new body was the Reverend James Finlay, outspoken minister of Toronto's Carlton Street United Church, who was among the first clergymen to take up the Nikkei cause. He would chair the committee for the next six years and would open his church to frequent CCJC meetings and public assemblies. The committee secretary, Donalda MacMillan, had lived in Formosa (a Japanese-occupied territory now known as Taiwan) for some time with her husband, a United Church missionary, and was active in the CCJC from its inception as the CCJC-AT.

Reverend Finlay was alerted to the Japanese Canadian situation by Olive Pannell, one of his Carlton Street parishioners, who regularly corresponded with Muriel Kitagawa, noted Japanese Canadian writer and activist. Upon hearing some of their correspondence read in church detailing the chaotic process of "evacuation" on the west coast, Finlay and others were roused to action. As Kitagawa commented later, in a *Nisei Affairs* article, the "initial support, spurred on by Mrs. Pannell, gradually became the spearhead of the protests against injustice arising all over the country." The CCJC resolved to send a delegation to Ottawa to protest the repatriation plan. Those chosen for the delegation included members of the Interchurch Advisory Committee and representatives of various secular agencies; among them were J.H. Fowler, of the National YMCA; B.K. Sandwell, editor of *Saturday Night* and member of the Civil Liberties Association of Toronto (CLAT); Don Franco, a University of Toronto graduate student and president of the Humanist Club; Kinzie Tanaka, of the JCCD (brother of George Tanaka of the National JCCA, the successor of the JCCD); and Donalda MacMillan, of the CCJC. The committee also decided to broaden its membership further by inviting participation from fraternal organizations.[16]

On Monday, 25 July, the delegation (which was joined in Ottawa by Eugene Forsey, of the Canadian Congress of Labour, and the Reverend George Reany, of the Hamilton CCJC) secured a series of meetings over the course of two days with Humphrey Mitchell, minister of labour, Norman Robertson, the undersecretary of state for external affairs, and Arthur Brown, solicitor for the Labour Department. Although the first day began well, with a sumptuous breakfast at the Chateau Laurier, the meetings were a frustrating exercise. Norman Robertson (the only official who met with the delegation that day) staunchly defended Ottawa's policy and expressed ignorance of any public opposition to it. He admitted that the Canadian government had done a "poor job with the matter of the Japanese since day one and that it might be in the best interest for them to return to Japan." This was certainly a disappointing response from an Ottawa mandarin who often took a liberal position. Robertson has been described as a "civil libertarian ... a humanist ... a gentle man who operated in the world of power ... and King's 'closest adviser.'" However sympathetic he may have been on other issues of the time, he acted in fine Janus-faced form in the case of the Nikkei.[17]

Next day, meetings with other officials would yield similar unsatisfactory results. For example, Humphrey Mitchell stated that it was not in the interest of the government to educate Canadians about prejudice, but that the CCJC was doing "a fine job." As a result of these meetings, the CCJC decided that it would have to rouse widespread public opposition before effective changes to government policy could be considered. Various committee members visited other organizations to discuss the situation, press releases went out to the media, and copies of a pamphlet titled *What about the Japanese Canadians?* were sent to interested groups across the country, as well as to members of Parliament.[18]

It was at this point in its career that the CCJC began to assume the role it would play in Canada's first major post-war human rights effort. The repatriation plan galvanized CCJC members into realizing that the Japanese Canadian problem involved more than merely coping with resettlement issues (although that would remain one of the committee's major tasks): it demanded action to ensure that these citizens be treated in a "just and democratic manner." Moreover, Ottawa's policy had implications beyond Canada's system of democracy: the nation's treatment of persons of Japanese ancestry would affect its reputation abroad.[19]

This new focus on human rights appears in the CCJC's first brief to the federal government. While congratulating Prime Minister King for upholding the ideals of the Atlantic Charter in his 4 August 1944 policy statement, specifically with regard to his pledge "to encourage respect for human rights and for fundamental freedoms for all without distinction as to race, language, religion or sex," the CCJC castigated him for the practical results of that policy. Canada was, the CCJC asserted, "already unwittingly a party to the Nazi treatment of an innocent and highly reputable minority."[20]

Yet it is also evident that the CCJC's egalitarian ideals, insofar as applied to persons of Japanese ancestry, were limited. At this point, in mid-1945, no one was pressing for the rights of *all* Nikkei in Canada. Restricting its efforts to the support of Japanese Canadians, the CCJC brought Japanese nationals into the discussion only when it encouraged the government to allow them to apply for Canadian citizenship.[21]

"We Must Not, in the Fighting, Lose the Freedoms for Which We Fight"

Although the activities of the CCJC were just gearing up in mid-1945, and as Canadian government policies were becoming increasingly oppressive, the operations of the ACLU on behalf of Japanese Americans were already well under way, and the discriminatory policies of the American government were slowly being revoked. The ACLU was a party to a few Supreme Court cases contesting the exclusion and relocation orders, and it was coordinating the efforts of several advocacy groups across the country, including its own affiliates on the Pacific coast and the Japanese American Citizens League (JACL), a prominent lobby group. Members were in constant contact with government officials who were sympathetic to the plight of the Nikkei, and the group was conducting a sophisticated public relations campaign through friendly newspapers.

The ACLU's move to involve itself in the relocation question had not been a foregone conclusion. From its beginning in 1942 and throughout the war, the removal of the Nikkei was one of the most contentious issues ever to confront the ACLU. Unlike the CCJC, which was formed largely in an ad hoc fashion around the single issue of justice for Japanese Canadians, the ACLU was a long-established, more broad-based interest group, concerned with safeguarding the rights of Americans as guaranteed in the Bill of Rights. The removal of Japanese Americans was but one of many issues that engaged the ACLU over the course of the Second World War. Whereas the decision of CCJC members to expand their organization from a local to a national lobby group was uncomplicated in that no disagreement occurred among the membership, the ACLU faced a schism over its involvement in the removal and relocation issues, both within its national executive board and from its west coast affiliates, particularly the Northern California and Southern California branches. These internal debates reveal much about the nature of the ACLU as an organization, and principally about the limits of liberalism in time of war, even within a civil liberties organization.

When the ACLU was formed on 19 January 1920 from the earlier National Civil Liberties Bureau, it was unique among the small group of civil rights organizations that already existed: these included the National Association for the Advancement of Colored People (NAACP, 1909), the Anti-Defamation League (1913), and the American Jewish Congress (1916).[22] These served as specific interest groups, whereas the ACLU adopted as its mission the impartial defence of civil liberties, especially free speech.[23] The ACLU enlarged the range of its concerns over time as issues shifted and expanded. It ventured from defending the right of free speech into such areas as radio, press, movie, and stage censorship; the civil rights of organized labour, employers, and unorganized workers; the defence of radical, racial, and religious minorities; academic freedom; and the rights of conscientious objectors.[24]

If war in 1917 gave the ACLU its start, war in 1941 would present a serious challenge to its ability to address multiple concurrent threats to civil liberties. Anti-communist fever swept through the ACLU following the Hitler-Stalin pact in 1939 and produced a decision that deviated from its principles: a policy enacted in 1940 that barred anyone who supported totalitarian regimes from holding official positions within the ACLU. The first and only casualty of this policy was Elizabeth Gurley Flynn, a colourful radical and founding member of the ACLU who also belonged to the Communist Party's National Committee. The decision on 7 May 1940 to purge Flynn from its ranks bitterly divided the ACLU board and demonstrated the uncertain state of civil liberties on the eve of the country's entrance into war.[25] At the same time, the ACLU maintained its policy of defending free speech for German American Nazis. "Persecute the Nazis," cautioned one ACLU publication, "and attract to them hundreds of sympathizers with the persecuted who would have otherwise been indifferent." Once war was declared, however, the ACLU board issued a statement asserting that not all speech deserved defence in wartime.[26]

In 1941, even as President Roosevelt declared 15 December as Bill of Rights Day, and as the chair of the Baltimore American Bar Association's Bill of Rights Committee remarked that the Bill of Rights "is an accepted and integral part of everyday and ordinary use," Americans were still unclear about the scope of the first ten amendments to the US Constitution.[27] "American" ideas were acceptable, but "un-American" concepts such as communism and fascism were not; to preserve democracy, the manifestations of those suspect concepts, such as political groups, would have to be excluded, or at least restricted, from the democratic process.

Like the CCJC, the ACLU as an organization attracted members from a confined spectrum of American society, including religious and social justice organizations and left-leaning members of the media. In particular, the ACLU often reflected the views of its main founder, Roger Nash Baldwin. Active throughout his life in various social justice organizations, Baldwin was an influential player in the National Urban League, the pacifist Fellowship of Reconciliation (FOR), the International Committee for Political Prisoners, the League against Imperialism, the League for Peace and Democracy, and the Friends of the Soviet Union. He has been characterized by many biographers and contemporaries as a political man who could inspire and manipulate followers and as a practical idealist who could work within the system for an unpopular cause.[28]

The legal profession was well represented in the ACLU through the membership of such notable talents as Arthur Garfield Hays, a successful corporate attorney who worked for free on ACLU cases; John Finerty, a counsel in the Sacco-Vanzetti case; Thurgood Marshall, counsel for the NAACP; Whitney North Seymour, former assistant solicitor general of the United States; and Raymond S. Wise, formerly the special assistant US attorney. By 1951, 47 percent of the ACLU board of directors came from the legal profession. Throughout the country, the ACLU was able to enlist prominent lawyers as volunteers on cases that aroused their interest or their indignation. The majority of the more faithful ACLU lawyers were less well known. Their "race," ethnicity, religion, and/or politics inclined them to the causes that the ACLU supported. In general, they were "liberals genuinely devoted to principle."[29]

Although ACLU members were drawn from religious institutions and organizations, they were not in the majority, as in the CCJC. Additionally, the ACLU attracted individuals from a variety of religious denominations, whereas the CCJC drew heavily from the Protestant churches. Harry Binsse, for example, was editor of *Commonweal*, a Roman Catholic weekly; Allan Knight Chalmers was pastor of the Broadway Tabernacle Congregational Church in New York City; John Haynes Holmes, chair of the ACLU board at this time, was founder and minister of the Community Church (Unitarian) in New York City and also served as vice-president of the NAACP; pacifist Episcopal minister John Nevin Sayre, a member of the ACLU executive, was co-director of the FOR; and William Spofford was president of the Christian Social Justice Fund and executive secretary of the Church League for Industrial Democracy. Norman Thomas, who ran unsuccessfully for the presidency on eight occasions as the Socialist Party candidate, was also a Presbyterian minister.[30]

At the beginning of the Second World War, the ACLU was, as it had always been, a loose coalition of respectable socialists, political radicals, religious pacifists, and lawyers and law professors who were concerned with civil liberties in general and favourite causes in particular. An internal survey of the National Committee conducted in 1935 listed twenty-eight socialists, twenty-two Democrats, four communist sympathizers, and three Republicans.[31] This diversity of membership would have a significant impact on the ACLU's response to the relocation orders. The decidedly left-of-centre board found itself in a remarkable situation: facing a membership that included a coalition of Roosevelt loyalists and conservative lawyers who strongly approved of US participation in the war.

The 19 February 1942 announcement of Executive Order 9066 and the 20 February military takeover of the "Japanese problem" was greeted with joy and relief by west coast newspapers and anti-Asian groups. The president authorized the secretary of war to designate military zones "from which any or all persons may be excluded," thus delegating to the military sweeping powers over American citizens. It was not yet clear what form of treatment the military intended, but popular opinion favoured mass imprisonment or deportation. Away from the west coast, reaction in the eastern media was fairly muted by comparison.[32]

The Japanese American Citizens League (JACL), the leading organization for Japanese Americans, decided not to oppose the relocation orders and instructed its members not to contest them in the courts. Opposition to the orders, it advised, was unpatriotic and would be harmful to the war effort.[33] Eventually, the JACL pursued a more activist policy and cooperated closely with the ACLU.[34] From the beginning, however, the ACLU and the American Friends Service Committee (AFSC) were the only national organizations to protest the orders as unconstitutional and unjust.

The ACLU did not immediately back up its swift condemnation of Executive Order 9066 with effective lobbying. Rather, in a remarkable turnaround in the months that followed, it moved from total condemnation of the presidential order to a more tepid disapproval of "evacuation" and the breakup of families. Its initial confusion can perhaps be explained by the fact that Baldwin and other ACLU members were confident that American ideals would prevail. Editorials calling for "tolerance" in the wake of the attack on Pearl Harbor persuaded Baldwin and others that Japanese Americans would probably escape the repression suffered by German Americans during the First World War.[35]

The press releases issued by the ACLU in the first week of March illustrate the group's confused stand. Although the ACLU criticized the "unnecessarily sweeping powers" of the presidential edict, it professed "not the slightest intention of interfering with any necessary moves to protect the West Coast area." At the same time, ACLU telegrams to affiliates in Los Angeles and San Francisco urged them to find litigation through which the ACLU could test the validity of the orders.[36] Three weeks later, in a fuller statement, the ACLU declared the order "open to grave question" on constitutional grounds, called for individual hearings, and expressed the hope that there would be "an effort to reconcile, as far as possible, civil rights with military necessities."[37] These statements represent the sum total of ACLU public activities on this issue during the crucial early months while removal was under way.

Deep factional differences surfaced during the board's initial discussions of the Japanese American issue on 2 March. Members ratified two of Baldwin's suggestions: the "creation of influential national and California committees to secure modification" of military orders and "an immediate court test of legality" of the expected orders.[38] Later in March, Baldwin drafted for the board a public letter to Roosevelt in which he set out the ACLU's concern that Executive Order 9066 was "open to grave question on the constitutional grounds of depriving American citizens of their liberty and use of their property without due process of law." The letter also urged Washington to establish a system of individual loyalty hearings for Japanese Americans who were subject to removal orders. The most notable part of the letter, however, pointed out the contradictory position of the government and observed that Executive Order 9066 "will add substance to the agitation abroad of Axis propagandists who constantly attack racial prejudice and discrimination here as revealing the insincerity of our democratic professions."[39]

The letter to Roosevelt was approved at the 23 March ACLU board meeting, but five members registered dissent. Among them were lawyers Morris Ernst and Raymond Wise, who represented the board's conservative faction adamantly loyal to Roosevelt, and Corliss Lamont, the heir to a railroad fortune and a vocal left-wing gadfly. Lamont voted not from partisan attachment but in support of Roosevelt as leader of the nation in wartime alliance with the Soviet Union, as occasioned by Nazi Germany's 1941 invasion of the Soviet Union. This coalition comprised of Roosevelt loyalists and fellow travellers failed to block the board's decision to send the letter to the president, but it complicated Baldwin's efforts to find a test case by continually trying to reverse the board's stand on Executive Order 9066. Some of these board members even favoured incarceration.[40]

While the ACLU affiliates on the west coast searched for test cases, the rift among the ACLU board members deepened. Those opposed to challenging the president's order were from the conservative, liberal, and leftist ranks of the ACLU, a seemingly inconceivable alliance. Whitney North Seymour led the conservative faction, which automatically deferred to wartime presidential authority. The liberals felt both loyalty to Roosevelt and revulsion for Nazi Germany. These conservatives and liberals were reluctant to question the judgment of the commander-in-chief, lest the successful prosecution of the war be hampered by dissent. Other liberals questioned the ACLU's ability to gauge "military necessity." On the other hand, ACLU leftists and fellow travellers were influenced by their concern for the Soviet Union, which they felt was carrying the full burden of the campaign against Germany. They charged the ACLU with being "obstructionist."[41]

The negative reaction to the Roosevelt letter by the conservative, liberal, and leftist ranks of the ACLU also reflects the pervasiveness of contemporary thinking on race, which focused on biological explanations of the behaviour of certain racial groups. In their letters to Baldwin recommending that the ACLU not lodge a protest against relocation, some ACLU members suggested that loyalty tests administered to Japanese Americans would be ineffective because the test subjects "have a general type of feature which makes it very difficult for the average European to distinguish one Japanese from another." Others cited Pearl Harbor as evidence enough of the necessity of the measures, implying the old adage that blood is thicker than water.[42] Alexander Meiklejohn expressed the attitudes about race held by both conservative and liberal factions when he wrote to Baldwin: "For us to say that they are taking away civil rights, would have as much sense as protesting because a 'measles' house is isolated. The Japanese citizens, as a group, are dangerous both to themselves and to their fellow-citizens. And, that being true, discriminatory action is justified." In making such a statement, Meiklejohn was highlighting a common belief of the day that relocation was "justified" as it would promote the assimilation of the Japanese into American life.[43]

The strongest opposition to the executive order came from the "old pacifists" in the ACLU, a group that included Roger Baldwin, Norman Thomas, John Haynes Holmes, and Arthur Garfield Hays. These men recognized the contradiction inherent in the president's policy: it exemplified the growing centralization of government power that could also be found in totalitarian societies. To them, Executive Order 9066 was particularly disturbing because it was identified with a war being fought for the preservation of democracy and against totalitarianism. Of these men, Norman Thomas stands out as a veritable "Cassandra." Long before the issuance of Executive Order 9066, Thomas was warning of precisely what occurred – the removal and incarceration of persons of Japanese ancestry on the west coast.[44]

At this point, no one, save for Thomas, was articulating the idea that the civil rights of the Nikkei were being violated. Still, some ACLU members recognized that the removal orders were setting a precedent that had wider implications for other minority groups.[45] For this element in the ACLU, the issue of removal was more than a question of the abrogation of minority group civil rights: it involved the complete abandonment of the principle of egalitarianism. During the crisis of wartime, the real protection of minority groups – recognition of equal rights under the law – becomes contentious and is therefore difficult to safeguard.

The ACLU recognized the need for minority group cooperation in its efforts to seek justice for Japanese Americans. ACLU manuscript records reveal press releases and suggestions for editorial comments directed specifically towards African American presses. One such release for editorial comment mused that

> Many other minority groups e.g. the Negroes have become seriously concerned with what we are doing to the Japanese minority group. The degree to which various groups within the United States are anxious as to their future in the American Republic, determines the degree to which they will aggressively defend it. For a united home front, all groups within it, racial, religious and political must have a firm sense of security that in fighting for the US they are also fighting for their own security.[46]

Baldwin also released similar commentary specifically for publication in the *Pacific Citizen*, the newspaper of the JACL.[47]

The unity on the home front that the ACLU so desired was certainly elusive within its own membership. In general, the variance in ACLU responses to Executive Order 9066 can be explained by the diverse nature of this organization, as Baldwin himself noted:

> Unlike many other agencies, we did not represent the self-interest of members to inspire loyalty, nor did we represent a single program to bind people together in common understanding. Civil liberties covered so many areas and activities that people interested in academic freedom, for example, would commonly show little interest in defending Jehovah's Witnesses or in censorship or in Communist cases. Our very divergence and catholicity of purpose was our weakness.[48]

The discord within the ACLU board became a major policy debate when the conservative-liberal-left coalition[49] forced a vote on two resolutions that symbolized the markedly different approaches to the removal question. Resolution 1, drafted by Arthur Garfield Hays of the "old pacifists" coalition, opposed the president's order in its entirety, asserting that, in "the absence of any conditions justifying a declaration of martial law, any order ... investing either military or civil authorities with power to remove any *citizen* or *group of citizens* from any zone established by such authorities ... constitutes a violation of civil liberties." The proposal for loyalty hearings, included in the original letter to Roosevelt, was now repudiated on constitutional grounds. The resolution closed with a warning that the president's order, if "pushed to its logical conclusion would justify even the adoption of Fascism in the United States to beat the Fascism of our enemies."[50] Those in favour of this resolution believed that the removal program violated the civil rights of American citizens on account of their race.

Resolution 2, favoured by the conservative-liberal-left coalition, reflected a compromise between those who wished the ACLU to remain noncommittal on the issue and those who wanted to reconcile their loyalty to a homeland engaged in a "just" war with their loyalty to civil liberties principles that would undoubtedly suffer during that war. The drafters negotiated these muddy waters by accepting the president's order but qualified it with procedural constraints. Resolution 2 conceded the government's right during wartime "to establish military zones and to remove persons, either citizens or aliens, from such zones when their presence may endanger national security, even in the absence of martial law." The qualifying conditions for ACLU support were that removal must be "directly necessary to the prosecution of the war or the defense of national security" and that the removal of individuals be "based upon a classification having a reasonable relationship to the danger intended to be met," thus implying that racial categorizations were still objectionable.[51]

The strong support given to Resolution 2 by several Jewish members (with the important exception of Arthur Garfield Hays) caused despair among the pacifists. In a hastily written letter, John Haynes Holmes lamented the loss of Jewish support but recognized the rationale behind the Jewish community's response. Norman Thomas likened supporting the president to treating "the children of Japanese as Stalin treated the German colonies along the Volga and as Hitler treats Jews."[52]

The governing bodies of the ACLU approved Resolution 2 by a precise two to one margin.[53] The Northern California branch, however, favoured Resolution 1 by a vote of six to four. Although this vote did not count in the final tally because only the national board vote was binding, it foreshadowed difficulties between the California branches and the national branch in New York City.[54] Approval of Resolution 2 indicated overwhelming acceptance of the government's right to subordinate civil liberties to wartime conditions and military needs but did not exclude all legal questions regarding the relocation program. The government could be challenged to show the necessity of the wholesale removal of Japanese Americans from their homes, and lawyers could argue that the order unlawfully singled out the Nikkei solely on race. Yet the vote represented a retreat from the ACLU's earlier position, as outlined in the letter to Roosevelt. From a public relations standpoint, it appeared that the ACLU endorsed the policy of the government and ignored the problem.

Interestingly, an earlier vote on compulsory civilian service in wartime revealed a similar reticence to address issues of civil liberties during a condition of war. In an almost two to one vote, the ACLU endorsed the idea, determining that "the United States has a right to mobilize all persons subject to its jurisdiction for the purposes of the prosecution of a war, whether for combatant or civilian service."[55]

The vote forced civil libertarians to define the specific substance of their beliefs. Should government power be constrained in wartime? What were the responsibilities of civil libertarians during wartime? Whatever their feelings about Executive Order 9066, most ACLU members could nevertheless agree that relocation would provide at least one benefit: the assimilation of Japanese citizens into American life. Like their Canadian counterparts, liberals in the United States identified the congregation of Japanese Americans on the Pacific coast as a problem.[56] It is also note-worthy that the ACLU decision not to condemn the presidential order of 19 February had an impact on the manner in which other groups would perceive and articulate their own responses. In particular, during an internal struggle within the National Council of Jewish Women, its president cited ACLU acceptance of the presidential order as a reason why liberals in the council must approve of relocation.[57]

The ACLU both lost and gained members as a result of the May vote. Perhaps most significantly, Norman Thomas nearly ended his long-standing affiliation with the ACLU over its failure to challenge the removal policy or the legality of the conscription of Japanese Americans. He considered the Nikkei relocation to be one of the most egregious violations of civil liberties ever committed by the United States government. Entreaties by Baldwin and Holmes persuaded Thomas to remain in the ACLU, but he demonstrated his disgust with the May decision by advising the Northern California and Seattle branches on how to circumvent the party line. He also attempted to impart his own critique through the Post War World Council, of which he was a founding member. In this group, he again found it necessary to temper his criticism in order to reach out to a broad liberal constituency.[58] Holmes, too, was able to reconcile himself to the repudiation of a principle of constitutional law basic to civil liberties by concluding that, although the ACLU "failed theoretically in the matter of principle," it was vindicated "practically in the matter of public action."[59]

Organizational difficulties also hampered the ACLU's handling of the removal issue. The national body had to contend with two very stubborn and warring branches in California. The main problems were the feuds between northern and southern branch lawyers who represented Japanese American clients, and the desire of the branches themselves for autonomy from the head office. Each California branch believed that its "proximity" to the problem gave it a more competent and effective understanding of the situation than the main branch. On 22 June, the national board of directors ordered Baldwin to inform the west coast affiliates that "local communities are not free to sponsor cases in which the position is taken that the government has no constitutional right to remove citizens from

military areas."[60] This dictum angered the branches and served to undermine the litigation they had already solicited. Mary Farquharson of the
Seattle branch wrote to Baldwin that she "was very much disappointed –
and shocked – to learn of the action" of the ACLU board.[61]

The Northern California Civil Liberties Union (NCCLU), based in San
Francisco, maintained the most uncompromising opposition to the
national board. The NCCLU board of directors, led by Ernest Besig, decided
to accept the results of the vote on the resolutions as binding on future
litigation but not on cases already open.[62] The NCCLU's determination to
prosecute its single test case, as promised to its members and to Fred Korematsu, the subject, amounted to a complete repudiation of the referendum
and the national board directive. For the next two years, angry letters flew
between Baldwin and Besig, who vowed, "We don't intend to trim our
sails to suit the Board's vacillating policy."[63] The national board, however,
wanted to maintain ACLU solidarity. Eventually, the NCCLU agreed to
submit briefs under its lawyer's name without mentioning any affiliation
with the ACLU.[64] Nevertheless, the acrimonious relations continued, and
the NCCLU nearly severed its ties with the national board in 1944.[65]

Faced with a divided national board and a local branch that disregarded
its authority, Baldwin kept the ACLU closely focused on aspects of the
removal and incarceration that it could address successfully. The ACLU
was one of the few organizations still speaking out for the civil liberties
of the incarcerated. For about a year, while keeping channels open with
the San Francisco board, Baldwin maintained pressure at the Justice Department to improve conditions for Japanese Americans and to develop a
release and furlough program that would ease the economic hardship
caused by detention. He also attempted to influence the army's administration of the program but went too far when he sent congratulatory letters to Lieutenant General John DeWitt, praising his handling of the
removal program for its "efficiency." Norman Thomas attacked him as
being "more agent than gadfly to the army."[66]

Three test cases – *Korematsu, Hirabayashi,* and *Yasui* (known collectively
as the Japanese American cases) – slowly developed over 1942 and 1943,
in no small way due to the persistence of the ACLU affiliates.[67] Eventually, they arrived at the Supreme Court, which heard the oral arguments
on 10 and 11 May 1943. The Seattle chapter of the ACLU filed an amicus curiae brief in *Hirabayashi,* and the NCCLU continued with its support of *Korematsu.* This legal term, Latin for "friend of the court," refers
to a party or organization that, though not a litigant, is nonetheless interested in an issue raised by the case. An amicus curiae may file a brief or
participate in an argument regarding the issue. An organization wishing to
take the amicus role must usually receive the court's permission and must
also secure the agreement of the party it desires to support. Additionally,

the amicus curiae argument is presented during the courtroom time allot-
ted to the litigant. The national ACLU refused to partner with the JACL
in the test cases, however, a decision that reflected its desire to appear
only in matters affecting the civil liberties of all Americans. As ACLU general counsel Clifford Forster put it, if "the JACL were to act jointly with
us it might appear we are taking these cases up only because the issues
affect Japanese Americans."[68] The national board did not participate until
1944, in *Ex Parte Endo*, the fourth test case.

These four test cases raised the basic questions of constitutional government that had previously stymied the ACLU. What were the limits of
the war powers in the Constitution? How far could the president and Congress compromise the rights of citizens in order to prosecute a war?
Although the Supreme Court upheld the government's authority in *Korematsu, Hirabayashi,* and *Yasui,* it finally reached a favourable decision with
Ex Parte Endo. This was delivered, however, on the day after the War Department rescinded the mass exclusion orders, allowing Japanese Americans to return to their Pacific coast homes as of 2 January 1945.[69]

The unwillingness of the US Supreme Court to strike down the removal
program is often viewed as a wartime aberration. If unwillingness is seen
as wartime aberration, opinions mirror ACLU conflict. Regardless, the diverg-
ence in the court decisions mirrored the conflict of allegiance that ACLU
members themselves had attempted to reconcile: how can the total war
needs of the state be harmonized with the protection of civil liberties and
the rights of citizens as outlined in the Constitution?

"It Is No Time to Cease Activity": The Maturation of the CCJC

For the ACLU, the incarceration of Japanese Americans was, from the
beginning, a clear-cut abrogation of civil liberties. For the CCJC, on the
other hand, the meaning of Nikkei removal and expatriation evolved over
the course of the war. Its initial assimilationist focus soon gave way to a
stronger defence of the human rights of Japanese Canadians. This development reflected the awareness of rights that grew throughout the period,
which also led to a very Canadian response to removal and expatriation.
In particular, the expatriation of Japanese Canadians, both naturalized and
citizens, incited the most vocal and overwhelming public opposition to
the actions of Ottawa.

Throughout 1944 and 1945, the CCJC sought to influence the government indirectly, by rousing public opinion. As already noted, it circulated
thousands of petitions, held numerous public meetings across the country, sent press releases to the media, and distributed copies of Howard
Norman's *What about the Japanese Canadians?* to cooperating groups
Canada-wide, as well as to all MPs, Prime Minister King, and his Cabinet.
In a letter accompanying the pamphlet, the CCJC once again referred to

human rights discourse in urging the government to consider carefully how it planned to deal with the "problem," for the answer "determines the measure of our ability to fulfill the pledge [to respect human rights in the United Nations Charter] made with other nations at San Francisco."[70]

The King government, however, was under direct political pressure from other sources. According to a confidential memorandum addressed to King, these included "large and influential groups in British Columbia, many of whom are determined that the Japanese shall never be allowed to return to that province." Among them were the *Vancouver Sun* and Liberal politicians, such as King's own Cabinet minister Ian Alistair Mackenzie, MP for Vancouver Centre. Other Liberal politicians from British Columbia, such as Tom Reid (New Westminster) and George Cruickshank (Fraser Valley), were also among those who pressured Ottawa to take a harder line on the Japanese "problem." Gabrielle Nishiguchi has noted that deportation became a convenient solution to King's political problem with British Columbia and the uncooperative stance taken by many provinces regarding the permanent dispersal of Japanese Canadians. Most of the provinces had agreed to accept relocatees only for the duration of the war, and they had extracted a promise from the King government to this effect.[71]

By mid-1945, the CCJC was evolving towards a highly politicized organization. Its membership was no longer dominated by former missionaries and members of religious institutions (see Appendix 1 list). As Ross Lambertson has pointed out, a majority of CCJC members were representatives of the Civil Liberties Association of Toronto (CLAT); these included its president, George Tatham, of the University of Toronto, Jarvis McCurdy, another University of Toronto academic, journalist Margaret Gould, CCF activist and lawyer F. Andrew Brewin, and B.K. Sandwell.[72]

The CCJC also broadened its advocacy in November 1945, following a statement made in the House of Commons by Minister of Labour Humphrey Mitchell clarifying the government's commitment to "repatriate" most of the individuals who had signed the forms declaring their intention to go to Japan. He announced that the government would accept applications for revocation made by Canadian-born and naturalized citizens before 2 September 1945, the date of Japan's surrender, but made no mention on the fate of those who had applied after that date. Although a small victory was gained with the promise to review the cases of Canadian-born Japanese, the provisions regarding naturalized citizens and Japanese nationals – that they were still under threat of deportation – remained unsatisfactory. Many of them were parents of Canadian-born children. Basing its stance on information from many Japanese Canadians and their supporters in British Columbia, the CCJC also alleged that duress was involved in the signing of the repatriation forms. Unimpressed by Mitchell's stratagem, the CCJC sent a telegram to the prime minister requesting that *all* applications for the cancellation of deportation, notwithstanding their date of request, be submitted to the courts for adjudication. The CCJC's criticism of such distinctions marked its willingness to defend all Canadian Nikkei, not just Canadian citizens of Japanese ancestry.[73]

As a result of the CCJC's continued public education campaign, more letters flowed into the offices of the prime minister, Cabinet ministers, and MPs protesting the deportation and demanding the removal of restrictions on Japanese Canadians. In particular, many felt the deportation orders were at odds with the principles of Bill 20, the Canadian Citizenship Act, introduced in Parliament on 22 October 1945. This act expressed the growing belief that legal distinctions between Canadians on racial or any other grounds were very "un-Canadian." In introducing the bill, however, Secretary of State Paul Martin had assured Parliament that its passage would not stand in the way of the deportation of Japanese Canadians.[74] To achieve this, Parliament introduced the National Emergency Transitional Powers Act, Bill 15, with clause G, section 3 authorizing deportations and revocation of nationality. Although the term "Japanese" did not appear in the bill, the intended targets were clear. Due to opposition from MPs, the Cooperative Commonwealth Federation, and religious organizations, clause G, section 3 was eventually withdrawn when Bill 15 was passed on 7 December. This victory was encouraging, but the CCJC continued its efforts to keep the issue alive in the press and the minds of Canadians.[75]

Just a week later, on 15 December, the King government bypassed Parliament and issued three Orders-in-Council (P.C. 7355, 7356, and 7357) that extended the government's broad powers to conduct deportations under the soon-to-lapse War Measures Act. As of 1 January 1946, under the National Emergency Transitional Powers Act, the Orders-in-Council empowered the government to carry out its "repatriation" plan.[76]

When, despite the public appeal, the Orders-in-Council authorizing the deportations were announced, the CCJC resolved to take legal action. This decision was a major step for a small executive representing a loosely knit group of organizations. F. Andrew Brewin was asked to serve as legal counsel for the committee.[77] The CCJC then took advocacy to the courts. What began as a writ issued by the CCJC against the attorney general of Canada testing the legality of the Orders-in-Council was soon referred by the Cabinet to the Supreme Court.

The CCJC began an intensive fundraising campaign to finance the case. Within a month, $10,000 was subscribed, with $20,000 collected in total over the course of the campaign. The CCJC also initiated a series of public meetings. On 10 January 1946, for example, nearly a thousand people attended a meeting held at Jarvis Collegiate in Toronto to hear addresses by Liberal senators Cairine Wilson and Arthur Roebuck, well-known human rights supporters. In her speech, Wilson asserted that "I would not like to

CANADIANS CONDEMNED
Without Trial-Without Justice

23,000 have been forced from their homes—have had their property seized and sold — are still denied the right to rent or buy land, houses or business — to travel and live where they wish.

74 Per Cent are Canadian citizens. Many others would be, but citizenship is refused them.

Their Crime?

They are of Japanese racial origin.

Are they therefore responsible for the crimes of Japan's war-lords? No responsible person asserts this.

Many have lived here 35 to 40 years.

No such charge is laid against Canadians of German or Italian descent.

Their Guilt?

They are good citizens, law-abiding, industrious.

They are loyal Canadians. Many Japanese-Canadians served in our armed forces.

On the authority of the Prime Minister of Canada, there is no charge of sabotage against them.

Yet thousands of these Canadians are being forced to move to Japan—a country over half of them have never seen.

JOIN THE PROTEST AGAINST THIS INJUSTICE
Public Meeting For Action

JARVIS COLLEGIATE
JARVIS ST. AT WELLESLEY

Thursday, Jan. 10, at 8 p.m.

SPEAKERS:
Senator ARTHUR ROEBUCK, K.C.   Senator CAIRINE WILSON
Rabbi A. FEINBERG   B. K. SANDWELL, Chairman

INFORMATION - DISCUSSION - ACTION

Sponsored Jointly by
CIVIL LIBERTIES ASSOCIATION OF TORONTO
CO-OPERATIVE COMMITTEE ON JAPANESE-CANADIANS

A CCJC poster calls citizens to meet in protest of injustices against Japanese Canadians.
Toronto Globe and Mail, 9 January 1946

think that after Canada's endorsation of the Atlantic Charter that we are about to violate these pledges." Rabbi Abraham Feinberg of Toronto's Holy Blossom Temple declared his support for rectifying the deportation injustice on behalf of "six million Jews who have been slaughtered in Europe for no other reason than that they were Jews."[78] Andrew Brewin spoke about the legal issues at hand. Both Wilson and Roebuck serve as good examples of influential Canadians, particularly politicians, who were involved in the CCJC, a topic that will be developed later. Similarly, Feinberg provides an example of the nature of minority and ethnic group cooperation in the burgeoning human rights movement, another theme to be explored in the pages to come.

Two resolutions came out of this meeting. One was sent to Prime Minister King; the other, delivered to Premier George A. Drew of Ontario, challenged the provincial government "to accept the citizenship and residence of Canadians of Japanese origin on a basis of equality with Canadians of other national origins." The intent of both resolutions was to demonstrate to the two governments that, as the eastern provinces, particularly Ontario, received increasing numbers of Japanese Canadian relocatees, the "Japanese problem" need not advance as far as expatriation. Even Ontario attorney general Leslie Blackwell (Conservative MPP, Eglinton) stated that he did not have the power to exclude Japanese Canadians from the province.[79]

A CCJC-sponsored meeting held on 24 February at Toronto's Carlton Street United Church specifically addressed the issue of expatriation. Brewin, Charles Millard, a CCJC member and CIO–United Steelworkers director, Hugh MacMillan, Reverend Finlay, and businessman J. Charles Haugh were all speakers. With the lone dissenting voice at that open meeting coming from a former POW of the Japanese, attendees endorsed a resolution asking the federal government to refrain from taking any further action in "deporting" Japanese Canadians.[80]

Across the country, informal committees were formalized by early 1946, resulting in the creation of regional committees in Vancouver, Calgary, Edmonton, Lethbridge, Regina, Saskatoon, Winnipeg, Ottawa, and Montreal, joining the committees that already existed in southwestern Ontario. The CCJC was thus organized on a federated basis, much as the ACLU operated. The regional committees kept in fairly regular contact with the main group in Toronto, which in turn suggested tactics and advised them about activities and lobbying efforts. These groups would also become central to the fundraising efforts for the litigation.[81] The cooperating CCJC groups also provided Andrew Brewin with the names of lawyers who could advise him, as CCJC general counsel, on the development of legal arguments to present to the Supreme Court of Canada. Many of these lawyers, already sympathetic to the situation of the Japanese Canadians, were concerned about the challenge to citizenship represented by the government's policy.[82]

As in the four US Supreme Court cases, the argument in the case before the Supreme Court of Canada centred on the limits of power. The case, formally titled *In the Matter of a Reference as to the Validity of Orders in Council of the 15th Day of December, 1945 (P.C. 7355, 7356 and 7357) in Relation to Persons of Japanese Race* (1946) and hereafter cited as *In the Matter of a Reference*, called on the Supreme Court to consider certain issues: Did the British North America Act's "peace, order and good government" clause and the associated War Measures Act, under which the deportation orders were issued, confer unlimited powers on the federal government? In this case, what were the limits on Parliament and, specifically, on the Cabinet, when Parliament delegated certain powers to that body?

In the court's 20 February 1946 ruling, a majority of the justices decided that the Orders-in-Council were valid in part. In practical terms, this meant that the male deportees would still be deported, but their dependants – wives and children – could remain in Canada. The CCJC then decided to launch an immediate appeal to the Judicial Committee of the Privy Council in London, the final court of appeal in the British Commonwealth. Pamphleteering and lobbying continued afresh for *Co-operative Committee on Japanese Canadians v. Attorney-General of Canada et al.*, the Privy Council case, as did fundraising, which was especially successful at the regional

---

PUBLIC MEETING

"Conscience may not give sanction to acts that have the sanction of the law."

● Will the Canadian People allow the Government to use its powers under the War Measures Act to deport THOUSANDS OF JAPANESE-CANADIANS – in peace time?

● Since the Supreme Court has decreed that women and children can not be deported, will the Government be allowed to separate 3,500 Canadian children from their fathers?

● The majority decision of the Supreme Court justifies the proposed deportation on the grounds of consent, but did the Japanese-Canadians really consent?

HEAR THE FACTS DISCUSSED AT

CARLTON UNITED CHURCH
(Yonge and Carlton)

SUNDAY, FEB. 24th — 8:30 P.M.

Prepare for Further Action

Speakers:
ANDREW BREWIN   C. H. MILLARD
HUGH MACMILLAN   REV. J. M. FINLAY

Under the auspices of the Co-operative Committee on Japanese-Canadians.

A CCJC poster advertises for a meeting to discuss "the facts." *Toronto Globe and Mail*, 23 February 1946

level. A delegation met with the prime minister and several members of his Cabinet in Ottawa, where Andrew Brewin explained the CCJC position on deportation. To the obvious legal argument against the policy – the emergency wartime situation no longer existed – Brewin added several others that took morality as their common thread: the policy disparaged Canadian citizenship; it discriminated on the basis of race; and it was unjust and inhumane. These arguments were clearly stated in a CCJC leaflet titled *Our Japanese Canadians: Citizens, Not Exiles,* of which fifty thousand copies were distributed across the country. The author of the pamphlet, Forrest LaViolette, an American who worked at Wyoming's Heart Mountain camp, was a sociology professor at McGill and a member of the Montreal branch of the CCJC. The pamphlet cited the United Nations Charter in support of the CCJC conclusion that the expatriation/deportation policy violated the commitments to human rights made by the Canadian government. It also noted that the Orders-in-Council would "threaten the security of every minority in Canada, a land of minorities."[83] Following up on this meeting, the CCJC sent a memorandum to all MPs in which it accused the government of employing "the methods of Nazism" and claimed that such powers of exile had not been seen in civilized countries since the days of the Stuarts. The CCJC also challenged MPs and senators to consider carefully the ramifications of carrying out deportation, for deportation "on racial grounds has been defined as a crime against humanity, and the war criminals of Germany and Japan are being tried precisely for this offence."[84]

The Privy Council heard the appeal for four days in July 1946, with Andrew Brewin assisted by two eminent British barristers. The Privy Council's 2 December decision was a disappointment for the CCJC and its supporters. It ruled entirely in favour of Ottawa, concluding that the Orders-in-Council were valid because, under the War Measures Act and Transitional Powers Act, the government could legally do anything it considered necessary for the safety of the country.[85] As in the American cases, the outcome of the Privy Council appeal demonstrated that the nation's highest courts had no power in wartime to prevent the abrogation of civil liberties. Although these cases will be discussed more fully in Chapter 5, it is important to note here that the decisions of both the Supreme Court of Canada and the Judicial Committee of the Privy Council were based upon the principle of parliamentary supremacy: that elected representatives of the people were responsible for passing and revoking legislation. As long as such legislation does not violate the federal-provincial division of powers in the constitution, a parliament can pass virtually any law it wishes, no matter how unjust it may seem to be. Furthermore, when the Canadian decision was appealed to the Privy Council, the sovereignty of Parliament was undisputed and the lords of the council would not impinge upon the exclusive authority of the Parliament of Canada.

The CCJC was preparing for yet another meeting with the prime minister when, on 24 January 1947, the government declared that its deportation policy was "no longer necessary" and that the Orders-in-Council providing for the "deportation" of Japanese Canadians were repealed. Still, restrictions remained on the movement of Japanese Canadians within Canada, as did a host of others, and the CCJC vowed further action, "until Japanese Canadians enjoy the same rights and privileges as their fellow citizens of other races." The CCJC would also become involved in the Bird Commission (1947-50), which presided over the question of restitution for property losses, as a later chapter will detail. However, these subjects did not capture the degree of public support that had propelled the deportation issue, and the CCJC quietly wound up its affairs in the early 1950s.[86]

"I Am Painfully Familiar with the Canadian Japanese Situation"
On 15 January 1946, Andrew Brewin sent an urgently worded letter to Arthur Garfield Hays on "an issue of great importance." In brief, Brewin detailed the mechanisms by which Ottawa was proposing to deport "certain classes of Canadian citizens both naturalized and Canadian born 'of the Japanese race.'" Brewin requested the advice of his American counterparts as to the constitutional position in the United States in regard to the forcible deportation of American citizens, particularly those "of the Japanese race," by executive action. Brewin was quite reasonably well informed on the subject, noting that American law did not allow for the deportation of citizens against their will. Remarking that "your constitutional provisions are different from ours," he indicated that the CCJC position would be strengthened if it could refer to the fact that Congress, or at least the executive branch of the US government, did not have the power to do what Ottawa was proposing to do. He added that time was of the essence, as *In the Matter of a Reference* would be held on 24 January, implying that any helpful information would probably be used in the CCJC brief to the federal government.[87] Thus began a series of correspondence between the ACLU and the CCJC, as well as the Canadian government, over the course of 1946 and 1947 on the issue of deportation.

What Brewin did not realize was that, technically, the American situation differed markedly from that of Canada. In the US, the deportation involved only those Nikkei who had formally renounced their American citizenship. As mentioned previously, the ACLU extended its assistance only towards Japanese Americans. As the Nisei renunciants were legally considered aliens ineligible for American citizenship, the ACLU was bound by previous policy to withhold its support.

On 25 April 1946, Pearl Buck (who was also head of the ACLU committee on race relations) asked Roger Baldwin about the Japanese Canadian deportation proceedings. Declaring that "the policy is exactly what went on under Adolf Hitler in regard to the Jews," she asked, "is there any way of making intelligent Canadians realize this? There is a whole-sale feeling of race in Canada that is really very bad ... But I think that some recognition ought to be made of this by your office, even though it is outside of the direct jurisdiction of our country."[88] In his response to Buck, Baldwin wrote that he was "painfully familiar with the Canadian Japanese situation." Although he noted, quite correctly, that "there is a very strong movement in Canada against present policy and it has been well aired in Parliament," he promised to take up the matter with the Inter-national League for the Rights of Man, "which has jurisdiction anywhere," and to obtain up-to-date information "from our Canadian friends."[89]

Among US groups such as the ACLU and the JACL, interest in the sit-uation of the Canadian Nikkei was piqued by the deportation issue and more so by Brewin's repeated requests for information on the American matter. Earlier in the war, however, Roger Baldwin had corresponded on behalf of the ACLU with several government agencies and officials, attempt-ing to obtain information on Ottawa's removal plans and those specifi-cally related to Canadian citizens of Japanese ancestry.[90] It is unclear how or for what purpose Baldwin intended to use the information that he received; ACLU records do not indicate that the Canadian situation was referred to in ACLU board meetings, or in strategy.

The questions of how Ottawa would deal with the expatriation of Nikkei citizens and how the CCJC would deal with the matter were of immediate practical interest to the ACLU. In 1946, Washington began to deport nearly 5,400 Japanese Americans who had renounced their citizenship under duress. Many subsequently changed their minds and sought to regain their American citizenship. The information that Brewin could supply on both the rights of citizenship in Canada and the appeal to the Privy Council was of great interest to the ACLU and to Japanese Americans: as Baldwin noted, "your situation would be helpful in dealing with ours."[91]

The ACLU did manage, after another bitter internal dispute, to repre-sent three clients who were under the threat of deportation. But it was largely due to the efforts of Wayne Collins, a lawyer loosely affiliated with the Northern California branch of the ACLU, that the courts eventually halted immediate deportations and, in a series of cases that lingered until 1951, ordered the restoration of citizenship to the renunciants.[92] The ACLU's lack of involvement in this issue demonstrates that its commit-ment to the defence of civil liberties extended to American citizens only.

Whether Brewin's information proved directly helpful to the ACLU is uncertain. Nonetheless, the evidence of mutual cognizance of the issues facing both Canadian and American Nikkei is germane to Brewin's obser-vation to Baldwin that "Parliament can delegate almost any power at all however extreme to the executive and the courts will not interfere. This decision has added interest to the movement in Canada for incorporating a Bill of Rights in the British North America Act ... Hitherto the prevailing opinion in Canada has been that we can rely upon the British system of entrusting these matters entirely to Parliament, but the experience of the Japanese Canadians has proved that this is not satisfactory."[93]

Even as the CCJC espoused the principles of the emerging human rights discourse, these Canadian advocates recognized the need for a Canadian-style bill of rights for future campaigns to fight racial discrimination. Although the United Nations Charter encouraged respect for human rights and minority concerns, it did not provide specific measures for their promotion. The Committee for a Bill of Rights, for example, which followed closely on the heels of the Japanese Canadian campaign and shared many committee members with the CCJC, used the example of the Japanese Canadian issue in connection with the wider issue of the passage of a Canadian bill of rights. In building upon the success of the campaign to end deportations, Canadian advocates began to forward the idea that, in light of events at home and abroad, it was necessary to demonstrate clearly to all minorities and all Canadians the urgency of a "basic law which recognizes human personality and the right to freedom under the law of every Canadian citizen irrespective of race."[94] The enshrining of a bill of rights in the Constitution was a popular idea among advocates in post-war Canada and even received serious attention in the Senate.[95]

Indeed, the deportation struggle marked the beginning of a number of important human rights battles that would occur during the post-war period. Although Ramsay Cook has concluded that, during the war, the drastic curtailment of civil liberties under the Defence of Canada Regulations "was made possible by indifference or lack of faith and understanding of liberal institutions on the part of the majority of the Canadian people," the efforts of the CCJC and similar organizations appear to indicate that this situation had begun to change by the late 1940s.[96] Following in the wake of the CCJC success came the Committee for the Repeal of the Chinese Immigration Act (CRCIA). It included seventy-nine prominent Canadians, of whom 80 percent were non-Chinese. The CRCIA included CCJC members and had the support of religious organizations, several MPs, and labour groups. Largely as a result of an intensive campaign styled after that of the CCJC, the Chinese Immigration Act was repealed in May 1947. The CRCIA managed its efforts by employing a great many techniques: massaging the news media, producing and distributing pamphlets, coordinating letter-writing campaigns, obtaining the support of influential people, and sending delegations to Ottawa. Significantly, the CRCIA successfully appealed to the public conscience and to that of government officials by promoting the human rights discourse that had previously roused the Canadian public against the deportation policy.[97]

As previously noted, the ACLU's relative success in the courts and the public opinion backlash against the US relocation affected other issues involving Japanese Americans. The ACLU played a minor role in assisting renunciants to regain their American citizenship. A.L. Wirin, representing the SC-ACLU in *Oyama v. California,* was successful in challenging the 1913 California Alien Land Act, which prohibited alien Japanese from owning land. One year later, in 1948, Wirin was victorious once again in the Supreme Court, this time in convincing the court to overturn a 1943 California law denying fishing licences to resident alien Japanese.[98]

But this is not to suggest that the ACLU involvement in this issue left any significant legacy. The Japanese American issue was but one of many that occupied the ACLU throughout the war; nor, for an organization devoted to the protection of civil liberties, was it the most important one. The ACLU was caught up in such pressing concerns as conscientious objectors and freedom of speech in wartime. Years later, in fact, Baldwin would regret his own and the ACLU's stance regarding the removal. The influence of the ACLU itself declined after the war, as the attack on all radical and liberal agencies gained momentum under the pressures of the Cold War.[99]

The ACLU and the CCJC engaged in varying degrees of activism during and throughout the Second World War in relation to the incarceration and deportation of the Nikkei in their respective countries. However, they did not function in isolation. Religious bodies of various faiths, informal committees, citizens' groups, organizations dedicated to civil liberties, student associations, and others joined the ACLU and the CCJC in opposing the policies directed against Japanese Americans and Japanese Canadians. The efforts of the CCJC and the ACLU were also formally and informally aided by political parties and government officials. Eventually, the mainstream media took notice of the situation, and in the case of the CCJC, were especially instrumental in disseminating information to Canadians regarding its activities. The participation of these other factions in the fight to secure justice for the Nikkei had a significant impact on the nature and utility of coalition building in the post-war period and will be more fully discussed below. These groups were also instrumental in voicing the accepted rhetoric in each nation – the long-standing doctrine of civil liberties in the United States, and the emerging discourse of human rights in Canada.

3
"Dear Friend": Advocacy Expanded

> Groups of Canadians throughout Canada are publicly appealing
> against the deportation. Newspapers are decrying it. Churches
> plead against it. This is not public pressure?
>
> – Muriel Kitagawa, "Deportation Is a Violation
> of Human Rights," *New Canadian*, November
> 1946

In both Canada and the United States, groups other than the CCJC and
the ACLU agitated for the fair treatment of persons of Japanese ancestry,
as Muriel Kitagawa's comment reveals. In many cases, the support of these
groups and individuals was activated by a simple letter starting with the
salutation "Dear Friend." Many of these bodies were religious organizations,
especially Christian groups such as the American Friends Service Committee and, in both countries, the YMCA. In Canada's House of Commons, the
Co-operative Commonwealth Federation (CCF) openly denounced many
of the Japanese Canadian policies from their inception (with the exception of the expulsion policy); it was the only political party to do so. In
the United States, no elected member of a political party condemned Executive Order 9066, but several members of the Socialist Party, then headed
by Norman Thomas (a founding member of the ACLU), publicly criticized
the incarceration process in several newspaper editorials and radio debates.
For the most part, the American and Canadian media were unanimous in
their support for relocation; it was only later in the war effort, as Allied
victories in the Far East were more numerous, that this unanimity started
to unravel. It began in Canada with traditionally liberal newspapers such
as the *Winnipeg Free Press* and the *Toronto Daily Star*, as well as the weekly
newsmagazine *Saturday Night*. Gradually, letters to the editor and editorials
opposing the disfranchisement and, in 1946, the deportation of Canadian citizens of Japanese descent, appeared in other newspapers across the
country. In the United States, the *Call*, the Socialist Party's weekly newspaper, was the first in 1942 to protest Roosevelt's executive order. Some
religious periodicals followed suit, including the *Christian Century* and
Commonweal. Opposition to Executive Order 9066 was expressed in the
African American press.[1] Most mainstream newspapers in the United States
did not register opposition until 1943.

The role of religious groups, political parties, the media, and government moderates in advocating for the rights of the Nikkei was a significant aspect of the public pressure that Muriel Kitagawa so noted. Although the efforts of some who opposed removal and relocation were unquestionably inadequate and largely represented compromised positions, the activities of these supporters of Nikkei rights must be understood within their difficult political context. In combination with the submissions made to government officials, the pamphleteering, day-to-day ministering to the incarcerated, numerous petition campaigns, and letters to the editor embodied a creative and eventually effective opposition to the rigid anti-Japanese racism of the day. Many of these individuals and organizations cooperated with the CCJC and the ACLU, which was an effective means of coordinating public pressure on the federal governments.

Onward Christian Soldiers: Christian Groups and Advocacy

The role of the North American Christian churches in the relocation (and, in Canada, the expatriation) debate has been largely ignored in many leading historical accounts of the relocation.[2] Other historians and commentators have accused the churches of supporting government policy on racial or other grounds. Forrest E. LaViolette, for example, argues that religious leaders and laity shared some of the anti-Asian stereotypes that long marked both British Columbian and Canadian society.[3] Only recently has the role of the churches in mobilizing opposition to government persecution of the Nikkei been examined in a detailed manner. Regarding the Canadian turn of events, Ross Lambertson chronicles the support by various Christian groups for the work of the CCJC, and Michael Hemmings outlines the response of many religious denominations across Canada to both resettlement and deportation.[4] On the American front, Michi Weglyn mentions the activities of the American Friends Service Committee (AFSC), Sandra Taylor comments on the varied Protestant church responses to incarceration, and Robert Shaffer has described the work of Protestant denominations as part of his analysis of the reactions of the American liberal-left to the relocation. Denominational unity, however, was not always the norm; Charles Lord has revealed that, within the American peace churches, opinion was not undifferentiated. The Mennonite Church took no official stance, whereas both the Society of Friends (Quakers) and the Church of the Brethren became steadfast advocates for Japanese Americans and their rights.[5]

The most numerous critics of the removal were church leaders. For both Canadian and American leaders and laity, opposition to government policies was remarkably similar in that the removal was viewed as an issue of the survival of morality and Christianity. Religious groups in North America were equally aware of the potential for Christianization and Canadianization/Americanization that the relocation policies afforded but also recognized their obvious racial discrimination. The reaction of the Canadian churches, however, was distinctive in its appeals to "British justice and fair play." Believing that Ottawa would adhere to these principles, the churches did not immediately oppose removal; their lack of response to the policy paralleled that of secular groups and individuals, whose opposition was virtually non-existent in the early months of 1942. Additionally, members of religious organizations initially supported the removal because it was linked with the policy of dispersal. Subscribing to contemporary thinking – that assimilation could assist minorities to integrate into Canadian and American society – religious leaders and laity withheld criticism of relocation on the grounds that the policy could achieve this beneficial result.

How supporters of Japanese American rights, including religious organizations, reacted to relocation is illustrated in the transcripts of the 1942 hearings held before the House Select Committee Investigating National Defense Migration. Also known as the Tolan Committee (for Congressman John H. Tolan, its chair), it was established by American liberals three days after the issuance of Executive Order 9066 in an effort to avert radical actions by anti-Japanese groups. By contrast, the sentiments of Canadian religious representatives can best be gauged through the letters they exchanged and the church publications they produced.

Religious groups in Canada and the United States had interacted with the Nikkei long before the advent of the February 1942 removal policies. In particular, various missionaries founded schools and other institutions specifically for the Japanese residing on the west coast. Indeed, along with the educational process came proselytizing. Although most Japanese immigrants were Buddhists, Christianity made considerable inroads among them throughout the early twentieth century, particularly through the Anglican and United Churches in Canada and the Episcopalian and Unitarian Churches, among others, in the United States. Missionaries were also sent overseas to minister to and convert the Japanese. Christians of Japanese ancestry eventually established their own network of Japanese churches throughout the Pacific coast.[6]

Thus, due to their overseas missions, church officials were suitably positioned to appreciate the increasing tension in East Asia in 1940, and the developments in American and Canadian Japanese diplomatic relationships. In Canada and the United States, they sent notices to various religious organizations and periodicals urging that a Christian attitude be maintained "toward these Japanese within our midst."[7] The issue was given more serious attention when the Home Missions Council and the Foreign Missions Conference of the Presbyterian Church in North America held an informal conference in March 1941 between Canadian and American representatives. Although these delegates resolved to establish a committee to deal with the problem of maintaining a Christian attitude towards the Nikkei, their immediate responses were characterized by a preoccupation with "Christianizing"

the Japanese. In particular, the Nisei were singled out for Christian attention, not only for religious purposes but also "from the standpoint of civic
unity and good citizenship."[8] Thus, Christian values were not only "correct" in a religious meaning but were also useful as a means of "Ameri-
canizing" or "Canadianizing" persons of Japanese ancestry.

Immediately following the 7 December 1941 bombing of Pearl Harbor,
many North American churches called for calm and fair treatment of *all*
Americans and Canadians. For example, in the United States, the Federal
Council of Churches issued a press release on 9 December urging Americans to maintain a Christian attitude "toward the Japanese in America,
many of whom are loyal patriotic American citizens." The statement also
counselled Washington to follow "a discipline which, while carefully observing the precautions necessary to national safety, has no place for vin-
dictiveness."[9] This careful resolution is best contrasted with the criticism
of Floyd Schmoe, of the Seattle American Friends Service Committee
(AFSC), who would become one of the main activists on behalf of Japanese Americans during their incarceration. Schmoe was especially vocal
when the FBI began detaining Issei leaders in the immediate aftermath of
Pearl Harbor. Charging that these roundups served only to raise suspicions
of Japanese nationals, Schmoe also expressed concern that they would
jeopardize the safety of Japanese Americans.[10] Local church groups, particularly on the Pacific coast, promptly issued many appeals for fair-
ness. The Seattle Council of Churches and Christian Education, remarking
pointedly that many of the Japanese on the west coast had "assumed the
responsibilities of American citizens, and are no less a part of these United
States than are the rest of us," urged Americans to "remain Christian" in
"attitudes and actions."[11]

Cautionary pronouncements, mostly tepid in nature, were all that followed the attack on Pearl Harbor. When Washington and Ottawa
announced their removal policies in February 1942, church officials, with
a few exceptions, produced similarly qualified reactions. Like the ACLU
and CCJC liberals and leftists, many of them opposed incarceration, but
they, too, were reluctant to object to the wartime policies of the Roosevelt
and King administrations. In the United States, in particular, the popu-·
larity of the war increased after Pearl Harbor, and growing numbers of liberals and leftists supported Roosevelt's New Deal administration. As a result,
representatives of the various denominations faced difficult moral dilem-
mas as they publicly expressed their sentiments regarding removal. Many
of the faithful also had "faith" in the government itself; some could not
conceive that such policies would be adopted.[12] Officials of some pacifist
churches in the United States, however, were often more vocal than their
counterparts in other denominations, as they were principally opposed to
war and had little to lose when it came to criticizing the president.

Whatever their private thoughts, not one of the Canadian religious denominations spoke out publicly against the government action. The Vancouver Presbytery of the United Church, for example, declared its belief in the loyalty of Japanese Canadians and expressed its "regret" that the "exigencies of war" involved such disruption of their lives. It did, however, make a plea for the Nisei to be accepted into the army.[13] In British Columbia in early 1942, a few Protestant clergy and laypersons, along with some members of the CCF, formed the Vancouver Consultative Council (VCC), which eventually became a significant civil liberties organization in the fight against deportation/expatriation. In many respects, the VCC was the "western wing" of the CCJC, keeping those in Toronto informed of movements afoot on the west coast. The VCC did not question the nature of the removal policy but focused instead on the issue of just treatment for all Japanese Canadians and urged the federal government to enact policies that would quell anti-Asian sentiment.[14] Relocation was justified as necessary for the assimilation of persons of Japanese ancestry. The only cautionary comments, as mentioned above, referred to the process of dispersal being handled in a "just" manner. Although such an approach may be seen as cooperative, it is also fair to say that the churches did not completely support Ottawa's actions. Indeed, Hugh Keenleyside of the Department of External Affairs remarked on this in a scathing letter to Dr. Armstrong of the Anglican Church of Canada. He blamed the BC churches for not calming the local hysteria that "ultimately" forced Ottawa to take "more and more repressive actions in relation to the Japanese and Canadian-Japanese population of British Columbia." Raising the spectre of retaliation by Japan in a "pretty gruesome manner against our fellow citizens and prisoners of war who have fallen into their hands," Keenleyside suggested that "the Christian Churches in British Columbia must bear a certain responsibility for this unhappy development."[15]

Following the announcement of Executive Order 9066, several religious organizations in the United States issued strong cautionary public statements. A few completely opposed the principle of removal. For example, the New York Conference of the Methodist Church criticized the removal of American citizens as a violation of the Bill of Rights.[16] The United Christian Missionary Society of the Disciples of Christ declared that the "mass internment upon the basis of suspicion arising from race, color, or ancestry, is a form of reprisal no more to be condoned in the United States than in Germany." It also called for loyalty hearings and suggested that those who were released under such auspices be given government aid in securing jobs or farms, or in re-entering business or professional life. These statements were delivered at the society's convention, held in Grand Rapids, Michigan, in late July 1942.[17] In writing directly to Lieutenant General DeWitt on the subject of removal, a Mrs. Jacob C. Auernheimer pointed out that "we do not feel the attitude of 'let the government take care of the Japanese' is either Christian or patriotic. Most of them are our fellow citizens and should be treated as such by Christians."[18]

Several representatives of religious groups who appeared before the Tolan Committee held that the decision "contained an invidious racial distinction" and that thousands of American citizens were being treated on par with, and in some cases worse than, enemy aliens. Many pointed out the obvious contradiction of recognizing and maintaining racial distinctions while waging a "just" war. They also warned that these distinctions might jeopardize internal race relations and that the Axis alliance would capitalize on the removal policy as a means of spreading the ideology of a racial war.[19] Ministers of the Protestant churches in Santa Maria, California, called for an outright rejection of incarceration and warned that "Such Nazi methods will be destructive of love and country in those directly and indirectly affected."[20] Members of the Executive Committee of the Federal Council of the Churches of Christ (FCCC) issued a prudent letter to Roosevelt in which they pledged their loyalty and questioned neither the principle of military necessity nor the infringement of the civil rights of American citizens. At the same time, however, the FCCC pointed out that comparable treatment was not imposed upon citizens of German or Italian background, and it charged that the removal policy smacked of "race discrimination" and totalitarianism. It further suggested that loyal Japanese would be "de-Americanized" as a result of the relocation and that America's "prestige and influence" would be damaged by the continuation of racially discriminatory policies.[21]

Society of Friends periodicals devoted considerable space to the early days of the removal. Many in the historic peace churches believed that the issue would be a great test of Christian integrity. Followers were urged to claim personal responsibility, as one columnist suggested in a July 1942 issue of *American Friend:* "The fault rests squarely upon us as a people who have permitted prejudice, fear and hatred to flower into intolerance and violence, and now in a war situation have allowed the government to arrange this evacuation in direct violation of our heritage of social and racial justice."[22]

Unlike the Protestant churches, the Society of Friends did not take a specific position on the removal question. According to Floyd Schmoe's testimony at the Tolan Committee hearings, the American Friends Service Committee (AFSC) was concerned with the human condition in general, especially the innocent victims and bystanders of war. From that standpoint, the AFSC was interested in the situation of the Japanese Americans. Schmoe, however, was still careful to point out that "We have not officially taken a position ... except to have a humanitarian interest in anyone who is suffering for conditions beyond their control."[23]

The differences in the nature and amount of opposition voiced by religious groups to the announcement of the removal policy in the US and Canada can be attributed to considerations of time and secrecy. The US incarceration took longer to complete than that of Canada: consuming nine months, it ended on 3 November 1942, when all Japanese Americans once living in the protected west coast zones had been transferred inland to the War Relocation Authority camps. Nor could the idea of incarcerating Japanese Americans be considered a secret. In Canada, by comparison, the entire relocation process was completed slightly more quickly, in about seven months. By 16 March, the RCMP had begun to assemble Japanese Canadians at Vancouver's Hastings Park Assembly Centre; by 31 October, the Canadian evacuation process had concluded. In addition, the policy arose from a few secretive Cabinet meetings.[24] Michael Hemmings has suggested that surprised Canadian church officials took removal as a done deal from the outset and focused instead on the next issue – resettlement.[25] Indeed, this was true to a certain extent in both countries, for the churches were reluctant to give up on either their missionary activities or their flocks, and the idea of resettlement was supported by virtually all liberals, including those among church officials, in Canada and the United States.

It is also true that, in Canada, church officials were confident that Ottawa would uphold British precepts of justice and fair play as it carried out the removal and resettlement policies. Certainly, church officials in both nations felt that the war was a "just war" and defined it according to moral and Christian principles, but in Canada the degree of faith in British justice stifled any serious attempt at dissension regarding government policies. For example, the Provincial Board of Missions to Orientals in British Columbia, a body of the Anglican Church of Canada, sent a resolution to Prime Minister King, the mayors of Vancouver and New Westminster, the Canadian Press Association, and the United Church of Canada, among others, stating its trust "that the true British tradition of justice and fair play will operate in any protective measures the Government may feel necessary to adopt towards the Japanese residents of the Country."[26]

Although many religious groups in both countries opposed the very principle of incarceration, they were sympathetic to the rationale behind the voluntary resettlement programs.[27] As the previous chapter revealed, a tactical confusion existed among liberals on this issue. Even as many religious leaders opposed racially based mass removal, they expressed confidence in the government's handling of the process and offered to aid in the planning phase in order to effect a humane and successful outcome. Their support for voluntary resettlement sprang from their conviction that it would help the Nikkei assimilate into mainstream life. For an example of this prevalent belief, we need look no further than the War Relocation Authority (WRA) mandate: "In common with many social scientists," this held that "wide distribution of the evacuees, with opportunity for free enterprise, is a sounder social policy than mass segregation with controlled labor as it fosters Americanism, maintains morale, diminishes the difficulty of reintegration into normal life after the war, and results in increased production."[28] The degree to which religious groups readily offered aid to Nikkei who resettled away from the west coast and created hostels for young Nisei men and women represents a practical manifestation of their support for assimilation.[29] In addition, resettlement would be an essential remedy to west coast racism. Geographic concentration on the coast was thought to inhibit assimilation because it enabled the perpetuation of immigrant culture. This failure to jettison their old ways and blend into the dominant society prompted the racism directed at non-white minorities. Resettlement would solve the problem. Although today's multicultural society would not entertain such views, liberals of the day thought it common sense that non-white minorities could and should assimilate. Contemporary racists, it should be remembered, believed that non-whites could never do so.[30]

Perhaps the best Canadian example of broadly based religious support for resettlement was the National Interchurch Advisory Committee on the Resettlement of Japanese Canadians (NIAC). The mandate of this inter-denominational group, composed of representatives of the Roman Catholic Church, the United Church of Canada, and the Anglican Church of Canada, among others, was the promotion of resettlement, as its name aptly suggests. It cooperated with the British Columbia Security Commission (BCSC) on matters relating to that goal. The NIAC firmly believed that resettlement was the sole solution, not only to preclude the formation of "colonies" but also to enable Japanese Canadians to be "re-absorbed into productive life, living as normal Canadians in normal Canadian communities."[31] This group was not the only example of interdenominational cooperation. The United and Anglican Churches regularly cooperated at the diocesan level on the issue of settlement. On occasion, however, as in some of the Interior settlements, this cooperation could be compromised by a competition for souls![32]

In the United States, the AFSC, the Baptists, the Church of the Brethren, the Congregationalists, the Federal Council of Churches, the Methodists, the Presbyterians, and the YWCA were representative of the groups helping in the resettlement process. Like their Canadian brethren, many officials of these religious bodies did not approve of incarceration in principle but were eager to assist the WRA in the resettlement of Japanese Americans. To that end, the Protestant Church Commission for Japanese Service was established in February 1942. Both the army and the WRA recognized the commission as the authorized channel for all services delivered by Protestant agencies to the incarcerated Japanese Americans. The Reverend Gordon

K. Chapman, a former Presbyterian missionary in Japan, was named executive secretary.[33] In addition to this group, the Committee on Resettlement of Japanese Americans, which consisted mostly of Quakers, was formed on 7 October 1942 by several church representatives who had met in New York City. Its executive secretary, George E. Rundquist, was a Quaker businessman and historian who had given up his academic career to volunteer for the Japanese Americans in connection with the New York Committee for Japanese Work. This body, which assisted in coordinating and labouring with local resettlement committees, also engaged in public relations at the local level.[34] These organizations were only two of the largest groups attempting to further the Japanese American resettlement. There were a great many others, so many that they often worked at cross-purposes, which, from time to time, resulted in veritable "turf wars."[35]

The efforts of representatives and organizations of the American churches did not go unnoticed by many Japanese Americans. Larry Tajiri's editorial in the 14 January 1943 issue of the *Pacific Citizen* is suggestive:

> If the nisei believed the church has not kept up with the times, if ever he believed that Christianity was a Sunday-go-to-meeting thing, he knows better now. We have watched the church play a seven-day-a-week role in the war relocation centers. We know now they are making an active, aggressive and forward fight for justice for the evacuee ... We are glad they stand with us in these times. We feel stronger that they do. And our faith in the American way is entrenched even deeper by their example of justice and devotion.[36]

In a July 1944 editorial, Tajiri would return to this theme, noting the significant number of churches from around the United States that were proclaiming support for the complete restoration of the rights of the Nikkei. Bill Hosokawa, frequent columnist in the *Pacific Citizen* and, later, the first Japanese American editor of the *Denver Post,* titled one of his columns "Churches Bolster the Morale of Evacuees" and commented that if "American churches have a voice in the shape of the postwar world, some fine ideas will be made a part of the peace structure."[37] Ultimately, the increasing awareness of the American churches that their social responsibilities were as important as their spiritual ones resulted in many practical efforts to aid the Nikkei. As Tajiri remarked, when at last the Nikkei could return to the Pacific coast as free men and women, "the churches, the conscience of the Christian world, will have played no small part in that return."[38] Although not all Nikkei were churchgoers, the behaviour of the churches during this time may have drawn many into the Christian fold.

By 1944, Canadian church leaders had begun to doubt the wisdom of Ottawa's plans for Japanese Canadians. Although resettlement (especially voluntary resettlement) was widely accepted, disfranchisement and wholesale deportation were not, and some church leaders publicly voiced their opposition. Their increasing activism corresponded with Canadian public opinion in general. According to a February 1944 Canadian Institute of Public Opinion poll, only 33 percent of Canadians supported the idea of deportation. That result stood in stark contrast to a poll commissioned in December 1943, which indicated that slightly over 50 percent of Canadians, including a significant majority of British Columbians, favoured deportation.[39]

At this point, the response of the Canadian churches begins to represent the growing awareness of human rights as an issue of importance to Canadian society. It is also where the rhetoric of Canadian church leaders differs markedly from that of their American counterparts. Many prominent church members began to realize that religious institutions had an obligation to act when the state imposed oppressive measures. For example, the Fellowship for a Christian Social Order (FCSO), consisting mostly of United Church social radicals, embodied the idea of "religion as something that is concerned with community and democracy" and asserted "that religious life. should ... spill over into socio-political activities."[40] Other groups such as the Student Christian Movement and the Fellowship of Reconciliation (FOR), which also took an interest in the treatment of Japanese Canadians, approached this issue from the perspective of radical Christianity, a belief system rooted in the Social Gospel. As indicated in Chapter 2, these organizations were among the earliest supporters of the CCJC. Richard Allen has pointed out that the "conviction that Christianity required a passionate commitment to social involvement" was a core tenet of the Social Gospel and an important guiding standard for its adherents. Although the Social Gospel movement had begun to decline in the 1920s, some members of the United Church, in particular, continued to be influenced by its ideas. Radical Christianity espoused an egalitarian worldview that naturally prompted its believers to support human rights. Certainly, the conviction that all are equal in the eyes of the Lord led to the view that minorities in Canada should possess the rights and privileges enjoyed by other Canadians.[41]

The Canadian churches began their embryonic public campaigns and lobbying efforts with the issue of Japanese Canadian disfranchisement. Officials of the Board of Foreign Missions of the United Church of Canada sent letters to MPs and the prime minister in opposition to clause 5 of Bill 135, the Dominion Franchise Amendment. Initially, the bill proposed to disfranchise "all persons whose racial origin is that of a country at war with Canada."[42] However, its wording was changed slightly so that the effect was to remove voting rights of Canadian citizens of Japanese ancestry living east of the Rockies. Opponents of the bill, including the

Rev. A.E. Armstrong of the United Church of Canada, argued that those "who were born in this country are no more responsible for what the militarists of the country of their racial origin have done, or are doing, than are Canadian citizens of any other racial background. Why, therefore, discriminate against them and not against Canadians whose ancestry is German, Italian, Finnish, Hungarian, Romanian, or Bulgarian?" The letters also alluded to the Atlantic Charter and Canada's obligations to uphold international commitments to the prohibition of racial discrimination.[43] The FCSO also protested Bill 135 as part of its Racial Equality Program, arguing that Japanese Canadian citizens deserved the *same* legal rights and civil liberties as other British subjects.[44] Additionally, individual church leaders and members sent letters of protest to Ottawa. During June and July 1944, in fact, letters from approximately sixty persons and organizations were received and duly noted by the Office of the Prime Minister. The letters came from several branches of the YMCA, Women's Auxiliaries of the Anglican and United Churches, and some United and Anglican Church leaders.[45]

Long before King tabled the three Orders-in-Council (P.C. 7355, 7356, and 7357) that enabled the government to deport the Nikkei from Canada, including those born in the country, the churches and affiliated religious groups expressed their concerns about the idea of mass deportation. These were not simply pious statements or opportunistic declarations made once the defeat of Japan was assured, as some scholars have suggested.[46] Rather, they represented the church's view that the only humane and constructive way through which to address the Japanese Canadian "problem" was geographic dispersal. In addition to being "false, cruel, un-British and above all, un-Christian," deportation would work at cross-purposes with the church's commitment to the principle of dispersal.[47]

Church publications were the primary forum through which religious officials could voice their opposition. Government censors, in fact, were kept quite busy from 1944 onwards dealing with the terminology used, and the viewpoints made, in several of these magazines. In particular, the *Canadian Churchman*, an Anglican weekly published in Toronto, and Franciscan and Jesuit serials were noted by F. Charpentier, chief censor of publications, for being especially troublesome in this regard.[48]

In May 1944, the VCC added its voice to the growing opposition to any proposal for deportation. In a letter to the prime minister, VCC president Dr. Norman F. Black wrote,

> The proposal that all persons of Japanese stock should be forcibly expelled from this Dominion seems to us wicked and preposterous. We have difficulty in understanding how anyone can champion such a suggestion unless, consciously or unconsciously, he had surrendered to the characteristic

racial attitude of Nazism ... We feel that talk about "repatriation" is an abuse of language, and that the forcible exile of these 16,261 Canadian citizens would be an act of indefensible tyranny and folly ... Finally ... the proposed expulsion would do violence to the conscience of a large section of the Canadian people.[49]

Surely, the "conscience" to which Black referred was the growing acceptance of the concept of "human rights," a concept that was gaining recognition internationally and in Canada. This letter was also signed by leaders of the Anglican, United, Baptist, and Roman Catholic denominations in Vancouver.

In a similar fashion, the Student Christian Movement urged the federal government to "make it clear that [it] will not consider now or at any future date proposals for mass deportation of Canadian citizens of Japanese origin. Such treatment, besides being entirely foreign to British traditions, would be ... a major contribution to social and international unrest in the post war period."[50] Correspondingly, the Fellowship of Reconciliation declared that "forced exile of Canadian citizens of Japanese origin is unthinkable and inhumane"; it reminded Prime Minister King that, "if we are a Christian democratic nation, we have an obligation to act in accordance with the highest ideals we know. Canada's action towards this minority problem has not been exemplary."[51] Yet another Christian group comprised of youth from the YMCA, the YWCA, and the United, Anglican, Baptist, and Presbyterian Churches, informed the prime minister that it was "opposed to the suggestions made by certain members of parliament and others, that Canadians of Japanese origin be 'repatriated' to Japan ... [Banishment] to a country from which they or their ancestors originally emigrated is contrary to fundamental Christian principles and is tantamount to acceptance of Hitler's racial theory."[52] The Canadian Council of Churches petitioned the federal government to set up a commission to investigate the loyalties of Japanese Canadians. It also requested that those who had signed repatriation forms be given an opportunity to change their minds, that the proposed deportation not occur until this had transpired, and that full citizenship status be granted to loyal Japanese Canadians.[53] Additionally, the National Interchurch Advisory Committee, in attempting to secure an audience with King, Minister of Justice Louis St. Laurent, and Minister of Labour Humphrey Mitchell, sent them a letter and a memorandum stating its opposition to deportation by voicing its approval of Ottawa's actions thus far, particularly the policies of dispersal and assimilation.[54] Not all the faithful were pleased by these efforts; some expressed their dissatisfaction with the actions (or inaction!) of the churches on both removal and relocation.[55]

Various church leaders and religious groups continued their opposition to the principle of deportation into 1945. As before, leaders and laity supported the policy of geographic dispersal, believing it to be the only equitable solution, and denounced discrimination that was based upon racial prejudice.[56] It is not surprising, then, as church opposition to government policies escalated, that representatives of the various denominations comprised over half of the CCJC membership when it was officially formed in May 1945. Church leaders surmised that, adding its efforts to their own, the CCJC would be an effective pressure group and vehicle to promote the goals of resettlement; they also expected that it would assume "responsibility for influencing public opinion in favour of the resettlement of Canadians of Japanese origin."[57]

Despite increasing opposition, the plans for Nikkei expatriation were set once and for all when the three Orders-in-Council were tabled on 15 December 1945, three and a half months after the end of the war. With these measures, federal government actions against Japanese Canadians reached an unprecedented apogee; so too, did the criticism of the churches. The CCJC encouraged all cooperating groups to send form letters of protest to Ottawa; church leaders and laity eagerly obliged. These letters amply demonstrate the emergent democratic human rights discourse that was infusing the advocacy movement. Many of them cited the Atlantic Charter and the Charter of the United Nations as guidelines that the government should follow in handling the Japanese Canadians. Others implored King not to exercise any racial discrimination in the deportation policy.[58] Most expressed concern for Canadians of Japanese ancestry and suggested that loyalty be the test of Japanese nationals residing in Canada. However, some did not make any distinctions regarding citizenship. The Rev. George Webber voiced disapproval of the deportation of "any Japanese ... even those who were not born in Canada," and commented that "such treatment ... does not apply to other enemy nationals." In a pamphlet titled *Save Canadian Children and Canadian Honour,* the VCC made similar statements on behalf of Japanese nationals; so, too, did the Canadian Council of Churches in a 19 December press release.[59] The issue of citizenship became blurred as the need to protect human rights, irrespective of citizenship, gained recognition.

By early 1946, the churches and related religious organizations were cooperating quite closely with the CCJC.[60] A CCJC letter addressed to the ministers of Toronto and district appealed to them to make an issue of the deportation and expulsion of Japanese Canadians and requested that a communal day of worship be held on Sunday, 20 January.[61] Indeed, the Reverend J.L.W. MacLean of St. Andrew's Presbyterian Church, Victoria, BC, delivered a scathing indictment of federal deportation policy in a sermon that was aired on a local radio station and that caught the attention of the VCC, who duly passed it on to the CCJC. MacLean's sermon

THE NATIONAL INTERCHURCH ADVISORY COMMITTEE

REV. GEO. DOREY, D.D.
Chairman

REV. E. H. JOHNSON,
Secretary

on

RESETTLEMENT OF JAPANESE CANADIANS
100 Adelaide St. West, Room 801
Toronto 1, Ontario

REV. W. W. JUDD, D.C.L.

REV. FR. A. E. MCQUILLEN

REV. C. H. SCHUTT, D.D.

January 31, 1946.

On Behalf of Justice and Fair Play to all Japanese Canadians

Dear Fellow Worker:

Recent pronouncements made by high Government officials at Ottawa indicate that unless the tolerant, liberal thinking people of the country lodge vigorous protests, several hundred Japanese Canadians, many of them Canadian citizens, will be deported to Japan against their will. This would establish a vicious precedent, bringing dishonour to Canada and causing unnecessary suffering to a number of innocent people, in that, families would be broken up and the returnees landed in Japan where adequate food is lacking and housing practically non-existent. In the hope of arousing more individual and group protests against this wholly uncalled for and un-Christian action we send you this letter.

The present Government policy concerning those of Japanese origin now in Canada is as follows:

(a) All Canadian Born of proved loyalty, including those who have asked to go to Japan but have requested cancellation of their signatures before orders for their deportation are given, may stay in Canada.

(b) Nationals and Naturalized Canadians who have requested repatriation but who asked for cancellation of such requests after September 2nd, 1945, are to be deported—along with all minors in their families.

(c) Nationals and Naturalized citizens of proved loyalty who did not sign for repatriation or those who did but requested cancellation before September 2nd, 1945, will be allowed to stay in Canada.

A crescendo of disapproval is being expressed all over Canada regarding Section B above. Many questions are being asked. Why should the Japanese be treated differently from the Italians or Germans? If what Prime Minister King stated in the House on August 4, 1944, is true, namely, that none of them have been guilty of sabotage or other offence against the Government, on what basis other than that of pure racial discrimination are they to be so treated? If they are to be deported on that basis in what respect is such action different from what the Nazis in Europe did to the Jews? It has now come to the place where, not the Japanese, but Canada and Canada's honour are being put on trial.

It is the opinion of the members of our Committee that the only Christian way to handle the question is to give every person of Japanese origin in Canada against whom no evidence of disloyalty has been found, a chance to have his case considered by a properly constituted tribunal. To do less, in our view, would be to violate the United Nations Charter which expressly states its purpose as "The realization of human rights and fundamental freedoms *for all without distinction as to race, sex, language or religion.*"

If on reading the above you feel at all as we do, you can have a part in working for Christian justice in Canada, by sending a letter or telegram of protest to the Prime Minister either as an individual or as a member of your own church group or of any other group with which you have contacts. *Public opinion must be mobilized if a grave injustice is to be avoided.* Whatever is done should be done speedily before the Government policy hardens into action. Any communication should be addressed to The Right Honourable W. L. Mackenzie King, Ottawa.

If more information is required, please do not hesitate to write. Our services are at your disposal.

Sincerely yours,

Rev. George Dorey, D.D., 299 Queen St., W.
Rev. E. H. Johnson, 100 Adelaide St., W.
Rev. W. W. Judd, D.D., 604 Jarvis St.
Rev. Fr. A. E. McQuillen, 200 Church St.
Rev. C. H. Schutt, D.D., 223 Church St.

This letter from NIAC urged "Fellow Workers" to send letters or telegrams of protest to the prime minister.
Courtesy McMaster University Libraries, Co-operative Committee on Japanese Canadians fonds, folder 18

is particularly interesting in that it demonstrates how "modern" theories about race had permeated the mainstream:

"God hath made of ONE BLOOD all nations of men to dwell on all the face of the earth." (Acts 17: 26). Paul, the Christian Missionary made this statement 2000 years ago. Our 20th century scientists testify that this is LITERALLY TRUE. All people of the earth are a single family and have a common origin. Racial differences exist only in non-essentials. Physiology and Philology attest the fact that the race is one. Modern science has discovered that all races – whether Whites, Negroes, or Mongols – have ONE BLOOD, regardless of the colour of their skin: this skin colour is determined by the presence of 2 special chemicals – carotene and melanin – which every one human being possesses in varying degrees. The race of mankind is ONE family ... Therefore racial discrimination and antagonism is senseless and wrong.[62]

MacLean then went on to challenge the federal government "to put into practice" the purpose of the United Nations Charter with respect to the Japanese Canadian case. Although hints of modern race theories were present in religious writings, the significance in this example is that it was linked with the developing human rights rhetoric.[63]

The church leadership and laity also supported the CCJC when it decided in December 1945 to launch a Supreme Court legal campaign to contest the orders. By this time, over forty national and local organizations were cooperating with the CCJC, including all the major religious denominations in Canada, the Canadian Jewish Congress, the Fellowship of Reconciliation, the Presbyterian Young People's Organizations, the Religious Education Council of Canada, the Student Christian Movement, and the YMCA and YWCA.[64]

The newly emerging human rights conscience certainly influenced the decision to take the deportation matter to the Supreme Court. In solidarity, the churches, the Fellowship of Reconciliation, the Student Christian Movement, and the VCC undertook fundraising campaigns to solicit donations to help finance *In the Matter of a Reference*. In particular, the VCC issued a bulletin titled "Orders-in-Council Threaten Your Citizenship!" which emphasized the racialist nature of the government's measures as well as the despotic manner in which they were approved. Readers were asked to write to the prime minister and to send their test case contributions directly to the VCC.[65] The Fellowship of Reconciliation pledged its full support.[66] Additionally, the VCC borrowed the pressure tactics of its CCJC brethren, scheduling mass protest meetings in which Vancouver could object to the "arbitrary and unprecedented obstruction" of T.B. Pickersgill,

RCMP commissioner of Japanese placement, who had frustrated the activities of VCC members. Specifically, this protest turned on an incident in which Reverend Canon W.W. Judd, Alex Grant, of the University of British Columbia Student Christian Movement, and VCC counsel R.J. McMaster were all allegedly denied entry to the incarceration camp at Tashme, BC.[67]

The NIAC exhorted church leaders to send "a letter or telegram of protest to the Prime Minister either as an individual or as a member of your own church group" to protest the actions of the federal government. Reflecting human rights discourse, the letters cited the United Nations Charter and remarked on the similarities between the deportation policy, Nazism, and racial discrimination. Several individuals and organizations followed the NIAC suggestion, as the Department of External Affairs noted receiving increased numbers of these form petitions.[68] The churches committed "large sums" of money to financing the test case, and the Student Christian Movement raised funds and "kept the issue alive in University circles and in the local communities."[69] For example, the latter sent an impassioned plea to all Christian youth groups asking members to "stop and think what this [deportation] means in terms of the failure of Canadian democracy, the impotence of the Christian church, the degradation of Canada's position among the nations, the seeds of World War III, and the cost in human suffering to thousands of fellow Canadian citizens ... This is a challenge to the conscience of the Christian community to act in defence of *fundamental human rights*."[70] In early 1946, about a hundred students representing nine universities from across Canada served as delegates to the Student Christian Movement's western regional conference, where they denounced the deportation policy. On 18 January, a delegation from the Canadian Council of Churches waited on the prime minister to express their disapproval of the government's actions.[71]

Although the Supreme Court ruling was largely disappointing, the Canadian churches did not abandon their campaign to bring justice to Japanese Canadians: they joined the CCJC and its cooperating groups in appealing the matter of the offensive Orders-in-Council to the Privy Council, in London. As they had done with the Supreme Court challenge, church groups helped to raise the much-needed funds to launch the appeal *(CCJC v. Attorney-General of Canada et al.)*. A day of prayer was hastily arranged for Sunday, 5 January.[72] In a letter sent to church leaders throughout Canada, the VCC explained that "the task of the church is not completed": as well as preventing deportation, the church must "help to cure the mental and spiritual cancer that has resulted from the race prejudice of the past fifty years and especially during the years of the war." In an interesting public tactic, it asked church leaders to read an attached "open letter" to their congregations on Sunday, 7 April; signed by the congregations, the letters would be forwarded to the VCC. By collecting these thousands of signatures, the VCC hoped to show the Nikkei that Canadians deeply regretted the actions of the federal government.[73] The Canadian School of Missions even obtained international support for a resolution it sent to Ottawa. This included signatures from over eighty missionaries representing countries in all parts of the world.[74] Additionally, the churches, by way of the NIAC, continued to promote resettlement; to this end, they partnered with the Department of Labour in presenting a "Church Sponsored Placement Plan for Japanese Canadian Families."[75] Although liberal thought was coming to regard the deportation as an infringement of human rights, the idea of dispersal and the resultant benefits of assimilation remained ingrained in the minds of religious leaders and laity, as it was in the minds of their secular comrades.

When the Privy Council ruling of late 1946 entirely favoured the federal government, the churches and religious organizations continued to support the CCJC in its lobbying efforts. Individual members volunteered to join CCJC delegations to Ottawa to protest the continuation of the Orders-in-Council; however, these efforts would become moot by early 1947, when the Orders-in-Council were cancelled.[76] Of course, other issues remained, as the previous chapter revealed, and the voice of the churches as individual and cooperating lobby groups continued to sound over the next two years until Japanese Canadians received the franchise in 1949.[77]

Thus, the involvement of churches and religious organizations in the campaign to achieve justice for Japanese Canadians began early in the war and did not wind up until long after war's end. The participation of religious groups in CCJC activities demonstrates that, following the announcement of the removal policy in early 1942, the churches played a major role in opposing Ottawa's repressive policies.

In comparison to their Canadian counterparts, the leadership and laity of the American churches were certainly less politically active in petitioning the government for change. The exception to this statement, however, were the American peace churches. In particular, the Society of Friends (Quakers) made its presence known at all the relocation camps. However, though the American churches immediately opposed the removal policy following its mid-February 1942 announcement in Executive Order 9066, they were relatively quiet in terms of lobbying the government concerning it. The main reason for this is that the ACLU, as a long-established and well-known civil liberties group, was leading the charge in the political sphere. The American churches, by contrast, were more interested in resettlement and in implementing the government's policies in that regard.

The role of the churches in the US resettlement process was recognized as very important by government officials who, in fact, relied heavily on them to carry out this work. As Thomas W. Holland, a former WRA chief of employment, remarked,

> Representatives of various church organizations and service committees were among the very first to recognize the implications of the evacuation and were early in encouraging and assisting the evacuees to find new homes in other parts of the country. Clergymen and other church workers have been, and still are, a powerful influence in shaping the receptive public opinion which has made the relocation program possible in the middle west and east. Through hostels and other forms of practical assistance the churches have made possible the relocation of large numbers of evacuees who would not have been able otherwise to have left the projects.[78]

In his memoir detailing his WRA tenure, Director Dillon Myer thanked many of the individuals and organizations, including the churches, for their dedicated support of the WRA program.[79] This cooperative interaction between religious institutions and the state was central to the relatively quick (as compared with Canada) reversal of the relocation. It was also in marked contrast with the concern expressed in late 1942 by WRA officials who questioned and criticized the qualifications and conduct of former Christian missionaries in the relocation camps.[80]

The overall degree of cooperation between the religious organizations and the WRA was also central to the day-to-day workings of the relocation camps. This, in particular, is where religious Americans made the most difference. Whether they were ministering to internees or organizing Christmas parties, church groups attempted to spread the spirit of Christianity whenever possible, for both altruistic and practical reasons. The churches were largely responsible for acquiring a variety of equipment needed in the relocation camps, such as that for church and social requirements; music, arts, and crafts; libraries; and athletics and playgrounds. In addition, they established an elaborate hostel system across the country to aid resettlement. The ACLU branches on the west coast also assisted these religious agencies, as well as their secular counterparts, in the resettlement program and eventually with the return of the Japanese Americans to the coast.[81]

Religious agencies also cooperated with the ACLU on matters relating to resettlement. Their degree of cooperation, however, was not as close as that between the CCJC and the Canadian churches. Although the American churches provided important services in the relocation camps, only in 1943 did the ACLU began to rely on them for lobbying purposes. By this time, the ACLU's government connections had informed it that lobbying, as opposed to litigation, would be most useful in providing for the immediate return of the Japanese Americans to the coast.[82] Consequently, the ACLU held a conference with religious agencies assisting in the Japanese American resettlement, whereupon it was decided that these groups would contact press associations, influential columnists, and national radio programs in order to encourage public support for resettlement. They were also asked to draft petitions or statements supporting the WRA and its work.[83]

Buoyed by the need to make a more national commitment to the resettlement issue, various church organizations began to assume a more vocal stance. This was especially critical as Japanese Americans began to return to the west coast in 1945, only to meet the same degree of suspicion as when they had left it in 1942. Undue pressure by the WRA on the incarcerated to make permanent resettlement arrangements before they left the camps resulted in confusion and panic. Hostels became overcrowded, and finding suitable housing grew increasingly difficult as time passed.[84] The apprehension concerning this situation led the Protestant Church Commission for Japanese Service, for example, to adopt several resolutions calling for a federal assistance program for returning Japanese Americans, as well as a federal assistance fund for persons incapable of self-support. The commission linked the necessity of the programs with the warning that the US risked jeopardizing its "international moral leadership by ill-considered treatment of its own citizens." The Federal Council of Churches added to the alarm by urging Secretary of the Interior Harold Ickes to provide adequate provision for those returning to the coast. Through its Resettlement Division, the Home Missions Council also urged Washington to do everything possible to meet the needs of the returning Nikkei. Floyd Schmoe and the AFSC organized groups of local citizens to help clean up the vacant homes of Japanese Americans and to guard them against potential vandalism.[85]

The motivations of American church organizations in calling for programs to support Japanese Americans and their families were based on the same principle in 1945 as they had been in 1942: the Christian and democratic treatment of persons of Japanese ancestry. Nevertheless, their everyday grassroots commitment to the just and humane treatment of Japanese Americans demonstrated a substantial resistance to the prejudicial and segregationist dogma that had been practiced on the west coast for decades.[86] Conversely, Canadian church rhetoric underwent an alteration throughout the war. Believing initially that the government would treat the Nikkei in a Christian and just manner but subsequently hardened by the disfranchisement issue and shocked by the plans for "repatriation," church leaders and laity turned to the United Nations Charter to articulate and bolster their opposition. Their acceptance of the charter reflected Canadians' growing awareness of its principles of fundamental human rights and the influence of the CCJC in directing the opposition to deportation.

"For Action by Members and Friends":
The Work of Other Interested Organizations

Like the Christian and Jewish groups, a variety of civil liberties bodies, student organizations, concerned citizens' associations, and women's groups, among others, advocated on behalf of Japanese Americans and Japanese Canadians. Numerous individuals also made their opinions known by way of protest letters. These efforts were an essential component of the advocacy movements in Canada and the United States, as they alerted government officials to the widespread disapproval of the treatment of the Nikkei. These groups were also useful "arms" of the ACLU and the CCJC, for they provided a necessary extension to the work of these two leading bodies, especially in public education and fundraising. Analyzing the rhetoric employed by these groups and individuals provides another way to assess the impact of human rights discourse in both the United States and Canada.

In the US, faculty and students clearly mobilized to show their opposition to mass removal, whereas student groups in Canada actively protested deportation. From the beginning, some American faculty and students were critical of the government's action, as evidenced by the many impassioned pleas for tolerance in the records of the House Select Committee Investigating National Defense Migration, also known as the Tolan Committee hearings. Several academics, including Eric C. Bellquist of the Department of Political Science at the University of California, advocated the protection of minority rights and the apprehension of subversive elements on an individual basis. He called upon the committee "to endeavor to ascertain just what lies behind the present clamor."[87] Jesse F. Steiner, chair of the University of Washington sociology department, argued that government acceptance of mass evacuation amounted to bowing to race prejudice; like many others, he compared it to "the treatment of minorities by the totalitarian governments in Europe and Asia."[88] Two University of Washington students attested to the "American-ness" of the 250 Nisei students on campus and their great degree of involvement in campus life.[89] Their testimony thus challenged one of the main assumptions of relocation – the inassimilability of Japanese Americans into the mainstream.

In cooperation with the Quakers, American academics pressured the government to allow Japanese American college students to continue their studies at other colleges throughout the United States. Initial sporadic attempts at student relocation were eventually replaced by a more coordinated government-sanctioned program at the national level. At the urging of WRA director Milton S. Eisenhower, the National Japanese American Student Relocation Council was formed at a Chicago conference on 29 May 1942; it was led by Quaker Clarence E. Pickett, executive secretary of the AFSC between 1929 and 1950.[90] Pickett was well known and well respected among the Nisei; indeed, a *Pacific Citizen* article lauded him for his "greatness" and commented on the "warmth" that emanated from him. Pickett also had. a reportedly close relationship with both Franklin and Eleanor Roosevelt, which may explain why he became known to Eisenhower. Pickett appointed Robert W. O'Brien, assistant dean of arts and sciences at the University of Washington, to lead the joint voluntary effort of eminent west and east coast academics and churchmen who relied on personal contacts to open the doors to higher education for thousands of Nisei. Like Pickett, O'Brien was, from the outset, a keen advocate for the fair treatment of persons of Japanese ancestry, arguing in the *Intercollegian,* for example, that the "treatment of the Japanese minority is the acid test of the American system. Let only one group become the subject of persecution and the safety of every group is in jeopardy."[91] The council also solicited donations to establish a student relocation scholarship fund. It actively lobbied the Roosevelt government on behalf of equal treatment for Japanese American students. The Student Relocation Council was a pioneer in that it not only assisted the removal of students to other universities where they could continue their studies, but it also supported the government's general relocation program by returning Nisei students to the camps during the summer months to "interpret the outside" to the residents.[92] The work of this council underscored the liberal belief in the benefits of assimilation. As one chapter in Robert W. O'Brien's insider account of the council suggested, the goal of the many individuals involved was that the Nisei would become "Americans without question," as assimilation in the manner they envisioned would erase any shreds of "Japanness" remaining in the students.[93]

The National Japanese American Student Relocation Council is also interesting for the contradiction it represented in the incarceration program. In moving from "concentration camp to campus," as scholar Allan Austin describes it, the approximately four thousand student relocatees acted as pioneers in the larger WRA plan for resettlement. They also served as early examples in the desire to promote multiculturalism in their new communities. Some students were eager to help foster increased contacts between Nikkei and whites to mitigate the impact of historic prejudice against Asians. Thus, while their friends and families remained incarcerated, they were free to come and go as they pleased, and to be accepted as members of their new campus communities.[94]

No comparable student relocation program existed in Canada, but student opinion provides some interesting information as to the reaction on Canadian campuses to the incarceration program. A sampling of polls conducted throughout 1945 and 1946 reveals that Canadian students generally opposed the policy of deportation. At both McGill and Sir George Williams (Concordia) College, student opinion was almost wholly against the idea. Representative comments included "anti-Japanese actions are reminiscent of Nazi methods" and "such actions are unfair both democratically and religiously." Others modified their opinion by saying that non-Canadian-born Japanese or those hostile to Canada should be deported. At the University of Ottawa, 150 students were polled; of those, 9.3 percent favoured deportation, 82.6 percent opposed it, and 8.1 percent were undecided. Every student polled at the University of Saskatchewan supported a policy of "tolerance," whereas 65 percent of those polled at the University of Western Ontario (UWO) favoured deportation. Students at the University of Toronto, the city that represented the central locus for activity, demonstrated their disagreement with the deportation policy through their actions. The Students' Administrative Council, representing all the university's undergraduates, wired the acting prime minister to demand the deletion of clause G, section 3, from Bill 15, the National Emergency Transitional Powers Act. The council executive wrote to its counterparts at other universities, informing them of the step it had taken and advising them to do the same.[95]

Along with the Student Christian Movement, the YMCA, and the YWCA, individual university students were valuable assets to the CCJC coalition. Their widespread involvement took in "university student Organizations in all the leading Canadian Universities."[96] At the University of Toronto, students formed a committee on Japanese Canadians; its chair, Don Franco, who was also president of the university's Humanist Club, participated in the initial CCJC delegation to Ottawa in the summer of 1945.[97] Protest meetings were often held at universities. On 14 February 1946, a Students' Forum was held at the University of Toronto at which some CCJC members were invited speakers. On 1 March, a mass meeting of a thousand students at Queen's University "loudly cheered" a speech given by CCJC member B.K. Sandwell.[98] McGill's Students Society sponsored a mass meeting protesting the university's exclusion policy. It motivated the university Senate to lift the restrictions in autumn 1945.[99] Although these student groups were locally formed, they did not confine themselves to local issues. Their concerns were with national policy, and the various student groups across the country kept the issues alive not only on campus but also in their communities. Both campus and community newspapers were used, and petitions were crafted and sent to local MPs and the prime minister.

The CCJC encouraged student support and action because students devoted much time to studying the issues at hand; increasing the awareness of all Canadians regarding the problem of deportation was paramount in creating widespread criticism of Ottawa's actions. February 1946 polls sponsored by the Student Christian Movement at both UWO and the University of Toronto indicate the importance of education in this case. At UWO, where no student focus group had been established to promote awareness of the Japanese Canadian situation, the poll revealed that, though 65 percent of respondents favoured equal rights for Japanese Canadians, 63 percent felt that the 10,387 Nikkei who had signed repatriation forms should be sent to Japan. Only 30 percent approved of extending the opportunity to revoke the decision. Of those asked whether they had studied the Japanese Canadian question, 223 said that they had; 345 had not. On the issue of whether Japanese Canadians could be assimilated, 220 students replied that they could, but 292 believed they could not. A majority, however, expressed interest in learning more about the issue. At the University of Toronto, on the other hand, the results of a student campus poll indicated that 64.1 percent opposed deportation, whereas 28.7 percent favoured it; of those, nearly 70 percent felt that they "knew the facts," whereas 30 percent did not. The results of the University of Toronto poll were testament to the lobbying and awareness efforts undertaken by the university branch of the CCJC.[100]

The University of Toronto was also fertile ground for support from faculty. There, academics particularly approved the idea of dispersal and assimilation, as did their American counterparts, a stance that was consistent with contemporary liberal thought. For example, Dr. Griffith Taylor, head of geography, viewed the deportation issue as a problem caused by "racial indigestion" and suggested that the solution was to "swallow this minority group."[101]

Analogous responses to the relocation of American and Canadian Nikkei came from other organizations, such as women's groups, for example. In the United States, the Women's International League for Peace and Freedom (WILPF) initially gave the Roosevelt administration the benefit of the doubt on removal but later became an ardent critic of this policy. The New Jersey Citizens Committee on Japanese American Resettlement could count representatives from the National Council of Jewish Women among its leadership. The National Council of Women (NCW) and the WILPF in Canada, a left-leaning pacifist group with a long history of social activism, were among the women's organizations that lent their support to the CCJC. Women's associations across Canada sent resolutions to the federal government in protest of deportation policy. As noted above, women's associations and missionary societies of all the leading denominations also supported both the ACLU and the CCJC. Many of these groups initially approved the idea of resettlement and encouraged work to this end but eventually came to realize the inherent injustice in the various policies.[102]

Organized labour, specifically the more progressive "industrial" trade unions, also took a strong interest in the problems of removal and (in Canada) expatriation. Louis Goldblatt, secretary of the California Congress of Industrial Organizations (CIO), made a dramatic statement to the Tolan Committee in castigating what he believed was the acquiescence of state and local authorities to the nativism of the Hearst press. He remarked that the CIO supported a war against the Axis powers, not one against the "so-called yellow peril," and added quite ominously that "this entire episode of hysteria and mob-chant against the native-born Japanese will form a dark page of American history. It may well appear as one of the great victories won by the Axis powers." Even after the removal occurred, the California CIO also endorsed the ACLU plan for individual hearing boards for Japanese American citizens and enemy aliens subject to the orders, so that those who were described as "key men in their plants" could return to their defence production jobs. An August 1943 CIO council meeting in San Francisco focused on minorities and specifically on the issue of racial and national unity in wartime. Conference attendees discussed anti-Semitism, discrimination against African Americans, and the problems faced by loyal Japanese Americans. Later in the war, speaking at a forum co-sponsored by the Japanese American Committee for Democracy and the American Committee for Protection of Foreign Born, Goldblatt stated that bringing more Japanese into industrial unions would "establish a fundamental unity which will end any possibility of discrimination because of race or national origin." He again advocated the use of loyalty boards to enable the assimilation of Japanese Americans into the war effort. San Francisco CIO president George Wilson added his name to open letters of protest against the removal, and the Building Services Employees' International Union Local 6 of Seattle expressed its disapproval of removal, as Japanese Americans headed a large number of the hotels in that city. By 1944, the CIO's United Auto Workers (UAW), then the world's largest union, called for fair treatment of Japanese American workers in all its plants. The CIO and the American Federation of Labor (AFL) were often singled out by the Nikkei press for their efforts in promoting Japanese American equality. The CIO regularly sent representatives to meetings sponsored by the ACLU.[103]

CIO involvement in the issue of justice for Japanese Americans is hardly surprising, given the council's roots. The inclusive character of modern industrial unionism effected an egalitarianism that led it into the political arena and into alliances – often tentative – with other oppressed groups in society. The CIO advocated a modern version of "social unionism," one in which organized labour was conceived as a force that would improve the place of trade unions within the wider community and would raise the living standards of all Americans. The egalitarianism of industrial unionism and the broader vision of social unionism naturally led to support for the struggle against prejudice and discrimination. For example, unlike other unions, such as the AFL of the 1920s and 1930s, the CIO favoured organization of African Americans on a level equal to that of white workers; it also supported federal efforts towards fair employment practices. During

and immediately following the war, African Americans played an important role in such CIO member unions as the United Auto Workers and
the Steelworkers, Shipbuilders, and United Packinghouse Workers, even
though the CIO had no formal policy promoting their employment or
their place in its own membership. By 1946, over 10 percent of union
members were black, a degree of involvement unlikely to have been
achieved without CIO efforts.[104]

Some Canadian trade unions formally supported the CCJC, a fact that
Ross Lambertson associates with the emerging social unionism of Canada's
post-war period, a movement paralleled south of the border. CCJC union
supporters included the Toronto Labour Council, the United Electrical,
Radio and Machine Workers of America, the Canadian Congress of Labour
(CCL), and the United Steelworkers of America (USW). Other lesser-known
unions proved their support for justice for the Japanese Canadians by
sending resolutions to the prime minister.[105] Labour unions also believed
in the benefits of assimilation, and thus actively promoted resettlement
as a desirable policy. As a member of a CCJC delegation, Charles Millard
of the CCL indicated to the prime minister and a Cabinet committee that
anti-Japanese hostility in some branches of labour had decreased and moreover that labour would support any resettlement policy. Failure to cease
discriminatory policies would result in "future repercussions" in the World
Federation of Trade Unions.[106] The USW was a logical ally for the CCJC
because it was also closely associated with the CCF. The Toronto Labour
Council, a municipal umbrella organization for CCL unions, also brought
social unionism into the CCJC campaign. Its president, Murray Cotterill,
was the USW publicity director; he later became an active member of the
Toronto Joint Labour Committee to Combat Racial Intolerance.[107]

Civil liberties groups and citizens' committees of a varied nature also
offered assistance and support to the CCJC and the ACLU. Several other
bodies commented on the issues and thus contributed in their own way
to the advocacy rhetoric surrounding the removal policies in both Canada and the United States and the deportation policy in Canada. The positions taken by most of these groups regarding the removal issue once again
reflected not only the confusion of liberals of the day but also the "common sense" about assimilation.

The Committee on National Security and Fair Play, formerly known as
the Northern California Committee on Fair Play for Citizens and Aliens,
and later titled the Committee on American Principles and Fair Play, was
headed by Galen Fisher, a noted organizer on behalf of Japanese Americans.
Throughout his life, he worked for greater understanding between the
United States and Japan, first as a YMCA secretary to Japan and then as
chair of the Pacific School of Religion board of trustees, the major Northern California advisor to the Institute of Pacific Relations.[108] The committee

had a double purpose, reflective perhaps of the duality of liberal thought during wartime. Although its aim was to support the government and the armed forces in preserving national security and winning the war, it also concerned itself with fostering what it termed "fair play," "especially toward law-abiding and innocent aliens and citizens of alien parentage." Fisher himself opposed the harsh restrictions placed on Japanese Americans, but he nevertheless adopted a more flexible approach when their removal from the west coast seemed unavoidable. Even as Fisher stated his opposition to removal at the Tolan Committee hearings on 21 February 1942, he was cooperating with officials and organizations who were planning the resettlement of Japanese Americans. His tactical approach is revealed in a 3 March press release issued by his committee, which "welcomed" Roosevelt's executive order and cited military control as necessary due to the "extreme gravity of the situation." Military removal, on the other hand, was strongly rejected. Once it was in full swing, Fisher and his committee retreated to another compromised position, calling for hearing boards at which the Nisei could prove their loyalty to prevent further measures.[109]

Fisher continued to challenge the removal policy even as his committee voiced little criticism of the WRA. Throughout the war, he published numerous articles, which were given wide circulation by the committee. Although in private Fisher criticized the removal policy and the WRA in far harsher terms than he did in published form, this should not be interpreted as evidence of hypocrisy; Fisher and his committee were attempting to create a positive environment for the return of the Nikkei to the west coast. If they could not halt current government and WRA policies, they could direct their attempts towards achieving more humane ones in the future.[110] To this end, Fisher and his colleagues kept in contact with Roger Baldwin, advising him on the relative successes and limitations of the work of the committee.[111] When the committee underwent an April 1943 reorganization to become the Committee on American Principles and Fair Play, its letters and purpose began to take on greater urgency with regard to the citizenship and treatment of Japanese Americans. Still, even into 1944, when the Atlantic Charter's human rights language might have made its way into committee correspondence, the treatment of the Nikkei was instead articulated as contrary to "fundamental American principles." Perhaps the closest this organization came to applying human rights rhetoric was in a statement of its beliefs in which it briefly remarked that "attacks upon the rights of any minority tend to undermine the rights of the majority."[112]

The Post War World Council, headed by Norman Thomas and Oswald Garrison Villard, a long-time pacifist and former editor of the *Nation*, also tried to reach out to a broad liberal constituency by opposing the removal, on the one hand, and, on the other, calling for the use of hearing boards to enable loyal Japanese Americans to return to their homes. In April 1942, the council issued a statement enunciating these beliefs; it was signed by over two hundred prominent Americans, indicating the degree to which American liberals were torn between abhorrence of discrimination and loyalty to the administration. However, another Post War World Council publication, a 1942 pamphlet titled *Democracy and the Japanese Americans,* expressed more consistent feelings on the issue of incarceration. It exhorted the government to end the mass incarceration of Japanese Americans and to prevent any similar situation from occurring again. The Post War World Council issued strong statements urging the fair treatment of American citizens of Japanese ancestry lest the United States echo the principles of Nazism. The government was also urged to settle families and small groups together, where they could "be absorbed into the general American life." Astute readers would have discerned Thomas' activist agenda in the closing pages of the pamphlet: "This pamphlet is written, published and circulated not only to disseminate information but to arouse action."[113]

Civil liberties organizations in Canada, although not as established as the ACLU, lent a strong voice to the opposition to Japanese Canadian deportation. The Civil Liberties Association of Toronto (CLAT) was a central force in the CCJC in particular, specifically by 1945. Civil liberties organizations in Canada experienced difficulties in the early 1940s due to a number of morale-busting pieces of legislation passed both provincially and federally in the 1930s and early 1940s, such as Quebec's so-called Padlock Law of 1937. Many civil libertarians began to take interest in issues of discrimination and racism. The deportation issue became an important focal point and thus helped to rejuvenate the civil libertarian movement in Canada.[114]

The CLAT was the only civil liberties organization in Canada to formally support the CCJC. It was among the associations listed as supporting the CCJC in that group's briefs to Ottawa, in its communications to members, and in its published literature. Along with the CCJC, it co-sponsored a major meeting of organizations and interested parties in January 1946 and helped to collect more than $1,200 to help finance the Supreme Court challenge.[115] Its motives for involvement were to secure justice for the Japanese Canadians within the context of their successful "dispersal and rehabilitation." Early in 1945, like other North American organizations advocating for the Nikkei, the CLAT supported the government plan for Japanese Canadian assimilation and urged Ottawa to do more to this end.[116]

By late 1945, the Civil Liberties Association of Winnipeg (CLAW) also supported the advocacy movement for Japanese Canadians, arguing that Canadian citizenship in general would be jeopardized by the government's illiberal proposed actions. Although neither the CLAW letters to King nor the lengthy brief it addressed to King and the senators and MPs from Manitoba contain a direct appeal to human rights, they do indicate that popular concern for the fair treatment of Japanese Canadians had made its mark upon this group, consequently rousing it to address the deportation issue.[117]

In 1946, when the CCJC was involved in Supreme Court litigation, other new civil liberties organizations were established. The Ottawa Civil Liberties Association was formed in the spring of 1946 by a group of about two hundred concerned "respectable" citizens, including Harry Southam, publisher of the *Ottawa Citizen*, a liberal newspaper. Another member, Edith Holtom, active in the Ottawa branch of the Co-operative Committee on Japanese Canadians, was a committed pacifist with the Fellowship of Reconciliation and the Fellowship for a Christian Social Order; she also had a strong interest in human and civil rights issues.[118]

Other civil liberties groups such as the Montreal Committee on Canadian Citizenship/La Comité pour la défense de la citoyenneté canadienne and the Emergency Committee for Civil Rights also formed during this period. They were all newcomers to the campaign and thus played minor roles. Their membership came from the familiar ranks of supporters, such as the Canadian Jewish Congress and the YMCA, and even the Saint Jean-Baptiste Society, a nationalist French Canadian organization. A number of progressive French Canadian activists, including Thérèse Casgrain, Jacques Perrault, and Roger Ouimet, were named to the Montreal Committee's executive. In one of its first acts, the committee denounced the deportation policy as "dangerous and attacking the fundamental rights of minorities." According to the *Montreal Gazette*, its main goals were to mobilize public opinion against the expatriation and to raise funds for the Privy Council appeal. These groups also corresponded with the ACLU on matters pertaining to the treatment of the Nikkei.[119]

The Vancouver branch of the Canadian Civil Liberties Union (VCCLU), which entered the fray in the spring of 1947, made substantial use of the emerging human rights rhetoric throughout its briefs and letters to the prime minister. Although it did not protest the forcible resettlement policy in 1942, it turned to the deportation issue in 1945, probably due to the involvement of one of its leading members, Hunter Lewis, a UBC English professor who was also chair of the Vancouver branch of the CCJC. In its summary of the various egregious pieces of legislation that still controlled Japanese Canadians in 1947, the VCCLU urged the King government to remove the existing discriminatory laws because "they are unjust, immoral, and contrary to the doctrines of humanity" and because "they set precedents that threaten the fundamental freedoms and human rights of all individuals and groups in the country."[120]

Thus, by 1945, civil libertarians, labour unions, student groups, and women's organizations in Canada had joined the CCJC in protesting the deportation of the Nikkei. In the United States, American members of similar groups worked to create an environment of acceptance of Japanese Americans. In both countries, the liberal media would play a central role in promulgating the many views of these associations.

"They Indicate One Side of Public Reaction towards the Handling of the Japanese Problem": The Role of the Media

In the weeks immediately following the 1942 announcement of Canadian and US government plans for the Japanese minority, major newspapers in both countries generally voiced their approval of them. In fact, Canadian newspapers did not criticize the removal until about 1945, moving, like the public generally, towards a more favourable perception of Japanese Canadians. In the United States, religious presses and left/liberal newspapers offered critiques ranging from open objections to Roosevelt and his decision to acceptance of some of the major premises of the pro-removal argument. For many advocacy groups, the media became a valuable tool in promoting their opinions regarding injustices directed against the Nikkei and in educating a public that was largely unaware of the degree of illegitimacy of Washington's actions. The media acted as an important mouthpiece for these advocates and also reflected the way in which the problem was defined in each country.

Both the *Nation* and the *New Republic*, the two "flagship left/liberal weeklies," denounced removal as an option even before Executive Order 9066 was issued, and both criticized the exercise of removal and relocation once they were under way.[121] However, neither weekly launched any significant campaign on those major issues. Nevertheless, their limited contributions helped to publicize the injustices done in order to "protect" democracy at home. The *Nation* published a few articles immediately following the removal order that attacked "propagandists at work" on the west coast, expressing worry about the economic fallout from removal and the ability of the "country's capacity to keep its head."[122] Once most of the round-ups took place, however, the *Nation* no longer mentioned the incarceration. An article in its 25 July 1942 edition, commenting on the apparent contradiction between policies dealing with the mainland and Hawaiian Japanese populations, marked the last such column on the issue for that year.[123] It is likely that its editors felt unease at rebuking the Roosevelt administration on its handling of the Japanese American issue.

By contrast, the *New Republic* devoted more continual coverage to the removal and other issues facing Japanese Americans, but its articles before and immediately following the announcement of Executive Order 9066 were often contradictory. Some columnists expressed confidence that

Washington would somehow counter the racist hysteria on the west coast; others advocated more forceful measures to be taken against Japanese Americans in Hawaii. By mid-1942, however, the *New Republic* routinely denounced the removal. Dubbing the efforts to strip Japanese Americans of their citizenship as the "American Nuremberg Law," commentators repeatedly denounced the removal policy as spoiling America's record on civil liberties. Several articles even featured Japanese American writers describing the toll of life in the incarceration camps.[124]

In early February 1942, Chester Rowell, a California newspaperman prominent as the former editor of the *San Francisco Chronicle,* wrote an article in that newspaper warning of the folly in the newly announced policies. He made what the *Pacific Citizen* described as a "plea for sanity and reason in the treatment of Japanese aliens" and asserted that the use of martial law, in particular, "would mean the suspension of the civil rights, not merely of citizens of Japanese ancestry, but of everybody." He further stated that the results of those measures were "not only against all law, morals and justice, but against our own interests," presumably referring to the democratic war aims for which Americans were fighting.[125]

Other journals and newspapers also published articles that voiced opposition to the incarceration, generally amidst pieces detailing various race-related issues of the day, such as the need to end racist practices against African Americans. Religious periodicals and weeklies joined in expressing disdain for the removal policy. The *Commonweal,* a liberal Catholic weekly, likened the removal orders to "witchcraft" and repeatedly opposed efforts to strip Japanese Americans of their citizenship. It even printed the entire text of the ACLU's amicus brief in the *Korematsu* case, which challenged the exclusion order before the Supreme Court.[126] In early 1942, the *New York Times* published several letters to the editor that favoured "fair play" for Japanese Americans, although their regularity appears to have lessened once the removal process hit its peak in mid-1942.[127] *Common Sense,* a small but influential social-democratic monthly, urged its readers to support and participate in an ACLU-led letter-writing campaign to Secretary of Interior Harold Ickes urging the creation of hearing boards to assess the loyalty of persons of Japanese ancestry.[128] The *Christian Century,* however, provided the widest and most influential coverage of anti-removal viewpoints with impressive regularity in 1942 and throughout the war. This liberal Protestant weekly reflected the views of its readership, which had a long history of Christian relations with Japanese Americans. It also mirrored the anti-racism and anti-imperialism that motivated many liberals of the day, and played a unique role in expressing support for American participation in the war and delivering balanced information on the removal issue.[129]

In terms of local media response, Walter and Mildred Woodward were arguably the only small-town newspaper editors to regularly editorialize in defence of their Nikkei neighbours and to remind their readership of the importance of the Bill of Rights in light of the repercussions of Executive Order 9066. Additionally, their *Bainbridge Review* provided four incarcerated Nisei the opportunity to become "Camp Correspondents." Thus, Paul Ohtaki, Sa Nakata, Tony Joura, and Sada Omoto regularly reported on such daily events as births, deaths, marriages, baseball scores, and enlistments in the US Army. Such reportage created an important link between the Bainbridge Island incarcerated and their neighbours still residing on Bainbridge Island, Washington, "paving the way for [their] return," as one island elder recalled.[130]

By 1944, more American newspapers and journals were joining the ranks of media calling for just treatment of Japanese Americans, especially as they returned to the west coast. Japanese removal was often linked with other minority issues. The *Chicago Defender* pointed out that "Negro Americans cannot but watch with interest and apprehension at the outcome of the Korematsu case," and a broadcaster commented on the wider implications of what had been done to the Japanese Americans: "This is far from being just a Japanese question – it can affect the negro, the Jew, labor minorities, business minorities, intellectual minorities – any group that is different – and when such discrimination is fostered there is no telling when it will end. Let us continue to act American."[131] *Harper's* printed a scathing attack on the entirety of the removal policy, calling it a violation of the Bill of Rights. The *San Francisco News* denounced the removal as a product of hysteria but remarked that "the one good effect" of the assimilation of the Nisei was their dispersal throughout the United States.[132] *Fortune* magazine suspected that the ban on the return of the "evacuees" was for "reasons other than military." Citing the army policy of "protective custody" – ostensibly instigated due to army fears of Japanese American pogroms incited by such Californian elements as the Hearst papers and the Native Sons of the Golden West – *Fortune* noted ominously that

> The American custom in the past has been to lock up the citizen who commits violence, not the victim of his threats and blows. The doctrine of "protective custody" could prove altogether too convenient a weapon in many other situations. In California, a state with a long history of race hatred and vigilanteism [sic], antagonism is already building against the Negroes who have come in for war jobs. What is to prevent their removal to jails, to "protect them" from riots? Or Negroes in Detroit, Jews in Boston, Mexicans in Texas? The possibilities of "protective custody" are endless, as the Nazis have amply proved.[133]

The *Intermountain Catholic* (now the *Register*) called on Salt Lake City residents to pressure local government officials to suspend restrictions on Nisei business activities. In his column "Intermountain Daybook," editor Reverend Robert J. Dwyer likened efforts to build "race hatred" to "Fascistic measures."[134]

Although the American media variously linked the removal to the issues of democracy, fascism, totalitarianism, and Nazism, they did not employ the concept of human rights in their critique of government actions. Canadian media opinions, however, underwent a much more discernable transformation that reflected the increasing awareness of the importance of human rights as a principle applying to the treatment of the Nikkei. In particular, *Canadian Forum*, the *Toronto Daily Star*, the *Toronto Globe and Mail*, the *Winnipeg Free Press*, the *Ottawa Citizen*, and *Saturday Night* often provided effective published opposition to the federal government's policies.[135]

Unlike the American newspapers discussed above, the Canadian media expressed no significant opposition to policies targeting Japanese Canadians in late 1941 and into 1942. A number of Canadian newspapers began to voice criticism over the franchise issue only in 1944 and when rumours of Japanese Canadian deportation circulated in late 1945. In fact, the lack of media response was so marked that *New Canadian* editor Tom Shoyama commented on it in an April 1944 editorial. By late 1945, however, the *New Canadian's* tone had changed. The newly appointed editor, Kasey Oyama, loudly proclaimed the Canadian media's collective denouncement of the expatriation policy by pointing out that the *Winnipeg Free Press* was the most active, publishing three editorials in one week opposing "deportation."[136] Like the change in the nature of CCJC and coordinating group opposition, which had occurred by 1945, the transition in the media's language of rights can also be attributed to the influence of the United Nations Charter.

As it had for the churches, Bill 135 sparked the media's first major negative outburst regarding Ottawa's handling of the "Japanese problem." On 22 June 1944, the *Winnipeg Free Press* editorialist claimed that disfranchising those who cooperated with the "dispersal" would seriously undermine the future prospects of resettlement. More ominous were the far broader implications beyond that of disfranchising Japanese Canadians: the precedent would be set for any provincial legislature to disfranchise any minority belonging to the "racial stock" of a country at war with Canada. As of June 1944, the potential candidates for such treatment were not few in number: Germans, Italians, Bulgarians, Hungarians, Romanians, and Finns could all be subject to the unjust clause 5 of Bill 135. Another *Winnipeg Free Press* editorial sagely commented that "we are either building a democracy in Canada on terms of equality of citizenship, or we are sliding into the dark age in which Germany has been submerged, where no man is the equal of another before the law unless he has the stamp of approval of a ruling caste." Later that year, yet another *Winnipeg Free Press* editorial described Ian Mackenzie's slogan "no Japs from the Rockies to the Sea" as illogical and wrote that he had "raised the bloody shirt of racialism," alluding, perhaps, to the brownshirts, the brutal shock troops of the Nazis.[137]

The CCJC actively courted newspaper attention as a major method of promoting its views in order to increase public awareness and thus create favourable public opinion. Indeed, this was very necessary, as a Wartime Information Bureau survey of June 1945 suggested that "many Canadians are largely unaware of it [the "problem of what to do with Canada's 24,000 residents of Japanese ancestry"] as a problem."[138] As early as November 1943, the extent of *Saturday Night's* "one-sided" criticism of the plight of Japanese Canadians drew the attention of Department of External Affairs officials.[139] The editor of *Saturday Night*, B.K. Sandwell, was both president of CLAT and a key player in the CCJC. By late 1945, both *Saturday Night* and the *Toronto Daily Star* regularly published articles and letters pertaining to the anti-deportation position. The *Star* and the *Winnipeg Free Press* published several letters critical of government policies, some of which were equated with those of Nazism. They kept readers apprised of CCJC activities, including its representations to Ottawa. On 22 January 1946, the *Star* printed the CCJC brief to the Supreme Court in its entirety.[140] Other newspapers also picked up on the theme of equating Canadian government actions with Nazism.[141]

Canadian Forum, disposed by the 1940s to a social-democratic perspective, was another useful medium for the CCJC and its campaign. By the early 1940s, *Canadian Forum* had already begun to examine race-related issues, reviewing some publications that explained how modern science was debunking biological race theories. Articles critiquing racial and religious discrimination also appeared therein, dealing with the rights of Jews, blacks, First Nations people, and Japanese Canadians.[142] In particular, its editor, Edith Fowke, produced a few articles that dealt with the deportation orders. Perhaps the best of these was "Japanese Canadians," which appeared in the January 1946 *Forum*; a work of forceful rhetoric, it was later reprinted as a pamphlet and distributed to CCJC-supporting organizations to aid the generation of funds for the legal campaigns. More than any of her *Canadian Forum* articles, "Japanese Canadians" brought to the forefront allegations that the applications for "repatriation" were signed in less than unfettered circumstances.[143] The indefatigable Fowke, CCF partisan and CCJC and FOR member, was also the associate editor of *Magazine Digest* and a member of the editorial board of the FOR publication *Reconciliation*. In addition, she produced a history of the CCJC in 1951, titled *They Made Democracy Work: The Story of the Cooperative Committee on Japanese Canadians.*

It was Grace MacInnis, however, CCF MLA in British Columbia and daughter of CCF founder J.S. Woodsworth, who can lay claim to penning the first *Canadian Forum* article that addressed the Nikkei situation. In the June 1942 issue, she published "Wanted: A Country," which raised a number of questions with respect to the "Oriental problem," a matter on which she and her husband, Angus MacInnis, a CCF MP for Vancouver East, were considered authorities. Both were known for their long-standing support of equal rights for Asians, however qualified it may have been. In *Oriental Canadians: Outcasts or Citizens?* a pamphlet calling for an end to anti-Asian prejudice, the MacInnises argued that the policy of exclusion from the west coast existed for defence purposes; in addition, they claimed that continuation of such restrictions would have the beneficial effect of dispersing the Nikkei throughout Canada. Indeed, some forty years later, Grace MacInnis was still lauding the forced relocation, not, of course, because it was forced, but because it more evenly distributed the Nikkei across the country.[144]

In December 1943, *Maclean's* offered readers two interesting perspectives on the "Japanese problem" by inviting Angus MacInnis and Howard Green (Liberal, Vancouver South) to debate the issue in its pages. Both authors focused on "repatriation," and their responses exemplify the degree to which rights discourse was embraced at that time. The printed debate was provocatively titled "Should We Send the Japs Back?" Providing an overview of the provisions by which the Japanese came to Canada and the problematic nature of their subsequent domination of west coast fishing and other industries, Green generally reiterated many well-worn stereotypes concerning them. For him, the solution to the "problem" was continued resettlement in eastern Canada on an individual basis; for those Nikkei still in the incarceration camps, the "alternative seems to be for the Canadian Government to insist that one of the terms of any peace treaty with Japan shall be that those Japanese who have not been permanently resettled are to be returned to Japan ... Another term should be that neither Canadians nor Japanese shall in future settle in the country of the other on a permanent basis."[145]

Although Green's submission is useful for its reflection of anti-Asian rhetoric and for what it did not reveal about the emerging rights discourse, MacInnis' entry clearly demonstrated an inchoative awareness of the concepts of human rights and of Canadian citizenship. MacInnis opposed repatriation for three reasons: first, he "would not be party to discriminating against a people because of race or color"; second, the "repatriation" policy proposed to "remove" Canadians, but, as he pointed out, "citizens of Canada cannot be 'repatriated' to some other country"; and third, persons of Japanese ancestry came to Canada lawfully. Not unlike the intolerant Green and, indeed, many liberal-minded advocates, MacInnis held fast to the idea of resettlement in eastern Canada. His summation, however, hinted at egalitarian principles:

> To conclude, I advocate granting to those of Japanese origin in Canada all the rights and privileges that I have, on the sole basis that they are human beings. To deny them one iota of the rights and privileges enjoyed by ... individuals of the race to which I belong would be a denial of the brotherhood of man; a denial to fellow humans of rights and privileges which I enjoy for no better reason than that my race was here first.[146]

The deportation orders also received attention from the American media. In the *Washington Post*, a strongly worded editorial declared the deportation proposal to be an "odious manifestation of racialism ... Our own treatment of persons of Japanese ancestry was, in all conscience, harsh enough. The Canadian treatment has been even more severe ... Canada will refresh its own great traditions of freedom if it gives these harassed people a chance to make a genuinely free choice now the hysteria of war is ended."[147] The venerable *New York Times* passed judgment on the Canadian situation, citing the duress under which many Japanese Canadians signed their repatriation forms. It also urged that the deportation of loyal Japanese Canadians be stopped and that restrictions on those remaining in Canada should be dropped so that, according to King's August 1944 policy statement, they be free "to pursue the settled lives to which they are entitled."[148] Interestingly, the American decision to deport Japanese American renunciants did not elicit much by way of opposition, as recorded in the media. A general consensus existed in the United States that, because the renunciants had disavowed their American citizenship, they were no longer subject to either the Bill of Rights or the sympathy of the American people. Canadian newspapers also eyed the developments in the Japanese American situation, and by late 1945 journalists such as Lorne Greene, the "Voice of Canada," were remarking on the discrepancies between the American and Canadian positions.[149]

By late 1945 and into 1946, the media devoted a significant amount of attention to demands that the deportation orders be rescinded and that Ottawa treat Japanese Canadians in a fair and humane manner. A *Toronto Globe and Mail* editorial singled out the popular protest against the deportation policy. Also of import was its recommendation that the "simple and just course would be for the Government to reconsider the whole question in light of human rights."[150] Many commentators understood that, though legal principles were at stake, so too were moral principles. Others noted that both Canadian citizenship and the security of non-Japanese minority groups in Canada would be threatened if the orders were upheld. The 8 June 1946 issue of *Saturday Night* included a blistering attack on several MPs from British Columbia, linking their attitudes with those of Southerners in the pre–Civil War period:

> In effect they assert with one breath that all men are born free and equal and entitled to life, liberty and the pursuit of happiness, and with the next they assert that persons of a certain color are not so born, or in other words they do not belong to the class covered by the phrase, "all men." The odd thing is that they are entirely unconscious of any inconsistency. They have taught themselves to think of a Japanese – any Japanese – as something slightly less than human and so they have no difficulty in forgetting about him when they orate about the rights and liberties of men in general. Having got that far they will find no trouble, when the occasion arises, in similarly forgetting about Chinese, Negroes and ultimately a lot of other kinds of human beings whom they do not happen to like.[151]

A play published by the UN Society in Canada advised that Canadians "must correct their indifference to minority peoples," as the "denial of human rights ... is a threat to world peace." Following the December 1946 Supreme Court ruling *In the Matter of the Reference*, an *Ottawa Citizen* editorial observed that the deportation was not in keeping with British traditions and that although the CCJC had "lost the legal battle [this] in no way invalidates other arguments against compulsory deportation it has put forward on humanitarian and social grounds ... For Canada to carry out this deportation would make a mockery of UN idealism."[152] The latter point was well mined in many other newspapers and media broadcasts, as the continuation of restrictive measures against the Nikkei was presented as a source of embarrassment. This was especially the case as the rights of minorities became of increasing concern to many nations following the war. At the United Nations Conference at Flushing Meadows in early 1947, human rights and the protection of minorities were viewed not as matters of national sovereignty but as issues properly concerning the whole world. CBC reporter Burton Kierstead noted that the Canadian delegation had voiced clear and strong opinions on matters of relief, reduction in armaments, and other affairs at the conference. However, as the debate turned to the question of the rights of minorities, in particular the treatment of "Indians in South Africa," as Kierstead put it, the Canadian delegation was "embarrassed." A Canadian newspaper journalist explained that the delegation's hesitation was due to the desire not to have Canada's own "undemocratic abuse of human rights ... held up before world public opinion."[153]

Still, it should be remembered that, even as many Canadian liberals fought deportation, they remained confident in assimilation as a means to thwart racism. The *Vancouver Daily Province* published comments made by B.K. Sandwell at a CBC board of governors meeting (Sandwell was a board member) in which he noted that the CCJC campaign to recognize the human and citizenship rights of Japanese Canadians "does not include any proposal for future admission of Japanese immigrants." He also expressed his hope that the "current controversy" over deportation would "get the Japs a little better distributed across Canada."[154]

When newspapers that espoused both liberal and Liberal traditions began to oppose the deportation policy, Ottawa took notice. During House of Commons debates regarding Japanese Canadian policy, CCF MPs often cited *Winnipeg Free Press* editorials in particular.[155] As mentioned earlier, the *Free Press* began its persistent criticism of government policy with the issue of disfranchisement in 1944. It also argued in favour of voluntary dispersal and assimilation, like other liberal commentators of the day. When the idea of deportation was being contemplated, the *Free Press* provided significant coverage of the topic, including the activities of the Winnipeg branch of the CCJC. Its critique reflected both the evolving human rights discourse and traditionally liberal arguments about freedom and the rule of law. In an editorial titled "We Will Regret Racialism," the *Free Press* cautioned that, though the war was fought "to rid the world of racialism and all its hateful works ... the persecution of minorities, as the people of this world have surely learned by now, always begins with the weakest minority. Once started it proceeds remorselessly to engulf all minorities." This combination of human rights and anti-racism rhetoric figured prominently in another editorial exhorting the province of Manitoba to take a "useful and enlightened role" in extending equal citizenship rights to the Nikkei settled there and to "accept the citizenship and residence of Canadians of Japanese origin on the same basis of equality as it accepts the right of Canadians of Polish, Scottish, Irish or Ukrainian origin to live here and exercise the rights and responsibilities of their citizenship."[156]

Although Canadian civil liberties groups, Protestant church officials, certain members of the media, and others enthusiastically adopted the concept of human rights, Ottawa had its own reservations. The public campaign shifted the King government's position on deportation, but this was not a total victory for human rights, as was aptly evidenced by the reticence of the King and Louis St. Laurent governments to vote in favour of the Universal Declaration of Human Rights (UDHR) in 1948. Between 1945 and 1948, the King government attempted to follow a determined policy of avoiding any commitment to the protection of international human rights as enunciated in the UDHR. House of Commons debates revealed a particular reluctance on the part of some MPs to agree to anything that might interfere with the powers or the sovereignty of the Canadian state.

Indeed, some maintained that, in times of national security, the whole-sale curtailment of human rights should remain an option for the government. The position taken by the King and St. Laurent governments revealed the apparent hypocrisy of signing an international instrument designed to protect human rights while insisting that Canada did not need one at home. In the end, Canada chose to endorse the declaration due to its concern for its international image.[157]

Encouraged by their limited victory with the deportation issue, some activists who had fought for Nisei rights carried on to demand a national bill of rights. With the ratification of the UDHR on 10 December 1948, civil liberties bodies, women's groups, organized labour, ethnic associations, and religious organizations all pressed the government to pass a national bill of rights. Alistair Stewart, CCF MP from Winnipeg North, was the first to put the idea to the House of Commons. Citing the UDHR preamble, with its language of fundamental rights and freedoms, Stewart expressed his view that a bill of rights would be essential in eliminating racial and religious discrimination. In addition, certain MPs, most notably M.J. Cold-well and John G. Diefenbaker, were instrumental in promoting a national bill of rights in the House of Commons and the media, indicative of how Canadian politicians were increasingly seizing the opportunity to criticize the government's record on civil liberties.[158]

Keeping the Facts before Those in Authority: The Efforts of "Allies" in Government

Politicians also played a role in changing the policies affecting persons of Japanese ancestry. In the United States, opposition to the removal came from the Socialist Party, whose resistance to the incarceration policy rested on the issue of civil liberties. Only later in the war did individual politicians from other parties register their disapproval of Washington's Nikkei policies. In Canada, pressure mounted within the House of Commons, where the CCF, in particular, provided much of the criticism. Over the course of the war, the nature of CCF opposition changed; after 1945, it mirrored the growing awareness of human rights. CCF disapproval of Ottawa's actions also reflected its awareness of what the entire program really meant. Additionally, the CCF escalated its criticism once it realized that removal produced neither resettlement across Canada nor the associated benefit of assimilation.

The Socialist Party condemned Executive Order 9066 and the military's removal of Japanese Americans once this became official government policy. It also voiced opposition to the restrictive efforts aimed at Japanese Americans on the west coast prior to Pearl Harbor. In the *Call*, the Socialist Party's weekly newspaper, columnists criticized the efforts to evict Japanese American farmers from "strategic" areas as a ploy to enable a land grab by white farmers. In a later article, Norman Thomas denounced Roosevelt's executive order as the "worst blot" yet on civil liberties and foreshadowed the "establishment of military despotism." Another editorial described the Nikkei removal process as "the most humiliating and most brutal method of handling the problem short of mass execution." On official levels, at its state convention in early March 1942, the California Socialist Party decried the treatment of Japanese Americans. At its executive committee meeting in April and at its May national convention, the National Socialist Party weighed in with its censure.[159] Perceiving this political reality, Norman Thomas ensured that his advocacy efforts in more moderate groups, particularly the Post War World Council and, of course, the ACLU, had wider appeal.

Although mainstream American politicians generally remained silent on the incarceration policy, at least one did speak out and urge his constituents to exercise humanity in receiving Japanese Americans to his state. When the WRA decided to resettle the Nikkei in the Amache, Colorado, camp, Governor Ralph Carr went against popular anti-Japanese sentiment by urging Coloradans to welcome them. In a speech defending the rights of Japanese Americans, Carr said, "If you harm them, you must harm me. I was brought up in a small town where I knew the shame and dishonor of race hatred. I grew to despise it because it threatened the happiness of you and you and you [pointing to his audience]."[160] For his defence of Nikkei rights in Colorado, Carr's political career was irreparably damaged. In 1942, he narrowly lost his bid for a Senate seat to Democratic incumbent Ed Johnson. In an interview one year later, Carr declared that his stance was logical: "That part of the constitution about all men being created equal and being guaranteed equal rights as citizens had no amendment excluding Japs, Jews, Catholics, or anyone else." Although Carr speculated that other state governors felt the same way, their silence was motivated by a desire for political longevity. Several city councils even passed resolutions urging Carr to "behave like the other governors." Attempting to openly defy the prejudice of his fellow Coloradans, Carr hired a Japanese American woman from the Amache camp as his housekeeper, who was then able to continue her academic studies at Denver University. Most certainly an exception to the rule in his time, Carr is still considered a friend and hero in Asian American history.[161]

In Canada, the CCF, particularly the BC wing of the party, did not register its disapproval of incarceration until much later in the war. Comparisons with the Socialist Party are unfair, as the latter had no elected representatives, either in Congress or state legislatures, and thus had nothing to lose by incurring the indignation of the electorate. Unlike the CCF, it was a small party without any reasonable electoral prospects. As for other non-mainstream political parties, the Labor Progressive Party (LPP) in British Columbia abandoned its usual public stand against racism in the case of Japanese Canadian incarceration. This change may be attributable to the LPP's communist members: hoping to win support from the province's non-Japanese fishermen, who viewed the Japanese as their economic competitors, they may have influenced the LPP to revise its policy. Fred Rose (MP, Cartier, Quebec), the LPP's only MP, spoke out a few times in the House of Commons against the incarceration, even as the BC LPP stated its support for the post-war exclusion of all Japanese Canadians from the west coast.[162]

The pages of the *Federationist,* the BC CCF weekly paper, provide excellent material through which to examine the party's position on the removal issue. Immediately following the attack on Pearl Harbor, the *Federationist* called for understanding and for labour to resist racial prejudice. Two weeks later, it supported the government persecution of those who were deemed "guilty" and "doubtful." By early January, the *Federationist* had declared the removal to be necessary as a safety precaution to prevent fifth column activity. Correspondingly, the BC CCF convention in late March resolved that "it is in the public interest that this evacuation be conducted speedily, humanely, and with a minimum of family and social dislocation."[163] This resolution was not easily adopted, for, as David Lewis, CCF national secretary, remarked, CCF members supported three intellectual stances regarding the Nikkei:

> The position against the mishandling of the Japanese and their rights as Canadian citizens – that was Angus MacInnis' [CCF MP, Vancouver East] position, and that had the support of the majority of the CCF. The others [in British Columbia] were divided into two: the hysterical, which included strangely enough ... the left-wing Marxists, and then there were the people who were afraid of the local situation.[164]

The CCF support for removal is surprising, given its commitment to "equal treatment before the law of all residents of Canada irrespective of race, nationality or religious or political beliefs," as proudly espoused in its "Regina Manifesto." In the 1930s, the CCF took up the cause of second-generation Asian enfranchisement, becoming the only political party in Canada to openly advocate for the rights of Asian Canadians. It should be noted, however, that not all CCF members in British Columbia agreed with the enfranchisement of Asians.[165]

The CCF's uncritical stance regarding removal was short-lived: by late 1943, the party had begun to reprove Ottawa's policies with increasing intensity. In April 1943, the BC section of the CCF met at its annual convention to consider various problems, among them the Japanese Canadian issue. The focus turned to concern regarding the increasing calls for repatriation. The convention resolved that the "Japanese question" was "but part of the problem of all racial minorities in Canada" that had to be solved according to the definition of social justice as established in the Atlantic Charter. Subscribing to contemporary liberal thought, the convention advocated the resettlement of Japanese Canadians across Canada to prevent the recurrence of racial tensions caused by the economic insecurities of big business.[166]

The CCF also opposed Ottawa's efforts to federally disfranchise Japanese Canadians through Bill 135 and attacked the use of the repatriation survey and the subsequent refusal to consider applications for cancellation of deportation. In the House of Commons, three CCF MPs – Bert Herridge (Kootenay West), Angus MacInnis (Vancouver East), and Alistair Stewart (Winnipeg North) – provided the lone voices calling for fair treatment of Japanese Canadians. MacInnis, for example, criticized the government's deportation policy as a violation of democratic tradition, Christian principles, and the human rights concepts enshrined in the United Nations Charter. In a sharp exchange with King, Stewart condemned the Orders-in-Council as hypocritical and an official endorsement of racial discrimination.[167]

Various CCF members also cooperated with the CCJC. CCF leader M.J. Coldwell, CCF activist Charles Millard, and a number of other influential CCJC supporters accompanied CCJC member Hugh MacMillan to an audience with the prime minister. Saskatchewan's CCF government supported the *In the Matter of a Reference.* in its hearing in the Supreme Court and also contributed funds. Saskatchewan premier T.C. Douglas extended a public invitation to persons of Japanese ancestry to settle in his province. Of import was the fact that Douglas made this offer *before* the war with Japan had ended. Other regional sections of the CCF sent letters and resolutions to King. The Quebec Provincial Council called the deportations a "dark blot upon the honour of Canada ... reminiscent of the race hating practices of Fascism in Europe." The CCF Ontario section argued in a letter to King that the deportation issue was of concern to all Canadians "because if the government can take away the rights and citizenship of one minority, then no minority group is safe."[168] By late 1945, the Winnipeg branch of the CCJC had initiated contact with federal CCF members, notably Stanley Knowles (Winnipeg North Centre) and Alistair Stewart (Winnipeg North), who promised to keep pressuring the federal government regarding the proposed deportations.[169]

Later, individual Liberal politicians across Canada would become sharply critical of their own government's policies. For example, on 24 April 1947, Benoit Michaud (Restigouche-Madawaska) voted for a CCF motion to annul Bill 104, which proposed to keep in place restrictions on Japanese Canadians initially passed as Orders-in-Council in the early 1940s. The motion was defeated by 105 to 31, with only 2 Conservatives and 4 Liberals voting in support. Explaining his stance, Michaud commented that, "as a member of a minority race in Canada I must oppose such legislation." Evidently, he was aware of the wider implications of the government's actions, for he stated that the "restrictions today are directed against the Japanese in Canada; tomorrow they may be directed against someone else."[170]

A few senators and other parliamentarians who were long-time human rights supporters added their efforts to the individual and collective work of the CCF. In the House of Commons, Liberal MP David Croll never broke ranks with the government, but in a February 1946 speech at a CCJC forum at the University of Toronto, he argued that Ottawa's policy violated the principles of the United Nations Charter. Croll also accompanied CCJC secretary Hugh MacMillan and other CCJC supporters to their audience with the prime minister.[171] Later, Croll, in addition to Angus MacInnis and Ross Thatcher (CCF MP, Moose Jaw), spoke out in the House of Commons regarding the Liberal government's plans to extend the Transitional Powers Act.[172]

Liberal senators Arthur Roebuck and Cairine Wilson also supported the CCJC, speaking out with force against the expatriation policy at a mass CCJC and CLAT meeting in early January 1946. Arthur Roebuck was the only Liberal MP to condemn the disfranchisement of the Japanese Canadians in 1944. Due to Roebuck's long-standing support for human rights, first as a labour lawyer defending such undesirables as immigrant communists in the 1930s and then as Cabinet minister in Ontario premier Mitchell Hepburn's Liberal government, his words carried clout. After taking a liberal line regarding the Oshawa General Motors strike, he also supported the admission of Jewish refugees into Canada and argued against the DOCR. Cairine Wilson was among the few senators who voted against Japanese Canadian disfranchisement. Faithful, like Roebuck, to the human rights cause, she too was an important political figure in the campaign. She was active in the League of Nations Society and, in the 1930s, in the Canadian National Committee on Refugees and Victims of Political Persecution, which attempted (unsuccessfully) to persuade Ottawa to take in Jewish refugees from Nazi Germany. The latter effort was part of Wilson's commitment to fostering understanding, an effort that persisted throughout her career in forms such as her leadership of the Canadian-American Women's Committee.[173]

A "profit and loss" statement in the November-December 1945 issue of *Nisei Affairs*, the JCCD newspaper, boldly declared that the public outcry against the deportation policy was "phenomenal." The article went on to explain that support for the campaign,

> spearheaded by the Toronto CCJC and similar representative central organizations in other cities in different provinces, has come from all strata

of Canadian society. The progressive, the conservative, urban and rural, employees, trade unions, religious organizations, political groups, the young and the old; in fact, all the diverse elements which make up the Canadian community.[174]

The *Toronto Globe and Mail* was also moved to comment on the coordinated public effort. Editorializing about the withdrawal of the offending Orders-in-Council, it asserted that Ottawa had been "driven to it by an outcry of exceptional strength."[175]

Although the intent of the present study is to highlight the groups and individuals who promoted the rights of American and Canadian Nikkei, this should not be interpreted as an attempt to play down North American racism during the period in question, or to minimize the meaning of the incarceration and expatriation. Dissent did crystallize around certain Canadian and American government policies, but this did not necessarily affect the widespread racist assumptions regarding minorities. Although this section noted that most advocates for Nikkei rights conformed to a certain "type" – that is, they were usually white, male, religious, and/or professional – members from other groups also joined in the advocacy work. The cooperation between the CCJC and these groups, particularly those from the Jewish Canadian community, was especially significant in that it heralded the kind of coalition-building efforts that characterized the post-war human rights movement in Canada. The same can be said for the American side of the story. However, in terms of accepting minorities within its own ranks, the Canadian advocacy movement was more inclusive than its American counterpart, embracing persons of Japanese ancestry in non-Japanese organizations.

4
Advancing Their Rights: Minorities and Advocacy

There are many ways in which to act. Progressive action lies not only in organizational work, but in the day-to-day living of us all. It is very easy to condemn a troubling fault in everyone. It is so easy that it requires a strict restraint on our part, if we wish to be fair. Yet I would warn you against toleration, a conscious toleration that still implies a supercilious superiority in yourself and an inferiority in the other.

– Muriel Kitagawa "Damage While You Wait," *Nisei Affairs* (January 1947)

From 1945 to 1947, Muriel Kitagawa wrote numerous articles exhorting the Japanese Canadian community to respond to injustice, not unlike her call to action above. She believed that if those who advocated the denial of Nikkei rights remained unopposed, other groups would soon feel the sting of oppression, with the wholesale curtailment of their human rights. Although the leading Canadian and American public advocates for the Nikkei were almost exclusively white males from religious or professional backgrounds, they were not alone. American and Canadian Nikkei did not sit passively while others defended their rights. Instead, they typically expressed their activism through the organizations that represented them: the Japanese American Citizens League (JACL) and, in Canada (in order of date of formation), the Japanese Canadian Citizens League (JCCL), the Japanese Canadian Citizens Council (JCCC), and the Japanese Canadian Citizens for Democracy (JCCD). The Nikkei also conveyed their views through their community publications. In the United States, the *Pacific Citizen,* the so-called mouthpiece of the JACL, was perhaps the most important of these. In Canada, the *New Canadian,* initially Vancouver-based, voiced the opinions of the JCCL; the Toronto-based *Nisei Affairs* promulgated the largely Nisei views of the JCCD. These newspapers acted as important vessels for the Nikkei in North America, facilitating awareness of developments in both nations.

American and Canadian Nikkei involvement in the campaigns to safeguard their rights was not restricted to advocacy within organizations. In the United States, Gordon Hirabayashi, Minoru Yasui, Mitsuye Endo, Ernest and Toki Wakayama, and Fred Korematsu took very public and very individual actions to oppose Washington's orders. Had they not opted to resist, exercising an incredible degree of agency in doing so, the ACLU could never have sponsored test cases. To varying degrees, each of them believed that the Constitution would protect their rights; furthermore, they had such faith in the judicial system that they presumed their acts of resistance would result in a successful outcome. Their belief in "the system" is significant because it provides another example of how Americans looked to the Constitution and the Bill of Rights in their appeals for justice for Japanese Americans. Unlike its American counterparts, the Canadian litigation was a reference case and therefore had no identifiable defendant. Nonetheless, the Nikkei were involved there, too: the briefs and representations they made to government officials played an integral role in the development of human rights discourse.

African Americans and Jews developed their own responses to the Nikkei removal. As Morton Grodzins has written, "The sentiment against Japanese was not far removed from (and was thus interchangeable with) sentiments against Negroes and Jews."[1] African American and Jewish groups in both the United States and Canada came to recognize that the struggles of the Japanese resembled their own. For reasons that will be discussed later, few of these groups protested the government policies of the day; they barely responded to the Nikkei removal policy. This indicates that, for many of these groups, as for the organizations discussed in the previous chapter, removal was hardly a concern. In fact, some went so far as to support it, suggesting that even the most vulnerable social groups can be blind to racism, especially when the state and elites conceal it by appealing to self-interest. Ottawa's deportation policy, however, galvanized the opposition of Canadian non-Japanese minority groups. Like many Nikkei, who believed that their governments would proceed in as fair a manner as possible, members of other minorities trusted that the British and American systems were informed by justice and fair play.

Japanese Americans and Japanese Canadians: The Struggle to Attain Representation

In the United States, the Japanese American Citizens League (JACL) worked closely with the ACLU.[2] Eager to demonstrate its loyalty, the JACL complied with the removal orders and urged all Japanese Americans to follow suit, but it became more militant by the war's end. Canada had no counterpart of the JACL until late 1947, when the National Japanese Canadian Citizens Association (NJCCA) was created. Although several Japanese associations existed in British Columbia, none had enough organizational clout or resources to claim national representation of Japanese Canadians and Japanese nationals. Significantly, the CCJC welcomed Japanese Canadian members from its inception; in the United States, however, Japanese Americans, deterred from directly participating in "white" groups, were encouraged to form their own organizations instead. The degree of racial solidarity expressed in the Canadian situation would provide an important foundation for this country's human rights community; in the United States, the eventual cooperation would help to support the civil rights movement. The Japanese Canadian Citizens League (JCCL) was organized in 1936 to work for the repeal of the law that prevented BC Nisei from voting federally. Although government agencies almost immediately recognized the JACL as the logical "liaison group," and Nikkei leadership remained largely within the Nisei group and the JACL in particular, the JCCL obtained no such status. Due to its internal problems, several offshoots and splinter groups formed, such as the militant Nisei Mass Evacuation Group (NMEG), the Japanese Canadian Citizens Council (JCCC), and the more significant Japanese Canadian Committee for Democracy (JCCD). The JCCD, formed in Toronto in 1943 from two CCJC subcommittees, worked with the CCJC until 1947.

Nikkei community leaders recognized that racial disadvantage, as it was then understood, would have to be addressed. However, the only courses of action – resistance to removal or compliance with it – were charged with risks. For the Nikkei, how to prove their loyalty lay at the crux of the dilemma. The confusion among white liberals was nothing compared to that existing among Japanese American and Japanese Canadian leaders. In the end, both sets of Japanese-led organizations in Canada and the United States initially took remarkably similar approaches with regard to agency. The JACL and the Japanese Canadian groups focused on the conservative and accommodationist strategies of dispersal, assimilation, and patriotism. These responses reveal the degree of Nikkei faith in the two main traditions of justice in each country: the British sense of justice and fair play in Canada and the Bill of Rights in the United States. Indeed, these responses echoed the feelings of the ACLU and those of Canadian advocates in their approach to the removal policy. At the outset, the policies of removal and the associated resettlement were "justified" in the minds of Japanese and non-Japanese as having beneficial consequences – namely, that resettlement would help the Nikkei immerse themselves in the Canadian and American mainstream.

Prior to the Second World War, the Japanese Canadian community in British Columbia exhibited a certain amount of confusion and division regarding which organizations properly represented it. Indeed, the same can be said for the Japanese American community in California. These disagreements sprang largely from differences between the immigrant and native-born generations. Certainly, persons of Japanese ancestry did come to figure actively in their own defence, but a significant generational divide typified their involvement. Overall, the Nisei (the second generation) were the activists; their Issei parents remained firmly rooted in the Japanese tradition of *shigata-ga-nai* (it cannot be helped). In both the US and Canada, class and religious differences also marked the Nikkei, which added to the difficulty in creating organizations that could serve and properly represent them and, later, that could offer any sort of resistance to the removal policies.[3]

The earliest known Japanese Canadian organization, the Canadian Japanese Association (CJA), was established in 1897 primarily as a benevolent group for new immigrants. By about 1935, when it was reorganized to become the coordinating agency for all Japanese associations in British Columbia, the CJA could claim support from most Issei in Canada. The Nisei, on the other hand, had no organization through which to frame their politicization and eventually diverge from the attitudes of their Issei parents. Even though the Nisei were systematically denied full access to the Canadian system, they desired to conform to the majority culture. As Peter Nunoda has pointed out, the Nisei preference for accommodation and assimilation would significantly impact the platforms of all Nisei organizations from 1935 to 1950, including their approach to the removal and deportation policies of the federal government.[4]

Although the Nisei clearly wanted an organization that reflected the goals of their generation, their first group – the Japanese Canadian Citizens Association (JCCA) – established in 1932 in Vancouver, got off to a poor start. Its primary purpose was to work towards enfranchisement and to address related citizenship questions. According to the *New Canadian*, the JCCA failed because of "Nisei apathy and indifference."[5] Its leaders, primarily well-educated Nisei, were undaunted; they organized a larger group in 1936, the Japanese Canadian Citizens League (JCCL). The mandate of this group was broader than that of the JCCA, but it remained independent from the parental generation in order "to provide an adequate machinery which would ultimately enable [the Nisei] to qualify as an integral part of Canada."[6] To this end, it immediately began to advocate for the rights of its members. In the spring of 1936, the JCCL collected funds to produce a brief arguing for the revision of clause 6, section 4, of the Dominion Franchise Act, under which British subjects of Japanese ancestry could not vote in British Columbia. Because they were disfranchised at the provincial level, they could not vote federally. Vancouver lawyer T.G. Norris prepared the brief, which was remarkable for language that was both detached and emotional. It asserted that granting Japanese Canadians their civil liberties and political rights would result in their full assimilation, and stated that the "present refusal of the franchise on the grounds of race is comparable only to the policy of Hitler with regard to the Jews. Does enlightened Canada really want a 'blood purge'?"[7] Although the brief did not express concern for the human rights of the Nikkei, it did question racially based policies.

Additionally, in May 1936, the JCCL sent four members to Ottawa to appear before the House of Commons Special Committee on Elections and Franchise Acts. In contrast with the strongly worded brief, the four delegates – teacher Hideko Hyodo, insurance agent Minoru Kobayashi, dentist Edward Banno, and university professor Samuel I. Hayakawa – presented a more muted and personal appeal for enfranchisement.[8] In particular, they emphasized the adaptability of the Nisei and their "extraordinarily complete process of Canadianization," two factors that clearly showed their suitability to exercise the franchise. In part because the four Nisei presented their case so eloquently, the committee was skeptical as to whether they were representative of their constituents. Although some committee members undoubtedly had the image of the unassimilable "Oriental" as their model, this assessment was not wholly inaccurate. The JCCL was often accused of being "cliquish," as its members were largely associated in some manner with the University of British Columbia and the "elitist" JCCA. Thus, due to generational differences and because its members were hardly from the "rank and file," the JCCL found it quite difficult to become the "official" voice of the Nisei. In the summer of 1941, hoping to gain mass appeal, it publicized its work in the *New Canadian,* but to no avail; generational differences and factionalism among the Nisei themselves thwarted efforts to develop the political consciousness of the Japanese Canadian community.[9]

With confusion and dissension in British Columbia's Nikkei community, no single organization spoke on its behalf when the British Columbia Security Commission (BCSC) began looking for Nikkei representatives to sit on the Liaison Committee. The purpose of this committee was to establish a consensus among Japanese Canadians supporting the "evacuation"; the commission would tolerate no resistance.[10] When the BCSC appointed individuals who were viewed as questionable by some, this prompted the emergence of three new Japanese Canadian organizations. During March 1942, the Naturalized Japanese Canadian Association (NJCA), the Japanese Canadian Citizens Council (JCCC), and the Nisei Mass Evacuation Group (NMEG) were formed to address the concerns of various elements in British Columbia's Japanese community. The latter two exemplify the split in opinion within the Nisei population.

The JCCC grew out of an organizational meeting of fifty-two overlapping BC-based Nisei groups, with its leadership obtained from the defunct JCCL. Its initial purpose was to handle the emergency of the relocation and to make the transition from home to incarceration camp as trouble-free as possible. When the federal government ordered that all able-bodied males of Japanese origin be removed from British Columbia's 100-mile protected zone by 1 April, the prospect of disassembling family units made the JCCC's task even more challenging. Following the example of their JCCL predecessors, JCCC members chose to regard the relocation as an "'acid test' of Canadian democracy, of their loyalty to Canada and of their future status in the country."[11] To this end, they adopted a general policy of cooperation with the BCSC and related authorities, fearing that the consequences of resistance would be far greater than those of acquiescence.[12] This response is not dissimilar to that of the churches, individuals, and other groups in 1942; if relocation were carried out properly and humanely, these organizations were prepared to support the BCSC as it worked to assimilate Japanese Canadians by resettling them throughout the country.

Not all Nisei agreed with the JCCC approach. Disturbed by their general treatment and by the specific proposal to separate families and send many Nisei males to work camps, thus treating them as if they were enemy aliens, Nisei in Vancouver created the Nisei Mass Evacuation Group. The NMEG formation marked the first numerically significant resistance to the removal. In a 15 April 1942 letter to BCSC chair Austin Taylor, the NMEG firmly stated its scorn for the plan to break up family units:

When we say "NO" at this point, we request you to remember that we are British subjects by birth, that we are no less loyal to Canada than any other Canadian, that we have done nothing to deserve the break-up of our families, that we are law abiding Canadian citizens, and that we are willing to accept suspension of our civil rights – rights to retain our homes and businesses, boats, cars, radios and cameras. Incidentally, we are entitled as native sons to all civil rights of an ordinary Canadian within the limitations of Canada's war effort.[13]

The NMEG also pointed out the contradiction between the teachings of Canadian religious institutions – that family unity be regarded as a "God-given human right" – and a policy that would take away the freedom to live with their families. Even as the NMEG criticized this aspect of removal policy, it lauded the faith of its members in British fair play and justice.[14]

A power struggle ensued between the JCCC and the NMEG when the JCCC declared that NMEG activities were "contrary to the best interests of the Council." Indeed, this was certainly the case, as the NMEG was determined to resist family separation, whereas the JCCC felt that the consequences of resistance would prove far worse for the Nisei community than cooperation with the BCSC. Politics certainly played a part in the obvious acrimony between the two groups. Indeed, some JCCC members believed that the NMEG was comprised of two factions: Nisei fighting for their rights as Canadians and those using the issue as a front for other purposes, such as usurping the leadership role of the JCCC.[15] The NMEG continued to oppose Ottawa's scheme to remove all men, married or single, to road camp projects in eastern British Columbia. Work slowdowns and strikes ensued in the road camps. Realizing that the stalemate would continue unless family reunification could be enacted, BCSC and RCMP officials attempted to influence Ottawa to this end. The NMEG's protests achieved a degree of success when the federal government agreed to let married men return to their families, although single men would have to continue building roads.[16]

The NMEG victory was also significant in that the group managed to earn official recognition from the BCSC, much to the annoyance of the JCCC. It also indicates that, even in mid-1942, the BC Nisei and Issei still had no sole organization voicing their concerns to the appropriate authorities. Once resettlement east of the Rockies took place, the Nisei established new political groups. Two of these, the Alberta Contact Committee and the Manitoba Joint Japanese Council, provided provincial leadership, but creating a national organization was impossible because of government-imposed travel restrictions. The Nisei were a fragmented people in 1942, both geographically and politically; nonetheless, the few leaders and groups that did emerge, as well as their limited activism, would eventually form a valuable base upon which to build the rights campaign.

The eastward resettlement resulted in the formation of other Nisei-based groups, most notably the Japanese Canadian Committee for Democracy (JCCD). The JCCD sprang from two subcommittees of the Co-operative Committee on Japanese Canadian Arrivals to Toronto (CCJC-AT) that were organized in 1943, a period in which the Nikkei community was in disarray. Like the CCJC-AT in its early days, the Nisei Men's and Women's Sub-committees sought to reduce prejudice and increase the opportunities for Japanese Canadians in Toronto. Apolitical at this point in its history, the CCJC-AT functioned primarily as a benevolent association. The Nisei Men's and Women's Sub-committees also endeavoured to report back to the CCJC-AT on matters relating to the welfare and needs of Toronto's Japanese Canadians. The close cooperation between the Toronto Japanese Canadian community and the white, middle-class, politically active liberal members of the CCJC-AT evolved in the early years of the Second World War. Working together, Japanese and non-Japanese CCJC-AT members studied the Orders-in-Council relating to Japanese Canadians and established the Nisei Co-op Residence, a hostel with accommodation for twenty Japanese Canadian men.[17]

In 1944, the increasing politicization required to launch a serious campaign for Nikkei rights resulted in the maturation of the Co-operative Committee on Japanese Canadians and the official formation of the JCCD. Braving an "epic" snowstorm on 13 December, some forty Nisei gathered at the Church of All Nations in downtown Toronto to form the JCCD, which would ultimately become the leading Japanese Canadian organization. The purpose of the JCCD was fivefold: to publicize the Japanese Canadian question, to coordinate the activities of other Nisei organizations, to report on the educational and vocational trends of the Nisei, to provide for the social needs of the Nisei, and to promote the work of the CCJC. However, it did not speak for all Japanese Canadians. Groups in Manitoba rejected it as too Toronto-centred and not fully national; Japanese Canadians in Quebec rejected outright the notion of an organization. Soon *Nisei Affairs* began to print JCCD material; in fact, though *Nisei Affairs* billed itself as a "Journal of Opinion," viewpoints that deviated from the JCCD party line found no place in its pages.[18] The politicization of the CCJC and the creation of the JCCD were essential in drawing Ottawa's attention to the shameful nature of its deportation policy. Still, the cleavage remained between the Nisei and the Issei, and it was left to the CCJC and the Nisei members of the JCCD to articulate the meaning of citizenship and rights in post-war Canada.

In both Canada and the United States, nearly everyone had accepted, however reluctantly, that the removal was inevitable. Whereas the Japanese Canadian community fractured regarding the maintenance of family unity and the resistance to Ottawa's separation plan, the very nature of the Japanese American Citizens League instantly split Issei and Nisei in the United States. The JACL was for citizens only. It was also, as Roger Daniels states, a "hypernational" organization that rejected any cultural ties to Japan, an approach that tended not to appeal to Issei leaders. The JACL was less marked by power struggles among the Nisei generation than were its Nisei-run counterparts in Canada. Thus, it was able to become a strong organization that could address the needs of its constituents immediately following Pearl Harbor. The almost immediate recognition by government officials and the ACLU that the JACL was a logical liaison group lent it even more leadership power, thus weakening Issei familial authority.[19]

As in Canada, the Issei generation dominated Nikkei communities on the US west coast prior to December 1941. Their organizations were primarily benevolent associations designed to provide information for immigrants and for mutual aid and protection. Like their Canadian counterparts, the American Issei remained in firm control of their communities for many decades as the cultural and generational chasms between Issei and Nisei widened. As the Nisei population began to grow, the Nisei sought out their own organizations. The Japanese American Citizens League was formed in Seattle, Washington, in 1930 from an assortment of political and social groups in several Pacific coast cities. Common to all was the desire to "Americanize" the Nisei; this goal of assimilation was carried into the founding principles of the JACL. In its early stages, and until America went to war, the JACL had little impact on the Japanese community and almost none on the broader society.[20]

The JACL underwent a dramatic change of leadership in 1941, one that transformed the association itself: previously, it had operated through local chapters, but now it functioned as a regional organization. Saburo Kido, a young Nisei lawyer with a bustling San Francisco practice, became JACL president, and Mike Masaoka, a brash, well-connected university graduate from Utah, became its national secretary and first full-time employee. Under their leadership, JACL membership increased and became even more devoted to the conservative and accommodationist strategies of self-help and enterprise. The JACL urged its members to surpass their American colleagues in work ethic and love of country. "Patriotism" would become the means to open the door of acceptance. To this end, Masaoka wrote the "Japanese American Creed" for the JACL in 1940, which was later published in the *Congressional Record*. It stated in part,

> ·I am proud that I am an American Citizen of Japanese Ancestry, for my very background makes me appreciate more fully the wonderful advantages of this nation. I believe in her institutions, ideals and traditions; I glory in her heritage; I boast of her history; I trust in her future. She has granted me liberties and opportunities such as no individual enjoys in this world today.
>
> Although some individuals may discriminate against me, I shall never become bitter or lose faith ... I am firm in my belief that American sportsmanship and attitude of fair play will judge citizenship and patriotism on the basis of action and achievement, and not on the basis of physical characteristics.
>
> Because I believe in America, and I trust she believes in me, and because I have received innumerable benefits from her, I pledge myself to do honor to her at all times ... in the hope that I may become a better American in a greater America.[21]

Copies of the creed and of the JACL "Declaration of Policy" ("Justice, Americanism, Citizenship, Leadership") were sent to the president, members of Congress, state officials, the press, and others, including the ACLU. In spite of the JACL's increasing attempt at organization and politicization, the Issei remained at the helm of most Japanese communities until late 1941.[22]

Immediately following the attack on Pearl Harbor, FBI agents began to arrest "dangerous aliens," many of whom were Issei community leaders. Intelligence agents were aided by JACL members who were asked about the loyalties of certain Issei. According to Masaoka, the JACL contributed "facts or rumors relating to [various people's] ostensible business and sympathies, family relationships, and organization ties."[23] The Japanese community on the Pacific coast was left largely leaderless, and many Issei-run organizations simply collapsed. Of the remaining Nikkei associations, only the Japanese American Citizens League was in any position to deal with the aftermath.

The JACL responded to the emergency situation of the immediate post–December 7 period by adopting a new strategy. First, it sought to establish itself as the dominant authority. In their efforts to achieve this and to identify themselves as patriotic Americans, JACL leaders Saburo Kido and Make Masaoka actively encouraged transgressions of the civil liberties of their own community members. This might include spying on "suspicious" individuals. Second, the JACL sought to improve the image of Japanese Americans via public relations campaigns that focused on the Nisei. Third, JACL leaders attempted to establish links with various levels of government to influence public policy. And fourth, the organization sought to ameliorate distress in the Nisei community by focusing their efforts at the grassroots level. Although the Nisei were strongly pressured to join the JACL, many resisted. Those who abstained objected to its right-wing boosterism. These were mainly liberal intellectuals who were affiliated with large universities, and whose concern for the protection of civil liberties outweighed their need to demonstrate patriotism. The opposition to the JACL stance was unorganized in the early days of the evacuation, but was galvanized once all Nikkei were established in the relocation camps.[24]

In a letter to the Tolan Committee, the Los Angeles United Citizens Federation, a very small Nikkei group, officially criticized both the relocation program and the JACL leadership. This body, comprised of a few liberal Nisei, some of whom appeared before the committee, strongly opposed the incarceration. One of their number, a YMCA employee from San Francisco named Lincoln Seiichi Kanai, objected to the indiscriminate identification of American citizens of Japanese ancestry with alien enemies.[25] Another member, James Omura, a florist and part-time editor of a liberal Nisei magazine, gave an impassioned plea to the Tolan Committee that expressed his disdain for the JACL and his strong opposition to removal. He read excerpts from an unpublished editorial from his magazine, which admonished that "the forceful evacuation of citizen Americans on the synthetic theory of racial fidelity – 'Once a Jap, always a Jap' – would be an indictment against every racial minority in the United States." He also asserted that, to observers, Americanism would be identified as "a racial attribute and not a national symbol." He then asked the committee, "Has the Gestapo come to America? Have we not risen in righteous anger at Hitler's mistreatment of the Jews? Then, is it not incongruous that citizen Americans of Japanese descent should be similarly mistreated and persecuted?"[26] The critical stance of the Los Angeles United Citizens Federation ultimately led the JACL to withdraw its support for this group.

JACL chapters spent considerable time and effort in public relations work to promulgate their patriotism and support for the war. JACL leaders issued several public statements, corresponded with officials, participated in public meetings, and encouraged donations to war campaigns,

such as the Red Cross, in an effort to convince their white American neighbours of their loyalty. Notwithstanding these efforts, many realized by mid-
February 1942 that the removal of the Nikkei from the Pacific coast was
inevitable. Prior to the announcement of Executive Order 9066, the JACL
attempted to establish a working relationship with bureaucrats representing various levels of government. JACL national president Kido and Masaoka
wrote to Attorney General Francis Biddle and sent a telegram to President
Roosevelt pledging the loyalty of the JACL and its members. Their efforts,
however, were for naught as they failed to establish the desired working
relationship with any level of government. When the Tolan hearings came
to the west coast, many JACL members expressed the hope that the Nisei
would not suffer removal. In a frank and detailed official statement that
was also published in the *Pacific Citizen*, they assured committee members of Japanese American loyalty and of their cooperation with any government plan. This was as far as the JACL felt it could go; the military
authorities had warned the group earlier that Japanese Americans would
be removed by force within twenty-four hours if they recommended or
demonstrated any resistance.[27]

Certainly, there was no American equivalent of the Nisei Mass Evacuation Group, for Washington did not propose separating family units. If
the JACL did not openly resist government policy, it was nonetheless effective, through Mike Masaoka, in influencing those of the War Relocation
Authority (WRA) and thus the nature of the removal itself. It is also significant that WRA head Milton Eisenhower invited Mike Masaoka to lead
a Japanese American Advisory Council that would be staffed by other JACL
members. In his communications with Eisenhower, Masaoka described his
vision for the incarceration camps: these would develop into "model American communities" whose internees would exhibit a great degree of self-
sufficiency in forming cooperative activities, such as credit unions and
farms. He urged that ample recreational facilities be provided by the WRA.
Educational facilities would emphasize Americanism and democratic
ideals, and "residents" would enjoy local self-government. Masaoka also
voiced his concerns for the civil liberties and self-respect of the incarcerated, asking that "infringements on civil liberties should be kept at the
absolute minimum and should not be invoked unless necessary." Tellingly,
he added that "they should be applied to *all without regard to race, color,
creed, or national origin*."[28] This latter entreaty was naïve, considering that
the only "race, color, creed, or national origin" involved was Japanese. It
was also an unrealistic expectation of a government whose plans for Nikkei
incarceration were clearly grounded in the belief that Japanese Americans
were disloyal.

The eagerness with which the JACL demonstrated Japanese American
patriotism and loyalty made it difficult to launch an effective effort to

oppose removal. The JACL has been condemned for failing to dispute government policy, but it is more accurate to single out its collaborative approach – adopted before Pearl Harbor and sustained after the war began – as the problem. From there, JACL leaders Masaoka and Kido had little choice but to support the "military necessity" of the incarceration; resistance thus became futile once removal became a reality. Although JACL leaders adopted this policy with reluctance, their stance rendered the JACL unable to advocate for those individuals who resisted the removal orders. Just as problematic was the mixed response from American liberals to the JACL policy of collaboration/compliance.

Although the ACLU and the JACL cooperated closely in the latter years of the war, such was not the case in 1942. In early March, ACLU director Roger Baldwin asked ACLU affiliates in Northern and Southern California to confer with representatives of Japanese American organizations and to offer ACLU aid in launching court challenges to the forthcoming incarceration orders. However, he did not expect much cooperation from the JACL, which he felt was "in the hands of politicians." The directors of both affiliates found no support from their Japanese American contacts for any contestation of the orders. An irritated Ernest Besig of the Northern California ACLU branch wrote Baldwin that the Nikkei were "in favor of acquiescence ... even at the cost of their inherited liberties." He also noted that the JACL had recently advised its members "not to contest any action·by the local, state or federal authorities."[29] Additionally, in its April bulletin, the JACL notified agencies that it "unalterably opposed" test cases. Besig continued to solicit the San Francisco Nikkei community despite the disapproval of the governing board and membership of his branch. Later, in a frank letter to Baldwin, Besig indicated that it would be "a miracle" if a test case were found, adding with chagrin that, "when it comes to a showdown, without exception the Japanese refuse to resist."[30]

By July 1942, however, the JACL had slightly amended its approach, soliciting funds from the Japanese American community to support the test cases. In the *Pacific Citizen*, Saburo Kido referred to the fundraising work of anti-Japanese groups, such as the Native Sons, and Daughters, of the Golden West, commenting that the "Native Sons have raised $1000 and the Native Daughters, a similar amount to launch the movements to deprive us and our children of our citizenship rights. Are we going to do anything to defend what we have so that we may resume our role as citizens once the war is over?"[31] Kido's plea to the *Citizen*'s readers certainly did not amount to full support of the ACLU program, but it would set in motion, albeit much later in the war, closer cooperation between the ACLU and the JACL on the issue of test cases. By January 1943, the JACL was requesting the right to send representatives to the California state legislature in Sacramento to oppose bills that would strip away Nikkei citizenship rights. In a telegram to Lieutenant General John DeWitt, JACL national secretary Masaoka pointed out that persons of Japanese ancestry, both citizens and aliens alike, "cooperated fully with the entire evacuation program as our contribution to the nation's war effort ... This unprecedented sacrifice on our part of our homes, our businesses and our associations, bears testimony to our loyalty."[32] The inconsistencies in JACL activism at this stage of the war are interesting. Certainly, the JACL was careful to fulfill its patriotic duty in supporting the incarceration policy, but at the same time felt compelled, and perhaps well situated, to speak out against attempts to bar the Nikkei from citizenship.

The stance taken by Japanese Americans did not endear them to liberal organizations on the Pacific coast. In early September, Galen Fisher of the influential Committee on National Security and Fair Play, the direct successor to the Northern California Committee on Fair Play for Citizens and Aliens of Japanese Ancestry, voiced his disappointment in the Japanese American Committee for Democracy (JACD), a New York–based organization founded in 1940 and consisting of Issei, Nisei, and white members. The goals of the JACD were similar to those of the JACL and the Fair Play Committees on the west coast – namely, expressing pro-American sentiments and engaging in public relations to highlight Japanese American loyalty. Its initial board was comprised of such white liberals as Roger Baldwin and Pearl Buck. But, under the influence of the Communist Party, its communications with government officials and its public announcements also pledged support for "evacuation" as a military necessity; the JACD even went so far as to obstruct the efforts of non-Japanese to disagree. For the communist sympathizers in the JACD, this strategy fit into the effort to defeat fascism. They also encouraged the Nisei to look beyond their own interests to forge cooperative efforts with African Americans on equal rights for all. Although this represented an admirable goal in terms of interracial cooperation, such principles wedded the Nisei to an uncritical stance that served only to diminish the injustice done to Japanese Americans. By 13 September 1942, Fisher had resigned from the JACD advisory board because he did not agree with its "fundamental policy of accepting the evacuation without reservation or right to criticism." Roger Baldwin and John Haynes Holmes also resigned from the JACD advisory board due to their "contrary commitments" in the ACLU.[33]

In the early days of the removal, the ACLU was left to fight without the cooperation of the larger Japanese American community. Racial exclusivity among advocacy groups was much more pronounced in the United States than it was in Canada. The JACL, for example, was organized by the Japanese and for the Japanese. White advocates, many of whom were influential persons in other prominent organizations, served mainly on the advisory boards of the Japanese-based groups, with the Nisei in charge

of the decision-making process. This was, in fact, a strategic move to demonstrate that "important persons" could vouch for the Japanese organizations. In turn, association with such high-profile names conferred instant
acknowledgment and influence upon the groups themselves. Galen Fisher,
for example, advised the Committee for the Democratic Treatment for
Japanese Residents in Eastern States that it "would exert a far greater influence on American public opinion if the enterprise were composed exclusively of persons other than Japanese ancestry." Apparently, the committee
followed his advice, for shortly thereafter it successfully recruited Pearl
Buck, Fisher, and Roger Baldwin, among others, to join the advisory board.
In early 1944, the *Pacific Citizen* boldly proclaimed that "67 prominent Americans" supported the JACL. Their names (see Appendix 2) were mainly
recognizable ones from the campaign for fair play for the Nisei. With few
exceptions, however, organizations in the United States were reluctant to
accept Japanese American members. Even the Committee on National
Security and Fair Play, one of whose aims was to determine evacuee needs,
refused to accept Nikkei members, fearing that this might affect its influence.[34] Interestingly, some Japanese Americans at the Heart Mountain,
Wyoming, relocation camp were keen to start an ACLU chapter there, in
order "to cultivate a social awareness that the question of minorities is a
question not restricted to Japanese, Chinese, or Negroes, but that it is a
common fight against a common enemy who does not believe in the bill
of rights." ACLU lawyer Arthur Garfield Hays turned down their request.[35]
    Although Japanese Americans were encouraged to form and cultivate
their own organizations, and were generally excluded from participating
in those of non–Japanese Americans, they were not deterred from opening up the JACL, for example, to those of non-Japanese descent. On 16
June 1944, the JACL organized its first interracial chapter, in New York City.
The New York JACL was formed on the suggestion of Roger Baldwin, who
felt that an organization was needed to protect the rights of Japanese
Americans in the eastern states and to engage in public relations activities on their behalf. To its Japanese American members from New York City
and environs, the group added such notables as Baldwin, ACLU counsel
Clifford Forster, and former WRA officer Clara Clayman. The departure
from traditional JACL membership, formally recognized in an official policy statement of early December 1944, reflected the growing awareness on
the part of activist Nisei that interracial cooperation on civil rights issues
would enhance the JACL's ability to influence government policy makers.[36]
    The ACLU and the JACL functioned independently of each other. In
Canada, however, the CCJC had a Japanese Canadian subcommittee that
later developed into a formal organization known as the JCCD. It was,
therefore, an offshoot of the CCJC. Although the task of galvanizing public opinion was of necessity left to whites, persons of Japanese ancestry

were not excluded from membership and activism in the main Canadian advocacy groups. Later, the dependency of the relationship between the JCCD and the CCJC meant that the former moved in lockstep with the latter. Thus, some Nikkei shared in developing the human rights community in Canada and in articulating human rights discourse.

The cooperative relationship of Japanese Canadian and white CCJC members did take time to cultivate; in fact, it was formally acknowledged only on 1 November 1943 (in a report submitted to the CCJC by its Japanese Canadian subcommittees). The report included a pledge to cooperate actively with the CCJC and other groups. It also detailed the numerous rights restrictions placed on Japanese Canadians, especially in connection with owning and leasing property, as outlined in Order-in-Council P.C. 1457. Urging the CCJC to "take immediate and strong steps to bring about the repeal of this regulation," the subcommittee stated that "this curtailment of the most important civil right, i.e. of owning property, seems not only contrary to generally accepted ideas of British justice but an unwise precedent to set in Canada because it is based not on enemy nationality but on race only." The subcommittee also made specific recommendations regarding the employment, housing, and social situation of Nisei in Toronto, which the CCJC proceeded to act upon throughout the fall and winter of 1943-44.[37] In the early days of the Co-operative Committee, its Japanese Canadian members were instrumental in providing direction for its advocacy activities and in educating the broader CCJC membership about the hardships specific to the Nikkei community. Political activism, however, was not immediate. The collaboration was predicated upon resettlement issues, not opposition to the incarceration itself.

Although no evidence suggests that Japanese American and Japanese Canadian organizations were corresponding by late 1943 and early 1944, it is useful to observe the resemblance between the statements of the CCJC Japanese subcommittee and those of the Heart Mountain internees who attempted unsuccessfully to form an ACLU chapter and the Los Angeles United Citizens Federation cited above. The similarity of their appeals for justice indicates that Canadian and American Nikkei were fully aware of the link between their persecution and its wider implications, specifically, that "British justice and fair play" and the Bill of Rights would be sullied by the continuation and introduction of the racially based policies directed against them.

Members of the Nisei Men's and Women's Sub-committees of the CCJC felt the need for action that went beyond the very practical objectives of housing and employment. Many, looking to become politically organized, created the JCCD in 1944, with former subcommittee members Roger Obata and George Tanaka as its leaders. Meetings took place in the bedrooms of 84 Gerrard Street in Toronto. Its creation coincided with the

CCJC decision to become more politically active on behalf of Japanese Canadians. When the House of Commons passed Bill 135, in which the federal disfranchisement of BC Nikkei was extended to all those who had left the province to live elsewhere in Canada, the CCJC saw an opportunity to demonstrate its newfound political ambitions. Its impact was muted, however, as only individual members managed to express opposition by writing letters of protest to the government.[38]

JCCD representatives travelled to Ottawa to present a brief to the government. Notified by wire on Sunday, 16 July, that the House of Commons would debate Bill 135 the next day, the JCCD held an emergency meeting to assemble its delegation and its materials. A number of reasons lay behind the JCCD decision to make the journey to Ottawa to protest the bill. Most important was the desire to demonstrate to MPs that disfranchisement was of significant concern to the Japanese Canadian community. Anti-Nisei politicians had long alleged that the Nikkei were uninterested in exercising the franchise, and furthermore that they could not understand the level of Canadianism that correlated with the appreciation of the right to vote.[39] In their brief to the government, JCCD delegates George Tanaka and Roger Obata opposed the bill on seven grounds:

1　The proposed amendment was not given proper opportunity for discussion in the House of Commons.
2　The proposed amendment is an unwarranted abdication of Dominion Parliamentary powers and is unconstitutional.
3　The proposed amendment is a dangerous precedent not conducive to the welfare of Canada.
4　The proposed amendment is an unwarranted deprivation of the rights of Canadian citizens.
5　The proposed amendment is contrary to the expressed Governmental policy with respect to the geographical dispersion of persons of Japanese race in Canada.
6　The proposed amendment is contrary to the wishes of a large part of public opinion in Canada.
7　The proposed amendment is contrary to British justice, and contrary to the expressed war aims of the United Nations.[40]

In explaining the fourth point, the JCCD stated that it was arguing on behalf of "naturalized and native-born Canadians" only, not for the rights of enemy aliens, a stance in line with that of the CCJC and other advocacy groups in Canada. The brief also asserted that Ottawa's position on the franchise issue was out of step with American policy, which guaranteed Japanese Americans the right to vote and even allowed them to serve in the armed forces. Few Japanese Canadians were in the Canadian military, as many volunteers who attempted to enlist were rejected on the grounds of race. The seventh point of the JCCD brief also reflected the attitudes of the emerging human rights discourse: it pointed out that it was "commonplace to speak of broad general principles of justice and fair play which must win the peace after the war," referred to the United Nations, and warned (echoing sentiments voiced by other advocates) that, "in fighting oppression abroad we must also guard against injustice at home."[41]

Once again, the JCCD's brief bears some remarkable similarities to ideas of those Japanese Americans who did not support the JACL's accommodationist stance in 1942. In both actions and words, they were expressing the belief that no race-based legal distinctions should exist between the Nikkei and members of mainstream cultures. But, by 1944, Japanese Canadians could bolster their desire for equality by appealing to the Atlantic Charter. "British liberties" could go only so far to protect the rights of minorities. At this time, Canadian Nikkei also found it useful to contrast their situation with that in the US, specifically because the American government was beginning to reverse its discriminatory policies. In particular, the fact that American Nisei could vote and serve their country provided an especially effective means with which to alert the Canadian public to the state-imposed inequalities faced by Japanese Canadians. Ottawa's Japanese Canadian policies demonstrated that it did not fully accept the emerging international objective of promoting fundamental human rights. With its appeal to citizenship rights and the Atlantic Charter, the JCCD's brief on the disfranchisement clause "paved the way," thus contributing to the CCJC's eventual human rights activism.

The campaign against the disfranchisement clause was aided by the CCF and the National Interchurch Advisory Committee on the Resettlement of Japanese Canadians (NIAC); the *Toronto Daily Star* and the *Toronto Globe and Mail* opposed it as well.[42] In tandem with their activities, JCCD protests resulted in an amendment to Bill 135: the offending clause was reworded so that only those Japanese Canadians who had not been allowed to vote in the previous federal election were excluded from the franchise. Although, ultimately, only the Nikkei who had served in the First World War and those few who would serve as translators and interpreters as of January 1945 benefited from the amendment, the action taken by the JCCD in the matter of Bill 135 marked an important step in its evolution from a loosely based group to a formal organization capable of effective lobbying. The JCCD delegation to Ottawa also established the political connections necessary for possible future campaigns. Although they had not won the franchise, JCCD members were encouraged by the outcome of their political protest and were more confident of the benefits of organization. As one senior government official remarked to the JCCD delegates, "You have gained much more than you have lost in this matter of the franchise legislation, just from the stand-point of the favourable publicity created."[43]

The JCCD was also commended on the even-handed reportage of its newspaper, *Nisei Affairs*. Indeed, Japanese Americans and Japanese Canadians and their organizations would find both solace and stimulus in the pages of their own newspapers. Along with *Nisei Affairs*, the *New Canadian*, a JCCL-affiliated paper, served the needs of British Columbia's (and Canada's) Nisei population from November 1938 onwards. In the United States, the *Pacific Citizen* was the impressive voice of the Nisei and the print wing of the JACL.

While providing their constituents with community, national, and international news, the Canadian and American Nisei-run English-language newspapers also reported on events across the 49th parallel.[44] By early 1942, both the *New Canadian* and the *Pacific Citizen* were publishing articles detailing each nation's incarceration process (*Nisei Affairs* began publication only in July 1945).[45] Both newspapers were also aware of the reportage of the non-Japanese press.[46] Of additional note is the fact that each was "transplanted" from the west coast: as a result of the removal orders, the *New Canadian* relocated from Vancouver to the BC Interior town of Kaslo and would later move to Winnipeg; the *Pacific Citizen* was uprooted from San Francisco to Salt Lake City. Although many of their articles were reprints (that is, they borrowed material from other publications), their editorials condemning or praising, as the case may be, the Canadian or American situation are particularly interesting. In both these newspapers and, later, in *Nisei Affairs*, these were quite numerous.

In looking both northward and southward, the Nisei press revealed a marked degree of mutual envy. In 1942, the *New Canadian* commented on the "care and consideration" in the treatment of Japanese Americans; in 1943, *Pacific Citizen* editor Larry Tajiri wistfully acknowledged that the "relocation" centres in the BC Interior had "less the atmosphere of a concentration camp and more the spirit of a western frontier community, with all the major and minor inconveniences of pioneer life."[47] On more than one occasion, the *Pacific Citizen* also commented on the "longstanding and unequivocal" CCF support of Japanese Canadians.[48] In the early period of public policy dealing with the "Japanese problem," the *New Canadian* was most concerned with the enlistment of American Nisei and the failure of repeated requests for the same policy in Canada. It was not overly critical of government policies in the early days of the incarceration. Recognizing the newspaper as a "propaganda medium," the Department of Labour even sent Thomas Shoyama to Ontario and Takaichi Umezuki, the Japanese-language editor, to Alberta and Manitoba to report on the advantages of eastern settlement. But this amenable relationship did not last long. Over the course of 1944, the *New Canadian* expressed increasing disenchantment

On the cover of a 1946 *Nisei Affairs* issue, Canada's minorities reach out for tolerance and peace over shackles of "racial prejudice," "insecurity," and "restrictions."
Nisei Affairs 1, 10 (November-December 1946)

The dove of peace carries a list of "Injustices to Japanese Canadians" from
Canada to its southern neighbour on this 1947 *Nisei Affairs* cover.
Nisei Affairs 2, 2 (March 1947)

with the direction of Canadian policy and its movement away from coordination with American policy (the Nisei papers seemed to take coordination itself for granted). For example, Tom Shoyama's 15 July editorial (one of his many forthright pieces) stated that the forced liquidation of assets and property, the exclusion from the federal franchise, and the "continued restrictions on basic civil rights" set the Canadian policy decidedly apart from that of the US.[49]

However, by mid-1944 and certainly into 1945, the envious glances were no longer reciprocal. Due to progressive agitation for deportation in Canada by mid-1944, the fight for the federal franchise, and the 17 December revocation of the US exclusion order (to take effect on 2 January 1945), Nisei Canadians looked longingly to the benefits of the policy pursued by Canada's more moderate southern neighbour. Tom Shoyama said as much, remarking in a *New Canadian* editorial germanely titled "Nisei Go Forward" that the cancellation of the American exclusion order pointed "to the obvious truth that in Canada we still have a long way to go to measure up to the same consciousness of national spirit and democratic tradition which is revealed by the American example."[50] The American Nisei press was just as critical, noting that, with respect to the disfranchisement, "Canadian racists" had won a round. It expressed similar sentiments regarding the repatriation program, observing that "race-baiters have won another round."[51]

The emerging human rights discourse is also evident in the pages of the Nisei press. The *Pacific Citizen* observed wryly that, due to its past and present treatment of the Nikkei, "beautiful San Francisco" had failed in its campaign to become the home of the United Nations Organization (UNO). During the UNO conference meetings in that city, it reported, "certain Californians took to burning down the homes of evacuees, to shooting into their houses, and some of these incidents took place but a

By August 1943, even the man of steel was expressing his support for "loyal" Japanese Americans.
Pacific Citizen 17, 8 (28 August 1943)

"Christmas in the Camps," by Mine Okubo.
Pacific Citizen 17, 25 (25 December 1943)

few miles from the spot in which delegates from the entire world were planning a prejudice-free world."[52] Later, another editorial likened Canada's handling of the "evacuee problem" to the "German treatment of the Jews" and to "incipient Fascism." It wondered "whether or not she [Canada] will, in accord with her conscience and the dictates of democracy," settle the "Japanese Canadian problem" or would "reiterate a 'white supremacy' policy that will make permanent the intentions and plans of the race-conscious, fascistic minority in Canada."[53] *Nisei Affairs* borrowed from the Double-V campaign of the African American press, in which black activists asserted that, though many African Americans were serving their country overseas, prejudice remained strong at home. The paper remarked that, because young Nisei were attempting to volunteer for the Canadian army, Canadians on the home front should begin to address racial prejudice. "Nothing," it argued, "could smear the record of a country more than the stigma of race persecution." An editorial in another issue condemned the deportation policy as being against the values of Canadian citizenship. The bold title of a 3 November 1945 *New Canadian* column – "Deportations a Violation of Human Rights" – made that publication's stance entirely clear.[54]

ACLU and CCJC leaders, particularly Roger Daniels, A.L. Wirin, and Andrew Brewin, contributed frequently to the *Pacific Citizen,* the *New Canadian,* and *Nisei Affairs.*[55] Regardless of their independent organizational ambitions, both the JACL and the JCCD needed to cultivate ties with American and Canadian Caucasian groups to ensure that their concerns would be heard and taken seriously. In order to promote their causes, the JACL and the JCCD needed the broader political exposure that groups such as the ACLU and the CCJC offered. In fact, although the CCJC-JCCD connection dated back to 1942, with the two Nisei subcommittees, the 1944 JCCD protest against Bill 135 was the only instance in which this group acted independently of the CCJC in its dialogue with the federal government. Future campaigns would see a tighter alliance between the two associations. In particular, the repatriation policy roused both groups, transforming them into articulate crusaders for Nikkei rights and ultimately resulting in the formation of stronger political groups among the Japanese in Canada.

The cooperative efforts between the JACL and the ACLU took longer to cultivate, in part due to the JACL's accommodationist stance regarding government policies and the subsequent dissatisfaction of liberal groups such as the ACLU concerning this approach. Additionally, the resettlement resulted in the dislocation of the JACL leadership; thus, from mid-1942 to about mid-1943, the JACL struggled to regain its position. In the meantime, the ACLU and its Pacific coast affiliates continued to search for possible test cases, moving without the support of either the JACL or most

"Racist Ghouls," by Cpl. Hero Tamura. Even as Japanese Americans were serving
their country, the Native Sons of the Golden West and other groups persisted
with anti-Japanese sentiment.
Pacific Citizen 18, 22 (24 June 1944)

Nisei. The firm stance against test cases was continually promoted in the assembly centres.[56] Consequently, Japanese American defiance of the removal began as individual acts of resistance. Later, some Japanese Americans, such as the Topaz Relocation Center residents who collected $1,312 towards the expenses of the Japanese American cases, did offer their support.[57]

On the Legal Front: Nikkei in the Courts

By February 1943, the JACL had expanded its campaign to two legal fronts: the "fight to protect fundamental human rights and the struggle to preserve basic property rights, for both alien and American Japanese." As A.L. Wirin declared in a *Pacific Citizen* article, this represented a "step of major significance."[58] However, both campaigns concerned themselves solely with opposing the efforts by the Native Sons of the Golden West to cancel American-born Japanese citizenship. This move represented the increasingly activist stance taken by the JACL throughout 1943 and well into 1944. In response to rumours that the JACL caused and did not oppose the "evacuation," that it was responsible for sending the Issei to the camps, and that it profited from the entire process, Saburo Kido laid out the JACL aims of 1943 in a "Report to the Nisei" published in the 25 December *Pacific Citizen*. He also detailed its objectives for 1944, which included public relations work, the restoration of citizenship rights and privileges, campaigns for equal employment opportunities and against "un-American discrimination," and efforts towards post-war planning. Although Kido wrote that the JACL participated in many test cases, JACL policy regarding involvement in test cases remained unchanged. Due to financial considerations, "only those matters which affect our fundamental rights as citizens will be considered."[59] At the end of 1943, the ACLU still lacked full JACL support.

Even more problematic was the recurring issue of test case financing. Although the JACL officially pursued a no-contest policy, it unofficially supported the ACLU's entire legal program in the pages of the *Pacific Citizen*. Well into 1944, Larry Tajiri was editorializing about the Supreme Court challenges, touting their precedent-setting potential and overall importance to the Japanese American community. Ernest Besig, still frustrated at the lack of financial support for the test cases, declared in a letter to Tajiri that "not one cent" of the NC-ACLU $2,224.62 expenditure had "been contributed by any persons of Japanese ancestry."[60] In his editorial, Tajiri reiterated the unofficial party line: "Aside from those persons actively engaged in these test cases, Japanese Americans can show support in only one way, financially. We actively urge all Nisei who are interested in their future welfare to give some contribution, however small, to the American Civil Liberties Union, earmarked, if desired, for Japanese American test cases."[61]

Not all Japanese Americans supported the no-contest policy of the JACL. Minoru Yasui, Gordon Hirabayashi, Ernest and Toki Wakayama, Fred Korematsu, and Mitsuye Endo all engaged in acts of resistance that prompted Washington to take legal action against them.[62] Yasui and Hirabayashi deliberately opposed the curfew orders and asked local police officials to arrest them. The Wakayamas volunteered to be test cases for the Southern California ACLU to bring a habeas corpus petition that would seek their release from detention. Endo also tried this strategy, as she reported to the Tanforan Assembly Center near San Francisco and then filed a habeas corpus petition challenging her detention. The *Korematsu* case was unique in that Fred Korematsu, who wished to marry a Caucasian woman, underwent plastic surgery to alter his appearance and subsequently posed as a Spanish Hawaiian so that he might evade removal. Thus, he did not turn himself in to the authorities and, initially at least, had no desire to be engaged in a cause.[63]

In the end, only *Hirabayashi, Korematsu, Endo,* and *Yasui* became test cases, with the ACLU participating in only *Hirabayashi* and *Korematsu*. Hirabayashi's case was handled by the ACLU Seattle branch, whereas the Northern California affiliate assumed responsibility for *Korematsu*. The ACLU was initially very interested in Ernest and Toki Wakayama's habeas corpus challenge, but the national ACLU board withdrew support for them after they were arrested for holding an illegal meeting at the Santa Anita Assembly Center. Through A.L. Wirin, the NC-ACLU continued to press their case with federal authorities, much to the disapproval of the national board. In the meantime, the Wakayamas were sent to the Manzanar relocation camp. Ernest Wakayama became so resentful of the treatment of his family that he sought repatriation to Japan and abandoned their case.[64]

Neither the ACLU nor the JACL supported *Yasui*. Nevertheless, it has the distinction of raising the first legal test of the removal orders. Born in Hood River, Oregon, Minoru Yasui was an American of Japanese descent; he completed training as an army officer, was educated as a lawyer, was employed in a Japanese consular office, and was actively involved in the JACL. His continual rejection from the army and his father's internment on suspicion of disloyalty ultimately led Yasui to violate Military Order No. 3, issued on 24 March 1942, which directed all enemy aliens and Japanese American citizens to remain in their homes between the hours of 8:00 p.m. and 6:00 a.m. Yasui made this decision long before the incarceration orders were announced. He felt strongly that Military Order No. 3, which applied to all persons of Japanese ancestry, was wrong because "it makes no distinction between citizens on the basis of ancestry. That order infringed on my rights as a citizen." In spite of his constitutional challenge to the curfew order, Yasui maintained his avowals of patriotism and his commitment to the JACL.[65]

From the beginning, the JACL did what it could to discredit Yasui's actions, fearing that they would prompt other Japanese Americans to resist, a course that would only arouse further public hostility towards the Nikkei. In particular, Masaoka focused on Yasui's employment in the Japanese consulate in Chicago, and promulgated this in bulletins circulated to all JACL chapters. ACLU staff lawyer Clifford Forster recommended to Baldwin that the ACLU detach itself from the case because of Yasui's consular experience. Yasui had retained lawyer Earl Bernard, who did not approach the ACLU for assistance. Forced to retain independent counsel, Minoru Yasui was left to contest the curfew orders without the initial support of the JACL and the ACLU. The ACLU later reversed its decision, only when Besig filed an amicus brief for the NC-ACLU.[66]

Gordon Hirabayashi's decision to resist reflected his deep commitment to pacifism and social activism, as expressed in his adherence to Quakerism. While a student at the University of Washington in Seattle, Hirabayashi participated in religious and activist groups, such as the YMCA, and joined the Seattle chapter of the JACL. Later, Hirabayashi became involved with the pacifist Fellowship of Reconciliation, where his commitment to nonviolent but militant resistance to war and service in the forces was strengthened. In the spring of 1942, he volunteered with the American Friends Service Committee (AFSC), the social service branch of the Quakers, where he assisted Japanese American families in finding storage space for their furniture and belongings. Due to his principles and the practical requirements of his AFSC work, Hirabayashi decided to violate the registration orders. Mary Farquharson of the Seattle ACLU branch offered to support him. Upon presenting himself to FBI authorities for arrest, Hirabayashi submitted a prepared statement titled "Why I Refused to Register for Evacuation." It was a four-page manifesto that reflected his Quaker faith, his familiarity with the pains of the incarceration process, and his knowledge of the constitutional rights of citizenship:

> This order for the mass evacuation of all persons of Japanese descent denies them the right to live. It forces thousands of energetic, law-abiding individuals to exist in a miserable psychological and a horrible physical atmosphere. This order limits to almost full extent the creative expression of those subjected. It kills the desire for a higher life. Hope for the future is exterminated. Human personalities are poisoned.[67]

Hirabayashi added that, though more than 60 percent of the "evacuees" were American citizens, their rights "are denied on a wholesale scale without due process of law and civil liberties which are theirs." His conclusion highlighted the reasons behind his defiance: "If I were to register and cooperate under those circumstances, I would be giving helpless consent to the denial of practically all of the things which give me incentive to live. I must maintain my Christian principles. I consider it my duty to maintain the democratic standards for which this nation lives. Therefore, I must refuse this order for evacuation."[68]

Only following its 13 February 1943 presentation to the Court of Appeals did *Hirabayashi* manage to get the attention of the national ACLU and the JACL. As the national board attempted to regain control of the case, the JACL began to reconsider its stance on resistance. In particular, A.L. Wirin was instrumental in arranging this change in policy by organizing a series of meetings between Roger Baldwin and Mike Masaoka in late 1942. The JACL director moved from Salt Lake City to Washington to engage in lobbying. Baldwin convinced him that filing an amicus brief would strengthen ACLU efforts in connection with *Hirabayashi*. The JACL's *Hirabayashi* brief was significant because it represented a wholesale abandonment of the group's previous policy of withholding support from Japanese Americans who challenged the orders.[69]

Although Fred Toyosaburo Korematsu had not intended to become the focus of a test case regarding removal, his ultimate resolve in seeking constitutional justice parallels the premeditated commitment of both Gordon Hirabayashi and Minoru Yasui. Officials apprehended Korematsu in San Leandro, California, as he was walking with his girlfriend. Initially he gave a false name, but upon further questioning he revealed his real name and thus that he was in violation of the evacuation orders. Officials also discovered that Korematsu had undergone plastic surgery in an attempt to alter his most obvious Asian features so that he and his Italian American girlfriend might leave for the Midwest with little scrutiny. While Korematsu was in the San Francisco County Jail, Ernest Besig came to visit and asked if he would consider participating in a test case. Korematsu readily agreed. Although Korematsu was neither a legal theorist like Yasui nor philosophically polished like Hirabayashi, his reasons for carrying the case all the way to the US Supreme Court were no less valid, or less astute. In a short and spare statement given to Besig, Korematsu declared that Japanese Americans "should have been given a fair trial in order that they may defend their loyalty at court in a democratic way ... Many disloyal Germans and Italians were caught, but they were not all corralled under armed guard like the Japanese – is this a racial issue?" In declaring his rights as an American citizen and in participating in a test case, Fred Korematsu resisted what he felt was unjust treatment: "I figured I'd lived here all my life and I was going to stay here." Some have likened Korematsu's actions to those of African American Rosa Parks; both were examples of ordinary citizen resistors.[70] Initially, the JACL paid little attention to *Korematsu*, but, in 1944, when the case was heading towards the Supreme Court, A.L. Wirin convinced Morris Opler, a community analyst at the Manzanar Relocation

Center in California who also held an anthropology doctorate, to prepare an amicus brief on behalf of the JACL.[71]

Mitsuye Endo's legal challenge was similar to Korematsu's in that Endo's participation was solicited by a lawyer. Interest in such a challenge was sparked by the purge of Nisei employed by the state of California. Although the employees were American-born citizens, each was accused of being "a citizen of the Empire of Japan, and a subject of the Emperor of Japan." Because they had attended "a Japanese school conducted by the officials of the Buddhist Church," they were also alleged to have the ability to "read and write the Japanese language" and were accused of belonging to certain Japanese organizations that were "violently opposed to the Democratic form of Government of the United States and to its principles."[72] Mitsuye Endo was among those who were singled out.

In this case, the JACL offered legal support to the dismissed workers. JACL president Saburo Kido recruited lawyer James Purcell to find an appropriate candidate for whom a test case might be initiated; the case would seek redress and challenge his or her illegal detention at the Tanforan Assembly Center. Purcell later changed the legal strategy to focus on filing a habeas corpus petition in the Federal District Court on the grounds that the unlawful detention had deprived a state employee of the right to report for work. In conducting his research, Purcell found that Endo was a suitable candidate for the habeas corpus petition. A twenty-two-year-old clerical worker for the California Department of Motor Vehicles in Sacramento, Endo had been raised as a Methodist, could neither speak nor read Japanese, had never been to Japan, and had a brother serving in the army. Through correspondence, Endo permitted Purcell to file the necessary papers on her behalf.[73]

Like Fred Korematsu, Mitsuye Endo did not deliberately set out to challenge government policy. She marked her place in history when she agreed that her name be placed on an important petition. Like that of Korematsu, her resolve strengthened over time. When the WRA offered to release her from detention if she agreed not to return to the Pacific coast "restricted area" (the entire state of California), Endo refused. In doing so, she became another symbol of resistance in the Japanese American community. Declining to forsake her legal challenge, Endo remained incarcerated for another two years.[74]

The Japanese American cases that tested various aspects of American removal policy owed much to the individual desires of Minoru Yasui, Fred Korematsu, Gordon Hirabayashi, and Mitsuye Endo. Each had different reasons for resisting accommodation and the abeyance of his or her rights as an American citizen. Neither the JACL nor the larger Japanese American community fully supported them. The ACLU cautiously approached only the *Hirabayashi* and *Korematsu* cases. That these four cases ultimately made their way to the US Supreme Court was the result of important cooperative efforts among the Japanese American resistors and the advocates and lawyers who supported and believed in their position. Nevertheless, individual Japanese Americans steadfastly maintained these legal efforts. Unlike the American cases, the Canadian litigation that eventually made its way to the Privy Council grew from a collective decision taken by both Japanese Canadians and non-Japanese Canadians. The case did not involve an individual plaintiff: rather, it represented the efforts of a group who wanted Japanese Canadians to share equally in the rights and duties of other Canadians and who wished that no distinctions should be made between Canadians on racial grounds.

Prior to the decision to challenge Canadian government policies in court, Kinzie Tanaka of the JCCD joined various CCJC members and other interested individuals in a delegation sent to Ottawa to protest the deportation plan and the restrictions on travel and property ownership. That the JCCD requested and received representation on this delegation is testament to its vital interest in expressing its own concerns and to the continued cooperative efforts between the JCCD and the CCJC. The JCCD also prepared its own summary on the repatriation question but never presented it to the federal government. Although the report defended signatories of repatriation forms and offered some of their motives for signing, it completely supported resettlement and assimilation as beneficial to Japanese Canadians. As proof of the Nikkei population's 100 percent Canadianism, the report highlighted its ability to overcome local prejudice during wartime and to take an active part in Canadian unions, "political conscious groups," and the "Christian Church life of the Community." It also offered proof in economic terms – namely, the quaint but sage observation that "where a man earns his living is where he is likely to stay and put down his roots."[75]

Realizing that the struggle to overturn the deportation policy would need reinforcements, the *New Canadian* exhorted all Nisei, not merely those in the JCCD, to fight. It called on the support of Nisei across the country, including the Nisei Fellowship in Montreal, the Sophy-Ed Club in Hamilton, the Manisei group in Winnipeg, and the Youth Council in Lethbridge, as well as Nisei organizations in London, Chatham, Regina, and elsewhere. In the meantime, other Nisei-based groups began working towards the same goals, cooperating closely with the JCCD and the CCJC. The leadership of the Lemon Creek Housing Centre in the BC Interior alerted the CCJC to the duress involved in the repatriation survey and urged the committee to take immediate action. It was only through this letter that the CCJC learned of the problem. The JCCD and the Slocan Valley Nisei Organization, a group comprised of the Japanese committees of the five camps in the area (New Denver, Bay Farm, Lemon Creek, Slocan City, and Popoff), also kept in contact regarding a plan of action to fight the repatriation orders. The Slocan Valley group responded to Tanaka's prompting by sending petitions to Prime Minister King, the minister of labour, the minister of justice, and the secretary of state. Earlier in 1945, this group had petitioned King to allow parents to remain in Canada, on the grounds that they "appreciated the democratic way of life for their children and have urged them to assume the full obligations of citizenship."[76]

Government officials remained unmoved by the appeals and delegations. In early December 1945, Ottawa announced that the first nine hundred would be deported to Japan in early January. JCCD and CCJC members decided to employ litigation to overturn the deportation program. The JCCD sought out Andrew Brewin to prepare the case; he promised CCJC assistance if the JCCD found a suitable litigant. Kinzie Tanaka, Kunio Hidaka, and other members of a CCJC special committee planned the necessary legal strategy. Shortly thereafter, the CCJC issued writs on behalf of Yutaka Shimoyama, a Nisei, and Mrs. Yae Nasu, a naturalized Canadian. The JCCD appointed a special Citizenship Defence Committee (CDC) to raise funds from Japanese Canadians across Canada, thus helping other organizations collect over $10,000 to finance the Supreme Court challenge and, later, the Privy Council case. The CDC, comprised of Issei and Nisei members, served as a CCJC affiliate member. On its own, the JCCD, by way of the CDC, collected $1,486; by 23 January 1946, it had given $1,000 to the CCJC for legal expenses.[77]

The Slocan Valley Nisei Organization also proceeded to launch an attack on the expatriation issue. It hired Vancouver lawyer Dennis Murphy to contest the validity of the repatriation survey in the Supreme Court of British Columbia. Murphy, however, made a critical error that resulted in the dismissal of the case. Working from the premise that the repatriation survey was beyond the powers of the British Columbia Security Commission, he sued the commission. However, had Murphy consulted the relevant Order-in-Council, he would have discovered that it had been repealed, with the result that the BCSC had ceased to exist as of February 1943. Unhappily for his case, Murphy learned in court that the Department of Labour had assumed the duties of the BCSC. Therefore, as the named defendant no longer existed, the case was dismissed. The *New Canadian* noted all this with some degree of dissatisfaction.[78]

By the mid-1940s, the political organization of the Japanese Canadian community was undergoing a significant change. The clearest manifestation of this was the movement to create a larger national political association to replace the local groups. Although the JCCD was gradually becoming recognized by other Nikkei organizations and government officials, probably due to its proximity to Ottawa, it endeavoured to form a "truly national" organization of Japanese Canadians. Even its outlook became more international, as evidenced by the fact that it sent a twenty-five-dollar donation to the JACD in support of its activities.[79] As a result of the continual lobbying throughout the 1940s, Japanese associations across Canada realized that a unified effort was necessary to effectuate equal rights. For this, the JACL was consulted, and Mike Masaoka was partially influential in guiding the federated structure and the objectives of the new group. In an inspiring speech to those who gathered in Toronto to hear his advice on forming a new organization, Masaoka said, "Many of us Nisei in the States, who took on the thankless task of leading our people into the camps and out again back into civilian life, did so only because we knew that someone had to do it. Some of us were beaten up by our own people, but that didn't stop us from fighting for our rights as American citizens!"[80]

Thus, in September 1947, with the end of the expatriation issue, the Japanese Canadian Committee for Democracy was dissolved. It became part of the Toronto chapter of the Japanese Canadian Citizens Association (JCCA), but not before altering its rules to allow the Issei to join, indicating the degree to which some Nisei were willing to mend the intergenerational strife that had plagued the community for decades. Other Canadian groups followed suit, unifying under the National JCCA (NJCCA), which was, not surprisingly, Toronto-based and comprised mainly of former members of the JCCD. At Mike Masaoka's instigation, George Tanaka became its full-time executive secretary. By all accounts, Masaoka gave a rousing speech in support of Tanaka's appointment as executive secretary, indicative of the cooperative stance of the two organizations.[81]

Both the JACL and the NJCCA, in cooperation with the ACLU and the CCJC, respectively, sought financial redress for the sale and confiscation of property. In both cases, the JACL and the NJCCA assumed responsibility for coordinating the claims procedure. In this final chapter of the relocation process, the NJCCA benefited from the prior experience of the JACL. Delegates at the National Conference on Japanese Americans, held in New York on 8 November 1945, formally discussed the idea of restitution for property loss and sent a letter to President Harry Truman with a request for the consideration of the legitimate indemnity claims of Japanese Americans. The ACLU offered to coordinate, through its coastal and national offices, the collection of claims in order to build up a case for action by Congress. The JACL assisted Japanese Americans in filling out the necessary forms.[82]

In 1948, Congress passed the Japanese American Evacuation Claims Act, which gave the Nikkei the right to claim from the government "damage to or loss of real or personal property" not compensated by insurance that had occurred "as a reasonable and natural consequence of the evacuation or exclusion."[83] Claims pertaining to emotional losses, such as the stigma attached to the removal, the psychological impact of relocation, or even physical injury or death were not addressed, nor were the losses of earnings or profits. Under the act, 26,568 claims totalling US$148 million were filed; the total amount disbursed by the government was approximately US$37 million.[84] Adding to the problem of claims assessment was the fact that, by 1948, the IRS had destroyed most of the 1939-42 income tax returns of the affected Japanese Americans. Acting on this information, the JACL attempted in 1954 to widen the scope of the act but to no avail, as the necessary documentation no longer existed.[85]

By 1946, the CCJC and the JCCD had turned their attention to the problem of securing compensation for Japanese Canadian property losses. The JCCD modified a claims form used by the ACLU and the JACL. Local chapters distributed the JCCD Economic Losses Survey throughout Canada in order to gather details on the nature of property losses. The claims procedure involved the Canada-wide cooperation of local NJCCA and CCJC chapters. Later, the CCJC and the NJCCA would use this evidence in approaching the government to establish a claims commission. The CCJC was also responsible for hiring lawyers to help with the claims.[86] After a delegation consisting of Andrew Brewin, CCJC secretary Hugh MacMillan, and George Tanaka of the JCCD met with the prime minister on 27 May 1947,[87] the Honourable Mr. Justice Bird was appointed under the Public Inquiries Act to head a royal commission to investigate property losses, but *only* those arising from negligence or lack of care by the property custodian or his staff. Believing strongly that the commission's terms of reference were too narrow, Brewin lobbied Ottawa on behalf of the CCJC-NJCCA coalition to widen them. The government agreed but only in connection with losses incurred through the sale of property, both real and personal, by the custodian at less than its fair market value, or through the loss, destruction, or theft of personal property vested in the custodian (but not while in the care of someone else). In the end, over eleven hundred claims were handled by the CCJC-NJCCA counsel, and by 1950, Bird's final report was submitted to the Cabinet. The government stated that $1,222,829 would be paid in awards. In all, the overall recovery on the claims was estimated at 56 percent of the gross value claimed.[88]

The CCJC-NJCCA coalition continued to fight for further compensation, urging the government to pay interest on the awards recently granted. By this time, however, the public felt that "justice" had been served by the royal commission, and only the *Toronto Globe and Mail* took any notice of these efforts.[89] In September 1950, the NJCCA attempted to seek further redress by submitting a brief to the government that outlined the Bird Commission's narrow terms of inquiry. It proposed compensation for general losses, interest on all awards, the creation of an agency to address losses on forced sales, and percentage settlements on various other losses.

Prime Minister Louis St. Laurent put closure to the NJCCA appeals when he informed Reverend James Finlay of the CCJC that "in carrying out the recommendations of Mr. Justice Bird we feel we have discharged our obligation to both the Japanese Canadians and to the general public."[90]

The NJCCA-CCJC partnership ended with the disbanding of the CCJC in mid-1951. An important legacy of this cooperation, however, was the development of modest ties between the Japanese Canadian community and two other minority rights organizations – namely (and only) those fostered by Jews and blacks. Indeed, similar forms of cooperation between groups representing minorities were also evident in the United States. It is also significant that Canadian minority groups were influenced by the actions and successes of their American counterparts, a fact indicative of the border's irrelevance where unity on equality issues was concerned.

Japanese American and Japanese Canadian advocacy groups were often ahead of their non-Japanese comrades in articulating their rights. They were responsible for revealing the link between the discriminatory policies directed at them specifically and the problem of racial prejudice in general. Later, Japanese Canadians associated the advancement of their rights with the far-reaching belief in human rights that was being advocated internationally. For a variety of reasons, not the least of which involved timing, the Japanese American issue did not include this international paradigm shift, even though evidence reveals (particularly in the campaign for redress) that Japanese Americans were aware of the emerging human rights discourse.

Disinterest and Interest: Minority Groups and the Removal

In this period, minority groups such as African Americans, Chinese Americans, and Jews came to recognize that their own persecution was part of a larger problem of racial prejudice. Similarly, commentators of the day realized that the wartime treatment of the Nikkei had serious implications for other oppressed groups in Canada and the United States, namely, persons of African descent and Jews. Yet in the early days of the removal, black and Jewish organizations had very little to say about the incarceration, or in defence of the Nikkei. In the early days of the war, not unlike the Nikkei and Canadian and American non-Japanese advocates, African and Chinese Americans, as well as Jews in both countries, believed in their systems of governance, trusting that the tyrannical excesses and severe treatment of minorities that occurred in parts of Europe would not be repeated in North America. Still, it is worth noting that minority group support for the Nikkei was not widespread in either country.

By the Second World War, Jews had established rights groups in the US and Canada. Organizations representing African Americans professed strong support for the rights of and respect for their constituents. In 1938, for example, the National Association for the Advancement of Colored People (NAACP) encouraged wiping out racial discrimination "no matter who are the victims, nor where such bigotry and oppression exist."[91] In 1942, its newspaper, the *Crisis,* declared that, "with our country at war ... the *Crisis* would emphasize with all its strength that now is the time *not* to be silent about the breaches of democracy here in our own land. Now is the time to speak out, not in disloyalty, but in the truest patriotism." Later that year, a strongly worded *Crisis* article titled "Americans in Concentration Camps" connected the race-based erosion of American Nikkei citizenship rights with the possibility that the same could happen to African Americans.[92]

Although the various minority organizations were responsive to racism in their midst, evidence from the early period of the incarceration process shows that they did not associate the removal order with racial injustice. Certainly, part of the explanation for this lay in wartime patriotism and government rhetoric regarding "military necessity" and "national security." Not even the ACLU was immune from such sentiments. The detachment from the removal issue can also be understood as characteristic of the organizations themselves, in that self-interest during wartime seriously challenged many agencies in both Canada and the United States to maintain their anti-racism objectives. Additionally, these associations were not exempt from the rationale that assimilation of the Japanese was a beneficial outcome of resettlement. Only later in the war did other minority representative groups offer their support, due to a heightened commitment to general civil rights in the United States and human rights in Canada.

Before Executive Order 9066 was announced, individuals from the African and Jewish American communities spoke out against the removal as a proposal based on racial selection. For example, Louis Goldblatt, Jewish secretary of the California State CIO, expressed his belief in the loyalty of Japanese Americans. On 27 April, the *San Francisco Chronicle* published a letter signed by twenty-eight Protestant and Jewish clergymen in support of the Japanese. In June 1942, the Post War World Council met in New York to address "the Japanese situation." Members of such organizations as the National Council of Jewish Women (NCJW) and the American Jewish Congress Women's Division attended, though not necessarily in an official capacity. Although many at the meeting observed that the removal constituted an infringement of the democratic process, no one spoke out clearly against it. The NCJW indicated its support for loyalty hearings and requested that, as individuals were cleared, they be allowed to return home. In fact, the NCJW cited the JACL's non-confrontational policy and the ACLU resolve not to attack Executive Order 9066 as partially responsible for its own decision not to publicly challenge any step the military believed "absolutely necessary for the safety of our war effort."[93] As indicated earlier, the ACLU debate regarding whether it should adopt Resolution 1 or Resolution 2 in formulating its official response to Executive Order 9066 revealed a significant cleavage in opinion between Jewish and non-Jewish members. The fact that several Jewish members strongly favoured the pro-Roosevelt Resolution 2 prompted despair among the pacifists in the group. In a hastily written letter on the subject, John Haynes Holmes remarked that Jewish supporters had "collapsed completely under the Hitler attack, and thus have surrendered completely to the war and the militarism which accompanies it. I suppose this is understandable psychologically, but it is nonetheless dreadful spiritually."[94] Norman Thomas' reaction was equally impassioned, likening support for Roosevelt's plan for the Nikkei to the policies of Stalin and Hitler.

Chinese Americans were not completely silent regarding the incarceration, yet the available evidence suggests that their opposition to it was sporadic. Most probably, Chinese Americans were wary of supporting the Japanese for several reasons, not the least of which was historic antagonism stemming from wars and conflicts between China and Japan. Additionally, relations between the United States and China had improved since the two countries became war allies, a fact that benefited Chinese Americans, as evidenced by the 1943 repeal of the discriminatory 1923 Chinese Exclusion Act. Their reluctance to speak out against incarceration may also have sprung from a fear of being misidentified as Japanese. Shortly after the attack on Pearl Harbor, a *Life* magazine article attempted to help readers distinguish the Chinese from the Japanese. Interestingly, Chinese American actors in Hollywood refused to play Japanese parts in "atrocity pictures" and turned down roles depicting Japanese Americans as saboteurs because they believed such pictures and roles stimulated racial prejudice. Mistaken identity could work both ways, however, as a Nisei discovered when he entered a Denver, Colorado, hotel and was warmly received upon registering there. He later learned that a special Chinese government mission had arrived in Denver that day and was staying at the same hotel. The staff believed him to be part of the Chinese delegation.[95]

After the incarceration was under way, Chinese Americans began to voice their support for the Nikkei. This ranged in nature from "official" support from organized groups to individual and ad hoc efforts. An early January 1942 Post War World Council pamphlet titled *Democracy and Japanese Americans* quoted a Chinese American college student who described the feeling in San Francisco's Chinatown as one of silent opposition to the incarceration and a sense of "luck that the Chinese are not evacuees instead of the Japanese." This was repeated by other commentators. Some Chinese Americans were more demonstrative. The newly organized Los Angeles Chinese Girl Scouts, for example, sent a package of Scouting materials to Nikkei Girl Scouts in the Heart Mountain relocation centre. Julia

Chung, leader of the new group, explained their motivation: "We felt that in this way we could best express our conviction that in Girl Scouting there are no racial barriers." Interestingly, most of the positive sentiments from Chinese Americans came from young adults. The 1943 Lake Tahoe Chinese Christian Youth Conference passed a resolution opposing expressions of racial hatred and discrimination towards Japanese Americans. A Chinese American graduate student gave an address titled "Tolerance and Understanding" at the Utah State Agricultural College in which he warned that prejudice directed at Japanese Americans, Jews, and African Americans could easily be turned towards Chinese Americans with equal motivation. Looking beyond the historic Chinese-Japanese animosity, he stated that "I am not an apologist for the Japanese people – far from it. My people have suffered most from Japanese activities. But I cannot condone US persecution of American-born Japanese." Later, Chinese American advocates, specifically at a panel discussion between student members of the East and West Association addressing the issue of "America's race problems," stated support for the return of the Nisei to their California homes. When the Nikkei did return to the west coast, some Chinese Americans resisted pressures to participate in anti-Japanese boycotts and interethnic conflicts with other minority groups that had been inflamed by anti-Japanese organizations.[96] Although these responses do not indicate a significant amount of support from the Chinese American community, they do suggest an awareness that the "Japanese problem" had widespread implications.

Chinese Canadians did not support the Nikkei during the Second World War. Although historic antagonism was an issue in Canada as much as it was in the United States, Chinese Canadians were preoccupied with assisting the Allied war effort and later with their own human rights campaigns. Many Chinese Canadian men and women volunteered for service overseas, joined the Red Cross, or participated in loan drives. In fact, the Vancouver Chinese community oversubscribed every Victory Loan Drive, contributing more per person to the drive than any other Canadian group. Into the mid-1940s, some Chinese Canadians continued their activism to press for changes to their voting rights and to discriminatory immigration law. Pressing for extension of the franchise, Chinese Canadian organizations cited the compulsory military service of Chinese Canadians as a reason for their inclusion; accordingly, in early 1945 British Columbia enfranchised all persons who served in both world wars. The Committee for the Repeal of the Chinese Immigration Act (CRCIA), formed in 1946 and comprised of Chinese and non-Chinese members, worked for the removal of immigration law restrictions under which the wives and children of Chinese men already in Canada were prevented from emigrating to the country. Its lobbying techniques, which resembled those of the CCJC, achieved partial success in 1947 when the discriminatory 1923 Chinese Immigration Act was repealed. Continuing its work into 1951, the CRCIA gathered some activists from the CCJC campaign along the way, but mutual support from the Japanese Canadian community was not forthcoming.[97]

Although the reaction of African American and Jewish groups to the removal seems to have been rather muted, once the Canadian Nikkei were "evacuated" to communities east of the Rocky Mountains and once Japanese Americans began returning to the Pacific coast in 1945, Jewish and black residents offered their support, pointing to a difference between the public and private actions of these particular citizens. It was well known in Toronto, Montreal, and Winnipeg, for example, that the Jews were quite willing to employ Japanese Canadians and to rent property to them, even if it meant undergoing social censure.[98]

Although no national African Canadian organization existed at the time of the relocation, the Toronto Home Service Association and the Toronto Afro Community Church supported the work of the CCJC. For example, Reverend Mr. Stuart of the Afro Community Church and commissioner of the Supreme Court of Ontario was a guest speaker at a JCCD meeting in early 1947. Tellingly, he spoke of the need for all people to cooperate regardless of skin colour in combatting racial intolerance.[99] Aboriginal peoples, on the other hand, supported calls for relocation in 1942; in 1946, the Native Brotherhood argued for maintaining the exclusion of Japanese Canadians from the west coast. According to historian Carol Lee, the Aboriginal position on this issue was motivated by concerns regarding economic competition: Japanese Canadians, Native Indians, and whites historically feuded over coastal fishing rights.[100]

As the Co-operative Committee became more politicized over the course of the war, particularly in reaction to the deportation proposal, the coalition was joined by the Jewish community, represented by the Canadian Jewish Congress (CJC). Founded in 1919, the CJC originally focused on assisting Jewish refugees. It then became more politically aware with the outbreak of Nazism and the associated refugee crisis. Joining the CCJC represented the CJC's expanding commitment to human rights, especially in the immediate post-war era.[101] Additionally, Rabbi Abraham Feinberg of Toronto's Holy Blossom Temple lent his oratorical skills to a 10 January 1946 public meeting jointly organized by the CCJC and the Civil Liberties Association of Toronto. Joining other human rights supporters such as Senators Arthur Roebuck and Cairine Wilson, Feinberg publicly condemned the deportation Orders-in-Council at a mass rally organized by the CCJC. In his capacity as rabbi, chair of the Joint Public Relations Committee of B'nai Brith and the CJC, and member of the Civil Liberties Association of Toronto, Feinberg was a fixture in Canada's human rights community in the immediate post-war period. He firmly believed that the "plight of one persecuted group is the fight of all" and demonstrated this belief again when campaigning for anti-discrimination legislation in the late 1940s.[102]

Like other minority group organizations, the NAACP began to engage in debate over the removal, albeit internally, only when the process was well under way. At its July 1942 annual convention, the NAACP addressed the relocation issue and produced a critique of incarceration that "was the most forceful of any at the time."[103] Accepting Washington's claim of wartime military necessity, the NAACP confined its concern to citizens of Japanese ancestry, a position very similar to that taken by other organizations of the day, including the ACLU and the CCJC. The NAACP delegates, however, also directly acknowledged the racism of the removal:

> Whereas in the evacuation of persons from the West Coast, as a military measure, American citizens of Japanese extraction were evacuated along with Japanese aliens, and whereas, similar treatment was not accorded citizens and aliens of other foreign extractions, it is apparent that race and color were the sole basis for the arbitrary classification by which one group of citizens is being unfairly treated.[104]

Although they supported the administration on the issue of military necessity, both the NAACP and the NCJW publicly recorded their opposition to a Senate bill that proposed nationwide Japanese "internment" for the duration of the war. Aware of the NAACP stance, JACL national secretary Mike Masaoka contacted Walter White, chair of the Alameda (California) County Branch Legal Committee of the NAACP, for aid: "Knowing of your [White's] interest in Americanism, a square deal for all, and in the preservation of the cardinal tenets of our Constitution for all peoples, regardless of race, color, or creed," Masaoka asked the NAACP to "take whatever action you feel is appropriate."[105]

The implication of prejudice directed against the Nikkei was not lost on other minority groups. Renowned African American journalist George Schuyler expressed his concerns, and those of other African Americans, in a *Pittsburgh Courier* column:

> The drive to take away the citizenship of native-born Americans simply because of "race" is in full swing ... There is talk of sending these citizens back to Japan (where most of them have never been) after the war ... We should get out of our heads immediately the idea that this program cannot and will not be carried out ... Once the precedent is established with 70,000 Japanese-American citizens, it will be easy to denationalize millions of Afro-American citizens. So whether or not we care anything about the fate of the Japanese-American citizens, we must champion their cause as ours.[106]

In early 1944, Schuyler voiced similar sentiments in a letter to the *Pacific Citizen*, observing that, if "citizens can be torn from their homes on no grounds except that of 'race,' then no citizen is safe."[107] Hugh MacBeth, an African American attorney from Los Angeles and head of California's Race Relations Commission, was another frequent and outspoken defender of American Nikkei rights. At a March 1943 public forum in Los Angeles, MacBeth declared that the "question of racial identity of the Japanese is out of the question. It does not matter to me if they are Japanese, Jews, Negroes, or Germans ... To arbitrarily gather a group of people and send them to a concentration camp – that type of procedure violates democratic principles."[108] It is worth noting that MacBeth was partly responsible for alerting Thomas to anti-Japanese sentiment in California in mid-January 1942. He was also a signatory to the JACL amicus brief in the *Korematsu* case.[109]

Editor John Sengstacke's *Chicago Defender*, a "preeminent African-American weekly," also expressed its solidarity with the Japanese American population in its opinion columns and editorials. The *Defender's* columnists examined Nikkei oppression from various viewpoints, but their concern for minority rights and the ramifications of citizenship in an increasingly diverse nation reflected a shared perspective. Columnists such as Walter White, NAACP secretary, Langston Hughes, poet, novelist, and playwright, Samuel Hayakawa, and John Robert Badger, African American correspondent on foreign affairs, commented on the incarceration with some regularity. Both Hayakawa and Hughes, for example, questioned why similarly oppressed minority groups were not speaking out in defence of the Japanese and challenged these groups to avoid subscribing to the sanctimonious judgments of mainstream culture. Conflating race and nationality, a *Defender* editorial on *Korematsu* wondered whether an unfavourable court decision might result in similar treatment for black Americans should the US declare war on Liberia.[110]

As the Japanese began to return to the coast, agitators attempted to induce interracial outbreaks between those who wished to reclaim their homes and the African Americans who now occupied them. Under the direction of Reverend Harold Kingsley, a group of NAACP members issued a statement urging "all citizens to resist attempts to instigate ill feeling between returning Japanese and Negroes." The statement added that both groups were victims of "restrictive agreements, prejudices and traditions." By 1944, articles and information about the continued restrictions on the Nikkei and problems of race relations common to both Japanese Americans and African Americans appeared regularly in *Race Relations: A Monthly Summary of Events and Trends*, co-published by Negro Universities Press and the Institute of Race Relations at Fisk University.[111] In January 1945, during a two-day conference in San Francisco sponsored by the Pacific

Coast Committee on American Principles and Fair Play to plan for the return of Japanese Americans to the coast, African American organizations joined Filipino and Korean groups in declaring that "any attempt to make capital for their own racial groups at the expense of the Japanese would be sawing off limbs on which they themselves sat."[112]

In an interesting example of bi-national awareness, A. Philip Randolph of the Brotherhood of Sleeping Car Porters, an African American union, spoke out in support of Japanese Canadians. Randolph was in Vancouver for an interracial conference on 3 August 1945. In making a number of statements about the threat of racial prejudice to peace, he asserted that "Japanese Canadians should have no more discrimination against them than do German or Italian Canadians."[113] Quite obviously, Randolph recognized the importance of citizenship in shielding individuals from discriminatory treatment, as he faced similar challenges to African American rights during the Second World War.[114]

Many Japanese Americans were not unaware of the support proffered them by various minority groups; nor were they unappreciative. The pages of the *Pacific Citizen* over the course of 1943 to 1945 are testament to that fact. In March 1943, "Nisei USA," a regular column by editor Larry Tajiri, detailed the level of interest in the incarceration by African American press and scholars throughout the United States. Tajiri mentioned George Schuyler's *Pittsburgh Courier* columns, as well as certain *Crisis* articles, among which figured "one of the sharpest and most outspoken articles on the treatment of Japanese Americans." He also singled out the *New Republic* and the coverage by its African American writers of the treatment of Japanese Americans. In a March 1944 column, Tajiri returned to a discussion of the Nisei and minorities, remarking that "Jap Crow is the brother of Jim Crow." Several *Pacific Citizen* editorials also praised the American press and minority advocates in general for their degree of interracial advocacy regarding the Japanese American situation.[115]

As the ACLU did not promote race relations, minority organizations such as the JACL were responsible for pursuing anti-discrimination legislation. The rhetoric they employed in the struggle for racial equality was sometimes interchangeable with that of contemporary Canadian advocates for human rights, as evidenced by Mike Masaoka's comments at the hearings on immigration laws: "Our practice of designating certain 'races' and 'people' as 'inferior' and 'undesirable' as immigrants and citizens is contrary to our commitments under the United Nations Charter and smacks of the racist doctrines of Hitler and Tojo, not to mention its repugnance to the principles for which so many American soldiers of all nationalities fought and died."[116] The important distinction between American and Canadian advocacy for Nikkei rights is that cooperation was more inclusive and unified in Canada.

Persons of Japanese ancestry in the United States did not overwhelmingly support the activities of the JACL or the ACLU and its cooperating organizations. The important exceptions, however, were Gordon Hirabayashi, Fred Korematsu, Minoru Yasui, and Mitsuye Endo, who pursued individual acts of resistance. Their cases eventually made their way to the US Supreme Court and ultimately comprised a mitigating element in the cancellation of Executive Order 9066. In Canada, the decision of a select group of Nisei to join with the CCJC in protesting Ottawa's discriminatory treatment of them had important consequences in both the short and long term. It ensured an effective fight against Ottawa and heralded the types of broadly based coalitions that would prove integral to the emerging human rights community in Canada. In general, human rights were gaining recognition within the Canadian population. The decision of some Japanese Canadian and a few minority group organizations to join forces with the CCJC is significant because it assured the places of the Nikkei, African Canadians, and Jews in the shaping of human rights discourse in the post-war period.

The actions of both white and Japanese advocates fused in litigation that was appealed to the highest courts. The ACLU, the CCJC, and their cooperating groups saw the court challenges as a means of raising public ire on issues affecting persons of Japanese ancestry. Although the court cases represented the cornerstone of ACLU advocacy for Japanese Americans, the Supreme Court challenge was but part of the CCJC's overall scheme to obtain justice for Japanese Canadians. Tellingly, their reference to the courts revealed much about the nature of civil liberties, human rights, and the limits of government during wartime in Canada and the United States.

5

"The War Is Over. Long Live the War!" Legal Battles to Obtain Justice during and after the Second World War

Vindication of the faith that the Bill of Rights is a dynamic reality in American life, in war-time as in time of peace came on Dec. 18 in the decision by the Supreme Court of the United States holding unconstitutional the detention of an American citizen in a Relocation Center, solely because of ancestry. In ordering the unconditional release of Mitsuye Endo from the Central Utah Relocation Center, located at Topaz, Utah, the Court struck a vigorous blow against discrimination because of race.

– A.L. Wirin (special counsel, national JACL),
Pacific Citizen, 6 January 1945

When it became apparent that political pressure and public appeals would not be enough to change government policy, the American Civil Liberties Union (ACLU), the Co-operative Committee on Japanese Canadians (CCJC), and their respective cooperating agencies decided to challenge its legality. The most significant cases that reached the US Supreme Court were *Hiraba-yashi, Korematsu,* and *Yasui Ex Parte Endo* will also be discussed due to its importance to the issue of the relocation cases, even though it received no formal ACLU support. In Canada, the legal challenge brought by the CCJC initially took the shape of a reference by Parliament to the Supreme Court – *In the Matter of a Reference as to the Validity of Orders in Council of the 15th Day of December, 1945 (P.C. 7355, 7356 and 7357), in Relation to Persons of the Japanese Race [In the Matter of a Reference].* Under Canadian law, this type of case entails a process by which the government refers a legal or constitutional question to a court so as to obtain its decision regarding it. Reference cases often focus on the validity of legislation. This case was later appealed to the Judicial Committee of the Privy Council under the title *Co-operative Committee on Japanese Canadians et al. v. Attorney-General of Canada et al.*

The legal briefs submitted by the ACLU and the CCJC provide another avenue to determine the substance of their advocacy for the Nikkei. Useful tools in assessing the discourse employed by each group, they provide clear evidence of how the groups articulated their opposition to government policy. Although the ACLU held fast to its mandate of protecting the civil liberties of American citizens, the CCJC could not appeal to such a constitutional legacy as the American Bill of Rights. Its advocacy, outlined in its briefs to the Supreme Court of Canada and the Privy Council, was informed and influenced as much by the United Nations Charter as by principles of constitutional law to counter discriminatory government policy.

Although the CCJC and its cooperating groups appealed to human rights discourse in their legal briefs, the courts were hardly convinced by their arguments. Whereas the outcome of the litigation had a delayed effect on the Canadian campaign, *Endo,* the last of the US Supreme Court cases, conferred more immediate success on the American campaign, as A.L. Wirin triumphantly proclaimed in the *Pacific Citizen.* Even as the CCJC continued with its legal appeals, its main goal was reversing the odious government policy and building public momentum to promote that change. The CCJC was sufficiently aware that human rights rhetoric would not provide the courts with sufficient grounds to discredit government policy; instead, it hoped that victory might eventually be achieved through the court of public opinion.

One Step Forward, Three Steps Back:
The ACLU and the Test Cases

The ACLU realized that court proceedings would not reverse the evacuation orders. The goal, then, was to use the judicial review process to modify some of their features. ACLU members believed that it was the "obligation of the Union ... to raise the unprecedented constitutional issues in the courts."[1]

Gordon Hirabayashi defied a military order that required "all persons of Japanese ancestry" to register for evacuation to the state fairgrounds at Puyallup, south of Seattle. This individual act of resistance was fostered by his Quaker roots and his belief in the due process of law and in civil liberties. Before making the final decision to resist, Hirabayashi sought legal advice from Arthur Barnett, a lawyer and member of the American Friends Service Committee (AFSC) in Seattle. Hirabayashi was also counselled by Mary Farquharson, a lawyer and member of the local ACLU chapter. Unable to find a case to properly challenge the issues of citizenship and civil liberties as posed by the relocation, Farquharson saw *Hirabayashi* "as a vehicle to fight for citizens' rights."[2] With Hirabayashi's permission, the Seattle ACLU agreed to sponsor the case. An informal committee was then established to provide legal advice, to raise bail funds, and for the eventual legal services.

The national board also became interested in Hirabayashi's case when Farquharson brought it to Roger Baldwin's attention on 14 May 1942, just before Hirabayashi planned to submit to the local authorities. Baldwin responded enthusiastically to Farquharson's letter, assuring her that the national board would "pay any expenses of a test suit." Baldwin may have had his own reasons for offering the board's support: like Hirabayashi, he had once been a conscientious objector. Hirabayashi's Christian background was also advantageous in terms of public relations value: he could not be made to fit the Japanese Buddhist stereotype so reviled by anti-Japanese bigots. The ACLU board thus adopted Baldwin's recommendation that it sponsor the case.[3]

Baldwin learned of Minoru Yasui's case from Gus Solomon, a Portland, Oregon, lawyer who had proffered his services to the ACLU on other occasions. Baldwin delegated judgment on ACLU involvement in *Yasui* to staff lawyer Clifford Forster, who then recommended that the ACLU distance itself from the case for two reasons. First, Forster pointed out that Yasui's lawyer, Earl Bernard, had not approached the ACLU for assistance. Second, Forster was concerned with a report that Yasui had been employed by the Japanese consulate in Chicago, albeit before the attack on Pearl Harbor. Neither of these concerns deterred Ernest Besig of the ACLU Northern California branch (NC-ACLU) from advising the ACLU national board to support Yasui. Nonetheless, Forster notified Besig on 1 June that the ACLU "is in no wise interested in the Yasui case."[4]

The national ACLU did pursue *Korematsu*, although Baldwin felt less enthusiasm for it than for *Hirabayashi*. In particular, he was concerned that Korematsu's use of plastic surgery to alter his appearance might weaken his success in court, as well as in the court of public opinion. He inquired as to Korematsu's "attitude, background, connections and patriotism," to which Besig replied that Korematsu "has no political connections and is patriotic in the conventional sense," that he neither spoke nor understand Japanese, and that "his associates are largely outside the Japanese community."[5] On 4 June, the NC-ACLU agreed to provide legal defence for Korematsu's case. At this point, the ACLU board did not disallow the involvement of the San Francisco branch.[6]

Baldwin also hoped to find litigation that would challenge the incarceration itself. Thus, when he learned from Besig about the situation of Mitsuye Endo, he wished to have her case placed under ACLU control. Endo's lawyer, James Purcell, filed a habeas corpus petition on her behalf and informed Besig that he did not require ACLU aid. In the end, though it fully supported the contentions of the *Endo* petition, the ACLU was relegated to the position of amicus curiae in this case.[7]

Disagreement within the ACLU over its position on the constitutionality of Executive Order 9066, as stated in its March 1942 letter to Roosevelt, would eventually compromise ACLU support for the test cases.[8] Following intense and divisive debate within the ACLU board and its affiliates throughout May and June 1942, the ACLU voted to amend its position on Executive Order 9066. It now accepted that the government had the right, during wartime, "to establish military zones and to remove persons, either citizens or aliens, from such zones when their presence may endanger national security, even in the absence of a declaration of martial law." Although the incarceration was then under way, the new ACLU policy would support it only if it were "directly necessary to the prosecution of the war or the defense of national security" and were "based upon a classification having a reasonable relationship to the danger intended to be met."[9]

Baldwin then had the task of instructing the Pacific coast affiliates on the new policy, in particular that "local committees are not free to sponsor cases in which the position is taken that the government has no constitutional right to remove citizens from military areas." As articulated by the ACLU Lawyers Committee, counsel acting on behalf of the ACLU could contest only the following issues:

1 The question as to whether a military necessity existed to justify the action of the Military Commander;
2 The question whether a classification based on Japanese ancestry was reasonable under the circumstances;
3 The question whether failure to provide hearings for the evacuated Japanese-American citizens deprived them of due process of law.[10]

In letters to A.L. Wirin of the Southern California ACLU (SC-ACLU), Ernest Besig of the NC-ACLU, and Mary Farquharson of the Seattle ACLU (S-ACLU), Baldwin reluctantly advised them to have their test case lawyers act as individuals independent of the ACLU and to establish independent committees to support the litigation, also without ACLU association. In an attempt to soften this blow, Baldwin promised to ask the ACLU's wealthy friends for financial assistance for the test cases.[11]

Baldwin's letter met with a varied response. Wirin believed that challenging the unconstitutionality of the order was legally and psychologically inadvisable; instead, he planned to maintain his original course of action by contesting the Wakayamas' detention on the basis of "imprisonment without a hearing" and "imprisonment resulting from race or ancestry."[12] The S-ACLU and the NC-ACLU were less forgiving. Farquharson hastily notified Baldwin of her disappointment in the ACLU board action. Privately, she also informed Norman Thomas that the ACLU board had "jeopardized a very high tradition of more than twenty years standing in the position they have taken on the Japanese evacuation cases ... The legal hair-splitting involved seems artificial and unreal as far as actual merit is concerned." As per Baldwin's suggestion and as formal ACLU support was no longer available, Farquharson helped establish the Gordon

Hirabayashi Defense Committee, built on an earlier committee she her-self had founded.[13] On behalf of the NC-ACLU, Besig reported to Baldwin that the branch agreed to be "bound by the change in policy" with regard to any new cases; however, it had resolved to carry on with *Korematsu,* "because we cannot in good conscience withdraw from the case at this late date." He reminded Baldwin that, when the NC-ACLU had taken up *Korematsu,* it had proceeded with the full support of the national board. He also rejected Baldwin's suggestion to establish an independent commit-tee.[14] Thus, the new policy had serious ramifications for the cases under way. Both Besig and Farquharson had promised Korematsu and Hirabaya-shi that no restrictions would be placed on the issues raised in court. Besig, in particular, was determined to test the case on constitutional grounds.[15]

By the time the first Japanese American test cases reached the courts in June 1942, the national ACLU's new position meant that none of the lawyers representing Japanese American clients could claim national ACLU aid. Ironically, as Japanese Americans and their supporters confronted the eviction of an entire racial group from the Pacific states, the only Amer-ican organization that was fully dedicated to protecting civil liberties and the rights of racial, religious, and political minorities had withdrawn from the struggle due to a procedural matter.

In the first test case to go to court, Minoru Yasui and his lawyer Earl Bernard hoped to convince Judge James Alger Fee of the Federal District Court in Portland, Oregon, that Executive Order 9066, the legal founda-tion of the curfew order under which Yasui was originally charged, was unconstitutional because it discriminated against one group of American citizens. Because he was not receiving ACLU support, Bernard was at lib-erty to conduct the case as he pleased. Thus, when Judge Fee questioned Yasui as to why he felt that the curfew order need not be obeyed, Yasui could freely reply that "this country is dedicated to the proposition that all men are created equal, that every American citizen has a right to walk up and down the streets as a free man, and I felt that these regulations were not constitutional." In conclusion, Bernard asked the judge to find Yasui not guilty because the curfew regulations, in depriving him "of his liberty and his property without due process of law" and denying him equal protection of the law, were void as they applied to him.[16]

Equally unhindered by ACLU dicta, lawyer James Purcell filed a habeas corpus petition on behalf of Mitsuye Endo on 13 July 1942. Purcell argued that Endo's detention was a violation of due process and was unsupported by statutory sanction. He stressed that the president and the military had no authority to order evacuation and detention of citizens, and that Pub-lic Law 503, under which the Justice Department became responsible for ensuring that evacuation orders were enforced through criminal prosecu-tion, did not provide Lieutenant General DeWitt with the authority to order the detention of Japanese Americans. Purcell also attacked the idea of military necessity, pointing to Congress' own Tolan Committee report that no Japanese Americans had performed acts of sabotage in Hawaii before, during, or after the attack on Pearl Harbor. Finally, Purcell contended that "there had never been a Supreme Court decision upholding the power of a military commission to try a citizen or permitting the military to detain a citizen." Purcell based this assertion on the 1866 Supreme Court opinion in *Ex Parte Milligan*, in which the majority held that "martial law can never exist where the courts are open, and in the proper and unobstructed exercise of their jurisdiction." Military rule and its enforcement "cannot arise from a threatened invasion. The necessity must be actual and present, the invasion real, such as effectively closes the courts and deposes the civil administration." Thus, Purcell persuasively depicted Endo's detention as a form of "undeclared martial law," as she had obviously been detained by military order without a hearing and the courts had certainly not been closed at any point before, during, or after 7 December 1941.[17]

In a San Francisco Federal District Court, Wayne Collins and Clarence E. Rust threw in "everything from soup to nuts" in launching their 20 June 1942 attack on the charges against Fred Korematsu.[18] The brief directly targeted Executive Order 9066 as an unconstitutional exercise of the "war powers" assigned to the president. According to Collins, restraints on the movements of any citizen were unlawful without the enactment of martial law. Additionally, the brief noted that Korematsu was deprived of his liberty without due process provisions, and that the singling out of Japanese Americans for exclusion violated equal rights protections. Collins also included other legally foolish points, such as the claim that Public Law 503 constituted a "grant of Title of Nobility by the United States to all citizens whose birth or lineage makes them 'Aryan,' 'White,' 'Pink-Complexioned,' ... to the exclusion of citizens of Japanese ancestry who are descended from a mythical Sun-Goddess." With the national ACLU and the NC-ACLU at odds over the recent change in policy, Baldwin forwarded the brief to Osmond Fraenkel, the board's constitutional expert, who reported that Collins had gone "even beyond the position originally authorized by the Board." Still, Fraenkel sympathized with the predicament of the San Francisco branch.[19]

Gordon Hirabayashi would be the last of the Japanese American resistors to reach the first stage of their courtroom journeys. On 20 October 1942, Frank L. Walters, Hirabayashi's lawyer, presented his case. In his demurrer, Walters focused directly on the Fifth Amendment for much of his argument, asserting that the orders for curfew and evacuation violated its due process clause and the rights of Japanese Americans as a racial minority to equal protection of the law. However, as regards the latter point,

Walters appealed to the Fifth Amendment because he believed that the Fourteenth Amendment's equal protection guarantee had been incorporated into it. Therefore, his appeal to the Fifth Amendment would automatically invoke the equal protection clause of the Fourteenth. As historian Peter Irons notes, this claim had insufficient precedent. In fact, it would be two decades before the Supreme Court formally "incorporated" the Fourteenth Amendment's equal rights guarantees into the due process provisions of the Fifth Amendment.[20]

In the end, the courts ruled against Yasui, Hirabayashi, and Korematsu (the resolution of the Endo case will be detailed later). Subsequently, their appeals were sent to the US Court of Appeals in San Francisco to be addressed on 19 February 1943, the first anniversary of Executive Order 9066. A few weeks later, the appellate judges petitioned to the Supreme Court without decision, utilizing the writ of certiorari route.[21] Once again, the ACLU engaged in a round of soul-searching over what degree of support, if any, it would provide in the appeals process.

ACLU support for *Korematsu* was further compromised by continued infighting between the board and its San Francisco affiliate. Ernest Besig was again advised by Roger Baldwin to disassociate the name of the ACLU from the case if the appeal objected to Roosevelt's order on constitutional grounds. Besig would not comply, which prompted board chairman John Haynes Holmes to write to Bishop Edward Parsons, chair of the Northern California board. A series of friendly letters passed between the clerics, while adversarial letters continued to flow between New York and San Francisco during the autumn of 1942. By December, however, Besig had reconsidered his stance: he had begun to doubt Collins' ability to present the case as it made its way through appeal to the Supreme Court and felt that it was becoming far too costly for the branch to handle. He suggested to Baldwin that "we should carry the case through the Circuit Court and that from then on the National Office should handle it in the way in which they have suggested we might do it."[22]

The *Yasui* case was also victim, once more, to political machinations within the ACLU board. Although *Yasui* initially lacked ACLU support, Besig recommended that the ACLU file an amicus brief with the Court of Appeals. This latest suggestion was negated when the ACLU board unanimously adopted the Seymour Resolution on 19 October 1942. ACLU lawyer Whitney North Seymour had proposed the resolution in order to detach the ACLU from the Justice Department sedition prosecutions of alleged Nazi sympathizers. The resolution denied support to cases in which "there are grounds for a belief that the defendant is cooperating with or acting on behalf of the enemy, even though the particular charge against the defendant might otherwise be appropriate for intervention by the Union."[23] When Judge Fee concluded that Yasui's employment at the Japanese consulate equated with a renunciation of his American citizenship, the ACLU board voted against supporting Yasui's appeal, even in an amicus role, feeling that his association with Japan provided sufficient grounds for doing so. Again, strong protest came from the NC-ACLU, as Besig desired to file an amicus brief with the Court of Appeals. Throughout February 1943, telegrams flew daily between Besig and Baldwin. Eventually, Besig persuaded both Baldwin and staff lawyer Clifford Forster that the judge's decision regarding Yasui's citizenship constituted a flawed reading of international law, one that would raise important questions of civil liberties and ultimately open "the way for a wholesale expatriation of American-born citizens whom other nations claim."[24] Although it was too late for the ACLU to endorse the *Yasui* appeal, the conservatism that had marked its policy thus far in the war began to moderate following this change of heart.

Nonetheless, the national ACLU declined to formally support the *Hirabayashi* appeal, despite a request from A.L. Wirin of the Los Angeles branch to file an amicus brief. The national ACLU would not budge on its earlier decision to "publicly disassociate" itself from the case.[25] Thus, in this second round of Japanese American litigation, the national ACLU undertook no formal role in any of the cases appearing before the Court of Appeals.

When the Circuit Court of Appeals certified the cases directly to the Supreme Court, it gave everyone associated with them barely six weeks to prepare for oral argument on 10 May 1943. Divisions within the ACLU resulted in the filing of two *Hirabayashi* briefs to the Supreme Court: one came from the national board; the other, an amicus brief, originated with the NC-ACLU. The JACL filed an additional amicus brief.[26] A.L. Wirin did convince Earl Bernard to share his time before the Supreme Court. Thus, via its Southern California branch, the ACLU would have a presence in *Yasui*. Earlier problems with Wayne Collins' arguing of *Korematsu* led Ernest Besig to recommend that the national board take up the case in its Supreme Court appearance. In one way or another, the ACLU would have its name associated with the Japanese American cases.

There was a general feeling in the ACLU that Hirabayashi's lawyer, Frank Walters, was not competent enough to present arguments in the Supreme Court. After a good deal of backroom manoeuvring, Baldwin convinced the Hirabayashi Committee to have Walters share the case with Harold Evans, a Quaker lawyer from a prestigious Philadelphia law firm. This decision also meant that *Hirabayashi* now had to abide by the ACLU resolution that enjoined any constitutional attack on Executive Order 9066. As a result of this change in direction, ACLU general counsel Osmond Fraenkel rewrote the existing draft brief and submitted it to the Supreme Court.[27]

Accordingly, Fraenkel's revised *Hirabayashi* brief addressed two issues: that Public Law 503 exceeded the scope of the president's order because it was not required by military necessity, and that the removal program in its entirety was an unconstitutional form of racial discrimination. The latter argument proved far more challenging, as Walters had found out when he attempted to use it in the Circuit Court appeal. Fraenkel modified it to advance that, under the Fifth Amendment's due process clause, a "reasonable basis" must exist for the federal government to impose discriminatory treatment. Fraenkel argued that the "wholesale attribution of disloyalty to a racial group of citizens" solely because some Japanese Americans "may be under suspicion" could hardly be considered a "rational ground" for the discrimination inherent in the orders issued by Lieutenant General DeWitt. As mentioned earlier, Supreme Court precedents regarding federal law and race as "an improper basis of classification" were not yet available. Fraenkel issued a challenge to the court, demanding whether war abroad should affect the "fundamental liberties at home. Here is one occasion for this Court to give an unequivocal answer to that question and show the world that we can fight for democracy and preserve it too."[28] The issue of racial discrimination, then, formed only a modest part of Fraenkel's case.

The amicus brief submitted by Wayne Collins on behalf of the NC-ACLU, far more impassioned than its national board counterpart, prompted another round of discord between the local branch and the national office. It went against ACLU policy in attacking the constitutionality of Executive Order 9066, and its language was less than moderate. Collins equated DeWitt with "dictators" such as Attila the Hun, Genghis Khan, and Adolf Hitler. Calling the removal "brutish slavery," Collins warned the Supreme Court justices that, should they defend the removal policy, they would "forever be enshrined in the hall of infamy as a symbol of bigotry, intolerance and oppression."[29] Collins' brief was hardly a scholarly dissection of race and racial theory (unlike the JACL amicus brief, to be examined below). For that reason and due to the branch's lengthy history of disobeying national policy, the ACLU threatened to disaffiliate the NC-ACLU. A completely repentant Bishop Parsons, chairman of the NC-ACLU, managed to dissuade Roger Baldwin and other board members from following through on their threat.[30]

The JACL brief, drafted by Morris E. Opler, levelled a full charge of racial discrimination at the government's policy. Opler had already written a JACL amicus brief for Wirin in connection with the *Regan* case, in which the Native Sons of the Golden West tried unsuccessfully to dispossess Japanese Americans of their voting rights. Although the brief contained the usual citations of Supreme Court decisions, themselves supplied by Wirin, Opler drew heavily from the work of Franz Boas and more recent studies of the assimilation of the Japanese American population. Opler sought to demonstrate that Japanese Americans were no different from any other immigrant group in either their attempts to assimilate and seek acceptance in American society or their retention of old-world conventions such as language, religion, and cuisine. The JACL brief also questioned the motives behind the military orders. Opler cited Lieutenant General DeWitt's statements, such as "a Jap's a Jap" and his assertions that American citizenship did not guarantee loyalty, as evidence that racism, not military necessity, was the real issue in *Hirabayashi*. Indeed, the brief devoted over twenty pages to refuting the "myths" that, because they enjoyed dual citizenship, Japanese American citizens would remain loyal to Japan, and that the expulsion of the Japanese from the west coast was engineered by "a small but highly organized vigorously anti-Japanese element." In turn, Wirin argued that DeWitt had had no "reasonable" basis upon which to issue the military orders: hence, they were unconstitutional.[31]

The *Yasui* Supreme Court appeal posed less of a problem for the national ACLU, as Earl Bernard agreed to share his argument time with A.L. Wirin. Both kept their contentions within ACLU policy limits. A favourable ruling on a legal technicality opened the way for a later appeal of *Korematsu*, as the Supreme Court remanded it to the Court of Appeals for a decision on the legality of the exclusion order.[32] The Supreme Court had already ruled unfavourably in *Hirabayashi* and *Yasui*, leading some ACLU members to doubt the utility of pressing additional cases through that court. Clifford Forster, however, was determined to obtain a ruling on the exclusion orders, observing that it is "one thing for the court to say that you can impose a curfew on a racial basis; it's another for the court to say bluntly that citizens may be removed from their homes on a racial footing." In a letter to A.L. Wirin, he added that to press the court on such a ruling would make "that court look awfully bad after this war is over."[33] Additionally, both Forster and Baldwin were not impressed with how Collins and Purcell had handled their respective cases; neither were Department of Justice (DOJ) officials, who began working closely with the ACLU director on *Korematsu* and *Endo* strategy. Lawyer Charles Horsky, a close friend of Edward Ennis of the Department of Justice, was retained for both cases and served as ACLU-DOJ go-between. The approach employed by both sides in *Korematsu* was to get the court to consider the evacuation and detention issues together and to reverse the *Hirabayashi* opinion. This strategy was later confirmed in a meeting between DOJ lawyers and Baldwin, who informed Osmond Fraenkel that "they insist we file a brief amicus curiae in the Korematsu case. It need be practically only on one point – that evacuation meant detention."[34]

The brief that Wayne Collins submitted on behalf of the NC-ACLU made no attempt to join the two issues of evacuation and detention. Employing the "kitchen-sink" strategy that he had favoured in *Korematsu*, Collins built on his challenge to the constitutionality of DeWitt's exclusion order by citing twelve other constitutional charges. Under the Eighth Amendment, Collins claimed, the order inflicted "cruel and unusual punishment" on his client. He also argued that the order violated the "slavery and involuntary servitude" proscriptions of the Thirteenth Amendment and that it infracted Article 3 of the Constitution because it forced "a corruption of blood" upon Korematsu based "upon the theory of the constructive treason of his remote ancestors." As in his earlier *Korematsu* brief, Collins aimed his parting shots directly at the justices of the Supreme Court:

> General DeWitt let Terror out to plague these citizens but closed the lid on the Pandora box and left Hope to smother. It is your duty to raise the lid and revive Hope for these, our people, who have suffered at the hands of one of our servants. Do this speedily as the law commands you. History will not forget your opinion herein.[35]

In response to a suggestion from DOJ lawyers, Charles Horsky submitted an amicus brief of behalf of the ACLU, structuring it to target what they believed was the government's most vulnerable point. The removal order presented Korematsu with but two alternatives: he could refuse to report to the assembly centre and be arrested, or he could report to the assembly centre and be detained for an indefinite period of time. In either case, Korematsu would forfeit his freedom. The brief was also aimed at Lieutenant General DeWitt and his accusations of Japanese American espionage, which had provided the basis for the removal recommendation. Deciding that DeWitt's racism would not be addressed in the ACLU amicus brief, Roger Baldwin referred that task to the JACL, for whom A.L. Wirin and Morris Opler drafted an amicus brief, as they had in *Hirabayashi*. Together, the ACLU and JACL briefs effectively targeted DeWitt instead of the Constitution, questioning the factual basis for his evacuation order and his own racist motivations. This new strategy reflected lessons learned from *Hirabayashi*, in which constitutional objections to evacuation found little currency with the court. Taking the offensive and focusing on DeWitt could present Korematsu as "a victim of military error and racism."[36]

As he had in his *Hirabayashi* brief, Opler relied heavily on scholarly analysis and less on legal precedent. He modelled his approach on Swedish economist Gunnar Myrdal's *An American Dilemma*, a 1944 study of race relations in the United States. In it, Myrdal detailed the obstacles to full participation in American society faced by African Americans in the 1940s. Opler compared the west coast Nikkei with the African Americans of Harlem in terms of their pattern of residential segregation, asserting that, in the instance of the Nikkei, "there is no more reason than it is in the case of the Negro to assume that they were not there conforming to genuine American habits of thought and action." In this way, Opler sought to counter DeWitt's rationalization for removal – that Japanese Americans comprised "a large, unassimilated, tightly knit racial group, bound to an enemy nation by strong ties of race, culture, custom and religion." Opler's *Korematsu* brief was far more aggressive than his *Hirabayashi* brief, for it relied more heavily on accusations of race prejudice aimed directly at DeWitt. Opler also provided newspaper evidence of the economic greed that underlaid the evacuation. In concluding his brief, Opler capitalized on the example of DeWitt to reveal how racism had induced removal:

> We contend that General DeWitt accepted the views of racists instead of the principles of democracy because he is himself a confessed racist. This is no discovery of ours and it requires no extended argument on our part to prove this. General DeWitt has gone to unusual lengths to make perfectly clear his unalterable hostility, on racial grounds, to all persons of Japanese ancestry, regardless of citizenship and regardless of evidences of loyalty.[37]

Wayne Collins' rhetorical excesses also prompted the national ACLU to intervene in the *Endo* case. He had been delegated the brief by Endo's original lawyer, James Purcell. In condemning the abuse of power that led President Roosevelt to authorize DeWitt to deprive Mitsuye Endo of her liberty, Collins linked Roosevelt with Hitler. "To find a parallel in modern times we are bound to look in the concentration camps of Germany," he wrote, and "the example of the Madman of Berchtesgaden."[38] Collins also fashioned the amicus brief for the NC-ACLU, which vehemently attacked DeWitt for his "a Jap's a Jap" statement, positing that "the General cannot be an American either but necessarily must be of the foreign nationality that attached to his own ancestors." This brief, however, did make the more effective contention that the orders for the detention of Japanese Americans disregarded their constitutional rights and liberties.[39]

As a result of Collins' impropriety, Baldwin decided to convince the ACLU board to intervene in *Endo*. Osmond Fraenkel was once again charged with drafting an amicus brief on behalf of the national ACLU. He adhered to the merits of the case, namely, that because Endo was found neither disloyal nor dangerous, nothing justified her continued detention, or the detention of other Nikkei citizens who were found neither disloyal nor dangerous. In his only lapse of self-control, Fraenkel lashed out against the government's contention that detention was necessary to protect Japanese Americans from public violence, remarking that "this is the outrageous doctrine of 'protective custody' invented by the Nazis in their persecution of the Jews ... It has no place in American life."[40]

By late 1944, the ACLU appeared to have come full circle in its support for Japanese American litigation. The irony of this was not lost on Whitney

North Seymour, who had pushed for the resolution that restricted ACLU involvement in the cases.[41] At this late point in the war, an Allied victory seemed almost assured, causing many to wonder whether this would affect the court's ruling in *Korematsu* and *Endo*, leading to an outcome that differed from those of *Hirabayashi* and *Yasui*, only a year earlier. The majority and dissenting opinions delivered in the Supreme Court reveal the route from great disappointment in *Hirabayashi* to a perceived victory in *Endo*.

On 21 June 1943, Chief Justice Harlan Fiske Stone had delivered the majority opinion for *Hirabayashi*, which declared that the power to wage war was "power to wage war successfully" and that the court should defer to the commander-in-chief's requirement for broad discretion in the conduct of the war, including "some infringement on individual liberty." Stone then addressed the issue of racial discrimination, conceding that "distinctions between citizens solely because of their ancestry are by their very nature odious to a free people." Nevertheless, Stone asserted that "we cannot close our eyes to the fact ... that in a time of war residents having ethnic affiliations with an invading enemy may be a greater source of danger than those of a different ancestry." In fact, Stone went further to assert that, in his view, racism was not barred by the Constitution:

> The adoption by Government, in crisis of war and of threatened invasion, of measures for public safety, based upon recognition of facts and circumstances which indicate that a group of one national extraction may menace that safety more than others, is not wholly beyond the limits of the Constitution and is not to be condemned merely because in other and in most circumstances racial distinctions are irrelevant.[42]

In reaching these conclusions about the unlimited wartime powers of government and the sanctioning of racial prejudice, Chief Justice Stone's opinion drew broadly from the history of persons of Japanese ancestry residing in the United States. He linked their inability to assimilate with their tendency to concentrate in certain geographic areas and the discrimination they had suffered, such as the California Alien Land Act, miscegenation statutes, and employment restrictions. His reasoning was also influenced by the notion that "blood is thicker than water." He strongly suggested that dual citizenship issues and the propaganda disseminated by Japanese consuls, Buddhist priests, and other leaders could influence Nikkei loyalty. Stone stated that, in light of these factors, the president and Congress could "reasonably have concluded that these conditions ... encouraged the continued attachment of members of this group to Japan and Japanese institutions."[43] Thus, according to Chief Justice Stone, persons of Japanese ancestry could be considered culpable because of their perceived racial attachments.

Three other concurring opinions were published, all of which read almost like dissents.[44] Justice William O. Douglas, for example, commented that the court "cannot sit in judgment of the military requirements of that hour." Nor could it condone racism: Douglas maintained that "loyalty is a matter of mind and of heart not of race ... Moreover, guilt is personal under our constitutional system. Detention for reasonable cause is one thing. Detention on account of ancestry is another."[45] Justice Wiley B. Rutledge added that an officer such as DeWitt "must have wide discretion ... But it does not follow [that] there may be bounds beyond which the courts cannot go and, if he oversteps them, that the courts may have power to protect the civilian citizen."[46] It was the third concurrence by Justice Frank Murphy, however, that left its mark on the *Hirabayashi* decision.

Initially drafted as a dissent, Murphy's concurrence criticized many of the premises of the majority opinion. According to Murphy, the imposition of the curfew restriction may have been warranted at the time, as "modern war does not always wait for the observance of procedural requirements that are considered essential and appropriate under normal circumstances." In disputing whether the restrictions were still valid, Murphy argued that

> It does not follow ... that the broad guarantees of the Bill of Rights and other provisions of the Constitution protecting essential liberties are suspended by the mere existence of a state of war ... Distinctions based on color and ancestry are utterly inconsistent with our traditions and ideals. They are at variance with the principles for which we are now waging war ... Today is the first time, so far as I am aware, that we have sustained a substantial restriction of the personal liberty of citizens of the United States based upon the accident of race or ancestry ... It bears a melancholy resemblance to members of the Jewish race in Germany and in other parts of Europe ... This goes to the very brink of constitutional power.[47]

Murphy also took exception to the opinion that the inassimilability of Japanese Americans was a mitigating factor in the issuance of the curfew order. He viewed it as an unfortunate admission: "To say that any group cannot be assimilated is to admit that the great American experiment has failed ... As a nation we embrace many groups."[48]

To remark that *Hirabayashi* was a significant disappointment to those who had hoped for a different outcome is a serious understatement. As Peter Irons and Jerry Kang have observed, the court managed to avoid interfering with the incarceration while simultaneously refraining from granting it judicial approval. Indeed, the same can be said for the other Japanese American cases, in which the wartime Supreme Court acted as a full participant in the "internment machinery."[49] Using a legal technique known as *segmentation,* the Supreme Court divided the entire incarceration process into three separate steps: curfew, exclusion, and relocation.[50] In *Hirabaya-shi*, decision on the evacuation was avoided because sentences for viola-tion of both the curfew and the evacuation orders ran concurrently. Irons claims that Chief Justice Harlan Stone was eager to avoid the issue of exclu-sion for fear that addressing it would open up the entire incarceration pro-gram, obliging the court to pronounce on the entire program. So, the court framed the case entirely around the curfew issue and maintained that a curfew, even if ethnically targeted, was not a significant burden in time of war. In its wisdom, the court explained that the Japanese propensity for disloyalty had resulted from their historic prejudicial treatment in the US, which had prevented their assimilation. In other words, American dis-crimination had led to Japanese disloyalty. Today, the legitimization of an ethnic-specific curfew would be referred to as racial profiling. In its ami-cus brief, the JACL noted as much: "By [this line of reasoning], the Nazi treatment of the Jews is vindicated, for the Jews of Germany had suffered civil and social disabilities and therefore, by the sadistic turn of logic, should have been ripe for treason to the Reich precisely as Herr Hitler declared."[51]

In comparison to *Hirabayashi*, the *Yasui* decision is notable only for the reversal of the ruling of Oregon Federal District Court judge James Alger Fee that Yasui had forfeited his American citizenship when he worked for the Japanese government. The Supreme Court upheld the conviction of curfew violation, basing its decision upon the reasons cited in *Hirabaya-shi*. In returning the case to the District Court, "to afford that court an opportunity to strike its findings as to appellant's loss of United States cit-izenship," the Supreme Court also recommended a lighter sentence.[52]

Japanese Americans and their advocates would have to wait until 18 December 1944 for the Supreme Court to hand down the *Korematsu* and *Endo* rulings, in which it determined the legality of the removal. Accord-ing to the ACLU amicus brief, the issue at stake in *Korematsu* was for the court to rule "whether or not a citizen of the United States may, because he is of Japanese ancestry, be confined in barbed-wire stockades euphemisti-cally termed Assembly Centers or Relocation Centers – actually concen-tration camps."[53] The majority opinion, with six justices concurring and three dissenting, was written by Justice Hugo Black: it upheld Korematsu's conviction for failing to report for evacuation. Citing *Hirabayashi*, the court sustained the constitutionality of the evacuation.

The basis of Black's argument was that mass incarceration was neces-sary because "it was impossible to bring about an immediate segregation of the disloyal from the loyal." According to Black, "Hardships are part of war, and war is an aggregation of hardships. All citizens alike, both in and out of uniform, feel the impact of war in greater or lesser measure. Citizenship has its responsibilities as well as its privileges, and in time of war the burden is always heavier."[54]

The burden, however, was heavier for persons of Japanese ancestry. Likewise, in *Hirabayashi,* the court had rationalized differential treatment by asserting that it would be "needless" to "inflict hardship on the many" (namely, German and Italian Americans) by subjecting them all to curfew. More so than deft legal evasion of constitutional issues, the *Hirabayashi* and *Yasui* judgments reveal the incredible extent to which racial animus influenced some justices of the United States Supreme Court. This is even evident in the *Hirabayashi* amicus brief submitted by the attorneys general of California, Oregon, and Washington, who maintained that "the Japanese of the Pacific Coast area on the whole have remained a group apart and inscrutable to their neighbors, as they represent an unassimilated, homogenous element which in varying degrees is closely related through ties of race, language, religion, custom and ideology to the Japanese Empire." In this light of common sense concerning race, then, the following statement in the *Korematsu* decision appears understandable: "Korematsu was not excluded from the Military Area because of hostility to him or his race. He was excluded because we are at war with the Japanese Empire."[55]

The ACLU had argued that the evacuation centres were concentration camps, but Black rejected this assertion due to "the ugly connotations that term implies." He also rebuffed the contention that racism and prejudice were at the root of the evacuation, claiming that "to cast this case into outlines of racial prejudice, without reference to the real military dangers which were presented merely confuses the issue." Black's decision, then, went even further than that of *Hirabayashi* in deferring to the powers of military authorities.[56]

Of the three dissenting *Korematsu* opinions, those submitted by Justice Owen Roberts and Justice Frank Murphy (the *Hirabayashi* justice) are most notable. Contrasting *Korematsu* with *Hirabayashi,* Roberts presented Korematsu's treatment as a violation of the Constitution: "This is not a case of keeping people off the streets at night as was Kiyoshi Hirabayashi ... It is the case of convicting a citizen ... for not submitting to imprisonment in a concentration camp, based on his ancestry and solely because of his ancestry."[57] He also highlighted the contradictions inherent in the removal program: one order criminalized Korematsu if he left the zone in which he resided; the other criminalized him if he did not leave. Thus, Roberts concluded that the two orders were merely part of a larger program cleverly disguising the "real purpose" of the military authority – to lock Korematsu and others in a concentration camp.[58]

Justice Murphy's dissent was the most critical of the deference to military power, arguing that, as the exclusion order was made when the state and federal courts were still open (martial law had not been declared), it went beyond "the very brink of constitutional power" and entered "the ugly abyss of racism." The exercise of military discretion needed to be checked, especially when martial law had not been declared. Murphy concluded that, because little in the actual situation at hand could justify DeWitt's orders, the evacuation order was "an obvious racial discrimination." Murphy accepted the ACLU contention that the order deprived Japanese Americans of equal protection under the law, as guaranteed by the Fifth Amendment. He also accepted that it deprived them of other constitutional guarantees, such as the right to live and work where they chose, the right to freedom of movement, and the right to habeas corpus. Addressing the various premises upon which the evacuation orders were based, including those that were fictitious or *ex post facto*, as well as the many racial remarks and epithets voiced by DeWitt, Murphy observed that

> A military judgment based upon such racial and sociological considera-
> tions is not entitled to the great weight ordinarily given the judgments
> based upon strictly military considerations. Especially is this so when every
> charge relative to race, religion, culture, geographical location, and legal
> and economic status has been substantially discredited by independent
> studies made by experts in these matters.[59]

Murphy also pointed to the dangers of sanctioning the premise that individual disloyalty proved group disloyalty and thus justified discriminatory action against the group. Such a sanction undermined the basic premise of the legal system – that individual guilt is the sole basis for the deprivation of rights. According to Murphy, it dangerously paralleled the state ideology of America's enemies and portended discriminatory actions against other minority groups "in the passions of tomorrow." His dissent ended on a highly charged note:

> I dissent, therefore, from this legalization of racism. Racial discrimination
> in any form has no justifiable part whatever in our democratic way of life.
> It is unattractive in any setting but it is utterly revolting among a free
> people who have embraced the principles set forth in the Constitution of
> the United States. All residents of this nation are kin in some way by
> blood or culture to a foreign land. Yet they are ... part of the new and
> distinct civilization of the United States. They must accordingly be treated
> at all times as the heirs of the American experiment and as entitled to all
> the rights and freedoms guaranteed by the Constitution.[60]

The third dissenting opinion, delivered by Justice Robert Jackson, was perhaps the most prophetic, affirming that once the judiciary rationalized the constitutionality of such an order as evacuation, "the Court for all time has validated the principle of racial discrimination ... The principle then lies about like a loaded weapon ready for the hand of any authority that can bring forward a plausible claim of an urgent need."[61] Jackson also nodded to the very foundations of American constitutional law, and indeed, of the nation itself, when he wrote that

> if any fundamental assumption underlies our system, it is that guilt is personal and not inheritable ... But here is an attempt to make an otherwise innocent act a crime merely because this prisoner is a son of parents as to whom he had no choice, and belongs to a race from which there is no way to resign.[62]

Incidentally, Justice Jackson's dissent is usually recalled less frequently than those of his senior colleagues Roberts and Murphy. As John Barrett has explained, the second half of Jackson's dissent is problematic. In it, Jackson expresses resignation about judicial powerlessness and pessimism concerning the courts' ability to protect constitutional liberties from the pressure of military command. Furthermore, Jackson mused that perhaps all courts, even the Supreme Court, should abstain from holding military commanders to constitutional limits in times of war.[63]

Nevertheless, the court narrowed the issue in *Korematsu*, replicating the *Hirabayashi* strategy. What it had done the year before with the issue of curfew, it repeated with that of evacuation. In *Hirabayashi*, the court had held that a curfew order lay within Washington's legitimate wartime powers and that the singling out of the Japanese was not an act of racial discrimination; in *Korematsu*, it explained that, in light "of the principles we announced in the *Hirabayashi* case, *we are unable to conclude* that it was beyond the war power of Congress and the Executive to exclude those of Japanese ancestry from the West Coast war area at the time they did."[64] Segmentation struck again.

Hirabayashi and *Korematsu* are also alike in their approach to "strict scrutiny," which is part of a hierarchy of standards that courts must employ to measure an alleged government interest against a constitutional right or policy that conflicts with that interest. The two main contexts for strict scrutiny are the violation of a constitutional right, particularly one listed in the Bill of Rights, and the government use of suspect classifications such as race or national origin that may render such government interests void under the equal protection clause. In *Hirabayashi*, Chief Justice Stone provided specific detail, arguing that, though the war emergency made race-based classification imperative in this instance, in general, "Distinctions between citizens solely because of their ancestry are by their very nature odious to a free people whose institutions are founded upon the doctrine of equality. For that reason, legislative classification or discrimination based on race alone has often been held to be a denial of equal protection."[65]

In *Korematsu,* Black justified the court's ruling on the basis of extraordinary military urgency but stressed that "All legal restrictions which curtail the civil rights of a single racial group are immediately suspect ... Courts must subject them to the most rigid scrutiny. *Pressing public necessity may sometimes justify the existence of such restrictions; racial antagonism never can.*"[66] Thus, *Hirabayashi* and especially *Korematsu* are essential components of equal protection jurisprudence in the United States, although both are much criticized for the ways in which they applied the rule to the facts.[67]

On the same day as the *Korematsu* court upheld the evacuation itself, the *Ex Parte Endo* justices unanimously agreed that loyal citizens of Japanese ancestry could not be detained in the relocation centres against their will. They did not, however, rule on the constitutionality of Executive Order 9066 and the rights of citizens in relation to the military in wartime. Instead, Justice Douglas, who delivered the concurring opinion, pointed the finger of blame at WRA authorities on mere procedural grounds. In this, the Supreme Court shielded the executive and legislative branches from blame. Neither Endo nor the 110,000 incarcerated persons of Japanese ancestry received acknowledgment that their *constitutional* rights had been violated.

Justice Douglas delivered the opinion, which opened with three apparently obfuscating statements:

> We are of the view that Mitsuye Endo should be given her liberty. In reaching that conclusion we do not come to the underlying constitutional issues which have been argued. For we conclude that, whatever power the War Relocation Authority may have to detain other classes of citizens, it has no authority to subject citizens who are concededly loyal to its leave procedure.[68]

In terms of enigmatic reasoning, the decision did not improve from there. Douglas continued with what has been termed a "literalist stance." Observing that the documents relevant to the case (Executive Order 9066, Executive Order 9102, which had created the WRA, and Public Law 503) did not authorize mass detention, Douglas concluded that neither the president nor Congress authorized mass detention. The WRA was authorized only "to provide for the removal from designated areas of persons whose removal is necessary in the interests of national security."[69] The court then applied the avoidance protocol of reading legislation to avoid "constitutionally worrisome meanings." That is, it presumed that the president and Congress were "sensitive to and respectful of the liberties of the citizen." To read the executive orders otherwise "would be to assume that the Congress and the President intended that this discriminatory action should be taken against these people wholly on account of their ancestry even though the government conceded their loyalty to this country. *We cannot make such an assumption.*[70] Justice Douglas then went on to quote from President Roosevelt's government pronouncements on the loyalty of Americans of Japanese ancestry, thereby placing the president beyond reproach for his positive views.[71]

Justices Murphy and Roberts both felt compelled to file concurrences that addressed their difficulties with the majority opinion as expressed by Justice Douglas. Murphy declared that the detention of citizens of Japanese ancestry was clearly authorized by Congress and the executive, and that it constituted "another example of the unconstitutional resort to racism inherent in the entire evacuation program." Justice Roberts similarly refused the suggestion that "some inferior public servant exceeded the authority granted by executive order in this case." The court, Roberts noted, was asked to determine if Mitsuye Endo's detention violated the guarantees of the Bill of Rights, but it chose not to clearly address this issue. Roberts, however, had no such qualms: "There can be but one answer to that question. An admittedly loyal citizen has been deprived of her liberty for a period of years. Under the Constitution she should be free to come and go as she pleases."[72]

Some eighteen years later, in a 1962 interview, Douglas claimed that, despite his petition, backroom politics prevented him from getting the court to address constitutional issues, as Justices Black, Frankfurter, and Stone were strongly opposed to taking that route. It was his "biggest disappointment" that the court "wouldn't, in *Endo,* go to the constitutional ground but just stick to the conventional way of deciding the case a strain to construe a regulation to avoid a constitutional question. I'm the author of that but I did it under the necessities of the situation. But it seemed to me to be a much more wholesome thing from the point of view of the Court as an educating influence just to say what you can and can't do."[73]

With *Ex Parte Endo,* the Supreme Court of the United States had finally ruled on the incarceration of Japanese Americans. Two years later, the Supreme Court of Canada would have to rule on a more dire concern – Nikkei deportation.

Halting Deportation: The CCJC and the Courts

In 1945, when the Co-operative Committee on Japanese Canadians entered the judicial fray with a lawsuit contesting the legality of Orders-in-Council P.C. 7355, 7356, and 7357, the war had ended. In the United States, persons of Japanese ancestry were free of their bonds of relocation and were allowed to return to the Pacific coast. CCJC lawyer F. Andrew Brewin was charged with the task of aiding the CCJC in its legal challenge. Plans to complete a writ were carried out on Christmas Eve at the home of B.K. Sandwell.[74] On 27 December 1945, the CCJC issued the writ at Osgoode

Hall in Toronto against the attorney general of Canada in the name of Yutaka Shimoyama, a Canadian-born Nisei, and Yae Nasu, a naturalized Japanese Canadian. The writ claimed that Orders-in-Council P.C. 7355, 7356, and 7357, authorizing deportation, were ultra vires (beyond the scope of legal authority) and invalid on a number of grounds, such as habeas corpus.[75]

In addition to the national CCJC action, three more test cases were planned by the Winnipeg branch of the CCJC. However, when the federal Cabinet announced on 9 January 1946 that, in response to a national CCJC request, it was referring the Orders-in-Council to the Supreme Court, the Winnipeg committee put its litigation on hold. Its three test cases concerned Shoji Minamidi, a Canadian-born person of Japanese ancestry, Mitsuo Yagi, a Japanese national with a wife and three Canadian-born children, and Masajiro Ibuki, a naturalized Canadian with three children born in Canada.[76]

Time was of the essence for the CCJC, as a ship transporting deportees was scheduled to depart for Japan on 6 January.[77] In addition to issuing its legal action, the CCJC met with government officials to ask that the case be referred to the Supreme Court. On 4 January, a delegation consisting of Sandwell, George Tatham, Brewin, and Donalda MacMillan met with the acting minister of justice and his deputy minister. The delegation impressed upon the government representatives that numerous organizations across Canada supported CCJC actions and had protested the Orders-in-Council. It also argued that the orders threatened civil liberties and were "morally wrong." Lastly, Brewin pointed out that since Ottawa had the power to deport aliens only, the deportation orders for Canadian citizens were unconstitutional. They asked the two bureaucrats to convey this information to the Cabinet, with the intention that the matter be submitted to the Supreme Court as a reference case. If their request were not granted, the CCJC threatened to issue thousands of writs of habeas corpus against the government.[78]

As a result, and after the CCJC and its affiliated committees undertook to withdraw all writs issued against Ottawa, the Cabinet agreed to refer the orders to the Supreme Court to test their legality. In addition, it suspended the enforcement of the deportation orders, except for those Nikkei who desired to go to Japan. It became increasingly apparent to Ottawa that the CCJC had strong public support and could no longer be ignored. The King government also saw the legal reference as an opportunity to abdicate its responsibility to the Supreme Court on the issue of deportation.[79]

The argument was heard before the Supreme Court on 24 and 25 January. CCJC counsel F. Andrew Brewin and J.R. Cartwright, a noted constitutional authority who would later be appointed as a chief justice of the Supreme Court, acted on behalf of the CCJC, as did J.A. MacLennan. Brewin also represented the CCF Government of Saskatchewan in support of the CCJC; the Province of British Columbia supported the attorney general of

Canada against the appeal.[80] The question referred to the Supreme Court for hearing and consideration was the following: "Are the Orders-in-Council, dated the 15th day of December, 1945, being P.C. 7355, 7356, and 7357, *ultra vires* of the Governor in Council either in whole or in part and, if so, in what particular or particulars and to what extent?"[81] In formulating his argument, Brewin appealed to his colleagues in the legal profession for assistance; these included F.R. Scott, a McGill University law professor, R.J. McMaster, KC, a Vancouver lawyer, and Arnold Campbell, KC, of Winnipeg, with whom Brewin was well acquainted.[82] Brewin also corresponded with Dillon Myer of the WRA and Arthur Garfield Hays of the ACLU, in regards to the American situation.[83]

In making their case to the Supreme Court, the CCJC representatives submitted that the question referred to it should be answered in the affirmative – the Orders-in-Council were entirely ultra vires of the powers of Parliament. The CCJC sought to prove that the federal government was not granted unlimited powers under the "peace, order and good government" clause of the British North America Act (BNA) and the pursuant War Measures Act. Unhindered by internal strife, unlike the ACLU, the CCJC could directly challenge Ottawa on the issue of constitutionality.

In particular, it argued that the terms of the War Measures Act did not enable Parliament to delegate to the governor-in-council the power to order British subjects, whether by birth or naturalization, into exile in Japan. It observed that the United States Congress did not possess the authority to exile American citizens, and that not even in the gravest emergency had the British Parliament found it necessary to assume such a power. Under the War Measures Act, the CCJC claimed, government authority was limited to "arrest, detention, exclusion and deportation"; deportation was defined as "the return of an alien to the country from whence he came." The government, therefore, had exceeded its powers when it deported citizens of Canada. Furthermore, Brewin and Cartwright informed the justices that, although citizens could legitimately be deported due to felony conviction, their deportation for any other reason was considered expressly forbidden by habeas corpus. Additionally, the question of war emergency was posed, with special note that the orders were not made "by reason of war or apprehended war."[84] Brewin felt strongly that the issue of jurisdiction would be a difficult one for the government to defend. Brewin capitalized upon Ottawa's decision to incorporate certain War Measures Act powers into the National Emergency Transitional Powers Act. Highlighting the contradictions of this, Brewin remarked, "Parliament cannot say in the same breath that the 'war emergency' is over but that legislation can be passed not related to the 'post-war emergency' but related to the 'war emergency.' That amounts to saying 'The war is over, long live the war.'"[85]

The CCJC also contested the orders on the basis of race, arguing that the words "Japanese Race" were so vague as to be meaningless, therefore rendering the orders unenforceable. This line of reasoning sprang from Cartwright's suggestion that the Crown might be unable to prove that any particular individual was of the "Japanese Race." In incorporating this argument, Brewin, who had examined the works of many leading anthropologists and ethnologists on the subject of race, commented that they "are not at all agreed as to what is the proper test."[86] According to anthropologist Ralph Linton, whose *The Study of Man* Brewin had consulted, "races and stocks ... are abstractions." In *We Europeans*, ethnologists Julian S. Huxley and A.C. Haddon declared that "the word 'race' as applied scientifically to human groupings, has lost any sharpness of meaning."[87] Interestingly, in its examination of the term "race," the CCJC brief bore a remarkable similarity to the JACL brief drafted by Morris Opler. The current debates on the meaning of race found their way into the arguments of both the CCJC and the JACL. That the ACLU did not address the subject can perhaps be attributed to its desire to focus on civil liberties rather than conceptual issues concerning race.

Brewin and Cartwright also contested the orders on other grounds, claiming that, because they authorized the forcible removal of British subjects to a foreign country, they violated "acceptable principles of international law" and infringed on the authority of the receiving nations. In appealing to humanitarian principles, counsel for the CCJC contended that "there is a presumption that Parliament does not assert or assume jurisdiction which goes beyond the limits established by the common consent of nations" and that deportation of citizens on racial grounds had been declared a "crime against humanity" by the United Nations. Brewin and Cartwright added that, because the orders for deportation and revocation of citizenship threatened the citizenship rights of British subjects, they interfered with British law, namely, the British Nationality and Status of Aliens Act, which extended to the Dominion of Canada.[88]

Anticipating an adverse decision from the Supreme Court, the CCJC solicited advice from its affiliated committees across the country. All agreed that if the judgment were unfavourable, the CCJC would carry the appeal to the highest court, the Privy Council. On 20 February 1946, the Supreme Court announced its decision in *In the Matter of a Reference*. It satisfied no one, as a majority of the court held that the Orders-in-Council were partially valid. The CCJC immediately decided to appeal.[89] The Canadian justices' opinions were "confusing," it argued, and the "issue involved is of such crucial importance to the liberties of Canadians generally and especially to minority groups."[90]

The seven Supreme Court justices unanimously declared that the deportation of Japanese aliens and naturalized Japanese Canadians was legal.

However, they disagreed in the case of the Nisei: five favoured deportation and two opposed it. Regarding those dependants of male deportees who did not wish to go to Japan, the justices were split four to three against deportation. In practical terms, this meant that Ottawa could now legally deport the 6,844 adults who had signed requests for repatriation, but their 3,500 dependants could remain in Canada. Chief Justice Thibaudeau Rinfret and Judges Patrick Kerwin and Robert Taschereau declared that the orders were completely valid in all respects; the remaining four justices, A.B. Hudson, J.W. Estey, I.C. Rand, and R.L. Kellock, contended with certain aspects of them. The court upheld the authority of the Cabinet as "the sole judge of the necessity or advisability of these measures" and ruled the orders legal simply because the government had power to issue them under the War Measures Act. However, a majority of the court found insufficient justification for the deportation of the wives and children of male deportees.[91] The ruling was thus wholly unacceptable to the activists. The government could still deport people, but it would have to face the political repercussions of separating families.

Chief Justice Rinfret delivered the highly legalistic defence of the government's position. It drew heavily from common law, as the court could not look to a written constitution for guidance, unlike its American counterparts. Rinfret held that, though "there is always ... some risk of abuse when wide powers are committed in general terms to any body of men," the Cabinet was "the sole judge of the necessity or advisability of these measures." The Supreme Court, or any court, for that matter, was not qualified to pass judgment on the use of such powers. He pronounced the CCJC argument on the meaning of the term "deportation" to be "really immaterial," as deportation generally came under the wide powers of the War Measures Act.[92]

Justices Rand and Kellock, on the other hand, both took issue with the proposal to deport or "repatriate" Canadian citizens. In their dissents, they pointed out the contradictions in the use of the terms "repatriation" and "deportation." Kellock reasoned that, if "repatriation" meant "return to one's country," it could not apply to Canadian-born persons of Japanese ancestry, as they had no country but Canada. Similarly, Rand determined "repatriation" to mean a return to one's fatherland, or *patria;* thus, it could not be applied to those born in Canada.[93]

Significantly, a majority of the justices (four out of seven) agreed that deportation of wives and children was neither justified nor warranted under the rubric of national security. Nowhere in the Supreme Court decision, however, did the seven justices offer any guidance or clarification on the nature of citizenship. In declaring the majority of the government's "repatriation" and "deportation" program intra vires, the Supreme Court missed the opportunity to create an important precedent like the *Endo* decision of its American counterpart.[94] As the ruling disappointed all parties involved, including the CCJC and Ottawa itself, and as deportation was increasingly becoming a hot political issue, the matter was appealed to the Judicial Committee of the Privy Council.

For the CCJC, and Brewin, the lesson of the Supreme Court judgments was that the courts were concerned only with the legality of the orders, not with the moral justice or injustice of the policy. Considerations of race, then, would have little impact on the lords of the Privy Council. In defining "Japanese race," they would approach the matter solely in practical terms, for their purpose was to rule specifically on the letter of the law. Thus, the material presented by Brewin over the four days in session, throughout which he was assisted by two British lawyers, Christopher Shawcross, MP, and Geoffrey Wilson, was confined largely to arguments dealing with jurisdiction. Indeed, Brewin's own impressions of the proceedings bore out this opinion, as revealed in a CCJC bulletin based on his report that "the Privy Council is not concerned with 'justice' but only with the question of the 'power to deport.'" The lords of the Privy Council did take seriously the CCJC contention that deportation" was not an apt word to apply to citizens, but "they did not take seriously the contention that the war-time emergency is over."[95]

The Privy Council handed down its ruling in December 1946. Lord Wright delivered the unanimous judgment that the Orders-in-Council were intra vires under the War Measures Act.[96] Simply put, the deportation orders were valid *in toto* because, according to the Judicial Committee, the Canadian government had unlimited powers under the War Measures Act to do anything it considered necessary for the safety of the country. According to Lord Wright

> It is not pertinent to the judiciary to consider the wisdom or propriety of the particular policy which is embodied in the emergency legislation. Determination of the policy to be followed is exclusively a matter for the Parliament of the Dominion and those to whom it has delivered its powers.[97]

Specifically, because the act dealt with emergencies, the Judicial Committee found no grounds or relevance to consider the pertinence of nationality when the matter of emergency was linked with the combination of such words as "arrest, detention, exclusion and deportation." The Judicial Committee further ruled that "the word 'deportation' is used in a general sense and as an action applicable to all persons irrespective of nationality." The committee recognized the difficulties in the construction of words such as "deportation" but nonetheless ruled that such difficulties were irrelevant to the validity of the War Measures Act. It exercised similar reasoning regarding the contention that the phrase "of the Japanese race" was so vague as to be incapable of application, ruling that "difficulties of construction do not affect the validity of the Orders."[98]

Although Lord Simon of the Judicial Committee pronounced that "this was one of the most important cases that has ever come before us," it was clear that the committee's ruling did not reflect the importance of the case. Dealing only with the legal points involved, the Privy Council declined to pronounce on the nature of the deportation policy itself, as Lord Wright's ruling indicated. In short, according to the Privy Council, Ottawa had the power to deport citizens. This was a difficult decision for Canadians to accept because the idea of citizenship was becoming increasingly significant to them and because the Canadian Citizenship Act would come into effect in less than one month, on 1 January 1947. Thus, the act *appeared* meaningless because citizenship could be revoked on racial grounds, among others, as the deportation of Japanese Canadians seemed to demonstrate to all. Yet, parliamentary supremacy was still a reigning constitutional principle, as frustrating as this may have been to those involved in the deportation case. The British North America Act set the division of powers between Parliament and the provincial legislatures; each legislature was supreme, such that within its jurisdiction no other institution could pass certain laws. Thus, if legislation were properly enacted by Parliament, it was valid, no matter how inflexible or seemingly illiberal. For the CCJC, the ruling also underlined the fact that "a nation can never depend upon laws or constitutions to defend its rights" and pointed to the need for a restrictive bill of rights like that of the United States, or some other constitutional limitation of the powers of Parliament or the Cabinet.[99]

Disorder in the Courts:
Judging the Incarceration and Expatriation Cases

The CCJC, the ACLU, and their cooperating groups saw the court challenges as a means of raising public ire on issues affecting persons of Japanese ancestry. The legal campaign to achieve justice for Japanese Canadians was but one facet of CCJC strategy; the group correctly perceived that public education on the immorality and inhumanity of the orders was the most effective route through which to halt the deportations/expatriations. Indeed, the committee regarded the legal proceedings as merely a "holding operation," one launched while the people of Canada, and the Parliament of Canada, realized the gravity of the expatriation issue and conveyed their opinions to the prime minister and his Cabinet. The reference to the courts, though legally unsuccessful, did provide a cover behind which public opinion was harnessed, leading Ottawa to pursue an alternative policy of dispersal and resettlement across Canada.

For the ACLU, on the other hand, the court cases represented the cornerstone of its Japanese American advocacy. The ACLU's legal defence of persons of Japanese ancestry was both laudatory and contradictory in its attitudes towards civil liberties. Due to procedural constraints imposed by the ACLU itself, its lawyers were unable to address the obvious constitutional violations of presidential authority and had to limit themselves largely to arguments relating to equal rights and racial prejudice. Although race was important in the Japanese American cases, racial discrimination was not linked to any broader issue such as human rights, for the ACLU lawyers strictly dealt with the entire curfew-removal-relocation program as an unconstitutional form of racial discrimination.

As ACLU general counsel Osmond K. Fraenkel observed, "War is a notorious interferer with liberty"; thus, it was not surprising that both the Supreme Court of Canada and the Supreme Court of the United States were called upon to resolve conflicts between the liberties of the individual and the war powers of the state.[100] The Japanese American cases and the Japanese Canadian deportation case wound their way through their respective judicial systems. Following three largely unsuccessful appeals to the US Supreme Court, the *Endo* decision finally brought about the desired effect when the Supreme Court justices all agreed that loyal citizens of Japanese ancestry could not be detained against their will in the relocation centres to which they had been evacuated after Pearl Harbor. The dissenting views in the three American cases, and the single Canadian case, reflect the schisms within American and Canadian society over race, rights, and the nature of citizenship. Indeed, they also mirror the divisions and principles within the organizations that acted on behalf of persons of Japanese ancestry in North America.

In the Japanese American cases, the Supreme Court moved from a unanimous decision in *Hirabayashi,* in which it upheld the curfew orders that were issued as a preliminary to the evacuation of the Pacific coast, to a unanimous decision in *Endo,* in which it refused to sanction the detention of a citizen of Japanese ancestry who was considered to be loyal. Whereas the Supreme Court of Canada and the Privy Council did not check the powers of government in wartime or provide any guidance on the issue of citizenship, their decisions would, in fact, have little impact on the overall outcome of the offending Orders-in-Council. The case made by the CCJC, its affiliates, and coordinating groups would find a more favourable hearing in the court of public opinion. Ultimately, appealing to this court proved to be the more successful tactic.

In the United States, the outcome of the court cases was of greater consequence. Due to the existence of constitutional protections, the US Supreme Court had the authority to pass judgment on the limits of power during wartime. However, because a procedure-bound ACLU and incompetent affiliate lawyers presented their cases ineffectively, and because the Supreme Court justices subscribed to the doctrine of race, the Nikkei would receive "justice" only in late 1944. While the American public opinion backlash had an impact and while the Nisei were serving bravely in their military roles, the government, anticipating defeat in the Supreme Court, had begun to dismantle the relocation program. The day before the *Endo* decision was announced, it issued Public Proclamation No. 21, which officially ended mass incarceration. With the exception of those identified by name, all the incarcerated were freed as of 20 January 1945. When the Supreme Court decided *Duncan v. Kahanamoku* in 1946, it passed judgment on an extraordinary phase in American history – the longest period of martial law to which residents of a state or territory had ever been subjected – and put some closure on the remainder of the wartime program targeting persons of Japanese ancestry. The court ruled that the military tribunals did not have the legal authority to try civilians imprisoned in Hawaii. Although the governor of Hawaii could declare martial law, the court refused to agree that he could close all the courts and supplant them with military tribunals, even with presidential authority.[101]

Ultimately, the Canadian cases had little impact on legal scholarship and precedent, and certainly so with the advent of the Canadian Charter of Rights and Freedoms in 1982. As former Supreme Court justice Claire L'Heureux-Dubé has written, early equality cases "do not loom over Canadian constitutional history" as they do in the United States.[102] The Japanese American litigation, on the other hand, has experienced a greater lifespan as case law for a variety of subsequent matters. Although no published defence of the US Supreme Court, the Supreme Court of Canada, or even the Judicial Committee of the Privy Council exists, the legal briefs composed by the ACLU, the JACL, the CCJC, and the JCCD constitute a far more enduring and important legacy. These indicate, quite clearly, how persons of Japanese ancestry and their advocates were affected by the growing commitment to rights during and following the Second World War. In particular, the documents composed by the JACL, the CCJC, and the JCCD provide strong evidence of the extent to which human rights discourse had made its way into the mainstream.

6
Conclusion: "They Made Democracy Work"

> But the world is not the same, nor will Japanese Americans
> return to the status quo of Dec. 6, 1941 ... The group
> identification of Japanese Americans has been strengthened and
> maintained through the exigencies of war and the promulgation
> of military restrictions based on the fact of ancestry.
>
> – Larry Tajiri, commenting on the "end" of
> incarceration in *Pacific Citizen*, 23 December
> 1944

Larry Tajiri's comments seem quite prophetic in light of a number of developments since the end of the Second World War. Before the war, few North Americans viewed Japanese Americans and Japanese Canadians as citizens. But the 1940s precipitated a fundamental re-evaluation of the rights of the Nikkei and their place in North American society. Similarly, the Nikkei would reconsider their place amongst their fellow Americans and Canadians.

The relocation and expatriation issues enabled minority groups in Canada and the United States to realize that the problems faced by one group, especially with regard to racial prejudice, would have implications for the others. As the war neared its end, marked by Allied victories, public opposition to such racially based policies as relocation and expatriation became more pronounced. As a result, dissent, including dissent from minority representative organizations, became more acceptable. When groups such as the NAACP, the NCJW, and the CJC joined other organizations in decrying the treatment of Japanese Americans and Japanese Canadians, it marked a significant step towards greater post-war cooperation on other matters of mutual interest. This was particularly the case in Canada.

Japanese Canadian organizations recognized the importance of support from Euro-Canadians and the necessity of offering full cooperation to them. The Canadian struggle to overcome racial disadvantage required a cooperative effort of minorities and whites. Thus, in 1947 when the CJC requested national JCCA support in pushing for the enactment of fair employment practices (FEP) legislation, the latter readily agreed "because," as its president George Tanaka put it, "we know what it is like to be discriminated against."[1] Indeed, shortly before the NJCCA was formed, Kinzie Tanaka, as editor of *Nisei Affairs*, was among the first to exhort the Japanese

Canadian community to work towards the "common good" and to stress that "we shall not attain *our* ends until we have fought unselfishly for *the other's* struggle for some basic human right." Calls for Japanese Canadians to be unselfish and to work for the rights of Jews and African Canadians were repeated in its pages. Writing in *Nisei Affairs* under the pen name Sue Sada, Muriel Kitagawa critiqued the government policy of continuing post-war restrictions on Japanese Canadians, conspicuously titling her piece "Today the Japanese – Tomorrow?" Not surprisingly, then, the national JCCA would also support the Canadian demand for a bill of rights and fair employment practices legislation. A brief submitted to Parliament by the Committee for a Bill of Rights even included a clause disallowing the exile of Canadian citizens, clearly an acknowledgment of the expatriation struggles of the Japanese Canadian community. With the campaign for FEP legislation, in Ontario in particular, ethnic communities realized the value of coalition building.[2] Although the CCJC had disbanded by 1951, its activists learned valuable lessons and applied them to other campaigns. Of equal importance is that the language of human rights, first tested in the Nikkei human rights struggle, had made its mark.

Representatives from US minority groups were not inactive in the post-war period, either. In many ways, American minority organizations were eager to point out existing state-imposed inequalities. As mentioned earlier, the JACL amended its membership policy in late 1944 to permit all Americans to enroll as active members, regardless of race. This new proposal reflected the broadened scope of JACL activities in recognizing the wider problems of minority groups. It also illustrated the desire on the part of activist Nisei to break down the barriers imposed on and by other minority groups. The words of A.L. Wirin, who became a JACL member, are illustrative:

> As a non-Japanese, as a Caucasian, as an American with full rights, it seems timely to emphasize that the fight for the restoration of your rights is a fight you are also carrying on for the Chinese in the United States, for the Negroes in the United States, for the Jews in the United States, and for all minority groups. The challenge ahead of us is a challenging fight for the preservation of such rights and not only for yourself. So I look for a continuing opportunity to carry on that fight.[3]

The JACL made further advances in interracial cooperation with the founding of the JACL Anti-discrimination Committee (JACL-ADC), incorporated in 1946 as its legislative activist agency. It was created with the following goals in mind: to push for legislation that, though it would be of interest to Nikkei groups, would "probably be initiated and receive its primary support from other organizations"; to advance "general civil rights and social legislation which ... may be expected to receive support from organizations interested in 'equal rights and equal opportunities for all'"; and to oppose legislation that the JACL-ADC deemed "inimical and detrimental to the welfare of this country or its people."[4] In 1947, the JACL-ADC was involved in the deliberations of the House of Representatives' Standing Subcommittee on Immigration and Naturalization of the Committee on the Judiciary, which examined various House resolutions designed to eliminate certain inequalities in immigration law. In urging the repeal of the last remaining racial barriers against naturalization, which would be in step with the 1943 and 1945 congressional policies regarding the naturalization of Chinese, Filipinos, and "British Indians" resident in the United States, Mike Masaoka pointed out that though he represented only American citizens of Japanese ancestry, he endeavoured to speak out for "other American citizens and their alien parents who are classed as races 'inadmissible to the United States and ineligible to naturalization.'" The American Jewish Congress supported American citizenship for the Japanese, a position derived from its interest in Jewish war refugees, which, in turn, resulted in its decision to promote easing *all* immigration laws, including those discriminating against Asians.[5]

Perhaps in response to its long-standing issue with, and criticism of, the test case financing, the JACL established the JACL Legal Defense Fund in late 1946. Its purpose, not surprisingly, was to defray legal and court costs in litigation involving civil and property rights of racial minority groups that the JACL would initiate or participate in as "friend of the court." To that end, the Legal Defense Fund was contemplating the submission of briefs in cases involving restrictive covenants against African Americans and members of other minority groups. In an interesting turnabout, the JACL executive expressed its interest in participating in any further test cases questioning Supreme Court decisions upholding the legality of the "mass evacuation" program.[6]

Like individual Nisei and their organizations, the US Supreme Court's *Korematsu* decision played an interesting role in the African American postwar struggle for civil rights. Its declaration that classifications based on race were inherently suspect under the Constitution would feature prominently in the legal struggle for civil rights where the doctrine of "strict scrutiny" became explicit rather than implied.

In the immediate post-war period, JACL and NAACP attorneys united to fight the California Alien Land Act and to challenge racially restrictive covenants, the latter of which was part of a larger multigroup struggle.[7] Racially restrictive covenants in both Canada and the United States have often been used for segregationist purposes. Such a covenant is imposed in a deed by the seller to prohibit the sale or lease of real property to designated racial, religious, or ethnic minorities. Long-time advocate and ally of the Japanese, A.L. Wirin played an important role in persuading the JACL to support a multi-ethnic campaign against restrictive covenants in the Los Angeles area, in cooperation with the NAACP. Wirin brought his considerable expertise in fighting restrictive covenants on behalf of the ACLU. The JACL formalized its involvement by submitting an amicus curiae brief in support of the NAACP in those cases. These, and other litigation concerning California's fishing law, which was based on racial classification, were part of the ongoing effort to employ the strict scrutiny doctrine as an instrument to eliminate Jim Crow.[8]

In the attempt to strike down the infamous "separate but equal" doctrine cited in the 1896 case of *Plessy v. Ferguson,* the NAACP's campaign against inequality involved both the Japanese American litigation and Japanese American advocates.[9] Once again, the JACL would unite with African American, liberal, labour, and Jewish groups in filing amicus briefs, a now standard tactic demonstrating racial solidarity to the courts. The road to fighting educational inequality began with challenging the exclusion of African Americans from higher education. For example, in *McLaurin v. Oklahoma,* a JACL brief referred to the Nikkei incarceration as part of its attack on Jim Crow: It maintained that the "unfortunate and mistaken exercise of the war power involving racial discrimination was allowed as a temporary emergency matter." It then cited *Oyama* (the California Alien Land Act litigation), as well as others, to show that the court had already condemned the unconstitutionality of racial discrimination and should do so again.[10] The NAACP brief also drew upon the Japanese American cases. In a unanimous ruling of 5 June 1950, the Supreme Court found that the educational facilities were indeed unequal, although it missed the opportunity to explicitly engage the *Plessy* doctrine.[11]

In the penultimate challenge to "separate but equal," the arguments in the five consolidated cases known as *Brown v. Board of Education of Topeka, Kansas* resembled those that had come before and included appeals for the court to exercise strict scrutiny in judging laws involving race or colour.[12] Although the JACL did not submit a separate brief in this case, it did join five other organizations in a consolidated amicus brief; these groups included the ACLU, the American Ethical Union, the American Jewish Committee, the Anti-Defamation League of B'nai Brith, and the Unitarian Fellowship for Social Justice. Like the NAACP brief, this amicus brief maintained that the court should apply strict scrutiny and overturn the school segregation laws because they made racial distinctions without grave necessity. An amicus brief in *Bolling v. Sharpe,* the companion case to *Brown,* made a similar argument.[13] In *Brown,* the court delivered the now celebrated decision that "We conclude that in the field of public education the doctrine of 'separate but equal' has no place. Separate educational facilities are inherently unequal."[14] It was in *Bolling,* however, that the doctrine of strict scrutiny was explicitly adopted and the earlier work of the JACL formally incorporated. Chief Justice Earl Warren cited *Hirabayashi* and *Korematsu* in an endote, but their influence was all over his judgment: "Classifications based solely upon race must be scrutinized with particular care, since they are contrary to our traditions and hence constitutionally suspect."[15] As scholars have pointed out, the role of the American Nikkei cases deserves greater attention from those who study the history of civil rights in the United States. It is clear that the Japanese American campaign for justice, including the work of its advocates, extends beyond its conventional wartime parameters.[16]

Conclusion

In Joy Kogawa's *Obasan*, the character Naomi details both the desperate efforts of the Canadian Nikkei to remain a community and the desperation of a different minority – the advocates – who came together from disparate regions and felt the need to lodge their dissent:

> Throughout the country, here and there, were a few people doing what they could. There were missionaries, sending telegrams, drafting petitions, meeting together in rooms to pray. There were a few politicians sitting up late into the night, weighing conscience against expedience. There were the young Nisei men and women, the idealists, the thinkers, the leaders, scattered across the country. In Toronto, there were the Jews who opened their businesses to employ the Nisei. But for every one who sought to help, there were thousands who didn't.[17]

For those who did help, however, their efforts had lasting effects.

The continuing tragedy of the Japanese Americans and the Japanese Canadians helped to raise public awareness of the presence of racial discrimination in both nations. By the mid-1940s, assumptions about race and racial discrimination had begun to change, provoking some Canadians and Americans to become active in the campaign for justice for the Nikkei. The membership of the Co-operative Committee on Japanese Canadians and the American Civil Liberties Union exemplifies the growing rejection of racism in the intellectual and left/liberal communities in the 1940s.

The fight for the rights of Japanese Canadians contributed to a change in the way Canadians viewed minority rights. The war confronted them with the realities that parliamentary supremacy could be carried to extremes and that democracy could not be relied upon to protect a minority from the will of a majority. During this period, the concept of, and reliance upon, "British liberties" was gradually replaced with a greater awareness of human rights and the embrace of its related discourse. In particular, this study suggests that the adoption of the Atlantic Charter (1941) and

the United Nations Charter (26 June 1945), as well as the associated acceptance of human rights as an important concept, represented significant
turning points in the manner in which advocates opposed racially based
government policies. The campaign against the expatriation of Japanese
Canadians provided Canadians with the first opportunity to recognize
and articulate these important changes using the language of the United
Nations Charter.

Not all Canadians, however, embraced the human rights discourse. Although the public campaign launched by the CCJC and other advocates
shifted the government's position on deportation, it did not win a total
victory for human rights. Indeed, Ottawa's own reluctance to vote in favour
of the Universal Declaration of Human Rights in December 1948 indicated that acceptance of human rights was not widespread. Many of the
participants in the CCJC carried on to related campaigns precisely because
the victory was incomplete and other problems, such as racially restrictive covenants, continued to exist.

It is also significant that persons of Japanese ancestry were active in their
own defence and participated in the articulation of human rights as an
important concept. Despite community pressures to abide by government
policy, some Japanese Americans and Japanese Canadians initiated much
of the early protests regarding the discriminatory policies directed at them.
Indeed, Japanese Canadians took leadership roles within the CCJC. In Canada, the two dynamics – that of the Japanese and non-Japanese movements – had to come together to be effective, demonstrating the importance
of ethnic and religious cooperation in this period and heralding the cooperative nature of the developing Canadian human rights community.

As Chapter 4 revealed, little distinguished the human rights discourse
of the JACL from that of Canadian human rights advocates, whether Japanese or non-Japanese. The decision of Nisei-based organizations to cooperate fully with other Canadian advocacy groups, particularly the CCJC, and
the evidence that the Nikkei were welcomed into these groups as relatively
equal participants both symbolize the nature of the fledgling human rights
movement in post-war Canada. Long before multiculturalism became a
state-sanctioned policy, certain Japanese Canadians were among the first
to champion the full participation of racial and ethnic minorities in Canadian democracy, alongside their Anglo-Canadian comrades.

An examination of the briefs drafted by Japanese organizations in Canada and the United States reveals a remarkably similar series of aims related
to the respect for human rights. Whereas the JACL was interested in es-
pousing human rights discourse, the ACLU was not. That the ACLU, dedicated as it was to the protection of civil liberties, took up the cause of
justice for Japanese Americans all but guaranteed that the issue would be
enveloped by the concept of civil liberties. The movement in Canada had

neither a model nor an organizational impetus; nor did the movement have a bill of rights to bolster its appeals for justice. Although some of the initial momentum for reform came from Japanese Americans and Japanese Canadians themselves, non-Japanese advocates led the offensive in both countries. Significantly, both the ACLU and the CCJC concerned themselves with protecting the rights of Japanese *Americans* and *Canadians* as citizens; thus, they emphasized citizenship in their private and public appeals. Some ACLU and CCJC members expressed discomfort with the thought of defending the nationals of an enemy nation; more reasoned opinion held that they could make gains only if they defended American or Canadian citizens. Appeals focusing on citizenship and the related notion of depriving citizens of inalienable rights would resonate more fully with the public than those in which citizenship status was not a factor. The ACLU agreed that, as enemy aliens, the Issei (first generation) could be indiscriminately removed but urged that after evacuation they be given trials before loyalty hearing boards, like other aliens. Once the government had "separated the goats from the sheep," as Winston Churchill and others described the separation of Britain's disloyal citizens from their loyal counterparts, the loyal aliens should be allowed to return to their homes.

Thus, civil liberties and human rights were for citizens only, and with this, deliberate distinctions were made. By mid-1942, the ACLU board agreed that in the future "Japanese-Americans" should be referred to as "American citizens of Japanese ancestry."[18] In most of its public documents, the CCJC was careful to state that it was advocating modest change only, as well as the securing of public support for just, humane, and Christian treatment of Japanese Canadian citizens. Although the CCJC argued for the right of Japanese Canadians to return to their homes, it also advocated and approved of Ottawa's resettlement policy. Japanese Canadians would be better off scattered throughout the nation, instead of returning to "ethnic ghettos" on the coast. Although the civil liberties orientation of the ACLU led it to stress the rights of citizens exclusively, one might have expected that, in Canada, the shift towards a human rights viewpoint would not have led to a similarly narrow focus. That the CCJC tended to ignore the rights of aliens reveals the selectivity of its concept of human rights. Nevertheless, in advocating for the rights of Japanese Canadians, the CCJC was heralding a more broadened concept of Canadian citizenship.

Patriotism and partisan attachment cannot fully explain the ACLU board's attitude towards the wartime removal of Japanese Americans. During the "Red Scare" that followed the First World War, for example, the ACLU battled prosecutions of anarchists and communist supporters of the Russian revolution, despite the sympathy of many ACLU members for the

Woodrow Wilson administration. In fighting for the rights of African Americans during the 1930s, the ACLU also criticized Roosevelt for his failure to support anti-lynching legislation.[19] Like most Americans, some ACLU board members were willing to countenance any effort that the government deemed necessary to win the war. Geographically separated from the bulk of the Japanese American population on the Pacific coast, some ACLU board members, all of whom lived in the New York City area, placed their hatred of the Axis above their concern for civil liberties. The individual who authorized the incarceration was not only the president but also the commander-in-chief of the troops who fought to preserve democracy. Those in the ACLU who supported the Japanese American challengers thus confronted the visceral sentiments of their fearful colleagues. A "shift in opinion," produced by the global crusade against Nazi and other fascist aggression and terror, was beginning to make its mark but only insofar as their concerns remained focused on civil liberties and appeals to the Bill of Rights.

In Canada, the realization that, in the absence of an American-style bill of rights, the concept of "traditional British liberties" as expressed through the constitutional principle of parliamentary supremacy would not provide adequate protection for minorities motivated liberal-minded Canadians to work with the idea of human rights. In the United States, though the JACL recognized the importance of human rights, most advocates remained focused on civil liberties and the protection's afforded minorities by the Constitution and specifically the Bill of Rights. Thus, they had no need to turn to a new concept. In a way this approach was correct, as *Ex Parte Endo* would prove that the Constitution could be relied upon to check (albeit too late in Endo's case) the power of the executive.

If anything, Americans became more "civil rights conscious" in the 1940s.[20] This study, then, supports the conclusions of one influential book on American politics, which argues that, though human rights discourse is generally viewed as a "universal language," certain "dialects" can exist. In particular, Americans employ an individualistic version of the language, whereas Canadians acknowledge individual and group rights claims.[21] Although evidence exists of a shared language of advocacy – anti-Nazi rhetoric, traditional British or American liberties, or appeals to fair play – this study suggests that human rights became the accepted form of discourse for the CCJC and other advocates. Thus, the complex nature of North American dissent in the 1940s suggests the development of a dynamic, but eventually different, discourse in each country.

Voices Raised in Protest also highlights the limits of the left/liberal movement on behalf of the North American Japanese. It must be acknowledged that many liberals did not protest these policies. Supporters of Japanese

American rights in the United States, for example, chose not to make the injustice perpetrated against the Nikkei an issue in the 1942 congressional elections. Moreover, many of the leaders mentioned herein spoke out as individuals without mounting major organizational campaigns on behalf of the Japanese. Wartime liberalism was bound by the difficulty of criticizing the president or the prime minister during a war that most Americans and Canadians, including the critics of removal and relocation, supported. The reactions of those liberals and leftists who believed that they were working for Japanese American and Japanese Canadian rights were confused, muted at times, and conflicting.

As this book has revealed, the Canadian churches differed from their American counterparts in that they chose not to raise public alarm over the 1942 removal of the Nikkei, remaining silent due to their belief in military necessity and their faith in British justice and fair play. Only when the threat of deportation came to the fore in 1943 did the churches respond in a confrontational manner. Church leaders were finally convinced that the federal government had ignored its Christian conscience and had violated the citizenship and human rights of the Japanese Canadian citizenry. Certainly, the Canadian churches were slow to provocation. In a significant fashion, they were forced to act when their Christian principles conflicted with the demands of the state.

As well as contributing to the growing awareness of human rights in Canadian society, the churches underwent significant internal transformations. Their "slow-to-boil" reaction to removal and deportation represented this change. As Michael Hemmings has pointed out, the clergy came to understand that the true purpose of the church was to act in a prophetic role, often against the state, in order to inhibit state repression and to advocate for oppressed peoples.[22] Indeed, this trend also informed the church response to Jewish refugees, as Alan Davies and Marilyn F. Nefsky have detailed, contrary to the criticism by some scholars that the church was virtually silent and did little to assuage the plight of these targets of racial discrimination.[23] The present study has demonstrated that a group within the churches did move to support the Nikkei, and that its motives, framed initially in terms of Christian principles, later expanded to include the belief that human rights also needed to be defended.

The deportation orders passed by the Canadian government in 1945 provoked a variety of responses from Canadians. The efforts of the CCJC and its cooperative committees in various parts of the country were instrumental in bringing about change; so too, was the work of numerous others. Indeed, the CCJC was well aware of the necessity and the effectiveness of its partners, and appreciated their efforts. CCJC secretary Donalda MacMillan expressed these sentiments in a CCJC news bulletin of early 1947:

All the churches, both their leadership and their rank and file, played a part consistent with the principles and values they represent in society. Groups of university students, other youth groups, young men and women in the services, and returned veterans played a part that gives us reason to be encouraged about the future of Canada. The trade union movement and its members showed once again that they are on the side of humanity and justice. A large part of the press and those Members of the House of Commons and the Senate who joined the fight against the orders deserve credit for their assistance. We also wish to express appreciation to the thousands of persons from all parts of the country who contributed money to pay the legal expenses of appeals ... We are glad to be able to give credit to the government for changing its mind and rescinding the orders. Thus a course of action that would have been a lasting cause for shame to Canada has been abandoned, and it has been abandoned because the sound judgment and the sense of decency of the people of Canada would not stand for it.[24]

By the mid-1940s, the campaign to secure just and humane treatment for Japanese Canadians involved the cooperation of many different groups and organizations. So, too, did the American struggle, but it was fought mainly in the courts. The movement for justice for the Nikkei was not as significant a turning point or revelation in the United States as it was in Canada, probably because of the impact and precedent-setting nature of the deportation policy. Additionally, the American government allowed persons of Japanese ancestry to return to the Pacific coast in 1945, whereas Japanese Canadians had to wait until 1949.[25] The CCJC and its cooperating groups found that lobbying the federal and provincial governments, and creating public awareness that demanded change, was more satisfactory than appealing to the courts.

Although evidence suggests that Canadians did "look south" in developing tactics and formulating strategy, in the final analysis it is clear that an identifiably Canadian response evolved. Out of necessity, the CCJC and its cooperating groups employed the new international concept of human rights, since they could point to no constitutional legacy of the American Bill of Rights when fashioning appeals to the public conscience and to politicians. At the peak of its active life, the CCJC demonstrated that, by arousing the indignation of the Canadian people and using its power as leverage against the state, a small group of activists could initiate a fundamental reconsideration of the concepts of democracy and equality.

Whereas, in terms of its practical legacy, the treatment of Japanese Americans remains largely in the realm of legal history, the treatment of Japanese Canadians and the efforts of Canadian advocates, both whites and minorities, developed into a launching pad for future human rights and minority rights campaigns. Although Japanese Americans would support the civil rights movement, and though the texts of the Japanese American cases found important currency in some of the major court cases of the 1950s, the US advocacy movement on behalf of the Nikkei did not leave the same lasting impression as did the Canadian movement. The efforts of the CCJC and its cooperating groups in the crusade for justice for persons of Japanese ancestry must be understood within the context of both the international paradigm shift in human rights discourse and practice and in its Canadian applications. Groups of Canadians "made democracy work" by advancing the idea that every human individual had rights that must not be violated. Although notable for their aims, the CCJC and its associated groups did not advocate for the rights of *all* minorities, for this was a movement dedicated to furthering the rights of its own narrow constituency. Nevertheless, the campaign would eventually have a wider impact. Although Canada and the United States followed similar policies with respect to the wartime treatment of the Nikkei, their paths diverged over the legacies that developed due to the way in which advocates framed their opposition. Canadians came to embrace the human rights discourse that was trumpeted in the attempt to discontinue Ottawa's deportation of Japanese Canadians. Future efforts to repeal the Chinese Immigration Act, to discontinue the practice of restrictive covenants, to achieve the passage of fair employment and fair accommodation practices legislation, and to agitate for a "Canadian" bill of rights were based upon the foundations laid in the campaign to secure justice for Japanese Canadians. Those Canadian advocates who helped to articulate human rights discourse in the immediate post-war period were committed to an idea of Canada that we still share today – a belief in fundamental freedoms and acceptance of all people.

Afterword

Someday, people will be making a study of the matter.

– Andrew Brewin to Saul M. Cherniack,
11 February 1976

Andrew Brewin and Saul Cherniack would probably be pleased to know that, in fact, many people have made a "study of the matter," examining policies dealing with the wartime incarceration, internment, and expatriation of the Nikkei. This book challenges Canadians and Americans to remember. If one group can be singled out because it is perceived as different or dangerous, so can another group. If North Americans forget, or, worse, become indifferent to what happened to persons of Japanese ancestry during the Second World War, we are doomed to repeat mistakes each time we are faced with an emergency or crisis situation, or whenever "military necessity" is cited as a compelling reason.

This "study of the matter" also reminds Canadians and Americans of their democratic right to dissent. Groups of Canadians and Americans, including those of Japanese ancestry and other minorities, raised their voices in protest and prompted government officials to re-evaluate, alter, or abandon their discriminatory policies altogether. Have the lessons from the past been forgotten?

Confronting the Wrongs of the Past in the Twentieth Century
Much evidence indicates that the wartime treatment of the Nikkei is, in some ways, woven into our memories of the disturbing aspects of North American history. But, equally so, much suggests that it has faded from our awareness. In evaluating the meaning of the incarceration program, perhaps the best place to begin is with redress, the most public acknowledgment of the policy's miscreancy.

Some forty years after the Second World War ended, Japanese Americans and Japanese Canadians would be at the forefront of another significant human rights campaign — for redress. In 1988, both Canada and the United States officially endorsed redress, their actions forty-three days apart. On 10 August (in an election year), Republican president Ronald Reagan formally announced that under the Civil Liberties Act each survivor of the incarceration would receive an apology and US$20,000 tax-free as com- pensation. On 22 September (also in an election year), the Progressive Conservative government of Brian Mulroney unveiled a similar policy. It agreed to pay $21,000 to each survivor. Furthermore, it created what is now known as the Canadian Race Relations Foundation to serve as a memorial for the Japanese Canadian community and in an investigative capacity for historic injustice. The year 1988 was also notable in Canada, as the War Measures Act was revoked in July. It was replaced by the Emer- gencies Act, which prohibits discriminatory emergency orders and provides for payments of compensation to victims of discriminatory government actions. Whereas the Canadian payments were issued almost immediately, American Nikkei survivors had to wait two more years for their compen- sation, due to partisan and ideological battles over the budget in 1988 and 1989. Unfortunately, many who had been incarcerated had died before redress was officially passed.[1]

Canadian activism in relation to redress was a factor of circumstance and serendipity. The National Association of Japanese Canadians (NAJC), headed by Art Miki, became the predominant organization in the redress move- ment. A number of developments in the late 1970s and early 1980s helped to make it possible for Japanese Canadians to call for justice. The year 1977 marked the centennial of the arrival in Canada of Manzo Nagano, the first person of Japanese ancestry to come to the country. In honour of this, the Japanese Canadian Centennial Project prepared a photo exhibit, *A Dream of Riches: The Japanese Canadians, 1877-1977*, which was later published in book form. This marked a significant step in breaking the silence of the past. The Canadian Broadcasting Corporation (CBC) helped further the process. *A Call for Justice*, a 1982 CBC TV documentary film produced for *Journal*, endorsed some form of redress for Japanese Canad- ians. Additionally, the Commission on the Wartime Relocation and Intern- ment of Civilians (CWRIC) hearings prompted much interest on the part of Japanese Canadian organizations. They understood the motivation for community empowerment advocated by their American colleagues and believed in the importance of engaging the Japanese Canadian commu- nity in a discussion of redress.[2]

Although redress represented a significant acknowledgment of the wartime incarceration, it was marked by controversy and encountered opposition in both countries. In the United States, opposition to redress was some- times linked to demands that Japan should compensate the bombing of Pearl Harbor. In Canada, the most famous statement against redress came from former prime minister Pierre Elliott Trudeau: "I do not think it is a purpose of a government to right the past. It cannot re-write history. It is our purpose to be just in our time."[3] But redress was suitable justice for what was done decades ago. However, as Roy Miki has observed, the language of Canadian redress was not as apologetic as it might have been, and certainly not in comparison with that of the US. In signing the Civil Liberties Act of 1988, President Reagan offered the nation's apology. President George Herbert Walker Bush followed up with a letter, albeit impersonal, that accompanied the redress cheques:

> A monetary sum and words alone cannot restore lost years or erase painful memories; neither can they fully convey our Nation's resolve to rectify injustice and to uphold the rights of individuals. We can never fully right the wrongs of the past. But we can take a clear stand for justice and recognize that serious injustices were done to Japanese Americans during World War II. In enacting a law calling for restitution and *offering a sincere apology,* your fellow Americans have, in a very real sense, renewed their traditional commitment to the ideals of freedom, equality, and justice.[4]

This is a significant statement. The Canadian redress announcement, on the other hand, was not as magnanimous, equitable, or straightforward. Instead of an apology, it offered the Government of Canada's "regrets that at times throughout our history Canadians representing minority communities have been victims of discrimination and intolerance." In addressing (presumably) the incarceration, property losses, and expatriation, it voiced the government's "regret regarding the deprivation and hardship suffered by most members of the Japanese-Canadian community during the Second World War and in its immediate aftermath, and in particular by the Issei generation." Expressions of regret are not equivalent to an apology. The statement was suitably vague on the particulars of "deprivation and hardship." In singling out the Issei generation, it misrepresented the fact that most of those affected by the incarceration were Canadian-born.[5]

The issue of redress for historic discrimination was revived in June 2006 when Ottawa formally apologized to Chinese immigrants who had paid the racially motivated head tax between 1885 and 1923 and were thereafter subjected to isolation from their families, who were barred from Canada after the 1923 imposition of the Chinese Immigration Act. "Symbolic" payments to survivors and widows of the men who paid the head tax were also promised.[6]

In reaching the point of redress, Japanese Canadians and Japanese Americans made some important progress along the way. Much of that had to do with the generational shift within the Nikkei community. In both Canada and the United States, the leadership of Nikkei organizations shifted from the Nisei to the Sansei, the third generation, moving from a generation that experienced the wartime incarceration and attendant ordeals to one that experienced them, if at all, through the reminiscences of parents and grandparents. In 1980, Congress established the Commission on the

Wartime Relocation and Internment of Civilians (CWRIC) in response to JACL requests for a then undetermined redress. The commission presented its conclusions in *Personal Justice Denied*, which provided the basis for redress as proclaimed in the Civil Liberties Act of 1988. To some extent, this reawakened sense of justice and activism on the part of Japanese Americans was based on international developments – namely, that the West German government was engaging in a redress process by paying compensation to Jews and Jewish organizations. The JACL also linked its call for redress to wider domestic issues; it desired public acknowledgment of the injustice so as to prevent its reoccurrence in any form. The successes of the civil rights movement would help to energize the push for redress in the US and Canada.[7]

The Japanese American groups also demonstrated their organizational fervour in the *coram nobis* cases of 1983, which served as an important parallel to the redress campaign. A writ of error *coram nobis* (the error before us) is a legal device that allows a person convicted of a crime to challenge the conviction on certain grounds after having served the sentence. This litigation sprang from a discovery made by Aiko Herzig-Yoshinaga, a

Not unlike the letter that accompanied the redress cheques, the wording of this commemorative plaque of the Minidoka Relocation Center is indicative of American frankness regarding this chapter in their history. Stephanie Bangarth photo

clerical worker turned researcher, and Peter Irons, a university professor, civil rights lawyer, and political activist.[8] When the two learned that War Department and Justice Department officials had knowingly altered, suppressed, and destroyed evidence in the wartime Japanese American cases, Fred Korematsu, Gordon Hirabayashi, and Minoru Yasui filed *coram nobis* petitions in early 1983 that sought to set aside their convictions. (Mitsuye Endo did not submit a petition, because she had won her 1944 case.) As well, recently uncovered evidence had proved irrefutably that Washington had suppressed certain information emanating from the Office of Naval Intelligence: this had contradicted the army's claim of widespread disloyalty among Japanese Americans, a claim upon which the rationale of military necessity was based. In actuality, not one Japanese American was ever convicted of Second World War sabotage or espionage. The fact that Korematsu, Hirabayashi, and Yasui were willing once again to reprise their roles as public figures demonstrates that in 1983, as in 1943, some Japanese Americans were activists, not passive victims.[9]

Although the *coram nobis* litigation discredited the factual basis of the 1943 cases and the convictions were vacated, the Supreme Court rulings still stand, specifically that of *Korematsu*, with its expansive interpretation of the wartime powers of government. None of the *coram nobis* cases reached the Supreme Court for final verdict, as the Reagan administration's Department of Justice refused to appeal the reversals of *Korematsu* and *Hirabayashi*; Minoru Yasui's death in November 1986 rendered his case moot. In light of this, a number of legal scholars have suggested that the cases have taken on an added relevance in the context of the so-called war on terror and debates over ethnic profiling and US government confinement of "enemy combatants." Their research has revealed that the wartime Japanese American litigation has been employed to support and deny the use of "national security" and "imminent danger" rhetoric as a substitute for consistent legal reasoning. One scholar uses the term "national security fundamentalism" to describe the belief that, according to the Constitution, the president must be permitted to do whatever is necessary to protect the country when national security is threatened. Other scholars have posited that the revival of *Korematsu* and *Hirabayashi* in particular reveals much about contemporary racist sentiment towards Arabs and Arab Americans.[10]

Indeed, the principles that Fred Korematsu, Min Yasui, and Gordon Hirabayashi followed during the war are now being taken up by their children in an amicus brief in support of a class action lawsuit accusing federal officials of racial profiling and wrongful detainment. The class action lawsuit *(Turkmen v. Ashcroft)* was filed by Ibrahim Turkmen and Akhil Sachedva, who were among hundreds of immigrants detained in the months following the terrorist attacks on 11 September 2001. Many were arrested in secret with no charges, and they were not allowed to contact anyone. The authorities eventually cleared Ibrahim and Sachdeva of the accusations, but they deported the two men on visa violations. All of those detained were kept locked up for months as the FBI investigated them. Of the approximately 6,000 foreign nationals targeted for such treatment in the two years following September 11, not one has been been convicted of a terrorism-related crime; in effect, the detainees were presumed guilty until proven innocent, reversing legal procedure in the United States. In the lawsuit, the detainees argued that the government denied them equal protection before the law because they were targeted on the grounds of race and religion and that their due process rights were violated because they were detained after the resolution of their immigration hearings. Both claims were rejected by the District Court of New York.

For Eric Muller, a noted legal historian who filed the amicus brief, and for Karen Korematsu-Haigh, Holly Yasui, and Jay Hirabayashi, the similarities between the plight of the Issei in the aftermath of the bombing of Pearl Harbor on 7 December 1941 and the struggle of Arab and Muslim immigrants after September 11 cannot be ignored. The brief presents the argument that the Issei, much like Arab and Muslim immigrants in today's political climate, were singled out by the government because of race and that the federal trial judge who dismissed the case (*Turkmen v. Ashcroft*) resorted to the same legal theory that had justified the incarceration of Japanese aliens in the Second World War. The judge concluded that it was acceptable to use race and religion to distinguish foreign nationals and subject them to detainment because the 9/11 perpetrators were Arab foreign nationals who belonged to an Islamic fundamentalist group. Indeed, the *Turkmen* decision appears to justify the legality of racial profiling in circumstances where the government can claim urgent need in response to a perceived "enemy."[11]

Although it is not possible to revive the precise aspects of the Japanese Canadian reference case, as the decisions would be largely inconsistent with the 1982 Charter of Rights and Freedoms, reference cases have the same precedential value as do others. The war on terror has re-engaged Canadians in deliberations about the extent of government power in relation to the civil liberties and human rights of citizens. During a Supreme Court case that considered the use of security certificates to detain suspected terrorists, Crown counsel argued that the interests of national security are so vital that they trump all others. Indeed, a poll commissioned by the Canadian Defence and Foreign Affairs Institute indicated that many Canadians think preserving national security is more important than protecting civil liberties. Fully 67 percent agreed strongly or somewhat with the view that without national security, all other individual rights become theoretical, echoing the argument made in the Crown's case. In a unanimous judgment, however, all nine Supreme Court justices found that the system of federal security certificates was unconstitutional, violating the Charter of Rights section under which an accused must receive a fair trial and have access to the evidence against him or her.[12]

More recently, memories of the incarceration were revived with the campaign to save Joy Kogawa's childhood home from demolition, slated for 1 May 2006. Located in Vancouver's Marpole neighbourhood, the house figured prominently in *Obasan*, Kogawa's evocative and acclaimed novel of the incarceration and Canada's treatment of its citizens of Japanese ancestry. A fundraising drive initiated through the Land Conservancy of British Columbia required $1.25 million to buy the house, renovate it, and create a writer-in-residence centre, as well as a place for schoolchildren to learn about the Japanese Canadian experience. Perhaps due to collective indifference to preserving heritage sites that recall Canada's less celebrated past, the campaign progressed slowly, achieving its goal only when it received an anonymous donation of $500,000. Although the house was saved, money is still being raised to assure its place as a physical reminder of injustice and as a haven where writers facing persecution in their homelands may challenge it.[13]

The NAJC and Frank Moritsugu, a retired journalist and former Nisei volunteer of the Second World War, have set their sights on altering Canada's collective memory of the war through recognition of Nisei contributions at the Canadian War Museum in Ottawa. From the perpective of Moritsugu and NAJC activists, not only is the museum's interpretation of the persecution of Japanese Canadians in the 1940s insufficient, but it completely ignores the experiences of the approximately 150 Japanese Canadians who volunteered to serve in the armed forces of Canada. These volunteers served as translators and interpreters who assisted the British forces in the Asian theatre of war, but their efforts were not publicized by the Canadian government. In this latest example of Japanese Canadian activism, those involved hope to convince the museum to give visitors some information about the Japanese Canadian volunteers.[14]

Provocation

The story of the wartime discrimination against the Nikkei must be told in as many forms as possible. There is no single master account. It is important to understand the process by which incarceration, internment, confiscation and loss of property, disfranchisement, and expatriation took place, as well as the nature and composition of those individuals and groups who opposed them. Only by making the North American populace aware of both the wartime miscarriage of justice *and* the extraordinary dissent that ultimately overcame some of it can we ensure that such injustices will never impact another group of Americans and Canadians.

We North Americans have ties to many foreign national or ethnic groups; these connections, depending on the context, can be used to discriminate against individuals. In another time, prompted by another calamitous event, such injustice has the potential to reappear and torment another group of citizens. This study has demonstrated that when collective voices are raised in protest, they can make a difference. In the words of Edith Fowke,

> Here is one clear-cut example of how individual citizens, by banding together, managed to change the course of events in a very significant way. They made democracy work because they cared enough about it to make it work. *What they did can be repeated.*[15]

Appendix 1: Organizations Cooperating with or Interested in the Work of the CCJC by 1945

American Federation of Labor
Canadian Friends Service Committee
Canadian Jewish Congress
CCF Women's Section
Church of All Nations
Civil Liberties Association of Toronto
Committee on Refugees
Co-operative Commonwealth Youth Federation
Democratic Youth Federation
Fellowship for Christian Social Order   .
Fellowship of Reconciliation
Home Service Association
Humanist Club University of Toronto
Japanese Canadian Committee for Democracy
National Boys Work Board
National Council of YMCA
National Council of YWCA
National Girls Work Board
National Interchurch Advisory Committee on the Resettlement of
   Japanese Canadians
National Young Peoples Board
Ontario Boys Work Board
Ontario Christian Endeavour Union
Ontario Girls Work Board
Ontario Religious Education Council
Racial Equality and Equal Rights Committee
Religion and Labour Foundation
St. Christopher House
Student Christian Movement of Canada
Student Christian Movement University of Toronto

Toronto Boys Work Board
Toronto Christian Endeavour Union
Toronto Christian Youth Committee
Toronto Fellowship of Professional Women in the United Church of
  Canada
Toronto Girls Work Board
Toronto Saturday Night
Unitarian Fellowship for Social Justice
United Farmers Co-operative
United Nations Society of Toronto
United Nations Society of Women's Section
United Welfare Council
University Settlement
United Steelworkers of America
Workers' Educational Association
YMCA of Toronto
YWCA of Toronto

Baptist Church
General Secretary
Missionary Education
Women's Missionary Society

Church of England in Canada
Anglican Young Peoples Union Toronto
Council for Social Service
Dominion Board Women's Auxiliary
Women's Auxiliary for Social Service

Presbyterian Church of Canada
Board of Evangelism and Social Service
General Board of Mission Secretary
Missionary Education Secretary
Toronto Young Peoples
Women's Missionary Society
Young People's Society Secretary

United Church of Canada
Board of Evangelism and Social Service
Vigilantes Carleton Church
Women's Missionary Society
Young Peoples Board

Appendix 2: JACL Sponsors as of 12 February 1944

William Agar, chairman, Freedom House, New York
Mrs. Mary B. Alexander, Orinda, CA
Dr. Will W. Alexander, special assistant, War Manpower Commission.
    Formerly director, Interracial Commission
Roger Baldwin, national director, ACLU, New York
Eugene Barnett, general secretary, International Committee, YMCA,
    New York
Barry Lorin Binsse, editor, *Commonweal*, New York
Benjamin W. Black, MD, Alameda County Hospital, Oakland, CA
Pearl S. Buck, author, Perkasi, PA
Dr. Harry Woodburn Chase, chancellor, New York University, New York
Rev. Dr. David de Sola Pool, Spanish and Portuguese synagogue,
    New York
Dr. Monroe Deutsch, provost, University of California, Berkeley
Dr. Edwin R. Embree, director, Rosenwald Foundation, Chicago
Dorothy Canfield Fisher, author, Arlington, VT
Rev. Dr. Harry Emerson Fosdick, pastor, Riverside Church, New York
Arthur Gaeth, vice-president, Intermountain Radio network, Salt Lake
    City
Louis Goldblatt, secretary, IBWU-CIO, San Francisco
Dr. Frank P. Graham, president, University of North Carolina
Bishop W.E. Hammaker, Denver, CO
Dr. Hamilton Holt, president, Rollins College, Winter Park, FL
Dr. Rufus M. Jones, Haverford College, Haverford, PA
Benjamin H. Kizer, attorney, chairman, State Planning Commission,
    Spokane, WA
Read Lewis, director, Common Council for American Unity, New York
E.B. MacNaughton, First National Bank, Portland, OR
Rev. Dr. J.W. Marshall, Foreign Missions Board, Southern Baptist
    Convention, Richmond, VA

Dr. Felix Moreley, president, Haverford College, Haverford, PA

Mrs. Burton W. Musser, National YWCA Board, Salt Lake City

Charles Clayton Morrison, editor, *Christian Century*

Dr. John W. Nason, president, Swarthmore College, Swarthmore, PA

Dr. Reinhold Niebuhr, Union Theological Seminary, New York

Dr. William Allen Nielson, Falls Village, CT

Dr. Howard D. Odum, Institute for Research in Social Science,
University of North Carolina

The Most Rev. Edwin V. O'Hara, bishop of Kansas City, MO

Kirby Page, Fellowship of Reconciliation, La Habra, CA

Rev. Dr. Albert W. Palmer, president, Chicago Theological Seminary,
Chicago

Rt. Rev. Edward L. Parsons, former Episcopal bishop of California,
San Francisco

James G. Patton, president, National Farmers Union, Denver, CO

James L. Paxton Jr., president, Paxton-Mitchell Co., Omaha, NB

Jennings Perry, editor, *Tennesseean*, Nashville, TN

Dr. Ralph Barton Perry, chairman, American Defense, Harvard Group,
Cambridge, MA

Clarence E. Pickett, American Friends Service Committee, Philadelphia

Rev. Dr. E. McNeill Poteat, president, Colgate Rochester Theological
Seminary, Rochester, NY

Dr. Homer P. Rainey, president, University of Texas, Austin

Rabbi Irving P. Reichert, Congregation Emanuel, San Francisco

Rt. Rev. Charles F. Reifsnider, Pasadena, CA

Bishop William Scarlett, diocese of Missouri, Christ Church Cathedral,
St. Louis, MO

Gus Scholle, president, Michigan State CIO, Detroit

George Schuyler, associate editor, *Pittsburgh Courier*

Mr. and Mrs. Harper Sibley, Rochester, NY

Hon. Charles S. Sprague, editor, *Oregon Statesman*, Salem, OR

Dr. Jesse F. Steiner, University of Washington, Seattle

Rt. Rev. W. Bertrand Stevens, Episcopal bishop of Southern California,
Los Angeles

Monroe Sweetland, American Red Cross, Washington, DC

Raymond Gram Swing, Washington, DC

Mr. and Mrs. Charles P. Taft, Washington, DC

Dr. John W. Thomas, secretary, Department of Cities, American Baptist
Home Mission Society, New York

Norman Thomas, Post War World Council, New York

Joseph S. Thompson, president, Pacific Electric Mfg., San Francisco

Willard Townsend, president, United Transport Service Employees of
America, CIO, Chicago

George Trundle Jr., Cleveland, OH
Rt. Rev. Henry St. George Tucker, presiding bishop, Protestant Episcopal
  Church, president, Federal Council of Churches of Christ
August Vollmer, Berkeley, CA
The Most Rev. James E. Walsh, bishop and superior-general of the
  Catholic Maryknoll Missions
Richard J. Walsh, president, John Day Publishing Co., New York
Annie Clo Watson, executive secretary, International Institute,
  San Francisco
Dr. Ray Lyman Wilbur, Stanford University, Palo Alto, CA

Source: Pacific Citizen 18, 6 (12 February 1944)

Notes

Introduction

1 Herbert Marx, "The Emergency Power and Civil Liberties in Canada," *McGill Law Journal* 16, 39 (1970): 83, quoted in Lorraine E. Weinrib, "Terrorism's Challenge to the Constitutional Order," in Ronald Daniels, Patrick Macklem, and Kent Roach, eds., *The Security of Freedom: Essays on Canada's Anti-terrorism Bill* (Toronto: University of Toronto Press, 2001), 99.

2 Presidential Proclamation 4417, 19 February 1976.

3 Quoted in John Robert Columbo, *The Dictionary of Canadian Quotations* (Toronto: Stoddart, 1991), 475.

4 Carmela Patrias and Ruth Frager, "'This Is Our Country, These Are Our Rights': Minorities and the Origins of Ontario's Human Rights Campaigns," *Canadian Historical Review* 82, 1 (March 2001): 2; R. Brian Howe, "The Evolution of Human Rights Policy in Ontario," *Canadian Journal of Political Science* 24, 4 (December 1991): 783-802; James W. St. G. Walker, *"Race," Rights and the Law in the Supreme Court of Canada: Historical Case Studies* (Waterloo and Toronto: Osgoode Society for Canadian Legal History and Wilfrid Laurier University Press, 1997), 31; and Ross Lambertson, *Repression and Resistance: Canadian Human Rights Activists, 1930-1960* (Toronto: University of Toronto Press, 2005), chap. 3.

5 A more detailed discussion of the distinctive rights terminology employed in this study is provided in the pages that follow.

6 Chapter 1 offers a more detailed accounting of the similarities and differences developed here.

7 "Kiri's Piano" is on James Keelaghan's 1993 album *My Skies* (Green Linnet). The complete reference for David Guterson's novel is *Snow Falling on Cedars* (New York: Vintage Books, 1995). More information about *The Gull* can be found in Jean Miyake Downey, "Healing Japanese Canadian Diasporan History: Multicultural Noh Play *The Gull* Premieres in Vancouver," *Kyoto Journal* 62 (2006), http://www.kyotojournal.org/10,000things/043.html. I am grateful to Jean Miyake Downey for this reference and for our discussions over the course of May and June 2006.

8 On works of fiction, see, for example, Joy Kogawa, *Obasan* (Toronto: Penguin, 1983); Lauren Kessler, *Stubborn Twig: Three Generations in the Life of a Japanese American Family* (New York: Penguin Books, 1994); and Kerri Sakamoto, *The Electrical Field* (Toronto: Alfred A. Knopf, 1998).

9 On the victimization thesis in general, see, for example, James W. St. G. Walker, "The Fall and Rise of Africville," *Literary Review of Canada* 2 (July 1993): 3-5. On the methodological move from "objects" to "subjects" in history, the field of African American history is particularly illustrative. Sylvia Frey, *Water from the Rock: Black Resistance in a Revolutionary Age* (Princeton, NJ: Princeton University Press, 1991), explores themes of agency and resistance in her study of the American Revolution and its impact on slavery. In an interesting discussion of Afro-Christianity, Frey demonstrates that though whites had hoped that Christianity would have a civilizing effect on slaves, the slaves in turn gradually

incorporated African cultural elements into their worship as a means of exercising their independence. Instead of functioning as a tool of assimilation, Christianity, and particularly Afro-Christianity, became a vehicle through which African Americans were able to extricate themselves from white society and create a different value system and community.

10 Roger Daniels, *Asian America: Chinese and Japanese in the United States since 1850* (Seattle: University of Washington Press, 1989), 4. This remark is a reiterated statement from his earlier work *The Politics of Prejudice: The Anti-Japanese Movement in California and the Struggle for Japanese Exclusion*, 2nd ed. (Berkeley and Los Angeles: University of California Press 1977). See the preface in the latter work.

11 On resistance, see, for example, Gary Y. Okihiro, "Japanese Resistance in America's Concentration Camps: A Re-evaluation," *Amerasia Journal* 2 (Fall 1973): 20-34; Leslie T. Hatamiya, *Righting a Wrong: Japanese Americans and the Passage of the Civil Liberties Act of 1988* (Stanford, CA: Stanford University Press, 1993); Sandra C. Taylor, *Jewel of the Desert: Japanese American Internment at Topaz* (Berkeley: University of California Press, 1993); Richard Nishimoto, *Inside an American Concentration Camp: Japanese American Resistance at Poston, Arizona* (Tucson: University of Arizona Press, 1995). Brian Masaru Hayashi examines the accommodation, resistance, or avoidance strategies of the incarcerated in *Democratizing the Enemy: The Japanese American Internment* (Princeton, NJ, and Oxford: Princeton University Press, 2004). On the Nisei Mass Evacuation Group and their specific strategies of resistance, see Yon Shimizu, *The Exiles: An Archival History of the World War II Japanese Road Camps in British Columbia and Ontario* (Wallaceburg, ON: Shimizu Consulting and Publishing, 1993), chap. 2, and Roy Miki, *Redress: Inside the Japanese Canadian Call for Justice* (Vancouver: Raincoast Books, 2004), chap. 3.

12 Ad Hoc Committee for "Japanese Canadian Redress: The Toronto Story," *Japanese Canadian Redress: The Toronto Story* (Toronto: Hpf Press, 2000); Roy Miki and Cassandra Kobayashi, *Justice in Our Time: The Japanese Canadian Redress Settlement* (Vancouver: Talonbooks, 1991); Maryka Omatsu, *Bittersweet Passage: Redress and the Japanese Canadian Experience* (Toronto: Between the Lines, 1992); Miki, *Redress;* and William Minoru Hohri, *Repairing America: An Account of the Movement for Japanese-American Redress* (Pullman: Washington State University Press, 1988).

13 Robert Shaffer, "Cracks in the Consensus: Defending the Rights of Japanese Americans during World War II," *Radical History Review* 72 (1998): 84-120.

14 Ibid., 86.

15 For textbook accounts, see Mary Beth Norton, David M. Katzman, and David W. Blight, *A People and a Nation: A History of the United States*, 4th ed. (Boston: Houghton Mifflin, 1994), 834-35; Paul S. Boyer et al., *The Enduring Vision: A History of the American People* (Lexington, MA: D.C. Heath, 1990), 957; Norman Hillmer and J.L. Granatstein, *Empire to Umpire: Canada and the World to the 1990s* (Toronto: Copp Clark Longman, 1994), 170. In the scholarly literature, see W. Peter Ward, "British Columbia and the Japanese Evacuation," *Canadian Historical Review* 57, 3 (September 1976): 298, and Ken Adachi, *The Enemy That Never Was: A History of the Japanese Canadians*, rev. ed. (Toronto: McClelland and Stewart, 1991), 226-27.

16 Michi Nishiura Weglyn mentions the activities of the American Friends Service Committee and of some educators in *Years of Infamy: The Untold Story of America's Concentration Camps* (Seattle: University of Washington Press, 1996). On Norman Thomas' role, see Weglyn, *Years of Infamy;* Richard Drinnon, *Keeper of Concentration Camps: Dillon S. Myer and American Racism* (Berkeley and Los Angeles: University of California Press, 1987); W.A. Swanberg, *Norman Thomas: The Last Idealist* (New York: Charles Scribner's Sons, 1976), 266-70; and Gordon Chang, "'Superman Is About to Visit the Relocation Centers' and the Limits of Wartime Liberalism," *Amerasia Journal* 19, 1 (1993): 37-59. See John Christgau, "Collins versus the World: The Fight to Restore Citizenship to Japanese American Renunciants of World War II," *Pacific Historical Review* 54, 1 (February 1985): 1-31, and Donald E. Collins, *Native American Aliens: Disloyalty and the Renunciation of Citizenship by Japanese Americans during World War II* (Westport, CT: Greenwood Press, 1985), on one lawyer's work. In *Fragile Freedoms: Human Rights and Dissent in Canada*, rev. ed. (Toronto: Irwin, 1982), 106, Thomas R. Berger briefly notes the singular defence

of Japanese Canadians voiced in the House of Commons by Angus MacInnis, a Co-operative Commonwealth Federation MP from British Columbia. Ann Gomer Sunahara briefly refers to the "churches," as well as to a "movement" afoot to protest the sale of the internees' belongings, in "The Wartime Experience of North American Japanese: Some Canadian and American Comparisons" (paper presented at the Canadian Historical Association annual meeting, Montreal, June 1980), 24-25. See also Patricia E. Roy, "The Christian Churches and the Japanese-Canadians during and after World War II," in Ludgard De Decker, ed., *Toward a Just Society: The Interplay of Power and Influence* (Victoria, BC: Centre for Studies in Religion and Society, University of Victoria, 1998), 27-62.

Works that discuss – but minimize – opposition to FDR's policy are Sandra Taylor, "'Fellow-Feelers with the Afflicted': The Christian Churches and the Relocation of the Japanese during World War II," in Roger Daniels et al., eds., *Japanese Americans: From Relocation to Redress*, (Salt Lake City: University of Utah Press, 1986), 123-29, and Cheryl Greenberg, "Black and Jewish Responses to Japanese Internment," *Journal of American Ethnic History* 14 (Winter 1995): 3-37. See also Roger Daniels, *Concentration Camps USA: Japanese Americans and World War II* (New York: Holt Rinehart and Winston, 1972), 78-80, 148-51, and 158-64. On the protest made to the Government of Canada, see Patricia E. Roy et al., eds., *Mutual Hostages: Canadians and Japanese during the Second World War* (Toronto: University of Toronto Press, 1990), 155, 168, 175.

17 Drinnon, *Keeper of Concentration Camps,* 110-11; for a more balanced view, see Peter Irons, *Justice at War: The Story of the Japanese American Internment Cases* (Berkeley: University of California Press, 1983), and Samuel Walker, *In Defense of American Liberties: A History of the ACLU* (New York: Oxford University Press, 1990).

18 Shaffer, "Cracks in the Consensus," 84-85.

19 See, for example, Lester E. Suzuki, *Ministry in the Assembly and Relocation Centers of World War II* (Berkeley: Yardbird, 1979); Taylor, "'Fellow-Feelers with the Afflicted,'" 123-29; Gerald Sittser, *A Cautious Patriotism: The American Churches and the Second World War* (Chapel Hill: University of North Carolina Press, 1997); and Charles R. Lord, "The Response of the Historic Peace Churches to the Internment of the Japanese Americans during World War II" (MA thesis, Associated Mennonite Biblical Seminaries, 1981). No comparable Canadian studies exist, although Ann Gomer Sunahara, *The Politics of Racism: The Uprooting of Japanese Canadians during the Second World War* (Toronto: James Lorimer, 1981), 134, and Ross Lambertson, "Activists in the Age of Rights: The Struggle for Human Rights in Canada – 1945-1960" (PhD diss., University of Victoria, 1997), chap. 6, refer to the concern of Christian church members. See also Roy, "The Christian Churches." For a generalized overview of religious organizations in Canada during the period under study, see George Egerton, "Entering the Age of Human Rights: Religion, Politics, and Canadian Liberalism," *Canadian Historical Review* 85, 3 (September 2004): 451-79.

For biographies and autobiographies of individual members of religious organizations that are useful in this regard, see, for example, Sandra C. Taylor, *Advocate of Understanding: Sidney Gulick and the Search for Peace with Japan* (Kent, OH: Kent State University Press, 1984), and Abraham L. Feinberg, *Storm the Gates of Jericho* (Toronto and Montreal: McClelland and Stewart, 1964).

20 Ellen Eisenberg, "'As Truly American as Your Son': Voicing Opposition to Internment in Three West Coast Cities," *Oregon Historical Quarterly* 104, 4 (Winter 2003): 542-65.

21 On the ACLU and the incarceration, see Thomas McDaid, "The Response of the American Civil Liberties Union to the Japanese-American Internment" (MA thesis, Columbia University, 1969); Peter Irons, *The Courage of Their Convictions* (New York: Free Press, 1988), which includes an examination of the *Hirabayashi* case and the ACLU; Walker, *In Defense of American Liberties*, especially chap. 7; Diane Garey, *Defending Everybody: A History of the American Civil Liberties Union* (New York: TV Books, 1998), especially chap. 8; and Barton Bean, "Pressure for Freedom: The American Civil Liberties Union" (PhD diss., Cornell University, 1955), passim.

Less balanced accounts of the ACLU include William A. Donohue, *The Politics of the American Civil Liberties Union* (New Brunswick, NJ: Transaction Books, 1985), and Daniel

J. Popeo, *Not OUR America: The ACLU Exposed!* (Washington, DC: Washington Legal Foundation, 1989).

Individual accounts of ACLU members include the following: On Roger Baldwin, see, for example, Peggy Lamson, *Roger Baldwin: Founder of the American Civil Liberties Union: A Portrait* (Boston: Houghton Mifflin, 1976), an extremely episodic account based on little original research, probably because of the friction between writer and subject regarding the content of the book. On Norman Thomas, see Swanberg, *Norman Thomas*, 266-70; Chang, "'Superman Is About to Visit the Relocation Centers,'" 37-59; and Murray B. Seidler, *Norman Thomas: Respectable Rebel*, 2nd ed. (Syracuse: Syracuse University Press, 1967). On Arthur Garfield Hays, see Arthur Garfield Hays, *City Lawyer: The Autobiography of a Law Practice* (New York: Simon and Schuster, 1942).

22 Sunahara, *The Politics of Racism*, chap. 7; Forrest E. LaViolette, *The Canadian Japanese and World War II: A Sociological and Psychological Account* (Toronto: University of Toronto Press, 1948), 34-35, 215-25, 249-51, for example; Lambertson, *Repression and Resistance*, chap. 3; Peter Takaji Nunoda, "A Community in Transition and Conflict: The Japanese Canadians, 1935-1951" (PhD diss., University of Manitoba, 1991), chap. 5; Sidney Olyan, "Democracy in Action: A Study of the Co-operative Committee on Japanese Canadians" (MA thesis, University of Toronto School of Social Work, 1951); and Feinberg, *Storm the Gates of Jericho*.

23 Herbert A. Sohn, "Human Rights Policy in Ontario: A Case Study" (PhD diss., University of Toronto, 1975); John Charles Bagnall, "The Ontario Conservatives and the Development of Anti-discrimination Policy, 1944 to 1962" (PhD diss., Queen's University, 1984); Howe, "The Evolution of Human Rights Policy," 783-802, and R. Brian Howe, "Incrementalism and Human Rights Reform," *Journal of Canadian Studies* 28, 3 (Autumn 1993): 29-44.

24 See, for example, J. Petryshyn, "Class Conflict and Civil Liberties: The Origins and Activities of the Canadian Labour Defense League, 1925-1940," *Labour/Le Travail* 10 (Autumn 1982): 39-63; Michiel Horn, "'Free Speech within the Law': The Letter of the Sixty-Eight Toronto Professors, 1931," *Ontario History* 72, 1 (March 1980): 27-48, and Horn, *The League for Social Reconstruction: Intellectual Origins of the Democratic Left in Canada 1930-1942* (Toronto: University of Toronto Press, 1980).

25 Walker, *"Race," Rights and the Law*.

26 Ross Lambertson, "Aroused by Injustice: The Canadian Human Rights Policy Community, 1945-1955" (paper presented at the Canadian Ethnic Studies Conference, Toronto, 24-26 March 2000), and Lambertson, *Repression and Resistance*, chap. 2.

27 Patrias and Frager, "'This Is Our Country,'" 1-35; Stuart Svonkin, *Jews against Prejudice: American Jews and the Fight for Civil Liberties* (New York: Columbia University Press, 1997); and Philip Gleason, *Speaking of Diversity: Language and Ethnicity in Twentieth-Century America* (Baltimore: Johns Hopkins University Press, 1992). See also James W. St. G. Walker, "The 'Jewish Phase' in the Movement for Racial Equality in Canada," *Canadian Ethnic Studies* 34, 1 (2002): especially 6-10, and Ross Lambertson, "'The Dresden Story': Racism, Human Rights, and the Jewish Labour Committee of Canada," *Labour/Le Travail* 47 (Spring 2001): 43-82.

28 Roger Daniels, *Concentration Camps, North America: Japanese in the United States and Canada during World War II* (Malabar, FL: R.E. Krieger, 1981); Daniels, "The Japanese Experience in North America: An Essay in Comparative Racism," *Canadian Ethnic Studies* 9, 2 (1977): 91-100; and Daniels, "The Decision to Relocate the North American Japanese: Another Look," *Pacific Historical Review* 51 (February 1982): 71-77. For another comparative article by Daniels, see "Chinese and Japanese in North America: The Canadian and American Experiences Compared," *Canadian Review of American Studies* 17, 2 (Summer 1986): 173-87. See also Sunahara, "The Wartime Experience of North American Japanese"; Sunahara, "The Japanese American and Japanese Canadian Relocation in World War II: Historical Records and Comparisons," *Canadian Ethnic Studies* 10, 31 (1978): 126-28; and Claudia Frances Ayres Wright, "Legitimation by the Supreme Courts of Canada and the United States: A Case Study of Japanese Exclusion" (PhD diss., Claremont Graduate School, Claremont, CA, 1973).

29 Douglas A. Schmeiser, *Civil Liberties in Canada* (London: Oxford University Press, 1964), 13, and Peter W. Hogg, *Constitutional Law of Canada,* 2nd ed. (Toronto: Carswell, 1985), chap. 28.
30 Freedom of expression takes in the fundamental freedoms of speech, religion, assembly, and association. Voting rights refer to the right to vote and to be a candidate for elected office. Mobility rights address the freedom to enter and leave Canada and to move from one province to another. Legal rights include the right to legal counsel, to remain silent, and to be brought before a magistrate within a reasonable length of time (habeas corpus). Hogg, *Constitutional Law,* chap. 28.
31 Ibid., 454-56.
32 This discussion is based on categories framed by Walter S. Tarnopolsky in *The Canadian Bill of Rights,* 2nd ed. (Toronto: McClelland and Stewart, 1978). Ross Lambertson's work re-examines the differences between "classical" and "modern" egalitarian rights. Lambertson, *Repression and Resistance,* introduction.
33 The original "bill of rights," passed by Congress in 1789, is comprised of the first ten amendments to the US Constitution. Other amendments were subsequently added over the years, the most notable being the Fourteenth Amendment, passed in 1868.
34 Robert O. Matthews and Cranford Pratt, eds., *Human Rights in Canadian Foreign Policy* (Montreal and Kingston: McGill-Queen's University Press, 1988), 5.
35 Ibid., 3-6. The question of whether civil and political rights should take precedence over economic, social, and cultural rights is still manifest today. After the Second World War, the United Nations was unable to reconcile these rights into a single document, so two covenants were created in 1966: the International Covenant on Civil and Political Rights and the International Covenant on Economic, Social, and Cultural Rights.
36 The concept of community has a diverse theoretical background. By community, I mean to suggest a group of individuals or organizations loosely or closely associated because of a common cause. This definition of community is informed by the community action approach, as posited by A. Glen, which focuses on the problems of power and the mobilization of interests. A. Glen, "Methods and Theories in Community Practice," in H. Butcher, A. Glen, P. Henderson, and J. Smith, eds., *Community and Public Policy* (London: Pluto Press, 1993).
37 Roger Daniels, "Words Do Matter: A Note on Inappropriate Terminology and the Incarceration of the Japanese Americans," in Louis Fiset and Gail M. Nomura, eds., *Nikkei in the Pacific Northwest: Japanese Americans and Japanese Canadians in the Twentieth Century* (Seattle and London: University of Washington Press, 2005), 190-214. See also Daniels, "The Forced Migration of West Coast Japanese Americans, 1942-1946: A Quantitative Note," in Daniels et al., eds., *Japanese Americans: From Relocation to Redress,* 72-74.
38 Daniels, "Words Do Matters," in Fiset and Nomura, eds., *Nikkei in the Pacific Northwest,* chap. 9; Tetsuden Kashima, *Judgment without Trial: Japanese American Imprisonment during World War II* (Seattle: University of Washington Press, 2003), 9-10.
39 *Nisei Affairs* 1, 8 (18 March 1946). In *Nisei Affairs* 1, 4 (31 October 1945), a letter to the editor also took issue with the application of the term "repatriation" to Japanese Canadians and challenged the newspaper to use "expatriation" instead.
40 *Nisei Affairs* 1, 8 (18 March 1946).

Chapter 1: A Practicable Coincidence of Policies?
1 For more on the "Yellow Peril" in American history, see Roger Daniels, "The Yellow Peril," in *The Politics of Prejudice: The Anti-Japanese Movement in California and the Struggle for Japanese Exclusion,* 2nd ed. (Berkeley and Los Angeles: University of California Press, 1977), 65-78. For a comparable Canadian treatment, see W. Peter Ward, *White Canada Forever: Popular Attitudes and Public Policy toward Orientals in British Columbia,* 2nd ed. (Montreal and Kingston: McGill-Queen's University Press, 1990), chap. 6; Patricia E. Roy, *A White Man's Province: British Columbia Politicians and Chinese and Japanese Immigrants, 1858-1914* (Vancouver: UBC Press, 1989); and Roy, "British Columbia's Fear of Asians: 1900-1950," *Histoire Sociale/Social History* 13, 25 (May 1980): 161-72. Roy's latest work,

The Oriental Question: Consolidating a White Man's Province, 1914-41 (Vancouver: UBC Press, 2003), examines the attitudes towards Asians during the interwar period.
2 Roger Daniels, "The Japanese Experience in North America: An Essay in Comparative Racism," *Canadian Ethnic Studies* 9, 2 (1977): 91-94.
3 Quoted in ibid., 95. See also Ronald Takaki, *Strangers from a Different Shore: A History of Asian Americans*, rev. ed. (Boston: Back Bay Books, 1998), 203-8.
4 Provincial Voters Act, c. 20.
5 For more on the case, see Andrea Geiger-Adams, "Pioneer Issei: Tomekichi Homma's Fight for the Franchise," *Nikkei Images* 8, 1 (Spring 2003): 1-5, and Geiger-Adams, "Writing Racial Barriers into Law: Upholding B.C.'s Denial of the Vote to Its Japanese Canadian Citizens, *Homma v. Cunningham*, 1902," in Louis Fiset and Gail M. Nomura, eds., *Nikkei in the Pacific Northwest: Japanese Americans and Japanese Canadians in the Twentieth Century* (Seattle and London: University of Washington Press, 2005), 20-43.
6 Olsen quoted in Roger Daniels, *Concentration Camps, North America: Japanese in the United States and Canada during World War II* (Malabar, FL: R.E. Krieger, 1981), 34; Ken Adachi, *The Enemy That Never Was: A History of the Japanese Canadians*, rev. ed. (Toronto: McClelland and Stewart, 1991), 199-202; Ward, *White Canada Forever*, 148-49. For a history of deteriorating diplomatic relations in the interwar period between Japan and Canada, and, by extension, increasingly negative attitudes of Canadians towards Japan and the Japanese, see John D. Meehan, *The Dominion and the Rising Sun: Canada Encounters Japan* (Vancouver: UBC Press, 2004). For a history of US-Japan relations, see Part 1 in R.S. Thompson, *Empires of the Pacific* (New York: Basic Books, 2001).
7 Kaoru Ikeda, "Slocan Diary," in Keibo Oiwa, ed., *Stone Voices: Wartime Writings of Japanese Canadian Issei* (Montreal: Vehicule Press, 1991), 120-21.
8 Canada, *Gazette*, P.C. 365, 16 January 1942 (27 January 1942); P.C. 1486, 24 February 1942 (27 February 1942); "Regulations of Minister of Justice Implementing the Evacuation," 26 February 1942 (7 March 1942).
9 Douglas A. Schmeiser, *Civil Liberties in Canada* (London: Oxford University Press, 1964), 257.
10 Ward, *White Canada Forever*, chap. 8; Adachi, *The Enemy That Never Was*, appendix 2, 424-27; Stephanie D. Bangarth, "Mackenzie King and Japanese Canadians," in John English, Kenneth McLaughlin, and P. Whitney Lackenbauer, eds., *Mackenzie King: Citizenship and Community* (Toronto: Robin Brass Studio Press, 2002), 99-123; Secret correspondence, F.J. Mead to Captain H.R. Stewart, 17 April 1945, LAC, RG 25, vol. 5195; Canada, Department of Labour, *Two Reports on Japanese Canadians in World War II, 1944/1947* (New York: Arno Press, 1978), 17.
   The government's policy of moving the Nikkei away from the west coast had a direct impact on the demographics of Montreal. By 1949, thirteen hundred Japanese Canadians – the largest Japanese community in the francophone world – lived in the city. Greg Robinson, "'Two Other Solitudes': Historical Encounters between Japanese Canadians and French Canadians," (2005), http://www.discovernikkei.org/wiki/index.php/Robinson_Two_Solitudes.
11 The White House turned the telegram over to the State Department, the arm of the government normally designated to communicate with foreigners. Its response by letter was cool: "your desire to cooperate has been carefully noted." Quoted in Daniels, *Concentration Camps, North America*, 40-41; Daniels, "The Japanese Experience in North America," 95-96. Japanese Canadians made similar affirmations of loyalty. See, for example, Thomas Shoyama to King, and K. Rikimaru, Northern BC Residential Fisherman's Association, to King, 12 December 1941, LAC, RG 25, Department of External Affairs Papers, vol. 2942; Vernon and District Japanese Community to King, 9 December 1941, and T. Mitsui to King, 10 December 1941, LAC, MG 26 J1, William Lyon Mackenzie King Papers, 271142, 264101-2. I am indebted to Dr. Patricia E. Roy for these references.
12 Samuel Walker, *In Defense of American Liberties: A History of the ACLU* (New York: Oxford University Press, 1990), 137.
13 Persons of Japanese ancestry living outside the boundaries named in Public Proclamation No. 1, including those on the east coast, were spared the exclusion orders. Although German and Italian aliens were also named in the orders, only individual German and

Italian "enemy aliens" who were deemed a threat were detained. No other American citizens of any ethnic background were treated in such a fashion.

14 United States, War Department, Chief of Staff, *Final Report: Japanese Evacuation from the West Coast, 1942* (Washington, DC: Government Printing, 1943), 34. For more on Alaska's incarcerated population, see Tetsuden Kashima, *Judgment without Trial: Japanese American Imprisonment during World War II* (Seattle: University of Washington Press, 2003), chap. 5. On Roosevelt's anti-Japanese prejudices, see Greg Robinson, *By Order of the President: FDR and the Internment of Japanese Americans* (Cambridge, MA: Harvard University Press, 2001), especially chap. 3. On 10 August 1936, Roosevelt wrote a memorandum to the chief of naval operations: "One obvious thought occurs to me – that every Japanese citizen or non-citizen on the island of Oahu who meets these Japanese ships [visiting Japanese merchant ships] or has any connection with their officers or men should be secretly but definitely identified and his or her name placed on a special list of those who would be the first to be placed in a concentration camp in the event of trouble." Quoted in Peter Irons, *Justice at War: The Story of the Japanese American Internment Cases* (Berkeley: University of California Press, 1983), 20.

15 The term is from Kashima, *Judgment without Trial,* 67. Chapter 4 of Kashima's work deals with the Hawaiian case study. For more on the history of the Hawaiian Nikkei, see the extensive work by Gary Y. Okihiro, *Cane Fires: The Anti-Japanese Movement in Hawaii, 1865-1945* (Philadelphia: Temple University Press, 1991).

16 Kashima, *Judgment without Trial,* 172-73; "The Nisei in Hawaii," *Pacific Citizen* 18, 13 (22 April 1944).

17 *Pacific Citizen* 18, 13 (22 April 1944).

18 Okihiro, *Cane Fires,* chaps. 9-11; Robinson, *By Order of the President,* chap. 4, especially 156; Kashima, *Judgment without Trial,* chap. 4.

19 Okihiro, *Cane Fires,* chap. 11; Robinson, *By Order of the President,* 155-56; Kashima, *Judgment without Trial,* 86-87.

20 Daniels, *Concentration Camps, North America,* 83-87.

21 Canada, Order-in-Council P.C. 1665, 4 March 1942, s. 11(1), 169.

22 Adachi, *The Enemy That Never Was,* 324.

23 Quoted in United States, Commission on Wartime Relocation and Internment of Civilians, *Personal Justice Denied: Report of the Commission on Wartime Relocation and Internment of Civilians,* rev. ed. (Seattle: University of Washington Press, 1997), 132.

24 Takaki, *Strangers from a Different Shore,* 392-93; Gabrielle Nishiguchi, "Innocence Lost: The Wartime Experience of Japanese-Canadian Children," *Archivist* 121 (2003): 9-13; Hugh Brogan, *The Pelican History of the United States of America* (London: Longman Group, 1985), 586; Muriel Kitagawa, *This Is My Own: Letters to Wes and Other Writings on Japanese Canadians, 1941-1948,* ed. Roy Miki (Vancouver: Talonbooks, 1985), 92.

25 Adachi, *The Enemy That Never Was,* 238-39.

26 Daniels, *Concentration Camps, North America,* 88-90.

27 Canada, House of Commons, *Debates* (4 August 1944), 5916; Press Conference 982, 21 November 1944, Princeton University, Seeley G. Mudd Manuscript Library, American Civil Liberties Union Papers, vol. 2444. As Greg Robinson notes, Roosevelt long had an interest in dispersing minority populations. In 1920, for example, as Democratic candidate for vice-president, he stated, "We have permitted the foreign elements to segregate in colonies. They have crowded into one district and they have brought congestion and racial prejudices to our large cities. The result is that they do not easily conform to the manners and the customs and the requirements of their new home. Now, the remedy for this should be the distribution of aliens in various parts of the country." Quoted in Robinson, *By Order of the President,* 236.

28 "Repatriation" was the term used by the government of the day. In fact, most Japanese resident in Canada were not born in Japan; nor had they ever lived in that country. The official terminology, therefore, was inaccurate and an interesting reflection of the misconceptions held by government officials across Canada, indicative of the stubborn link between "race" and loyalty.

29 Adachi,. *The Enemy That Never Was,* 301, 309; "Throwaway Citizens," *The Fifth Estate,* CBC, 24 October 1995.

30 British Columbia Security Commission, "Report on the Removal of Japanese from Protected Areas, March 4, 1942 to October 31, 1942" (1942), 11ff. For more on the experiences of those who participated in provincial work programs, see, for Alberta, David Iwaasa, "Canadian Japanese in Southern Alberta, 1905-1945," in Roger Daniels, ed., *Two Monographs on Japanese Canadians* (New York: Aldo Press, 1979), 99-155, and David J. Goa, "Redeeming the War on the Home Front: Alberta's Japanese Community during the Second World War and After," in K.W. Tingley, ed., *For King and Country: Alberta in the Second World War* (Edmonton: Provincial Museum of Alberta, 1995), 313-26. For Ontario, see Stephanie D. Bangarth, "The Long, Wet Summer of 1942: The Ontario Farm Service Force, Small-Town Ontario and the Nisei," *Canadian Ethnic Studies* 37, 1 (2005): 40-62, and Yon Shimizu, *The Exiles: An Archival History of the World War II Japanese Road Camps in British Columbia and Ontario* (Wallaceburg, ON: Shimizu Consulting and Publishing, 1993).

31 Major General Henry C. Pratt, head of the Western Defense Command, made the announcement, which was published in the *New York Times* on 17 December 1945. For more on the *Endo* case, see Irons, *Justice at War,* 307-10, 317-19, 323-25, and 341-45, as well as chap. 5 of this book.

32 Okihiro, *Cane Fires,* 250-52; Daniels, *Concentration Camps, North America,* 112-14; Robinson, *By Order of the President,* 172.

33 Quoted in Daniels, *Concentration Camps, North America,* 112-13.

34 *New Canadian,* 23 January 1943, 28 August 1943, 23 September 1944; Patricia E. Roy, "The Soldiers Canada Didn't Want: Her Chinese and Japanese Citizens," *Canadian Historical Review* 59, 3 (September 1978): 341-58.

35 Canada, House of Commons, *Debates* (15 July 1944), 5025.

36 J.W. Noseworthy, MP, to Rev. A.E. Armstrong, 12 July 1944, UCC, Board of Overseas Missions, box 10, file 368.

37 Canada, *Statutory Orders and Regulations, 1945,* v. 4, P.C. 7355, P.C. 7356, P.C. 7357, 15 December 1945. The War Measures Act, which dates to the First World War, was passed on 22 August 1914. It gave the federal government full authority to do everything deemed necessary "for the security, defense, peace, order, and welfare of Canada," including governing by decree, when it perceived the existence of "war, invasion or insurrection, real or apprehended." It was repealed in 1988.

38 On historic racist animus among high-ranking Canadian politicians, including Prime Minister William Lyon Mackenzie King, see Bangarth, "Mackenzie King and Japanese Canadians," 99-123.

39 Roger Daniels, "The Decision to Relocate the North American Japanese: Another Look," *Pacific Historical Review* 51 (February 1982): 77.

40 Ibid., 73. The Permanent Joint Board of Defense, comprised of both Canadian and American officials largely of military background, had a civilian chairman and a secretary from each country. It was established as the outcome of meetings between President Roosevelt and Prime Minister King at Ogdensburg, New York, on 17-18 August 1940.

41 Memorandum of a meeting of the Permanent Joint Board of Defense, 10-11 November 1941, LAC, MG 26 J4, vol. 320.

42 Gordon to Wrong, 5 February 1942, LAC, RG 25, series A-3-b, vol. 2798, file 773-B-1-40; Daniels, "The Decision to Relocate the North American Japanese," 75.

43 Even as war and incarceration were well under way, some American officials remained quite unaware of actions taken north of the 49th parallel. Asked during a congressional hearing if he knew of relocation programs in other countries, WRA director Dillon Myer replied, "I don't think there is any country doing what we are doing." US Senate, Subcommittee of Committee on Military Affairs, *Hearings on S444, Jan. 20, 1943* (Washington, DC: Government Printing Office, 1943), 45, quoted in Robinson, *By Order of the President,* 282n49.

44 Robinson, *By Order of the President,* 114; Michi Nishiura Weglyn, *Years of Infamy: The Untold Story of America's Concentration Camps,* rev. ed. (Seattle: University of Washington

Press, 1996), 191n; "Memorandum on Progress with Relation to the Japanese Problem in British Columbia," n.d. (January 1942?), prepared by the Department of External Affairs, LAC, RG 25, vol. 2798, file 3464-B-40, pt. 1

45 Secret memo for the prime minister, 20 August 1943, LAC, MG 26 J4, vol. 283, file 2965.

46 United States, *Congressional Record,* 78th Cong., 1st Sess. (14 September 1943), 7521-22.

47 "Memorandum for Dr. Keenleyside," 12 October 1943, LAC, RG 25, series G-2, vol. 3004, file 3464-B-40C, #2, pt. 2.

48 "Secret Memo from Mr. Clark, US Embassy," 23 October 1944, LAC, MG 26 J4, vol. 361, file 3850; Breckenridge Long, Asst. Secretary of State, 17 December 1943, cited in Weglyn, *Years of Infamy,* 190-91.

49 L.B. Pearson to secretary of state for external affairs, 10 May 1944, LAC, RG 25, vol. 5761, file 104(S) [part 1-1]; N. Robertson, "Memorandum for the Prime Minister: Position of the Japanese in Canada," 13 June 1944, LAC, MG 26 J4, reel H1536; N. Robertson, "Memorandum for the Prime Minister," 22 June 1944, LAC, MG 26 J4, reel H1536; Hugh L. Keenleyside, "Memorandum for the Under-Secretary," 15 August 1944, with attached memorandum, Miss Bridge, "The Treatment of Persons of Japanese Racial Origin in the United States since Pearl Harbour," 15 August 1944, LAC, RG 25, file 3464-B-402.

50 Canada, House of Commons, *Debates* (4 August 1944), 5915-18.

51 Ibid.

52 R.G. Robertson to L.B. Pearson, confidential, 30 March 1945, LAC, RG 25, series G-2, vol. 3004, file 3464-B-40C #3, file 3464-B-40C, pt.3; Memo for Mr. Baldwin, 30 October 1945, LAC, RG 2, Privy Council Office Records, series B-2, vol. 84, file J-25-1, 1945.

53 Donald E. Collins, *Native American Aliens: Disloyalty and the Renunciation of Citizenship by Japanese Americans during World War II* (Westport, CT: Greenwood Press, 1985), 123-33; Daniels, *Concentration Camps, North America,* chap. 6 passim, 166; Kashima, *Judgment without Trial,* 168-72.

54 Collins, *Native American Aliens,* 132-33. Readers who wish to know more about the renunciants should view Satsuki Ina's film *From a Silk Cocoon* (Hesono O Productions, 2005), a true story based on a series of letters exchanged between a young Japanese American couple, Itaru and Shizuko Ina. Separated in the incarceration camps, they renounced their citizenship and were deported to Japan.

55 Canadian reaction to the decision to incarcerate persons of Japanese ancestry will be discussed in greater detail in Chapters 3 and 4.

56 For more on the situation of civil libertarians and civil liberties groups prior to and immediately following the outbreak of the Second World War, see Ross Lambertson, *Repression and Resistance: Canadian Human Rights Activists, 1930-1960* (Toronto: University of Toronto Press, 2005), chaps. 1 and 2, and Laurence Hannant, *The Infernal Machine: Investigating the Loyalty of Canada's Citizens* (Toronto: University of Toronto Press, 1995). See also Suzanne Skebo, "Liberty and Authority: Civil Liberties in Toronto, 1929-1935" (MA thesis, University of British Columbia, 1968), for a discussion of civil liberties and interested organizations in the period prior to the war.

57 *Race Relations: A Monthly Summary of Events and Trends* (Negro Universities Press, New York) 2, 7 (February 1945): 197-98. See also Carol Anderson, *Eyes off the Prize: The United Nations and the African American Struggle for Human Rights, 1944-1955* (Cambridge: Oxford University Press, 2003).

58 Ruth Benedict, *Race: Science and Politics* (New York: Modern Age Books, 1940); Gunnar Dahlberg, *Race, Reason and Rubbish* (London: G. Allen and Unwin, 1942); and Ashley Montagu, *Man's Most Dangerous Myth: The Fallacy of Race,* 4th ed. (Cleveland: World Publishing, 1964).

59 Benedict, *Race: Science and Politics,,* 179-80.

60 House of Commons, *Debates* (17 July 1944), 4925-26.

61 *Vancouver Sun,* 1 May 1943, quoted in Kay J. Anderson, *Vancouver's Chinatown: Racial Discourse in Canada, 1875-1980* (Montreal and Kingston: McGill-Queen's University Press, 1991), 90.

62 Ross Lambertson, "Aroused by Injustice: The Canadian Human Rights Policy Community,

1945-1955" (paper presented at the Canadian Ethnic Studies Conference, Toronto, 24-26 March 2000), 6.

63 Quoted in ibid., 9.

64 Quoted in Lambertson, "Aroused by Injustice," 10-11.

65 Charter of the United Nations, 26 June 1945, Can. T.S. 1945 No. 7, preamble and art. 1.

66 J.S. Woodsworth, "Besco," *Canadian Forum*, March 1924; Kenneth McNaught, *A Prophet in Politics: A Biography of J.S. Woodsworth* (Toronto: University of Toronto Press, 1959), 125-35, especially 126; Robinson quoted in Judith Fingard, "From Sea to Rail: Black Transportation Workers and Their Families in Halifax, c. 1870-1916," *Acadiensis* 24, 2 (Spring 1995): 58. I am indebted to a generous and collegial anonymous peer reviewer supplied by UBC Press for these references.

67 As Arnold Bruner notes, Canada's Jewish Labour Committee "looked south" to the "fair practices" policy and legislative enactments passed by several American states from 1945 to 1949. These provided the committee with an effective working model to use in applying pressure for law reform that would resolve or minimize the effects on Jews of discrimination in employment, services, housing, business, professions, and higher education. Arnold Bruner, "The Genesis of Ontario's Human Rights Legislation: A Study in Law Reform," *University of Toronto Faculty of Law Review* 37, 236 (1979): 237.

Chapter 2: The CCJC and the ACLU

1 Ross Lambertson, "Activists in the Age of Rights: The Struggle for Human Rights in Canada – 1945-1960" (PhD diss., University of Victoria, 1997), 44-45.

2 Edith Fowke, *They Made Democracy Work: The Story of the Co-operative Committee on Japanese Canadians* (Toronto: Co-operative Committee on Japanese Canadians, 1951), 75. This item may be found in McMaster University Archives, Co-operative Committee on Japanese Canadians Papers [CCJC-MAC], file 12, and in Library and Archives Canada [LAC], MG 28, series 4, vol. 2, file 13; "A Record of the Work of the Cooperative Committee on Japanese Canadians," 1, LAC, MG 28 V2, series 1, 14, file 4. This document may also be found in CCJC-MAC, folder 12.

3 Co-operative Committee on Japanese Canadian Arrivals in Toronto, Minutes, 8 June 1943, 1, LAC, MG 28 V2, series 1, 14, file 1, pt. 2 of 2.

4 Ann Gomer Sunahara, *The Politics of Racism: The Uprooting of Japanese Canadians during the Second World War* (Toronto: James Lorimer, 1981), 131-32. For more on the assimilationist stance of Canadian and American Nisei, see Chapter 4 of this book.

5 Co-operative Committee on Japanese Canadian Arrivals in Toronto, Minutes, 8 June 1943, 1-2, LAC, MG 28 VI, series 1, 14, file 1, pt. 2 of 2. The committee noted that a "colony" of Japanese Canadians had already formed around the McCaul Street area in Toronto. Ernest Trueman issued a statement to the effect that the settlement must be dispersed, presumably with the help of the CCJC-AT.

6 Co-operative Committee on Japanese Canadian Arrivals in Toronto, Minutes, 8 June 1943, 2, LAC, MG 28 V1, series 1, 14, file 1, pt. 2 of 2; "A Record of the Work of the Cooperative Committee on Japanese Canadians," 1, LAC, MG 28 V2, series 1, 14, file 4, n.d.

7 The JCCD worked with the CCJC until 1947, when it was dissolved and its members joined the Toronto chapter of the Japanese Canadian Citizens Association (JCCA). This later became the National Japanese Canadian Citizens Association (NJCCA). The JCCA and the NJCCA will be discussed in Chapter 5. Jarnail Singh, "Wartime Toronto and Japanese Canadians," *Polyphony* 6, 1 (Summer 1984): 199-200. Singh's article was based on an interview by Gerry Shikatani with George Tanaka. I would like to thank P. Whitney Lackenbauer for this reference.

8 Quoted in LAC, MG 26 J1, Vol. 354, reel C7048, VCC to W.L.M. King, 29 May 1944. The Vancouver Consultative Council was founded to examine issues concerning Canadian citizenship. It will be discussed in greater detail in Chapter 3.

9 "A Record of the Work of the Cooperative Committee on Japanese Canadians," 1-2, LAC, MG 28, series 1, 14, vol. 2; Fowke, *They Made Democracy Work*, 7-8, LAC, MG 28, vol. 2, file 13; "Draft of Statement to Claimants from the Co-operative Committee," 1, CCJC-MAC,

folder 13; Norman F. Black, *A Challenge to Patriotism and Statesmanship* (Toronto: The Christian Social Council of Canada, July 1944), CCJC-MAC, folder 17. The full text of Black's discussion appeared in *Saturday Night*, 5 February 1944.

10 Canada, Order-in-Council P.C. 1457, 24 February 1942. Only those requests to purchase property initiated before February 1942 were approved. The Justice Department denied all other requests made between 1942 and 1944. See LAC, RG 27, Department of Labour, Japanese Division, vol. 642, file 23-2-12-1.

11 "A Record of the Work of the Cooperative Committee on Japanese Canadians," 2-3, LAC, MG 28 V2, series 1, 14, file 4; Fowke, *They Made Democracy Work*, 7, LAC, MG 28, vol. 2, file 13; CCJC, "Minutes, 1944," 25 May 1944, CCJC-MAC, folder 3.

12 "A Record of the Work of the Cooperative Committee on Japanese Canadians," 3, LAC, MG 28, series 1, 14, vol. 2, file 4; Fowke, *They Made Democracy Work*, 8.

13 "A Record of the Work of the Cooperative Committee on Japanese Canadians," 3, LAC, MG 28, series 1, 14, vol. 2, file 4; Fowke, *They Made Democracy Work*, 9; Canada, House of Commons, *Debates* (4 August 1944), 5917.

14 MG 28, "A Record of the Work of the Cooperative Committee on Japanese Canadians," 3, LAC, MG 28, series 1, 14, vol. 2, file 4; CCJC, "Correspondence and Minutes, 1943-56," LAC, MG 28, vol. 1, file 1, pt. 2 of 2; "Brief" submitted by Japanese Canadian Committee for Democracy in the interests of Canadians of Japanese origin in Canada, 24 June 1944, LAC, MG 28, vol. 1, series 1, file 3, pt. 2 of 2. Chapter 3 will provide more specific information on the campaign of religious organizations against disfranchisement.

15 Fowke, *They Made Democracy Work*, 10; "The Plight of Japanese-Canadians," *Toronto Daily Star*, 7 August 1945; Sunahara, *The Politics of Racism*, 123. For very good discussions of why many Japanese Canadians chose to move to Japan, see Sunahara, *The Politics of Racism*, 119-23, and Lemon Creek Japanese to Mrs. Hugh MacMillan, 29 October 1945, CCJC, "Correspondence and Minutes," LAC, MG 28, vol. 1, file 1, series 1, pt. 2 of 2.

16 Fowke, *They Made Democracy Work*, 11-12; "Notices of Enlarged Meetings," 22 May 1945, 19 June 1945, LAC, MG 28, vol. 1, file 1, series 1 pt. 2 of 2; Muriel Kitagawa, *This Is My Own: Letters to Wes and Other Writings on Japanese Canadians, 1941-1948*, ed. Roy Miki (Vancouver: Talonbooks, 1985), 212-13; Muriel Kitagawa, "Farewell to a Friend – Olive Pannell," *Nisei Affairs* 1, 7 (February 1946).

17 *Nisei Affairs* 1, 2 (28 August 1945); Kitagawa, *This Is My Own*, 210. The descriptive sentence about Robertson, from N.F. Dreisziger, is partly attributed therein to J.L. Granatstein. See N.F. Dreisziger, "7 December 1941: A Turning Point in Canadian Wartime Policy toward Enemy Ethnic Groups?" *Journal of Canadian Studies* 32, 1 (Spring 1997): 97. In relation to the DOCR and the federal government's policies regarding immigrants from enemy lands, Dreisziger has noted that "Fate had prepared Robertson for an important role in this process by giving him a humanistic upbringing and a pivotal position in wartime Ottawa." Dreisziger, "7 December 1941," 93. Paula Draper sees a "progressive public servant" in Robertson, in relation to federal policy on Jewish immigration. Paula Jean Draper, "Fragmented Loyalties: Canadian Jewry, the King Government and the Refugee Dilemma," in Norman Hillmer, Bohdan Kordan, and Lubomyr Luciuk, eds., *On Guard for Thee: War, Ethnicity and the Canadian State, 1939-1945* (Kingston, ON: Canadian Committee for the History of the Second World War, 1988), 167.

18 "Report on Delegation to Ottawa," 30 July 1945, LAC, MG 28 V7, Japanese Canadian Committee on Democracy (JCCD), JCCD Papers; Fowke, *They Made Democracy Work*, 12.

19 "What Is the Cooperative Committee?" n.d., CCJC-MAC, folder 11.

20 "Brief. Re: Repatriation of Japanese Canadians," 25 July 1945, CCJC-MAC, folder 12.

21 Ibid.

22 The Anti-Defamation League (ADL) has as its mission the cessation of defamation of the Jewish people.

23 Roger Nash Baldwin, *Memorandum on the Origins of the ACLU* (New York: American Civil Liberties Union, 1973), 1-3, Columbia University, Butler Library [BLCU]; Charles Lam Markmann, *The Noblest Cry* (New York: St. Martin's Press, 1965), 15-18.

24 Roger Nash Baldwin, "Presenting the American Civil Liberties Union: What Are Its

Principles? How Does It Work? Where Does It Get Its Money? Who Controls Its Policies?" April 1945, 1-2, BLCU (New York: The Union, 1945).

25 Flynn was ultimately vindicated when the anti-totalitarian resolution was abolished in
1968. Her supporters in the 1940 struggle won her posthumous reinstatement to the
board in 1976. ACLU board of directors, Minutes, 8 June 1964, 20-21 April 1974, 10-11
April 1976, Princeton University, Seeley G. Mudd Manuscript Library [Mudd Library],
American Civil Liberties Union [ACLU] Papers, boxes 35, 108, 114; Corliss Lamont Interview, BLCU, Oral History Collection.

26 Quoted in Diane Garey, *Defending Everybody: A History of the American Civil Liberties Union*
(New York: TV Books, 1998), 115-16.

27 *ACLU Weekly Bulletin*, 25 January 1941, Mudd Library, ACLU Papers, vol. 2256.

28 Ben Huebsch interview, Reminiscences of Ben W. Huebsch, BLCU, Oral History Collection; "Memo on Attitudes for Peggy," 1973, Mudd Library, MC 082, Peggy Lamson Collection on Roger Baldwin, box 1, folder 1.

29 Baldwin, *Presenting the American Civil Liberties Union*, 10-11, BLCU; Barton Bean, "Pressure for Freedom: The American Civil Liberties Union" (PhD diss., Cornell University,
1955), 165n19; Reminiscences of Roger Nash Baldwin, interview by Dr. Harlan Phillips,
November-December 1953, January 1954, 131-38, BLCU, Oral History Collection; "Liberal Lawyers List," September 1942, Mudd Library, MC 072, Arthur Garfield Hays Papers,
box 10, folder 3.

30 Baldwin, *Presenting the American Civil Liberties Union*, 10-11.

31 Samuel Walker, *In Defense of American Liberties: A History of the ACLU* (New York: Oxford
University Press, 1990), 68-69.

32 See Chapter 3 for a discussion of the reportage in the *New Republic* and the *Nation* over
the course of 1942. Quotes taken from Executive Order 9066.

33 Japanese American Citizens League, *Bulletin 142*, 7 April 1942, Mudd Library, ACLU
Papers, vol. 2394, 62. In the early days of March 1942, the Southern California branch
of the ACLU tried fruitlessly to find a Japanese American "guinea pig" who would launch
a court case. Clinton J. Taft to Baldwin, 4 March 1942 and 17 April 1942, Mudd Library,
ACLU Papers, vol. 2406. The reaction of the JACL to the relocation orders and its subsequent lobbying efforts later in the war will be examined in Chapter 4.

34 The nature of the cooperation between the ACLU and the JACL will be detailed in Chapter 4.

35 Arthur Garfield Hays to Morris Ernst, 5 January 1942, Mudd Library, box 10; "A Report
on American Democratic Liberties in War-time, June 1942: The Bill of Rights in War,"
June 1942, Mudd Library, ACLU Papers, box 1879, folder 16.

36 ACLU press release, 1 March 1942, 5 March 1942, Mudd Library, ACLU Papers, box 1915,
folder 6.

37 ACLU press release, 23 March 1942, Mudd Library, ACLU Papers, box 1915, folder 6.

38 ACLU board of directors, Minutes, 2 March 1942, Mudd Library, ACLU Papers, vol. 2363.

39 Roger Baldwin, John Haynes Holmes, Aylwyn Ross et al., to Roosevelt, 20 March 1942,
Mudd Library, ACLU Papers, vol. 2363.

40 Osmond K. Fraenkel diary, 30 April 1942, 25 June 1942, Mudd Library, MC 192, Osmond
K. Fraenkel Diary Excerpts, box 1, folder 1. Fraenkel's diary entry of 25 June 1942 indi-
cates his belief that some group removal was justified in the case of "Japs recently in
Japan, or who, though born here, ever claimed Japanese citizenship."

41 Meiklejohn to Baldwin, 17 March 1942, Mudd Library, ACLU Papers, vol. 2363; Morris
Ernst to Baldwin, 19 March 1942, Mudd Library, ACLU Papers, vol. 2363; Walker, *In
Defense of American Liberties*, 139; Peter Irons, *Justice at War: The Story of the Japanese
American Internment Cases* (Berkeley: University of California Press, 1983), 128. For more
on how American intellectuals confronted Stalinism in the 1940s, see William L. O'Neill,
A Better World: The Great Schism: Stalinism and the American Intellectuals (New York: Simon
and Schuster, 1983).

42 For examples, all in Mudd Library, ACLU Papers, vol. 2363, see Ernest Besig to Baldwin,
with enclosure, 9 March 1942; Stephen Vincent Benet to ACLU, 14 March 1942; Frida

Kirchway to Baldwin, 18 March 1942; and John P. Marquand to Baldwin, 14 March 1942. Several letters, both pro and con, can be found in vol. 2363.
43 Meiklejohn to Baldwin, 17 March 1942, Mudd Library, ACLU Papers, vol. 2363.
44 Walker, *In Defense of American Liberties,* 139-140. I make no claim to originality in applying the term "Cassandra" to Norman Thomas. For that, see Greg Robinson, "Norman Thomas and the Struggle against Internment," *Prospects 28* (2003): 2.
45 Hays to Percy Fridenberg, 29 June 1942, Mudd Library, MC 072, box 10.
46 Release for editorial comment, 25 November 1942, Mudd Library, ACLU Papers, box 1915, folder 6.
47 "Evacuation of Citizens, Aliens of Japanese Extraction," *Pacific Citizen* 15, 8 (23 July 1942).
48 Reminiscences of Roger Nash Baldwin, interview by Dr. Harlan Phillips, November-December 1953, January 1954, 187ff, BLCU, Oral History Collection.
49 This description is from Walker, *In Defense of American Liberties,* 140.
50 "To the Active Members of the Corporation," 22 May 1942, emphasis added, Mudd Library, ACLU Papers, vol. 2394. Also in Mudd Library, MC 072, box 10, folder 2. For a detailed discussion of the voting decisions of many ACLU members, see Thomas McDaid, "The Response of the American Civil Liberties Union to the Japanese American Internment" (MA thesis, Columbia University, 1969).
51 "To the Active Members of the Corporation," 22 May 1942, Mudd Library, ACLU Papers, vol. 2394.
52 Thomas to John Haynes Holmes, 11 March 1942, Princeton University, Firestone Library, Norman Thomas Papers [Firestone Library, NT Papers], microfilm reel 56, file 2:B:1; Holmes to Thomas, 12 March 1942, Firestone Library, NT Papers, microfilm reel 56, file 2:B:1. Thomas to Albert Hamilton, 20 March 1942, Firestone Library, NT Papers, microfilm reel 56, file 2:B:1. Holmes also noted in his letter that he had lost many Jewish friends on this issue and had practically ceased his lecturing for Jewish synagogues and centres.
53 "To the Members of the Board of Directors," 19 June 1942, Mudd Library, MC 072, box 10, folder 2.
54 Walker, *In Defense of American Liberties,* 406n19.
55 ACLU board of directors, Minutes, 25 May 1942, Mudd Library, ACLU Papers, vol. 2363; "To the Members of the National Committee and the Board of Directors," 27 May 1942, Mudd Library, MC 072, box 10, folder 2; Fraenkel diary, 4 May 1942, Mudd Library, MC 192.
56 Roger Baldwin to Alexander Meiklejohn, 30 June 1942, Mudd Library, ACLU Papers, box 1055; "Evacuations Product of Hysteria, Says Lawyer," *San Francisco News,* 22 November 1944, Mudd Library, ACLU Papers, vol. 2599; "Democracy and Japanese Americans," 1942, Mudd Library, Undergraduate Alumni Records, Norman Thomas, Class of 1905.
57 Thomas to John Haynes Holmes, 14 November 1942, Firestone Library, Norman Thomas (NT) Papers, microfilm reel 56, file 2:B:1. The advocacy positions assumed by other groups in Canada and the US with respect to the relocation will be examined in fuller detail in Chapter 3.
58 See the following, all in Firestone Library, NT Papers, microfilm reel 56, file 2:B:1: Thomas to Ernest Besig, 8 July 1942; Mary Farquharson to Thomas, 13 July 1942; Thomas to Farquharson, 11 August 1942; John Haynes Holmes to Thomas, 13 November 1942; Besig to Thomas, 17 November 1942; and Thomas to Besig, 21 November 1942. See also Robinson, "Norman Thomas and the Struggle against Internment," 10-12. I am grateful to Dr. Robinson for sharing this work with me.
   Two years later, writing to Baldwin on Post War World Council letterhead, Thomas was still vexed with the ACLU's "flip-flop" regarding the letter to Roosevelt, arguing that it caused confusion among opponents of relocation and "logically weakened the presentation of the case to the courts." Thomas to Baldwin, 18 March 1944, Mudd Library, ACLU Papers, vol. 2588.
59 John Haynes Holmes to Thomas, 13 November 1942, Firestone Library, NT Papers, microfilm reel 56, file 2:B:1.
60 ACLU board of directors, Minutes, 22 June 1942, Mudd Library, ACLU Papers, vol. 2356;

John Nevin Sayre to Mary Farquharson, 6 July 1942, Firestone Library, NT Papers, microfilm reel 56, file 2:B:1.

61 Farquharson to Baldwin, 24 June 1942, Mudd Library, ACLU Papers, vol. 2740.

62 Board of directors, Minutes of the Northern California Civil Liberties Union, 2 July 1942, Mudd Library, ACLU Papers, vol. 2356.

63 Besig to Clifford Forster, 10 July 1942, Mudd Library, ACLU Papers, vol. 2397. Most of the ACLU-NCCLU correspondence can be found in vol. 2356.

64 ACLU-NCCLU, board of directors meeting, Minutes, 21 December 1942, Mudd Library, ACLU Papers, vol. 2356.

65 Walker, *In Defense of American Liberties,* 141-42.

66 Baldwin to DeWitt, 3 November 1942, Mudd Library, ACLU Papers, vol. 2444; ACLU, board of directors, Minutes, 9 November 1942, Mudd Library, ACLU Papers, vol. 2444; 7 November 1942, Firestone Library, NT Papers, microfilm reel 56, file 2:B:1. In a recent PBS documentary on the *Korematsu* case, lawyer and scholar Peter alleged that, because the national board was friendly with the Roosevelt administration, Baldwin did not want to be perceived as "soft." "Of Civil Wrongs and Rights: The Fred Korematsu Story," *P.O.V.,* PBS, 11 July 2001. This tape was kindly loaned to me by Professor Emeritus Robert W. Babcock of the University of Maine.

67 The term was coined in Eugene V. Rostow, "The Japanese-American Cases – A Disaster," *Yale Law Journal* 54 (June 1945): 489-533.

68 Forster to Wirin, 6 January 1944, Mudd Library, ACLU Papers, vol. 2585.

69 *Korematsu v. United States,* 323 U.S. 214 (1944); *Hirabayashi v. United States,* 320 U.S. 81 (1943); *Yasui v. United States,* 320 U.S. 115 (1943); *Ex Parte Endo,* 323 U.S. 283 (1944).

70 CCJC to members of Parliament, 7 September 1945, LAC, MG 28, series 1, vol. 2, file 9, pt. 2 of 2. Numerous letters and petitions protesting the government's actions can be found in LAC, RG 25, Department of External Affairs Records, series G-2, vol. 3554, file 773-B-1-40, pt. 4.

71 "RE Treatment of Japanese Persons in Canada," 9 October 1945, LAC, MG 31 E87, R.G. Robertson Papers, vol. 1, file 12; R.L. Gabrielle Nishiguchi, "'Reducing the Numbers': The 'Transportation' of the Canadian Japanese (1941-1947)" (MA thesis, Carleton University, 1993), 115-16; Stephanie Bangarth, "The Long, Wet Summer of 1942: The Ontario Farm Service Force, Small-Town Ontario, and the Nisei," *Canadian Ethnic Studies* 37, 1 (2005): 45-46.

72 Lambertson, "Activists in the Age of Rights," 66.

73 Canada, House of Commons, *Debates* (21 November 1945), 2375-76, and (22 November 1945), 2405; CCJC to King, 24 November 1945, LAC, MG 26 J1, William Lyon Mackenzie King Papers,; Edith Fowke, *They Made Democracy Work,* 14-17.

74 For letters and petitions protesting the actions of the government, see LAC, RG 25, series G-2, vol. 3554, file 773-B-1-40, pt. 4; Memo, R. Gordon Robertson to the prime minister, 17 September 1945, LAC, MG 26 J1, vol. 387; Memo, R. Gordon Robertson to Norman Robertson, 6 December 1945, LAC, MG 26 J1, vol. 387; Memo, R. Gordon Robertson to Mr. Wrong, 24 October 1945, LAC, MG 26 J1, vol. 387. On Bill 20, see Canada, House of Commons, *Debates* (22 October 1945), 1335 (first reading). Martin's comments were made during the second reading of the bill, on 6 April 1946. The Canadian Citizenship Act was passed in 1946 and took effect on 1 January 1947. Prime Minister William Lyon Mackenzie King has the honour of being Canada's first citizen.

75 "A Record of the Work of the Cooperative Committee on Japanese Canadians," 8, CCJC-MAC, folder 16; Ken Adachi, *The Enemy That Never Was: A History of the Japanese Canadians,* rev. ed. (Toronto: McClelland and Stewart, 1991), 304-6.

76 Orders-in-Council P.C. 7355, P.C. 7356, P.C. 7357, 15 December 1945.

77 CCJC, Minutes, 10 November 1945, CCJC-MAC, folder 4; Minutes, 8 January 1946, LAC, MG 28 V1, series 1, 14, file 1, pt. 2 of 2.

78 Feinberg, a very visible human rights activist in the post-war period, also played an important role in the repeal of the 1923 Chinese Immigration Act and was central to the creation of anti-discrimination legislation in Ontario. Abraham L. Feinberg, *Storm the Gates*

of Jericho (Toronto and Montreal: McClelland and Stewart, 1964). Wilson and Feinburg quoted in "Mass Meeting Unit [sic] in Opposing Japanese Ousting," *Toronto Globe and Mail,* 11 January 1946.

79 "Programme," 10 January 1946, LAC, MG 28, vol. 1, series 1, file 1, pt. 2 of 2; "Permit," Jarvis Collegiate School, 10 January 1946, LAC, MG 28, vol. 1, file 1; Resolution, 10 January 1946, LAC, MG 28, vol. 1, series 1, file 1, pt. 2 of 2; "Committee Acts to Remove Ban on Entries into Toronto" and "Avoid Concentration Says Supervisor," *New Canadian,* 16 February 1946, LAC, MG 28, vol. 1, series 1, file 1, pt. 2 of 2.

80 "Former Captive Raises Lone Voice on Jap Issue," *Toronto Globe and Mail,* 25 February 1946. The lone dissenter was a member of the Royal Rifles of Canada who "wore the red shoulder patches of the Hong Kong force."

81 CCJC, Minutes, 19 September 1945, 5 April 1946, LAC, MG 28, vol. 1, series 1, file 1, pt. 2 of 2. A lively recollection of the formation of the Lethbridge Committee can be found in "Lethbridge Committee – Report on Activities," William S. Wallace to Mark Hopkins, archivist, 12 September 1977, LAC, MG 28, vol. 1, file 4. On the formation of the Montreal Committee on Japanese Canadians (MCJC), see, especially, Executive of the provisional Montreal Committee on Japanese Canadians to "Dear Fellow Citizen," 14 January 1946; Scott to Brewin, 21 January 1946; and Scott to G.A. Gariepy, Montreal Trades and Labour Council, 28 March 1946, all in LAC, MG 30 D211, Francis Reginald Scott Papers. See also *Saturday Night,* 2 March 1946, for publication of a statement of the MCJC.

82 Brewin to Arnold Campbell, KC, 5 January 1946, LAC, MG 32 C26, F. Andrew Brewin Papers, vol. 1. See also LAC, MG 30 E266, Saul M. Cherniack Papers, vol. 1.

83 Forrest LaViolette, *Our Japanese Canadians: Citizens, Not Exiles* (April 1946), LAC, MG 28, vol. 3, file 16; CCJC, Minutes, 22 January 1946, 22 March 1946, LAC, MG 28, vol. 1, file 1; *CCJC News Bulletin 7,* 14 September 1946, LAC, MG 28, vol. 1, file 1; BCSC, "Minute of a Meeting concerning the Problem of Japanese in Canada," 26 March 1946, LAC, RG 36/27, Boards, Offices and Commissions, series 27: British Columbia Security Commission, 1942-1948, vol. 104; "A Record of the Work of the Cooperative Committee on Japanese Canadians," n.d., 13, CCJC-MAC, folder 12.

84 "Co-operative Committee on Japanese Canadians Submission to Parliament," 26 March 1946, LAC, MG 32 C26, vol. 3, file 3-3.

85 Fowke, *They Made Democracy Work,* 23. For the Privy Council appeal, see *Co-operative Committee on Japanese Canadians v. A.G. Canada* (1947), A.C. 87, 1 D.L.R. 577.

86 Fowke, *They Made Democracy Work,* 23-25, 32; "Report of the Sub-committee on Restrictions and Property Losses," 26 October 1946, LAC, MG 28, series 1, vol. 1, file 1, pt. 2 of 2; CCJC to the prime minister, 11 April 1947, LAC, MG 28, series 1, vol. 1, file 1, pt. 2 of 2; *CCJC News Bulletin 8,* 10 February 1947, LAC, MG 28, series 1, vol. 2, file 13, Minutes, 21, 24, and 26 February 1947, 2 April 1947, CCJC-MAC, folder 6; CCJC, Minutes, 21 April 1950, CCJC-MAC, folder 9; "Statement to Claimants RE Origin, Nature and Work of the Co-operative Committee on Japanese Canadians," April 1950, 3, CCJC-MAC, folder 13.

87 Brewin to Hays, 15 January 1946, Mudd Library, ACLU Papers, box 14, folder 5. Replies to Brewin's letter include Hays to ACLU board, 18 January 1946; Hays to Brewin, 18 January 1946; and Clifford Forster, ACLU general counsel, to Brewin, 21 January 1946. ACLU Papers, box 14, folder 5.

88 Pearl Buck to Roger Baldwin, 25 April 1946, Mudd Library, ACLU Papers, box 11, folder 5.

89 Baldwin to Buck, 29 April 1946, Mudd Library, ACLU Papers, box 11, folder 5. It should be noted that, at this time, Baldwin was the American representative of the International League for the Rights of Man. ACLU concern regarding international situations was not restricted to the Canadian example: the ACLU also wrote letters of interest to the US State Department on the subject of the Peruvian Japanese who were interned at a camp in Texas. This population was also at risk for deportation to Japan. Peruvian Japanese, Mudd Library, ACLU Papers, box 11, folder 3. For more on the Peruvian Japanese, see Michi Nishiura Weglyn, *Years of Infamy: The Untold Story of America's Concentration Camps* rev. ed. (Seattle: University of Washington Press, 1996), chap. 2, and Tetsuden Kashima,

Judgment without Trial: Japanese American Imprisonment during World War II (Seattle: University of Washington Press, 2003), chap. 5.

90 See, all in Mudd Library, ACLU Papers, vol. 2464, Baldwin to director of public information, 25 June 1942; Baldwin to the undersecretary of state for external affairs (DEA), 10 July 1942; Mr. Rive, DEA, to Baldwin, 31 July 1942; Baldwin to Ernest L. Maag, Red Cross, 4 August 1942; Rive to Baldwin, 7 August 1942; Sally Avitabile (secretary to Roger Baldwin) to Canadian Wartime Information Board (WIB), 11 January 1943; A. Dunton, WIB, to Avitabile, 11 February 1943; A. MacNamara, deputy minister of labour, to Baldwin, 8 February 1943, with enclosure, *Removal of Japanese from Protected Areas;* Dunton to Baldwin, 4 March 1943; George Collins, BCSC commissioner, to ACLU, 20 May 1943, with enclosure, *Removal of Japanese from the Protected Areas of British Columbia.*

91 Baldwin to Brewin, 26 December 1946, Mudd Library, ACLU Papers, box 1055, folder 6. See Brewin's reply, 7 January 1947, in the same file.

92 "Annual Report," 1951, 58-59, Mudd Library, ACLU Papers, box 1880, folder 4; see also Frank Chuman, *Bamboo People* (Del Mar, CA: Japanese American Citizens, 1976), 270-78; John Christgau, "Collins versus the World: The Fight to Restore Citizenship to Japanese American Renunciants of World War II," *Pacific Historical Review* 54, 1 (February 1985): 1-32.

93 Brewin to Baldwin, 7 January 1947, Mudd Library, ACLU Papers, box 1055, folder 6. Further correspondence ensued on the issue of a Canadian bill of rights. See Mudd Library, ACLU Papers, box 1148, folder 7, and box 1149, folder 5. The latter includes letters written by Irving Himel of the Committee for a Bill of Rights.

94 Brewin to Baldwin, 3 February 1947, Mudd Library, ACLU Papers, box 1148, folder 7. The quote is from a 27 January 1947 speech delivered by Brewin to the Civil Liberties Association of Toronto, enclosed with this letter. For media support of this idea, see "Morally Indefensible," *Winnipeg Free Press,* 7 December 1946.

95 Journals of the Senate of Canada, no. 65 (25 June 1948), 512-15; Senate of Canada, *Official Report of Debates,* 1947-48, 20th Parl., 4th Sess. (25 June 1948), 165-67. See also Irving Abella, "Jews, Human Rights, and the Making of a New Canada," *Journal of the Canadian Historical Association* 11 (2000): 3-16. On Saskatchewan's 1947 Bill of Rights, see Carmela Patrias, "Socialists, Jews, and the 1947 Saskatchewan Bill of Rights," *Canadian Historical Review* 87, 2 (June 2006): 265-92.

96 Ramsay Cook, "Canadian Liberalism in Wartime: A Study of the Defence of Canada Regulations and Some Canadian Attitudes to Civil Liberties in Wartime 1939-1945" (MA thesis, Queen's University, 1955), 277. See also Cook, "Canadian Freedom in Wartime, 1939-1945," in W.H. Heick and Roger Graham, eds., *His Own Man: Essays in Honour of Arthur Reginald Lower* (Montreal and Kingston: McGill-Queen's University Press, 1974), 37-53.

97 Stephanie Bangarth, "'We Are Not Asking You to Open Wide the Gates for Chinese Immigration': The Committee for the Repeal of the Chinese Immigration Act and Early Human Rights Activism in Canada," *Canadian Historical Review* 84, 3 (September 2003): 395-422.

98 "Appellants' Opening Brief," *California v. Fred Y. Oyama et al.,* 1947, Mudd Library, MC 072, box 24, folder 4; *Oyama v. California,* 332 U.S. 633 (1948); *Takahashi v. Fish Commission,* 334 U.S. 410 (1948).

99 Peggy Lamson, *Roger Baldwin: Founder of the American Civil Liberties Union: A Portrait* (Boston: Houghton Mifflin, 1976), 238-40; Walker, *In Defense of American Liberties,* 149-60; Reminiscences of Roger Nash Baldwin, interview by Dr. Harlan Phillips, November-December 1953, January 1954, 152-67, BLCU, Oral History Collection.

Chapter 3: "Dear Friend"

1 The role of the African American press will be examined in Chapter 4.

2 See, for example, W. Peter Ward, *White Canada Forever: Popular Attitudes and Public Policy toward Orientals in British Columbia,* 2nd ed. (Montreal and Kingston: McGill-Queen's University Press, 1978), and Peter Takaji Nunoda, "A Community in Transition and Conflict: The Japanese Canadians, 1935-1951" (PhD diss., University of Manitoba, 1991), which make no mention of any opposition to the government orders; Patricia E. Roy et

al., eds. *Mutual Hostages: Canadians and Japanese during the Second World War* (Toronto: University of Toronto Press, 1990), details only the Christian churches' opposition to the deportation policy; for American scholarly accounts, see Jacobus ten Broek, Edward N. Barnhart, and Floyd W. Matson, *Prejudice, War, and the Constitution* (Berkeley: University of California Press, 1954); Allan Bosworth, *America's Concentration Camps* (New York: W.W. Norton, 1967); Roger Daniels, *Concentration Camps USA: Japanese Americans and World War II* (New York: Holt, Reinhart and Winston, 1972); and Peter Irons, *Justice at War: The Story of the Japanese American Internment Cases* (Berkeley: University of California Press, 1983).

3 Forrest E. LaViolette, *The Canadian Japanese and World War II: A Sociological and Psychological Account* (Toronto: University of Toronto Press, 1948), 5-23, 37. Ann Gomer Sunahara offers a similar, albeit brief, opinion in *The Politics of Racism: The Uprooting of Japanese Canadians during the Second World War* (Toronto: James Lorimer, 1981), 86. For background, see W. Peter Ward, "The Oriental Immigrant and Canada's Protestant Clergy, 1855-1925," *BC Studies* 22 (Summer 1974): 40-55.

4 Ross Lambertson, *Repression and Resistance: Canadian Human Rights Activists, 1930-1960* (Toronto: University of Toronto Press, 2005), chap. 3; Michael Hemmings, "The Church and the Japanese in Canada, 1941-1946: Ambulance Wagon to Embattled Army?" (M. Theol., Vancouver School of Theology, 1990).

5 Michi Nishiura Weglyn, *Years of Infamy: The Untold Story of America's Concentration Camps*, rev. ed. (Seattle: University of Washington Press, 1996); Sandra C. Taylor, "'Fellow-Feelers with the Afflicted': The Christian Churches and the Relocation of the Japanese during World War II," in Roger Daniels et al., eds., *Japanese Americans: From Relocation to Redress* (Salt Lake City: University of Utah Press, 1986), 123-29; Robert Shaffer, "Cracks in the Consensus: Defending the Rights of Japanese Americans during World War II," *Radical History Review* 72 (1998): 84-120; Charles R. Lord, "The Response of the Historic Peace Churches to the Internment of the Japanese Americans during World War II" (MA thesis, Associated Mennonite Biblical Seminaries, 1981).

6 Ken Adachi, *The Enemy That Never Was: A History of the Japanese Canadians*, rev. ed. (Toronto: McClelland and Stewart, 1991), 111-16; Toru Matsumoto, *Beyond Prejudice* (New York: Friendship Press, 1946), 13-14.

7 Emory Ross, general secretary, Foreign Missions Conference of North America, to Mark Dawber, Home Missions Council, 1 November 1940, Presbyterian Historical Society [PHS], RG 26, National Council of Churches Papers, box 8, folder 17.

8 Ross to Dawber, 11 March 1941, PHS, RG 26, box 8, folder 17; "Record of a Meeting of an Informal Group Concerned with the Matter of Christian Attitudes toward the Japanese in North America and in US Possessions," 19 March 1941, PHS, RG 26, box 8, folder 17; "Minutes of a Meeting of the Inter-council Committee on Japanese Christian Work in the United States," 10 April 1941, PHS, RG 26, box 8, folder 17.

9 Federal Council of Churches, "Church Leaders Urge Christian Attitude toward Japanese in US," press release, 9 December 1941, PHS, RG 26, box 8, folder 17. In 1908, thirty-one denominations representing most of the major Protestant and orthodox churches in the United States had joined this council. While the council was active in issuing pronouncements on social, economic, and political questions, many conservative churchmen criticized its liberal theology. In 1950, it was absorbed by a larger body, the National Council of Churches of Christ. Edgar C. Bundy, *Collectivism in the Churches: A Documented Account of the Political Activities of the Federal, National and World Council of Churches* (Wheaton, IL: Church League of America, 1958), introduction.

10 Schmoe, "Seattle's Peace Churches and Relocation," in Daniels et al., *Japanese Americans*, 117-22.

11 Commission on Aliens and Prisoners of War, "The Churches and the Japanese in America," 30 March 1942, 15, PHS, RG 26, box 8, folder 17.

12 Galen Fisher, of the Committee on American Principles and Fair Play (to be discussed later in this chapter), made a contemporary case for "faith" in the government in "Our Japanese Refugees," an article originally published in the *Christian Century* and reprinted

in the *Pacific Citizen* 15, 3 (18 June 1942). For the initial muted response from Protestant denominations, see Taylor, "'Fellow-Feelers with the Afflicted,'" 123-29.
13 *New Canadian,* 12 March 1942.
14 Norman F. Black, "A Challenge to Patriotism and Statesmanship," 1944, Library and Archives Canada [LAC], MG 28, series 6, vol. 3, file 16; Ward, *White Canada Forever,* 164. The earlier manifestation of the VCC, the Consultative Council for Cooperation in Wartime Problems of Canadian Citizenship, was formed on 20 March 1942. According to Rev. Howard Norman, its president, "The primary aim of the Council will be to facilitate the exchange of information between groups recognizing, in the situation of Japanese Canadians, a challenge to citizenship, Christianity and our common humanity." "The Consultative Council for Cooperation in Wartime Problems of Canadian Citizenship," n.d., LAC, MG 30 C69, Margaret Foster Papers, circular; Meeting of the Consultative Council for Cooperation in Wartime Problems of Canadian Citizenship, Minutes, 30 March 1942, LAC, MG 30 C69, Margaret Foster Papers.
15 H.L. Keenleyside to Dr. Armstrong ("strictly confidential"), 7 March 1942, Anglican Church of Canada, General Synod Archives [ACC], GS75-103, Missionary Society of the Church in Canada, box 72, file 2.
16 ACLU, Newsletter, 11 May 1942, 3, Princeton University, Seeley G. Mudd Manuscript Library [Mudd Library], American Civil Liberties Union [ACLU] Papers, vol. 2444.
17 Quoted in "Church Conference Resolution Hits Mass Evacuee Internment," *Pacific Citizen* 15, 10 (6 August 1942).
18 Quoted in Brian Masaru Hayashi, *Democratizing the Enemy: The Japanese American Internment* (Princeton, NJ, and Oxford: Princeton University Press, 2004), 85.
19 United States, House Select Committee Investigating National Defense Migration, *Preliminary Report and Recommendations on Problems of Evacuation of Citizens and Aliens from Military Areas* (H.R. Rep. No. 1911), 77th Cong., 2nd Sess. (Washington, DC: Government Printing Office, March 1942), 14-15; "The Churches and the Japanese in America," 30 March 1942, 18-19, PHS, RG 26, box 8, folder 17. Similar sentiments appear in "The Church and the Japanese Evacuation and Relocation," 25 September 1942, 1-2, PHS, RG 301.7, Board of National Missions, series 2: Department of City, Immigrant and Industrial Work, subseries 2: Jacob A. Long, Superintendent Files, 1910-57, box 12, folder 11. This is a review of the year's events by the Protestant Church Commission for Japanese Service, the central interdenominational agency (excluding the Seventh-day Adventists) to coordinate the activities of the various denominations with respect to the removal. Constituted by joint action of the Federal and Home Missions Council, and with the cooperation of the Foreign Missions Conference, it predated the announcement of removal policy. Matsumoto, *Beyond Prejudice,* 13-14.
20 Commission on Aliens and Prisoners of War, "The Churches and the Japanese in America," 30 March 1942, 16-17, PHS, RG 26, box 8, folder 17.
21 "Minutes of the Executive Committee of the Federal Council of the Churches of Christ in America," 15 May 1942, 12-13, PHS, NCC, RG 18, Federal Council of the Churches of Christ in America Records, box 1, folder 12. More church resolutions can be found in Fellowship of Reconciliation (Northern California Office), *The Church Measures the Evacuation: Three Recent Church Statements Opposing Continued Wholesale Detention of America's Japanese* (San Francisco: Northern California ACLU, 26 October 1942), Mudd Library, ACLU Papers, vol. 2396. The three statements were issued by the Disciples of Christ, the Synod of California of the Presbyterian Church, and the Methodist Church. See also "Resolution on Japanese Evacuation and Internment," adopted by the Board of Managers of the United Christian Missionary Society and the International Convention of the Disciples of Christ, 5 August 1942, Mudd Library, ACLU Papers, vol. 2396.
22 American Friends Service Committee, "A Message for Today," *American Friend,* 16 July 1942, 305, quoted in Lord, "The Response of the Historic Peace Churches," 11-12.
23 United States, Congress, House Select Committee Investigating National Defense Migration, *Problems of Evacuation of Enemy Aliens and Others from Prohibited Military Zones,* pt. 30, 77th Cong., 2nd Sess. (Washington, DC: Government Printing Office, 1942), 11530.

24 Roger Daniels, *Concentration Camps, North America: Japanese in the United States and Canada during World War II* (Malabar, FL: R.E. Krieger, 1981), 104-5, 184-85; Adachi, *The Enemy That Never Was*, 222-23.

25 Hemmings, "The Church and the Japanese in Canada," 29.

26 Minutes of the Administrative Committee of the Provincial Board of Missions to Orientals in British Columbia, 8 January 1942, ACC, GS75-103, series 3-3, Leonard A. Dixon Files, file 1.

27 It should be noted that many advocates of the principle of resettlement supported voluntary – not forcible – resettlement. Influenced by propaganda, Japanese Americans and Japanese Canadians believed in and promoted assimilation. This will be examined in greater detail in Chapter 4.

28 Quoted in "The Church and the Japanese Evacuation and Relocation," 25 September 1942, 5, PHS, RG 301.7, box 12, folder 11.

29 In Montreal, for example, Mother Saint-Pierre and the Soeurs du Christ-Roi opened a hostel for young Nisei women. The United Church in Montreal also organized aid to Japanese Canadians who resettled in the city. Greg Robinson, "'Two Other Solitudes': Historical Encounters between Japanese Canadians and French Canadians," (2005), http://www.discovernikkei.org/wiki/index.php/Robinson_Two_Solitudes.

30 *Resettlement Bulletin* 2, 3 (March 1944), Mudd Library, ACLU Papers, vol. 2586. This WRA circular profiled information regarding Canada, in which National Interchurch Advisory Committee leaders promoted dispersal and blamed the current situation on conditions on the west coast, where Japanese Canadians "found themselves segregated in colonies." For contemporary scholarly analysis in which assimilation was promoted, see Carey McWilliams, "Japanese Evacuation: Policy and Perspectives," *Common Ground* (Summer 1942): 1-8, Mudd Library, ACLU Papers, vol. 2396. For scholarly analysis of prevailing thought on the benefits of assimilation, see Sunahara, *The Politics of Racism*, 131-32. See also David R. Hughes and Evelyn Kallen, *The Anatomy of Racism: Canadian Dimensions* (Montreal: Harvest Books, 1974).

31 The National Interchurch Advisory Committee on the Resettlement of Japanese Canadians, "Planning Resettlement of Japanese Canadians," April 1944, ACC, GS75-103, series 9-14, box 137, file 9.

32 "Report of Work among Japanese-Canadians in Toronto, Niagara and Huron Dioceses: January-October 1946," ACC, GS75-103, box 93, file 1A; W.H. Gale to Dixon, 18 April 1942, ACC, GS75-103, series 3-3, box 72, file 2; "Mrs. Loveys' Report on New Japanese Centres," 1942, United Church of Canada [UCC], Central Archives, Victoria University, Women's Missionary Society, Home Missions, Oriental Work, 1927-1962, box 128, series 18, file 2. This report commented on the level of competition existing between United Church and Anglican workers. One United Church worker feared that the Anglicans "may make inroads on their UC [United Church] people." See also Home Mission executive secretary to Miss Mildred Matthewson, 11 June 1943, UCC, Central Archives, Victoria University, Women's Missionary Society, box 128, series 18, file 4, in which the Catholic Church was singled out: "It is the Roman Catholic situation which we all fear because they seem to have many people and much money to spend in all the areas." See also Anglican Japanese Mission Reports, "1942," "1943," "1944," LAC, MG 30 D200, Grace Tucker Papers, file 7.

33 "The Church and Japanese Evacuation and Relocation," 25 September 1942, 4, PHS, RG 301.7, box 12, folder 11; "Protestant Group Appeals for Materials to Aid Evacuees," *Pacific Citizen* 15, 25 (19 November 1942); "National Baptist Group Will Aid Relocation of Evacuees," *Pacific Citizen* 16, 2 (14 January 1943); Matsumoto, *Beyond Prejudice*, 13-14.

34 J. Quinter Miller to Dr. Jacob Long, 10 November 1942, PHS, RG 301.7, box 12, folder 4; Committee on Resettlement of Japanese Americans, "Planning Resettlement of Japanese Americans," July 1943, PHS, RG 26, box 8, folder 17; "New Committee Will Assist in Relocation," *Pacific Citizen* 15, 22 (29 October 1942); Matsumoto, *Beyond Prejudice*, 55.

35 Gordon K. Chapman, Protestant Church Commission for Japanese Service, to Dr. Mark A. Dawber, Home Missions Council of North America, 3 December 1942, PHS, RG 301.7,

box 12, folder 7; Dawber to members of the Committee on Administration of Japanese Christian Work, 26 January 1943, PHS, RG 301.7, box 12, folder 4; "Minutes of the Committee on Administration of Japanese Work," 24 March 1943, PHS, RG 301.7, box 12, folder 4.

36 Larry Tajiri, "Churches and Relocation," *Pacific Citizen* 16, 2 (14 January 1943), 4.

37 Larry Tajiri, "Churches Lead Again," *Pacific Citizen* 18, 22 (22 July 1944); Bill Hosokawa, "Churches Bolster the Morale of Evacuees," *Pacific Citizen* 18, 20 (10 June 1944).

38 Tajiri, "Churches Lead Again," *Pacific Citizen*.

39 "Slim Majority of Canadians Favour 'Repatriation' Says Poll," and "Public Opinion on 'Repatriation,'" *New Canadian*, 8 January 1944; "Cross-Country Poll against Deportation of Citizens," *New Canadian*, 26 February 1944.

40 Howard Norman to Rev. Dr. J. Arnup, 10 October 1943, UCC, Board of World Missions, Japan Mission, 1880-1971, box 6, file 136. See also FCSO, Vancouver Unit, Canada's Japanese, "Declaration of Purpose," n.d., McMaster University Archives, Co-operative Committee on Japanese Canadians Papers [CCJC-MAC], folder 20.

41 Richard Allen, *The Social Passion: Religion and Social Reform in Canada, 1914-1928* (Toronto: University of Toronto Press, 1971), 16. The Social Gospel movement led to off-shoots other than human rights activism, such as the social purity movement, which focused on the sexual and moral aspects of social life. For more on the social purity movement, see Marianna Valverde, *The Age of Soap, Light, and Water: Moral Reform in English Canada, 1885-1925* (Toronto: McClelland and Stewart, 1991).

42 Quoted in Carol F. Lee, "The Road to Enfranchisement: Chinese and Japanese in British Columbia," *BC Studies* 30 (Summer 1976): 52.

43 Rev. A.E. Armstrong to Hon. W.P. Mulock, MP, 12 July 1944, UCC, Board of Overseas Missions, Minutes and General Correspondence, box 10, file 368; Armstrong to Hon. William Lyon Mackenzie King, MP, 12 July 1944, UCC, Board of Overseas Missions, box 10, file 368; Rev. A.E. Armstrong to J.W. Noseworthy, 12 July 1944, UCC, Board of Overseas Missions, box 10, file 368; Armstrong to King, 12 June 1944, UCC, Board of Overseas Missions, box 10, file 368.

44 "Decisions of the Annual Conference," *Christian Social Action*, "Decisions of the Annual Conference," 3 (July-August 1943), UCC, FSCO, Fellowship for a Christian Social Order Papers; Rev. John W. Grant, "Disfranchisement Imperils Democracy," *Christian Social Action* 4 (July-August 1944).

45 Memorandum for Mr. Robertson re: treatment of Japanese in Canada, 20 July 1943, LAC, RG 25, Department of External Affairs, vol. 2798, file 773-B-1-40, pt. 3, mentions the "considerable concern among churches and missionary organizations"; W.J. Turnbull, "Memorandum for the Prime Minister," with enclosure, "List of Persons from Whom Protests Have Been Received, since June the 21st, regarding Section 5 of Bill 135," 7 July 1944, LAC, MG 26 J4, William Lyon Mackenzie King Papers, Notes and Memoranda, microfilm reel H1536.

46 M. Harrison, "The Social Influence of the United Church of Canada in British Columbia, 1930-1948" (MA thesis, University of British Columbia, 1975), 186-89; LaViolette, *The Canadian Japanese*, 196.

47 From a May 1944 meeting of the United Church Conference of British Columbia, quoted in Hemmings, "The Church and the Japanese in Canada," 108-9.

48 G. Glazebrook, undersecretary of state for external affairs, to F. Charpentier, chief censor of publications, Department of National War Services, 18 August 1944, LAC, RG 25, series G-2, vol. 3005, file 3464-B-40, pt. 1. This letter enclosed a copy of "Confirmation of Interned Japanese," a 27 July 1944 article from the *Canadian Churchman*. Criticizing its references to Tashme, BC, as an "Internment Camp" and to "Interned Anglicans" and "Interned Japanese," Glazebrook wrote, "As you know, Tashme is a Japanese 'settlement' and not an internment camp. The Japanese residing there possess considerable liberty so far as living conditions are concerned and are free to move to Eastern Canada to undertake employment under National Selective service requirements. The only internment camp for Japanese is at Angler, Ontario. The Japanese government has subjected Canadians and

other Allied nations nationals in Japan and Japanese occupied territory to severe restrictions. If articles such as the one which I am referring to you are published in Canada they might be used to justify the 'internment' of Canadian nationals in the Far East. You might consider advising the editor of the *Canadian Churchman* that his use of inaccurate terminology in this article could produce the unhappy results outlined above and suggest to him that the word 'settlement' be used in any future publicity on this subject."

See also F. Charpentier to T.A. Stone, secretary, Department of External Affairs, 19 January 1944, LAC, RG 25, series G-2, vol. 3005, file 3464-B-40, pt.1. Charpentier noted that "Every now and then we have some censorship difficulties with religious magazines published by congregations, either Protestant or Catholic. The Franciscans and the Jesuits have given us more trouble than the others in their defence of the Japanese." As an example, he appended the January 1944 issue of *Les Missions Franciscaines*, containing an article titled "Ceci se passe chez nous" by Fr. Maurice Gagnon, and remarked, "He blames the Cdn authorities for their treatment of the Japanese Canadians, and he invokes the democratic principles to appeal in their favour. He draws a parallel between the way we treat the Japs and the way the Germans treat the Jews, which is unfair, we think, in the present instance, because the real parallel should be drawn between our treatment of the Japs and the Jap treatment of the Canadians."

49 Black to King, 29 May 1944, LAC, RG 25, vol. 2798, file 773-B-1-40, pt. 3.
50 Gerald M. Hutchinson to King, 2 June 1944, LAC, RG 25, vol. 2798, file 773-B-1-40, pt. 3.
51 A.G. Watson to King, 14 July 1944, LAC, RG 25, vol. 2798, file 773-B-1-40, pt. 3.
52 A.G. Watson to King, 8 August 1944, LAC, RG 25, vol. 2798, file 773-B-1-40, pt. 3.
53 "Canadian Council of Churches on Japanese Canadians," *Canadian Churchman,* 17 January 1946, 5.
54 Rev. G. Dorey to King, 26 May 1944, LAC, RG 25, vol. 2798, file 773-B-1-40, pt. 3; "Memorandum to the Prime Minister," 3 July 1944, LAC, RG 25, vol. 2798, file 773-B-1-40, pt. 3.
55 Grace Tucker to Rev. H.G. Watts, 27 March 1945, LAC, MG 30 D200. Grace Tucker was an Anglican missionary who worked in the British Columbia relocation camps.
56 National Interchurch Advisory Committee to King, 3 October 1945, LAC, MG 28 V1, Co-operative Committee on Japanese Canadians Papers, series 1, vol. 1, file 1, pt. 2 of 2. This letter plainly asked the government to abandon its plans for deportation.
57 "Co-operative Committee for Japanese Canadians Formed," *New Canadian*, 30 June 1945, 1.
58 Rev. Philip Caiger-Watson to King, 23 February 1946, LAC, MG 26 J1, Primary Correspondence, vol. 400; Rev. J.T. Clarke to King, 8 March 1946, LAC, MG 26 J1, vol. 400; Women's Missionary Society Auxiliaries [WMS] of Pengarth, Duval, and Strasbourg, Saskatchewan, to King, 29 October 1945, LAC, RG 25, series G-2, vol. 3554, file 773-B-1-40; Rev. Allan Dixon to King, 31 October 1945, LAC, RG 25, series G-2, vol. 3554, file 773-B-1-40; University of Saskatchewan Student Christian Movement to King, 31 October 1945, LAC, RG 25, series G-2, vol. 3554, file 773-B-1-40. Other protest letters sent to King by religious organizations and churches, all in LAC, RG 25, series G-2, vol. 3554, file 773-B-1-40, include Women's International League for Peace and Freedom, Toronto, 15 October 1945; Ontario Christian Endeavour Union, 15 October 1945; Deer Park United Church, Toronto, 15 October 1945; Canadian Friends Service Committee/Fred Haslam, 17 July and 15 October 1945; WMS, Knox United Church, Edmonton, 2 October 1945; three petitions from Canadian Girls in Training (CGIT) branches in Saskatchewan, 30 August 1945; and more than a hundred generic petitions signed and sent by Canadians from Alberta, Saskatchewan, Manitoba, and Ontario. These petitions were mimeographed letters originally written by United Church officials in an organized effort to get Canadians to send letters of protest to Ottawa. In R.G. Robertson to the prime minister, n.d. but probably July 1945, the writer remarked that his office had received about thirty to thirty-five of the petitions during the last month. Further letters to King in LAC, RG 25, series G-2, vol. 3554, file 773-B-1-40, include Student Christian Movement of McGill University, 17 July 1945; United Church of Canada, Montreal Presbytery, 15 May 1945; Humanist Club, University of Toronto, 12 July 1945; and Harold Toye, for the Religion-Labour Foundation,

14 June 1945. The Religion-Labour Foundation was comprised of members of the American Federation of Labor and the Congress of Industrial Organizations, in addition to various Christian and Jewish members.

59 Women's Missionary Auxiliary of Fairfield United Church of Hamilton to King, 28 January 1946, LAC, MG 26 J1, vol. 400; Rev. A.E. Millson to King, 6 March 1946, LAC, MG 26 J1, vol. 403; Petition from the Inter-varsity Christian Fellowship Club, University of Alberta, to King, n.d., LAC, MG 26 J4, Memoranda and Notes, vol. 283, file 2965; Rev. George Webber to King, 8 August 1945, LAC, RG 25, series G-2, vol. 3554, file 773-B-1-40; VCC, "Save Canadian Children and Canadian Honour," 1945, CCJC-MAC, folder 19; Canadian Council of Churches, "Canadian Council of Churches on Japanese Canadians," press release, 19 December 1945, CCJC-MAC, folder 16.

60 By 1947, the following churches and religious organizations had given their support to the CCJC: the Baptist Federation of Canada, the Canadian Council of Churches, the Catholic Archdiocese of Toronto, the Church of Christ (Disciples), the Church of England in Canada, the Evangelical Lutheran Church, the Inter-varsity Christian Fellowship, the Presbyterian Church of Canada, the Salvation Army, the Society of Friends, the Student Christian Movement, the United Church of Canada, the YMCA, and the YWCA. "Memorandum for the Public Accounts Committee," 27 May 1947, LAC, MG 28, series 6, vol. 2, file 10, pt. 1.

61 D. MacMillan and Rev. J. Finlay to the ministers of Toronto and district, 14 January 1946, CCJC-MAC, folder 4.

62 Rev. J.L.W. MacLean, "Questions of the Hour: 3. What about the Japanese?" 3 March 1946 (emphasis in original), LAC, MG 28, series 6, vol. 3, file 16, pt. 1.

63 Ibid.

64 CCJC, "Memorandum for the Members of the House of Commons and Senate of Canada on the Orders-in-Council P.C. 7355, 7356, 7357, for the Deportation of Canadians of Japanese Racial Origin," April 1946, 3, LAC, MG 28, series 1, vol. 3, file 16, pt.1.

65 VCC, "Orders-in-Council Threaten Your Citizenship!" LAC, MG 28, series 6, vol. 3, file 16, pt. 1.

66 *Of Interest to You: Monthly News Bulletin of the FOR* 1, 1 (January 1946), CCJC-MAC, folder 20.

67 *Nisei Affairs* 1, 6 (19 January 1946).

68 NIAC, "On Behalf of Justice and Fair Play to All Japanese Canadians," 31 January 1946, LAC, MG 30 D200; DEA, Memorandum, 11 February 1946, LAC, RG 25, vol. 3405, file 773-B-1-40, pt. 5.

69 "A Record of the Work of the Cooperative Committee on Japanese Canadians," 11, CCJC-MAC, folder 12.

70 Student Christian Movement of Canada, "Emergency Bulletin of Japanese-Canadians," special bulletin to all Christian youth groups, 15 October 1945 (emphasis added), CCJC-MAC, folder 20. Members were encouraged to wire or write Prime Minister King, the minister of labour, the undersecretary of state, and provincial premiers, as well as to study the question of relocation and to disseminate information through campus-wide and local action. The Student Christian Movement also advised associated committees to ask local churches, faculty clubs, service clubs, and trade unions to take up "the cause" and make their voices heard by writing letters to campus and city papers.

71 The student delegates were from the "universities of British Columbia, Alberta, Saskatchewan and Manitoba and from Queen's College, McGill University, Toronto University, Brandon College and Guelph Agricultural College." *Pacific Citizen* 22, 4 (26 January 1946); *CCJC News Bulletin* 2, 24 January 1946, CCJC-MAC, folder 10.

72 Canon Davison, "A Rigorous Law and Rigorous Injustice," *Montreal Daily Star*, 4 December 1945, LAC, MG 28, series 1, vol. 3, file 14.

73 VCC, Open letter, 27 March 1946, CCJC-MAC, folder 19. Attached letter titled "To Men and Women of Japanese Origin Lawfully Residing in Canada."

74 *CCJC Bulletin* 4, 15 March 1946, CCJC-MAC, folder 10.

75 "Church Sponsored Placement Plan for Japanese Canadian Families under the Auspices

of the National Interchurch Advisory Committee on the Resettlement of Japanese Canadians," September 1946, CCJC-MAC, folder 18.

76 CCJC, Minutes, 12 December 1946, LAC, MG 28, series 1, vol. 1, file 1; VCC to "Dear Friend," 6 March 1947, LAC, MG 28, series 1, vol. 2, file 10.

77 Hemmings, "The Church and the Japanese in Canada," 124-25.

78 Holland quoted in George E. Rundquist, "The Churches Role in Resettlement," *Resettlement Bulletin*, October 1943, quoted in Lord, "The Response of the Historic Peace Churches," 74-75.

79 Dillon Myer, *Uprooted Americans: The Japanese Americans and the War Relocation Authority during World War II* (Tucson: University of Arizona Press, 1971), especially preface and 136-38.

80 WRA to Mark Dawber, 8 October 1942, PHS, RG 301.7, box 12, folder 4; Dawber to Rev. Gordon Chapman, 16 October 1942, passing on concerns regarding above letter from WRA.

81 Home Missions Council of North America to the general secretaries of Women's Home Missions Boards, 6 November 1942, PHS, RG 26, box 8, folder 17. The Women's Home Missions Boards were asked to arrange for forty thousand gifts to be sent to the children in the relocation camps and were urged to "think of what this could mean in building Christian friendship!" See also religious press release, 17 November 1942, PHS, RG 26, box 8, folder 17; Gordon Chapman, Protestant Church Commission for Japanese Service, to Edith Lowry, Home Missions Council, 23 November 1942, PHS, RG 26, box 8, folder 17; "Christmas Parties Assured for US Evacuee Children," *Pacific Citizen* 15, 26 (26 November 1942). The same calls for equipment and Christmas toys were repeated in 1943, and also for Thanksgiving. Commission on Aliens and Prisoners of War, Floyd W. Schmoe, *Japanese Americans and the Present Crisis* (n.p.: n.d. [late 1942?]), Mudd Library, ACLU Papers, vol. 2396. The purpose of this pamphlet, as detailed on its inside cover, was to assist the churches "in facing the situation more intelligently and in fulfilling their responsibilities." For more on the practical ministering in the camps, see Matsumoto, *Beyond Prejudice*, chap. 2. For a complete listing of all the hostels in the US, see Matsumoto, *Beyond Prejudice*, appendix 3, 144-45. For the pledge of ACLU branch cooperation, see *ACLU Bulletin 1159*, 2 January 1945, Mudd Library, ACLU Papers, vol. 2584.

82 See, for example, Philip Glick, WRA, to Forster, 17 November 1943, Mudd Library, ACLU Papers, vol. 2463.

83 Baldwin to Wirin, 23 June 1943, Mudd Library, ACLU Papers, vol. 2463.

84 The WRA officially ceased to exist on 30 June 1946, although its phase-out period lasted about eighteen months. Daniels, *Concentration Camps, North America*, 164-66; Matsumoto, *Beyond Prejudice*, 127-28. Government housing was made available to the relocatees, but it was not of a permanent nature. One such example was the accommodation at Seabrook Farms, New Jersey, to which a mass relocation of more than seventeen hundred Japanese Americans was sent in October 1945. They were placed in "relaxed internment" at this well-known frozen-food processing plant where the labour of German POWs had been used during the war years. Many found living in its camp-like atmosphere a wholly unsatisfactory experience. For more on Seabrook Farms, see correspondence in Mudd Library, ACLU Papers, vol. 2662, and Weglyn, *Years of Infamy*, 65.

85 "Crisis in Church Relations of Japanese-Americans," *Christian Century*, 23 January 1946; Letter, Philip M. Glick to Rev. Toru Matsumoto, 4 December 1945, PHS, RG 26, box 8, folder 18; Matsumoto, *Beyond Prejudice*, 129-31; Shaffer, "Cracks in the Consensus," 106.

86 American churches seem not to have noticed the parallel situation of the Canadian Nikkei. According to available sources, only the US Unitarian Association managed to criticize the actions of the Canadian government. In October 1948, it passed a resolution at its annual convention in which it deplored Ottawa's treatment of Japanese Canadians. In particular, it cited the requirement that the Nikkei obtain permits from the RCMP before entering British Columbia, and the denial of fishing rights. It called the continuation of these restrictions three years after the end of the war "a denial of the fundamental principles of democracy." Quoted in *New Canadian*, 13 October 1948, LAC, RG 36/27, Boards, Offices and Commissions, series 27: British Columbia Security Commission, 1942-48, vol. 39.

87 United States Congress, House Select Committee Investigating National Defense Migration, *Hearings before the Select Committee Investigating National Defense Migration,* 77th Cong., 2nd Sess. (Washington, DC: Government Printing Office, 1942), pt. 29, 11242.
88 United States Congress, *Hearings,* pt. 30, 11555, 11557-63.
89 United States Congress, *Hearings,* pt. 30, 11590-95, 11598-99.
90 Allan Austin, *From Concentration Camp to Campus: Japanese American Students and World War II* (Urbana: University of Illinois Press, 2004), provides a detailed examination of the development of the student relocation program. In particular, Austin quotes Eisenhower on the frustrating process of finding someone to helm the program: "I must confess that I am still distressed by the excuses I received from the educators I approached. All declined. Then someone suggested that I telephone Clarence Pickett, the prominent Quaker leader." Eisenhower, *The President Is Calling,* 120, quoted in Austin, *From Concentration Camp to Campus,* 184n63.
91 "Our Friends, the Friends," *Pacific Citizen* 15, 26 (26 November 1942); Robert W. O'Brien, "Nisei Face a Crisis," *Intercollegian,* April 1942, Mudd Library, ACLU Papers, vol. 2372.
92 Convincing schools to accept relocated Nikkei students was not an easy task. A Princeton spokesman wanted, at first, nothing to do with "American-born Japanese students even though they may be in good standing and not under suspicion." Other institutions demanded FBI and G-2 (military intelligence) clearance as part of entrance requirements. The president of Stanford University and the chancellor of the University of California, Berkeley stand out for their efforts in lobbying the Tolan Committee for fair treatment of Nisei students. Ray Lyman Wilbur, chancellor, Stanford University, to John Tolan, 13 April 1942, Mudd Library, vol. 2394; Weglyn, *Years of Infamy,* 105-10; Matsumoto, *Beyond Prejudice,* chap. 8. See also Robert W. O'Brien, *The College Nisei* (Palo Alto, CA: Pacific Books, 1949), and Austin, *From Concentration Camp to Campus.*
93 O'Brien, *The College Nisei,* 114-24.
94 Austin, *From Concentration Camps to Campus,* chap. 4.
95 "Students Hold Mixed Opinions on Japanese Canadian Problem," *New Canadian,* 24 November 1945.
96 See the list of groups in Edith Fowke, *They Made Democracy Work: The Story of the Co-operative Committee on Japanese Canadians* (Toronto: CCJC, 1951).
97 "Students Organize Committee to Protest Expatriation Move," *New Canadian,* 24 October 1945. An open letter from the Humanist Club to campus groups at other universities indicated that the club was organizing a committee to protest the unfair treatment of Japanese Canadians. Open letter, Humanist Club, 11 October 1945, LAC, MG 28, series 1, vol. 2, file 9.
98 *CCJC News Bulletin 4,* 15 March 1946, CCJC-MAC, folder 10. Speakers at the University of Toronto included Andrew Brewin, CCJC member Kinzie Tanaka, and Lt. Col. David Croll, MP.
99 Robinson, "Two Other Solitudes."
100 *Varsity,* 28 February 1946.
101 *Varsity,* 12 October 1945.
102 CCJC, "Memorandum for the Members of the House of Commons and Senate of Canada on the Orders-in-Council P.C. 7355, 7356, 7357 for the Deportation of Canadians of Japanese Racial Origin," April 1946, 3, LAC, MG 28, series 1, vol. 3, file 16, pt. 1; *CCJC Bulletin 4,* 16 March 1946, LAC, MG 28, series 1, vol. 3, file 15, pt. 1; Women's Christian Temperance Union, Vancouver District, to King, 26 February 1942, LAC, MG 26 J1, microfilm reel 6814; Corbetton Women's Missionary Society to King, 15 January 1945, LAC, MG 26 J1, microfilm reel 9168; F.E. Farquharson, Comber Women's Missionary Society, to King, 10 January 1946, LAC, MG 26 J1, microfilm reel 9168; Cottam Women's Missionary Society to King, 19 February 1946, LAC, MG 26 J1, microfilm reel 9168, vol. 403. Several letters from women's groups protesting deportation can also be found in LAC, RG 25, series G-2, vol. 3554, file 773-B-1-40, pt. 4. The Women's International League for Peace and Freedom sent its representatives to participate in the Consultative Council for Cooperation in Wartime Problems of Canadian Citizenship, the precursor to

the VCC. "Meeting of the Consultative Council for Cooperation in Wartime Problems of Canadian Citizenship," Minutes, 30 March 1942, LAC, MG 30 C69.

103 United States Congress, *Hearings*, pt. 30, 11611-12, 11178-90; "League Finds Ally in State CIO Head during Tolan Committee Hearing in San Francisco: Statement Given," *Pacific Citizen* 14, 2 (24 February 1942); "Case for Nisei Presented at CIO Conference," *Pacific Citizen* 17, 6 (14 August 1943); "CIO Auto Workers, World's Biggest Union, Urges Fair Play for Japanese Americans," *Pacific Citizen* 18, 15 (6 May 1944); "Nisei and Labor Unions," *Pacific Citizen* 17, 28 (15 January 1944); "What Side Are You On?" *Pacific Citizen* 18, 15 (6 May 1944); "Plea for Change in West Coast Order Gains Support," May 1942, Mudd Library, ACLU Papers, vol. 2395; *JACL Bulletin 19*, 15 July 1943, Mudd Library, ACLU Papers, vol. 2464; "List of Organizations Present at Meeting on April 24, 1944," Mudd Library, ACLU Papers, vol. 2585; Galen Fisher, "The Nisei Return," *Common Sense*, November 1945, 5, Mudd Library, ACLU Papers, vol. 2585.

104 Kim Moody, *An Injury to All: The Decline of American Unionism* (London: Verso/New Left Books, 1988), xiv-xvi, 21-22. My thanks to Julius N.J. Olajos for this reference. See also Philip S. Foner, *Organized Labor and the Black Worker, 1916-1973* (New York: Praeger, 1974), 238-69.

105 CCJC, "Memorandum for the Members of the House of Commons and Senate of Canada on the Orders-in-Council P.C. 7355, 7356, 7357 for the Deportation of Canadians of Japanese Racial Origin," April 1946, 3, LAC, MG 28, series 1, pt. 1. Lists of participating unions can also be found in "Memorandum for the Public Accounts Committee," 27 May 1942, LAC, MG 28, series 1, vol. 2, file 10, pt. 1. Resolutions came from the Moosejaw and District Labour Council and the Jewellery Workers Union of Toronto on 1 March 1946. *CCJC News Bulletin 4*, 15 March 1946, CCJC-MAC, folder 10.

106 "Minutes of a Meeting Concerning the Problem of Japanese in Canada," 26 March 1946, 3, LAC, RG 36/27, vol. 104, file 10.

107 The Toronto Joint Labour Committee to Combat Racial Intolerance was established with a great deal of manoeuvring by Kalmen Kaplansky, executive director of the Jewish Labour Committee. Officially the creation of both local Trades and Labor Congress and CCL trade unions, it included, for the most part, rank-and-file trade unionists. Very active in the campaign for fair accommodations practices, particularly in Dresden, Ontario, the committee also lent its support to the Committee for the Repeal of the Chinese Immigration Act (CRCIA). Lambertson, *Repression and Resistance*, 290-95. For more on the Dresden affair, see Lambertson, *Repression and Resistance*, chap. 7; Ross Lambertson, "'The Dresden Story': Racism, Human Rights, and the Jewish Labour Committee of Canada," *Labour/Le Travail* 47 (Spring 2001): 43-82; James W. St. G. Walker, *"Race," Rights and the Law in the Supreme Court of Canada: Historical Case Studies* (Waterloo: Wilfrid Laurier University Press, 1997), chap. 3, ss. 6 and 8; and Alan A. Borovoy, "Fair Accommodation Practices Act: The 'Dresden Affair,'" *University of Toronto Faculty of Law Review* 14 (January 1956): 13-23. On the CRCIA, see Stephanie D. Bangarth, "'We Are Not Asking You to Open Wide the Gates for Chinese Immigration': The Committee for the Repeal of the Chinese Immigration Act and Early Human Rights Activism in Canada," *Canadian Historical Review* 84, 3 (September 2003): 395-422.

108 *New York Herald-Tribune*, 13 August (1938?), Columbia University, Butler Library [BLCU], Department of Rare Books and Manuscripts, Institute of Pacific Relations [IPR] Collection, box 126.

109 United States Congress, *Hearings*, pt. 29, 11197-203, 11096-100; Committee on National Security and Fair Play, press release, 3 March 1942, BLCU, IPR Papers, box 59; "Galen Fisher Advises against Removal," *Pacific Citizen* 14, 1 (24 February 1942); Shaffer, "Cracks in the Consensus," 91-92.

110 Committee on National Security and Fair Play, "The Bottleneck in Japanese Resettlement," press release, 18 May 1942, Mudd Library, ACLU Papers, vol. 2394. Fisher did not always find it easy to publish his writing. William Lockwood, editor of the *Survey*, the Institute for Pacific Relations publication, refused to print one of his articles unless he altered an argument that made light of military necessity. Lockwood to Fisher, 6 June 1942, BLCU,

IPR Papers, box 168; Galen Fisher, "The Nisei Return," *Common Sense*, November 1945, Mudd Library, ACLU Papers, vol. 2693.

111 For correspondence between the committee and Baldwin, see Mudd Library, ACLU Papers, vol. 2463. When the committee was reorganized as the Committee on American Principles and Fair Play, Fisher became its assistant treasurer. In approval of this reorganization, Baldwin sent a financial contribution. It is unclear whether this was personal or on behalf of the ACLU. Baldwin to Galen Fisher, Committee on American Principles and Fair Play, 20 April 1943, Mudd Library, ACLU Papers, vol. 2463.

112 Fisher to Baldwin, 10 April 1943, with enclosure, "The Fair Play Committee," Mudd Library, ACLU Papers, vol. 2463; Committee on American Principles and Fair Play, "High Points in 1944 Activities," n.d., Mudd Library, ACLU Papers, vol. 2664.

113 Post War World Council to Roosevelt, 30 April 1942, Mudd Library, ACLU Papers, vol. 2394; *Common Sense*, June 1942, 215; Post War World Council, *Democracy and the Japanese Americans* (New York: Post War World Council, 1942), Mudd Library, Undergraduate Alumni Records, Norman Thomas, Class of 1905, folder 3; WRA proclamation, release no. 6-1, "Plea for Change in West Coast Order Gains Support," 1 June 1942, Mudd Library, ACLU Papers, vol. 2395; Greg Robinson, "Norman Thomas and the Struggle against Internment," *Prospects* 28 (2003): 7.

114 Lambertson, *Repression and Resistance*, 107-8.

115 CCJC, "Memorandum for the Members of the House of Commons and the Senate of Canada," April 1946, 3, LAC, MG 28, series 4, vol. 3, file 16, CCJC, Minutes of enlarged meeting, 10 January 1946, LAC, MG 28, series 4, vol. 1, file 1; CCJC, Minutes, 22 January 1946, LAC, MG 28, series 4, vol. 1, file 1; *CCJC News Bulletin 2*, 24 January 1946, CCJC-MAC, folder 10. The *CCJC News Bulletin* commented that the CLAT "is supporting us wholeheartedly."

116 W. Jarvis McCurdy and George Tatham, CLAT, to King, 23 February 1945, LAC, RG 25, vol. 11, file 773-B-1-40. In closing their letter, the writers pledged to King that, "In all of this we wish to assure you of our hearty support."

117 D. Owens, CLAW, to King, 30 November 1945, with enclosure, Brief to King and senators and MPs from Manitoba, LAC, MG 26 J1, microfilm reel C9879.

118 David Heaps, parliamentary secretary to M.J. Coldwell, MP, to Baldwin, 12 June 1946, Mudd Library, ACLU Papers, vol. 2732; for information regarding Edith Ellen Holtom, see LAC, MG 31 I1, Edith Ellen Holtom Papers. Records indicate that Holtom sent thirty-one dollars to the CCJC in 1946. The papers also include files pertaining to African Americans (1960s) and Chilean refugees (1970s).

119 Statement of the Montreal Committee, from *Montreal Gazette*, 28 February 1946, quoted in Robinson, "'Two Other Solitudes.'" For more on the Montreal Committee, see also Roy et al., *Mutual Hostages*, 178. On the correspondence between these groups and the ACLU, see Mudd Library, ACLU Papers, vol. 2732. On the Montreal Committee, see LAC, MG 30 D211, Francis Reginald Scott Papers, vol. 17, file 8.

120 Vancouver Canadian Civil Liberties Union, brief to King, 25 March 1947, LAC, MG 28 V7, vol. 2, file 4.

121 Shaffer, "Cracks in the Consensus," 97.

122 Robert Bendiner, "Cool Heads or Martial Law," *Nation* 154 (14 February 1942), 183, and Howard Costigan, "The Plight of the Nisei," *Nation* 154 (14 February 1942), 185.

123 Albert Horlings, "Hawaii's 150,000 Japanese," *Nation* 155 (25 July 1942): 69-71. Also of note is Charles Inglehart, "Citizens behind Barbed Wire," *Nation* 154 (6 June 1942): 649-51, which lamented the lack of educated response to the perceived threat from Japan.

124 Carey McWilliams, "California and the Japanese," *New Republic* 106 (2 March 1942); "Japanese Out of California," *New Republic* 106 (6 April 1942); Ted Nakashima, "Concentration Camps: US Style," *New Republic* 154 (15 June 1942); and I. Noguchi, "Trouble among Japanese-Americans," *New Republic* 162 (1 February 1943). For editorials citing the removal as a blemish on US civil liberties, see the *New Republic* 108 (15 June 1942); 113 (4 January 1943); and 130 (26 June 1944).

125   Quoted in "A Plea for Sanity in Treatment of Japanese," *Pacific Citizen* 14, 1 (14 February 1942).
126   "Native Born," *Commonweal* 35 (10 April 1942); "Native Born II," *Commonweal* 35 (17 April 1942); "Tolan Report," *Commonweal* 36 (5 June 1942); and special issue, *Commonweal* 40 (10 March 1944).
127   For letters to the *New York Times*, see 23 December 1941, 20; 15 January 1942, 18; 6 March 1942, 8; and 12 April 1942, 11.
128   *Common Sense*, June 1942. It even listed Eleanor Roosevelt on its masthead. Shaffer, "Cracks in the Consensus," 98.
129   The April 1942 *Christian Century* coverage of the removal issue, all in Mudd Library, ACLU Papers, vol. 2372, includes Galen Fisher, "Our Japanese Refugees," 1 April, 424-26; Galen Fisher, "Does Race Limit the Bill of Rights?" 15 April, 484-85; Galen Fisher "Citizens or Subjects?" 29 April, 551-53; Galen Fisher, "Ministers Express Good Will to Japanese Evacuees," 8 April. See also Shaffer, "Cracks in the Consensus," 100-101.
130   Gerald Elfendahl, "Remembering Walter Woodward (1910-2001)," *People's History Library*, n.d., http://www.historylink.org/essays/output.cfm?file_id=3111. Elfendahl also remarks that Walter Woodward was the basis for newspaper editor Arthur Chambers, in David Guterson's best-selling novel *Snow Falling on Cedars*.
131   "The Bill of Rights and Japanese-Americans," *Chicago Defender*, 22 April 1944, Mudd Library, ACLU Papers, vol. 2583; "Excerpts from the Broadcast of Arthur Gaeth," 21 February 1944, Intermountain Radio Network, Mudd Library, ACLU Papers, vol. 2585.
132   S. Burton Heath, "What about Hugh Kiino?" *Harper's* 187 (October 1943): 450-58; "Evacuations Production of Hysteria, Says Lawyer," *San Francisco News*, 22 November 1944, Mudd Library, ACLU Papers, vol. 2599.
133   Quoted in "Ban on Return of Evacuees May Be for Reasons Other Than Military, Declares 'Fortune,'" *Pacific Citizen* 18, 3 (22 April 1944). In the same issue of *Pacific Citizen*, Larry Tajiri followed up with a sharply worded editorial in which he asserted that the "evacuation has set a precedent for the detention of a selected group of American citizens without trial and without the filing of charges against them." Tajiri, "Dangerous Doctrine," *Pacific Citizen* 18, 3 (22 April 1944).
134   Quoted in "Intermountain Catholic Paper Denounces Anti-Nisei Prejudice," *Pacific Citizen* 18, 10 (11 March 1944).
135   Brewin to Baldwin, 3 February 1947, Mudd Library, ACLU Papers, box 1148, folder 7. In this letter, Brewin enclosed a 27 January 1947 speech he had given at a CLAT meeting in which he referred to the newspapers.
136   Tom Shoyama, editorial, *New Canadian*, 1 April 1944; Kasey Oyama, editorial "We Must Fight Deportation," *New Canadian*, 10 November 1945. An article in the 2 March 1946 edition of the *New Canadian* listed the following newspapers as critical of the Supreme Court ruling on "deportation": *Lethbridge Herald, Montreal Gazette, St. Thomas Times-Journal, Toronto Daily Star, Vancouver Daily Province, Vancouver Sun,* and *Winnipeg Free Press.*
137   *Winnipeg Free Press*, 21 June and 7 July 1944, 6 October 1944; *Toronto Daily Star*, 19 July 1944, all in LAC, MG 28 V7, Japanese Canadian Citizens Association (JCCA) Papers, vol. 17, reel C-12835.
138   CCJC, Minutes, 2 October 1945, LAC, MG 28, series 1, vol. 1, file 1, pt. 2 of 2; WIB Survey, no. 66, 30 June 1945, LAC, RG 36/27, series 217, vol. 41, file 2505.
139   DEA memo for file, 15 December 1943, LAC, RG 25, series G-2, vol. 3004, file 3464-B-40C. The memo describes two *Saturday Night* articles as voicing "one side of public reaction towards the handling of the Japanese problem in Canada." (Articles in 13 November and 20 November 1943 editions.)
140   "Delegation Asks Ottawa Consider Japs in Canada," *Toronto Daily Star*, 4 January 1946, p. 2; "Claim Deportation of Japs Violates International Law," *Toronto Daily Star*, 22 January 1946, p. 26; "'Citizens' Group on Japanese Meets Officials," *Winnipeg Free Press*, 7 January 1946; "Court Reserves Judgement on Deportation of Japs," *Winnipeg Free Press*, 26 January 1946.

141 R.L. Vincent, "The Disposal of Unwanted Citizens," *Toronto Daily Star,* 26 July 1945; "Let's Not Become as Nazis," *Ottawa Journal,* 19 June 1944, RG 25, series A-3-b, vol. 5761, file 104(s), pt. 1.1-2.2.

142 See, in *Canadian Forum,* "Scientific Aspects of the Race Problem," December 1942; Douglas MacLennan, "Racial Discrimination in Canada," October 1943; "Combatting Anti-Semitism," and "The Races of Mankind," February 1944; "Pandering to Prejudice," August 1944; and "The Red Man's Burden," October 1944.

143 Edith Fowke, "Japanese Canadians," *Canadian Forum,* January 1946. Other Fowke articles in *Canadian Forum* include Fowke with A.G. Watson, "Democracy and the Japanese Canadian," July 1945, and Fowke, "Justice and Japanese Canadians," January 1947.

144 Grace MacInnis, "Wanted: A Country," *Canadian Forum,* June 1942; Grace MacInnis and Angus MacInnis, *Oriental Canadians: Outcasts or Citizens?* (Vancouver: Federationist Publishing, [1944]), UCC, General Council Committees Section, Commission on the Church, Nation and World Order, box 2, file 17; Werner Cohn, "The Persecution of Japanese Canadians and the Political Left in British Columbia, December 1941-March 1942," *BC Studies* 68 (Winter 1985-86): 3-22.

145 Howard Green, "Should We Send the Japs Back? – Yes," *Maclean's,* 1 December 1943, 12, 34-35.

146 Angus MacInnis, "Should We Send the Japs Back? – No," *Maclean's,* 1 December 1943, 12, 37-38.

147 "Halt Exile of Japs, US Advice to Canada," *Washington Post,* 11 June 1945.

148 "Will Deport 1,500 Japanese," *New York Times,* 21 November 1945, p. 3, Mudd Library, ACLU Papers, vol. 2659.

149 See, all in LAC, MG 26 J4, "An Unseemly Auction," *Vancouver Daily Province,* 3 October 1944, microfilm reel H1536; Elmore Philpott, "Japanese War Scandal," *Vancouver Sun,* 8 December 1945, microfilm reel C249549-50; "Japanese on the Coast," *Vancouver Daily Province,* 18 December 1945, microfilm reel C249578-79. In a CBC Radio commentary, Lorne Greene contrasted the army admittance policies of the American government with those of the Canadian government. Lorne Greene, "Around the World," CBC Radio, 1 September 1945, LAC, MG 28, series 1, vol. 2, file 9. See also Senator Cairine Wilson's comments in "US Didn't Treat Its Japs as Harshly – Senator Wilson," *Toronto Daily Star,* 11 January 1946.

150 Editorial, "Unworthy of Canada," *Toronto Globe and Mail,* 14 January 1946.

151 "Basis of Liberty," *Saturday Night,* 8 June 1946.

152 Pattie Tanner, *Minority Groups VS. Canadian Public: A Mock Trial* (Toronto: UN Society in Canada, June 1946), LAC, MG 28, series 1, vol. 3, file 16, *Ottawa Citizen,* 3 December 1946; *Winnipeg Free Press,* 7 January 1946; *Montreal Star,* 4 December 1946; *Toronto Daily Star,* 3 December 1946; "Can Exile Any Group Prairie Farmer Fears," *Toronto Daily Star,* 20 February 1946.

153 Burton Kierstead, "Recent Developments Affecting Civil Liberties," *Canadian Commentary,* CBC Radio, 28 January 1947, LAC, MG 28, series 6, vol. 3, file 21.

154 *Vancouver Daily Province,* 26 January 1946, LAC, MG 30 C69. Edith Fowke voiced similar sentiments in "Justice and Japanese Canadians," *Canadian Forum,* January 1947, p. 225.

155 Canada, House of Commons, *Debates* (17 June 1944), 4918 (Knowles); (12 August 1944), 6414 (Knowles); (17 December 1945), 3702 (Stewart); (9 April 1946), 698 (Stewart).

156 Editorial, "We Will Regret Racialism," *Winnipeg Free Press,* 19 September 1945, p. 1; editorial, "Manitoba Can Take a Lead," *Winnipeg Free Press,* 18 October 1945, p. 1. See also editorial, "Our Japanese Issue, Vital," *Winnipeg Free Press,* 19 October 1945, and editorial, "Morally Indefensible," *Winnipeg Free Press,* 7 December 1946.

157 Canada, House of Commons, *Debates* (9 April 1948), 2842-46; (12 April 1948), 2854-96; (16 April 1948), 3038-3041; *Toronto Globe and Mail,* 27 September 1947, 17 December 1947, 18 February 1948, 14 April 1948; Christopher MacLennan, *Toward the Charter: Canadians and the Demand for a National Bill of Rights, 1929-1960* (Kingston and Montreal: McGill-Queen's University Press, 2003), chap. 3.

158 *Toronto Globe and Mail,* 1 December 1947; Canada, House of Commons, *Debates* (13 September 1945), 135-38, and (12 April 1948), 2864-68.

159 Norman Thomas, "On the President's Speech," *Call,* 7 March 1942, p. 5; "Persecution in a Democracy," *Call,* 14 March 1942, p. 4, quoted in Shaffer, "Cracks in the Consensus," 95. Other *Call* articles cited in Shaffer, "Cracks in the Consensus," 95, include Travers Clements, "The Re-winning of the West," 21 February 1942; "Socialists Rap Indiscriminate Evacuations," 25 April 1942; and "Socialist Resolution on War and Fascism," 12 June 1942.

160 Quoted in "Camp Amache Historic, Indeed," *DenverPost.com,* 8 May 2006, http://www.DenverPost.com.

161 "Former Governor of Colorado Says His Defense of Nisei Rights 'Finished Him Politically'," *Pacific Citizen* 18, 10 (11 September 1943); Arthur A. Hansen, "Peculiar Odyssey: Newsman Jimmie Omura's Removal from and Regeneration within Nikkei Society, History, and Memory," in Louis Fiset and Gail M. Nomura, eds., *Nikkei in the Pacific Northwest: Japanese Americans and Japanese Canadians in the Twentieth Century* (Seattle and London: University of Washington Press, 2005), 282; Jun Xing, "Governor Ralph Carr: An American and Colorado Hero," *CASAE News* (Center for Applied Studies in American Ethnicity) 4 (November-December 1996): 4. In 1976, a bust of Carr was erected in Denver's Sakura Square to commemorate his efforts on behalf of persons of Japanese ancestry. On 23 January 2002, the state of Colorado declared 11 December to be Governor Ralph Carr Day. More information about Governor Carr's stance can be found in Robert Harvey, *Amache: The Story of Japanese American Internment in Colorado during World War II* (New York: Roberts Reinhart, 2003).

162 Canada, House of Commons, *Debates* (22 November 1945), 2426; "Labour Progressive's Racist Platform Draws C.C.F. Fire," *New Canadian,* 13 January 1945; Lambertson, *Repression and Resistance,* 112.

163 Quoted in Cohn, "The Persecution of Japanese Canadians," 10.

164 Quoted in Sunahara, *The Politics of Racism,* 54-55; see also Grace MacInnis and Angus MacInnis, *Oriental Canadians: Outcasts or Citizens?* (Vancouver: Federationist Publishing, [1944]), UCC, General Council Committees Section, Commission on the Church, Nation and World Order, box 2, file 17.

165 Section 12, "Freedom," Co-operative Commonwealth Federation Programme, adopted at First National Convention, held at Regina, Saskatchewan, July 1933, quoted in J.K. McNaught, *A Prophet in Politics: A Biography of J.S. Woodsworth* (Toronto: University of Toronto Press, 1959), 328; Adachi, *The Enemy That Never Was,* 181-84.

166 CCF, *News Comment* 3, 18 (15 September 1943), LAC, MG 28, series 1, vol. 2, file 16; CCF, *News Comment* 5, 21 (1 November 1945), LAC, MG 28, series 1, vol. 2, file 16; Grace MacInnis and Angus MacInnis, *Oriental Canadians: Outcasts or Citizens?* (Vancouver: Federationist Publishing, [1944]), UCC, General Council Committees Section, Commission on the Church, Nation and World Order, box 2, file 17.

167 See Canada, House of Commons, *Debates* (21 November 1945), 2385, 2389 (MacInnis); (22 November 1945), 2400-2401 (Herridge); (17 December 1945), 3702-4 (Stewart). For condemnation from MacInnis and Stewart regarding the decision to use Orders-in-Council to enable deportation, see Canada, House of Commons, *Debates* (17 December 1945), 3695 (MacInnis), 3704 (Stewart).

168 M.J. Coldwell to Brewin, 18 April 1946, LAC, MG 32 C26, F. Andrew Brewin Papers, vol. 3; Brewin to Coldwell, 19 April 1946, LAC, MG 32 C26, vol. 3; CCJC, Minutes, 5 April 1946, LAC, MG 28, series 1, vol. 1, file 1; Carmela Patrias, "Socialists, Jews, and the 1947 Saskatchewan Bill of Rights," *Canadian Historical Review* 87, 2 (June 2006): 274-75; CCJC *News Bulletin* 7, 14 September 1946, MG 28, vol. 3, series 1, file 15; Quebec Provincial CCF Council Resolution, 27 January 1946, LAC, MG 31 E87, R.G. Robertson Papers, vol. 1; Norma Tracy, correspondence secretary, CCF, Ontario section, to King, 25 March 1946, LAC, MG 26 J1, microfilm reel C9168. In 1946, the Saskatchewan CCF government appointed a few Japanese Canadians to high-ranking civil service positions, much to the alarm of CCF politicians in that government and others. Patrias, "Socialists, Jews, and the 1947 Saskatchewan Bill of Rights," 276-77.

169 Stanley Knowles to Thelma Perry Scambler, 29 October 1945, LAC, MG 30 C160, Grace

Thompson Papers; Alistair Stewart to Scambler, 29 October 1945, LAC, MG 30 C160; Ralph Maybank to Scambler, 31 October 1945, LAC, MG 30 C160.
170 Quoted in *Nisei Affairs* 2, 3 (April 1947). Bill 104 extended Order-in-Council P.C. 251 (13 January 1942), which prohibited fishing licences for Japanese Canadians, and Order-in-Council P.C. 946 (5 February 1943), which authorized the minister of labour to control the movement, employment, and place of residence of all Nikkei.
171 "Habeas Corpus If Basis of Law, Order-in-Council Revokes This Decides Jap-Canadian Forum," *Varsity*, 15 February 1946, LAC, MG 28, series 1, vol. 3, file 20; Fowke, *They Made Democracy Work*, 22, CCJC-MAC, folder 12.
172 "No Room for Doctrine of 'White Supremacy,' Croll Insists in House," *Toronto Globe and Mail*, 18 March 1948. The usual supporters of this move were, not surprisingly, Tom Reid (Liberal, New Westminster) and George Cruickshank (Liberal, Fraser Valley).
173 CCJC, Minutes of executive meeting, 22 October 1945, LAC, MG 28, series 1, vol. 1, file 1, pt. 2 of 2; CCJC, Minutes, 23 November 1946, LAC, MG 28, series 1, vol. 1, file 1, pt. 2 of 2; "Japanese Question," speech delivered by Sen. A.W. Roebuck at Jarvis Collegiate, 10 January 1946, LAC, MG 28, series 1, vol. 2, file 13; *Toronto Daily Star*, 8 May 1947, LAC, MG 28, series 1, vol. 3, file 21; CCJC, Minutes, 21 February 1946, CCJC-MAC, folder 5; CCJC, Minutes, 28 April 1947, CCJC-MAC, folder 6; Franca Iacovetta, "'A Respectable Feminist': The Political Career of Senator Cairine Wilson, 1921-1962," in Linda Kealey and Joan Sangster, eds., *Beyond the Vote: Canadian Women and Politics* (Toronto: University of Toronto Press, 1989), 63-85; Lambertson, *Repression and Resistance*, 128-29; Andrew C. Holman, "'A Quietly Excellent Piece of International Goodwill': The Canadian-American Women's Committee, *Popular Diplomacy*, and Canadian-American Relations, 1941-69" (paper presented at the ACSUS biennial conference, St. Louis, Missouri, 16-21 November 2005).
174 "Profit and Loss Statement for 1945," *Nisei Affairs* 1, 5 (November-December 1945).
175 Editorial, "Retreat under Pressure," *Toronto Globe and Mail*, 25 January 1947.

Chapter 4: Advancing Their Rights
1 Morton Grodzins, *Americans Betrayed: Politics and the Japanese Evacuation* (Chicago: University of Chicago Press, 1949), 163.
2 Indeed, its executive secretary, Mike Masaoka, and ACLU director Roger Baldwin developed a very close relationship, with the former naming his first-born son after the latter.
3 The intergenerational divide has been chronicled by both Canadian and American scholars. On the American situation, see Jacobus ten Broek, Edward N. Barnhart, and Floyd W. Matson, *Prejudice, War, and the Constitution* (Berkeley: University of California Press, 1958); Grodzins, *Americans Betrayed;* Paul R. Spickard, "The Nisei Assume Power: The Japanese American Citizens League, 1941-1942," *Pacific Historical Review* 52, 2 (May 1983): 147-74; Roger Daniels, *Concentration Camps, North America: Japanese in the United States and Canada during World War II* (Malabar, FL: R.E. Krieger, 1981), chap. 1; and Ronald Takaki, *Strangers from a Different Shore: A History of Asian Americans* (Boston: Back Bay Books, 1998), chap. 5. On the Canadian situation, see Daniels, *Concentration Camps, North America*, chap. 9; Ken Adachi, *The Enemy That Never Was: A History of the Japanese Canadians*, rev. ed. (Toronto: McClelland and Stewart, 1991), chap. 5; and Peter Takaji Nunoda, "A Community in Transition and Conflict: The Japanese Canadians, 1935-1951" (PhD diss., University of Manitoba, 1991), chap. 2.
4 Interview, Dr. Wes Fujiwara by Ms. Gayle Shellard, 1989. My thanks to Gayle Shellard for sharing her interview with me. See also Nunoda, "A Community in Transition," 38-39, and Adachi, *The Enemy That Never Was*, 123-27, 157-58.
5 *New Canadian*, 17 July 1940; Nunoda, "A Community in Transition," 39-40; Adachi, *The Enemy That Never Was*, 164.
6 *New Canadian*, 27 May 1939.
7 Quoted in Adachi, *The Enemy That Never Was*, 160-61.
8 Vancouver-born Samuel I. Hayakawa was an English professor and semanticist who vaulted into fame when he successfully ended a strike at the San Francisco State College

campus in 1968. In 1976, at age seventy, he went on to serve as Republican senator for California. An ardent assimilationist, he also chaired a group called US English, dedicated to pressing for a constitutional amendment to make English the nation's official language. Government of Canada, *Wayfarers: Canadian Achievers*, Canada Heirloom Series, vol. 5, s.v. "Samuel I. Hayakawa," by Mel James, http://collections.ic.gc.ca/.

9 Adachi, *The Enemy That Never Was*, 161-65, quote on 162.

10 "Report on Activities of the Nisei Sub-committee to the Advisory Committee on Welfare," 31 March 1942, Library and Archives of Canada [LAC], RG 2, Privy Council Office Records, vol. 6, file "Circular Letters, 1942-1945"; "Report of Judge J.C.A. Cameron on Royal Commission to Investigate Activities of the Black Dragon Society in British Columbia," 19 December 1942, 10, LAC, RG 33/60, vol. 2.

11 Adachi, *The Enemy That Never Was*, 227.

12 "Minutes of the Japanese Canadian Citizens Council," 31 March 1942, LAC, MG 28 V7, National Japanese Canadian Citizens Association Papers, vol. 1, file 2; Nisei Mass Evacuation Group, "Survey of Development of Events Re: Evacuation of Canadians of Japanese Origin," 15 April 1942, LAC, RG 36/27, Boards, Offices and Commissions, series 27: British Columbia Security Commission, 1942-1948, vol. 3, series 27, file 66; Nunoda, "A Community in Transition," 69-70.

13 NMEG to Austin Taylor, BCSC, 15 April 1942, LAC, RG 36/27, vol. 3, series 27, file 66.

14 Ibid. Roy Miki devotes an entire chapter to the NMEG struggle in *Redress: Inside the Japanese Canadian Call for Justice* (Vancouver: Raincoast Books, 2004), chap. 3.

15 JCCC Minutes, 11 April 1942, 13 May 1942, LAC, MG 28 V7, vol. 1, file 2; Hill to Mead, *RCMP Intelligence Report*, 11 April 1942, LAC, RG 36/27, vol. 2, series, 27, file 53.

16 Ann Gomer Sunahara, "The Wartime Experience of North American Japanese: Some Canadian and American Comparisons" (paper presented at the Canadian Historical Association annual meeting, Montreal, June 1980), 4-6; Ann Gomer Sunahara, *The Politics of Racism: The Uprooting of Japanese Canadians during the Second World War* (Toronto: James Lorimer, 1981), 66-75; Nunoda, "A Community in Transition," chap. 3.

17 Cooperative Committee on Japanese-Canadian Arrivals in Toronto, Minutes, 8 June 1943, 2, LAC, MG 28, series 1, 14, vol. 1, file 1, pt. 2 of 2; "A Record of the Work of the Cooperative Committee on Japanese Canadians," 1, LAC, MG 28, series 1, 14, vol. 2, file 4. This document may also be found in the McMaster University Archives, Co-operative Committee on Japanese Canadians Papers [CCJC-MAC], folder 12. Jarnail Singh, "Wartime Toronto and Japanese Canadians," *Polyphony* 6, 1 (Summer 1984): 240-44. This article was based on an interview with George Tanaka. I would like to thank P. Whitney Lackenbauer for this reference. Ad Hoc Committee for "Japanese Canadian Redress: The Toronto Story," *Japanese Canadian Redress: The Toronto Story* (Toronto: Hpf Press, 2000), chap. 1, "The Roots of Our Struggle." My thanks to Myron Momryk of Library and Archives Canada for drawing my attention to this book.

18 Quote taken from masthead of *Nisei Affairs* 1, 1 (20 July 1945). For the JCCD's limited national appeal, see *Encyclopedia of Canada's Peoples*, s.v. "Japanese," by Midge Michiko Ayukawa and Patricia E. Roy, http://www.multiculturalcanada.ca/ecp/content/japanese.html.

19 Daniels, *Concentration Camps, North America*, 24-25; Adachi, *The Enemy That Never Was*, 236-37; Spickard, "The Nisei Assume Power," 147-48.

20 Spickard, "The Nisei Assume Power," 151-54; Takaki, *Strangers from a Different Shore*, chap. 5; Daniels, *Concentration Camps, North America*, 21-25.

21 Quoted in Daniels, *Concentration Camps, North America*, 24-25. The JACL creed was entered on page A2205 of the United States *Congressional Record* on 9 May 1941. On Saburo Kido, see "Biography of Saburo Kido," n.d., Princeton University, Firestone Library, Norman Thomas Papers [Firestone Library, NT Papers], series 5, subseries C, microfilm reel 82, file V:C:4 – Japanese Americans, 1934-1956; on Mike Masaoka, see Biographical sketch, Mike M. Masaoka, n.d., Princeton University, Seeley G. Mudd Manuscript Library [Mudd Library], American Civil Liberties Union [ACLU] Papers, series 3, box 1056, folder 9.

22 Spickard, "The Nisei Assume Power," 158-59.

23 Quoted in ibid., 157.
24 Spickard, "The Nisei Assume Power," 160-61.
25 United States Congress, House Select Committee Investigating National Defense Migration, *Hearings before the Select Committee Investigating National Defense Migration, 77th Congress, 2nd Sess.* (Washington, DC: Government Printing Office, 1942), p. 29, 11266-67; Grodzins, *Americans Betrayed,* 195-96. With the support of the ACLU, Lincoln Seiichi Kanai sued out a writ of habeas corpus on the grounds that imprisonment would deny him due process and equal protection of the law, and that compliance with the evacuation orders would be a negation of his citizenship status. Eventually charged with violation of the military orders, he was sentenced to six months in prison. The federal district judge in the case described him as a "full blooded Japanese." The ACLU did not appeal. "Memorandum on the Court Cases Contesting the Evacuation of American Citizens of Japanese Ancestry," January 1943, Mudd Library, MC 005, Roger N. Baldwin Papers, box 18, folder 9; Besig to Baldwin, 1 August 1942, Mudd Library, ACLU Papers, vol. 2397.
26 Quoted in United States Congress, *Hearings,* 11229-32. James Omura subsequently became editor of a newspaper called the *Denver Rocky Shimpo*. In 1944, after publishing statements issued by the Heart Mountain Fair Play Committee and supporting the committee in his editorials, he was indicted for conspiracy to violate the Selective Service Act and for counselling others to resist the draft. The statements had declared that Fair Play Committee members would not cooperate with the draft unless their citizenship rights were restored. The cost of the trial bankrupted Omura's newspaper. Takaki, *Strangers from a Different Shore,* 398-99.
27 Spickard, "The Nisei Assume Power," 162-64; United States Congress, *Hearings,* pt. 29, 11151, 11156, 11449-78; "Statement of the Japanese American Citizens League," *Pacific Citizen* 14, 1 (24 February 1942).
28 Spickard, "The Nisei Assume Power," 164-67; Masaoka quoted in Milton S. Eisenhower, *The President Is Calling* (Garden City: Doubleday Press, 1974), 117-24 (emphasis added).
29 Baldwin to Besig, 16 March 1942, Mudd Library, ACLU Papers, vol. 2363; Besig to Baldwin, 6 March 1942, 13 March 1942, Mudd Library, ACLU Papers, vol. 2363; Peter Irons, *Justice at War: The Story of the Japanese American Internment Cases* (Berkeley: University of California Press, 1983), 112; Samuel Walker, *In Defense of American Liberties: A History of the ACLU* (New York: Oxford University Press, 1990), 138.
30 "Re: Test Cases," *JACL Bulletin* 142 (7 April 1942), Mudd Library, ACLU Papers, vol. 2394; Besig to Baldwin, 4 April 1942, Mudd Library, ACLU Papers, vol. 2363.
31 Saburo Kido, "US Nisei Must Raise Funds to Fight Threats to Civil Liberties," *Pacific Citizen* 15, 6 (9 July 1942).
32 "JACL Asks Right to Send Representatives to California to Defend Nisei Citizenship," *Pacific Citizen* 16, 2 (14 January 1943).
33 Edward C. Carter to Galen Fisher, 8 September 1942, Columbia University, Butler Library [BLCU], Department of Rare Books and Manuscripts, Institute of Pacific Relations Collection [IPR], box 59; Fisher to Carter, 15 September 1942, BLCU, IPR, box 59; Baldwin to Mr. Yoshita Takagi, JACD, cc to Mary Hillyer, Seattle ACLU, 25 June 1942, Mudd Library, ACLU Papers, box 8, folder 12; Baldwin to Rt. Rev. Edward L. Parsons, SC-ACLU, 27 October 1942, Mudd Library, ACLU Papers, box 8, folder 12; Greg Robinson, "Nisei in Gotham: The JACD and Japanese Americans in 1940s New York," *Prospects* 30 (2006): 1-15.
34 Galen Fisher to Takeshi Haga, 3 October 1941, BLCU, IPR, box 59; Tom Kume to Edward C. Carter, 14 October 1941, BLCU, IPR, box 59; Tom Kume to ACLU, 23 August 1941, Mudd Library, ACLU Papers, vol. 2464; Baldwin to Kume, 26 August 1941, Mudd Library, ACLU Papers, vol. 2464; "67 Prominent Americans Sponsor JACL," *Pacific Citizen* 18, 6 (12 February 1944); "JACL Sponsors," *Pacific Citizen* 18, 6 (12 February 1944).
35 Paul Oyamada to Arthur Garfield Hays, 18 November 1942, Mudd Library, ACLU Papers, vol. 2396; Hays to Oyamada, 24 November 1942, Mudd Library, ACLU Papers, vol. 2396. Hays replied that he "did not believe that he [Oyamada] could be effective in a relocation center."
36 "JACL Chapter Organized on Inter-racial Basis in New York," *Pacific Citizen* 18, 23 (1 July

1944); "New JACL Policy," *Pacific Citizen* 19, 23 (9 December 1944). Sponsors of the group included leaders of church and labour organizations. Among them were B.F. McLaurin, international organizer of the Brotherhood of Sleeping Car Porters; Harry Binsse, editor of the *Commonweal;* Norman Thomas; and George Schuyler, editor of the *Pittsburgh Courier.*

37 "Combined Report of the Men's and Women's Sub-committees to Co-operative Committee for Japanese-Canadians," 1-4, CCJC-MAC, file 12.

38 Singh, "Wartime Toronto and Japanese Canadians," 2-3; Interview, Mr. George Tanaka by Mr. Gerry Shikatani, 17 May 1978, Multicultural History Society of Ontario Archives. See Chapter 3 for more information on the letter-writing campaign of individual CCJC members.

39 "Report of Nisei Delegation to Ottawa regarding Disfranchisement Bill #135," 24 July 1944, LAC, MG 28 V7, vol. 1.

40 *JCCD Brief in the Matter of the War Services Elector's Bill (#135 of 1944) Section 5 regarding Certain Amendment to Section 14 ss. 2 of the Dominion Elections Act, 1938 and in the Matter of the Proposed Disfranchisement of British Subjects and Canadian Citizens in Canada* [JCCD Brief], 24 June 1944, 2, LAC, MG 28 V7, vol. 1, file 23.

41 Ibid., 6-10.

42 CCF and NIAC opposition is mentioned in Chapter 4. Patricia E. Roy, "Citizens without Votes: East Asians in British Columbia, 1872-1947," in Jorgen Dahlie and Tissa Fernando, eds., *Ethnicity, Power, and Politics in Canada* (Toronto: Methuen Press, 1981), 162-63.

43 Nunoda, "A Community in Transition," 165-66; Roy Ito, We Went to War: The Story of the Japanese Canadians Who Served during the First and Second World Wars, 2nd ed. (Stittsville, ON: Canada's Wings, 1992), pt. 4. "A Record of the Work of the Cooperative Committee on Japanese Canadians," 3, LAC, MG 28, series 1, 14, vol. 2, file 4; CCJ6, "Correspondence and Minutes, 1943-56," LAC, MG 28, series 1, 14, vol. 1, file 1, pt. 2 of 2; JCCD Brief, 24 June 1944, LAC, MG 28 V7, vol. 1, file 23.

44 The *New Canadian* published a parallel copy in Japanese but only prior to the attack on Pearl Harbor and after 1945, when publishing in Japanese was no longer prohibited. Takaichi Umezuki was the Japanese-language editor.

45 The following 1942 issues of the *Pacific Citizen* contain articles detailing the Canadian situation: 15, 6 (9 July), "Manitoba Province Admits Nisei Children into Public Schools," 15, 16 (17 September), and "Canadian Evacuees Settled in Wartime Housing Projects in British Columbia Interior," (10 December). In 1942, the *New Canadian* published a number of articles about the US incarceration: "Give Local Japanese a Fair Chance is American Attitude," 12 January; "Storms Brewing in the US," 30 January; Editorial, 9 February; "U.S. Front," 25 February; Editorial, 3 March; "On the American Front," 5 March; 12 March; and 13 June.

46 See, for example, "Canadian Paper Opposes Move to Deport Japanese," *Pacific Citizen* 16, 11 (18 March 1943); *New Canadian,* 15 March 1943. See also Chapter 3 for a lengthier discussion.

47 *New Canadian,* 12 January 1942; Larry Tajiri, *Pacific Citizen* 16, 17 (29 April 1943).

48 For *Pacific Citizen* articles lauding CCF support of Japanese Canadians, see "A Lesson from the North," 16, 25 (24 June 1943); "Canadian CCF Official Backs Rights of Nisei," 17, 22 (4 December 1943); "Progressive Canadian Party Backs Rights of Dominion's Citizens of Japanese Ancestry," 18, 8 (26 February 1944); and "Canada's CCF Reaffirms 1943 Stand on Evacuee Problem," 18, 14 (29 April 1944).

49 Tom Shoyama, "Pressure Defeats Policy," *New Canadian,* 15 July 1944; Patricia E. Roy et al., eds., *Mutual Hostages: Canadians and Japanese during the Second World War* (Toronto: University of Toronto Press, 1990), 144-45. Thomas Shoyama died on 22 December 2006. Shortly thereafter, a *Toronto Globe and Mail* article described his impressive careers as close advisor to Tommy Douglas at the height of CCF power in Saskatchewan, where he also helped develop that province's Crown corporations and Medicare; as a deputy minister in Pierre Trudeau's government; and as a "cherished" academic at the University of Victoria's School of Public Administration and the Department of Asian and Pacific Studies.

.But nowhere does the article mention Shoyama's impressive work in advocating for the basic rights of Japanese Canadians during his tenure as *New Canadian* editor. See John Chaput, "Thomas Shoyama, Civil Servant and Teacher: 1916-2006," *Toronto Globe and Mail,* 30 December 2006.

50 Tom Shoyama, "Americans Go Forward," *New Canadian,* 6 January 1945.

51 *Pacific Citizen,* editorial, "Canadian Contrast," 18, 25 (15 July 1944); Larry Tajiri, "Canadian Racists," 18, 27 (29 July 1944); editorial, "Racism in Canada," 20, 12 (24 March 1945).

52 "World Capital," *Pacific Citizen* 22, 2 (12 January 1946).

53 "Canadian Problem," *Pacific Citizen* 22, 6 (9 February 1946).

54 Editorial, *Nisei Affairs* 1, 2 (28 August 1945), and editorial, 1, 4 (31 October 1945); "Deportations a Violation of Human Rights," *New Canadian,* 3 November 1945.

55 See, for example, Brewin's article, "Legal Aspects of the Proposed Deportation," *Nisei Affairs* 1, 8 (March 1946); A.L. Wirin, "The Supreme Court Decisions: U.S. High Court Vindicates Faith That Bill of Rights Is Dynamic Reality in Nation's Life," *Pacific Citizen* 20, 1 (6 January 1945); Roger Baldwin, "Civil Liberties in Wartime: Test Cases May Be Necessary to Define Legal Rights of Japanese American Group," *Pacific Citizen* 17, 25 (25 December 1943).

56 *The Evacuee Speaks* (Santa Anita Assembly Center newsletter), 1 August 1942, Mudd Library, ACLU Papers, vol. 2394.

57 ACLU national board, Minutes, 18 December 1944, Mudd Library, ACLU Papers, vol. 2584.

58 A.L. Wirin, "Wirin: JACL's Action Is Step of Major Significance toward Preserving Fundamental Rights," *Pacific Citizen* 16, 6 (11 February 1943). See also "JACL Brief in Regan Case Attacks Racial Nationalism of California Native Sons Group," *Pacific Citizen* 16, 7 (18 February 1943).

59 Saburo Kido, "Report to the Nisei: National President Refutes Rumors regarding JACL in Summarizing 1943 Activities," *Pacific Citizen* 17, 25 (25 December 1943). In the same issue, Joe Grant Masaoka, brother of Mike Masaoka, called on Japanese Americans to end their criticism of the JACL, cautioning that "Japanese Americans can ill afford to be disunited." Masaoka, "Joe Grant Masaoka's," *Pacific Citizen* 17, 25 (25 December 1943).

60 Larry Tajiri, "Financing Test Cases," *Pacific Citizen* 19, 18 (4 November 1944).

61 Ibid.

62 The *Hirabayashi, Korematsu,* and *Endo* cases will be examined in greater detail in Chapter 5, with special attention to the briefs and arguments presented by the ACLU. For the *Yasui* case and a history of three generations of the Yasui family, see Lauren Kessler's outstanding *Stubborn Twig: Three Generations in the Life of a Japanese American Family* (New York: Penguin Books, 1994). For the *Yasui* case specifically, see her Chapter 9. My thanks to Karolyn Smardz Frost for the gift òf this book. It should also be noted that Japanese American groups in the camps organized resistance to the removal. The example of the Heart Mountain Fair Play Committee, in particular, calls into question the stereotype of the Japanese American as victim of wartime oppression, responding only with patriotism and resignation. For full details regarding the Heart Mountain resistors, see Daniels, *Concentration Camps, North America,* 118-29. Tule Lake was also a centre of resistance, mainly by the Kibei, a group of young Nikkei who had been born in the US and educated in Japan. Dissatisfied with their situation, they saw renunciation of their citizenship as the best means by which to resist. For a description of the Tule Lake resistance, see Dorothy S. Thomas and Richard S. Nishimoto, *The Spoilage* (Berkeley and Los Angeles: University of California Press, 1946), and Gary Y. Okihiro, "Tule Lake under Martial Law: A Study in Japanese Resistance," *Journal of Ethnic Studies* 5, 3 (Fall 1977): 71-85. At the Manzanar Camp, a camp-wide riot broke out on 6 December 1942, largely at the instigation of anti-JACL-WRA "agitators" and joined by the majority of the camp population. After the military police were called in, two young males were killed and many others were treated for gunshot wounds. For differing accounts of the Manzanar riot, see Thomas and Nishimoto, *The Spoilage,* 49-52; Allan Bosworth, *America's Concentration Camps* (New York: W.W. Norton Press, 1967), 157-62; Audrie Girdner and Anne Loftis, *The Great Betrayal*

(New York: Macmillan Press, 1969), 263-66; and Michi Nishiura Weglyn, *Years of Infamy: The Untold Story of America's Concentration Camps*, rev. ed. (Seattle: University of Washington Press, 1996), 121-33.

63 Walker, *In Defense of American Liberties*, 138-39; Irons, *Justice at War*, chap. 7; "Of Civil Wrongs and Rights: The Fred Korematsu Story," *P.O.V.*, PBS, 11 July 2001.

64 Wirin to Fraenkel, 13 August 1942, Mudd Library, MC 072, Arthur Garfield Hays Papers, box 10, folder 3; Fraenkel memo, "With Regard to the Draft Brief," 17 August 1942, Mudd Library, MC 072, box 10, folder 3; *ACLU Bulletin 1032*, 6 July 1942, Mudd Library, ACLU Papers, vol. 2395; Wirin to Howard Lewis, 3 September 1942, Mudd Library, ACLU Papers, vol. 2398; Ernest Wakayama to Wirin, 1 September 1942, Mudd Library, ACLU Papers, vol. 2398; SC-ACLU, press release, 26 September 1942, Mudd Library, ACLU Papers, vol. 2398; Wakayama to Wirin, 14 February 1943, Mudd Library, ACLU Papers, vol. 2398; Wirin to Baldwin, 25 February 1943, Mudd Library, ACLU Papers, vol. 2398; Baldwin to Wirin, 1 March 1943, Mudd Library, ACLU Papers, vol. 2398; SC-ACLU, Minutes, 13 June 1942, Mudd Library, ACLU Papers, vol. 2463; Walker, *In Defense of American Liberties*, 138-39; Irons, *Justice at War*, 114-15.

65 Quoted in Irons, *Justice at War*, 84-87.

66 Irons, *Justice at War*, 114-15; Walker, *In Defense of American Liberties*, 138-39. Apparently, Yasui held no grudge against the ACLU regarding its lack of support for his case. In 1945, he sent a five-dollar donation to the ACLU and offered the assistance of the local Denver chapter of the JACL if it were needed. Minoru Yasui to ACLU, 8 February 1945, Mudd Library, ACLU Papers, vol. 2667.

67 Quoted in Irons, *Justice at War*, 87-88.

68 Ibid., 88; Hirabayashi to Baldwin, 18 July 1944, Mudd Library, ACLU Papers, vol. 2587.

69 US Circuit Court of Appeals, *John T. Regan vs. Cameron King, as Registrar of Voters in the City and County of San Francisco, State of California*, No. 10,299, Brief for Japanese American Citizens League, amicus curiae, 16 February 1943, Mudd Library, MC 072, box 24, folder 2; *Hirabayashi v. United States*, 320 U.S. 81 (1943), Brief, Japanese American Citizens League, amicus curiae; "National JACL to File Briefs in Evacuation Test Cases before US Supreme Court," *Pacific Citizen* 16, 17 (29 April 1943); Irons, *Justice at War*, 192-93.

70 Ernest Besig to Howard J. Lewis, 31 August 1942, Mudd Library, ACLU Papers, vol. 2397; Korematsu quoted in "Of Civil Wrongs and Rights: The Fred Korematsu Story" *P.O.V.*, PBS, 11 July 2001; Irons, *Justice at War*, 93-99.

71 Saburo Kido to Clifford Forster, 6 January 1944, Mudd Library, ACLU Papers, vol., 2587; Wirin to Baldwin, 24 April 1944, Mudd Library, ACLU Papers, vol. 2587.

72 Irons, *Justice at War*, 99-101.

73 Ibid., 101-2.

74 Ibid., 102-3.

75 JCCD, Minutes, 29 June 1945, LAC, MG 28 V7, vol. 1, file 7; Edith Fowke, *They Made Democracy Work: The Story of the Co-operative Committee on Japanese Canadians* (Toronto: Co-operative Committee on Japanese Canadians, 1951), 13-17; Report of G.J.A. Reany on visit of delegation to Ottawa re: the Japanese in Canada, 30 July 1945, LAC, MG 28, series 6, vol. 2, file 13; "In the Matter of Dispersal of the Japanese Canadians throughout Canada," n.d. (1945?), LAC, MG 28, series 6, vol. 1, file 5. In its introduction, this report noted that it was "the result of a consensus of opinion by twelve Japanese Canadians who have lived for the past three years in Eastern Canada and who have taken an active part in Nisei organizations which have, in the main, been set up for the following reasons: to fight for a one hundred percent Canadian Citizenship, to combat increasing Government restrictions on civil rights, to educate and seek the cooperation of the Canadian population in matters pertaining to the Japanese Canadian minority problem."

76 "We Must Fight Deportation," *New Canadian*, 10 November 1945; Japanese of Lemon Creek to Mrs. Hugh MacMillan, 29 October 1945, LAC, MG 28 V7, vol. 1, file 6; Slocan Valley Nisei Organization to Margaret Foster, 16 March 1946, LAC, MG 30 C69, Margaret Foster Papers; *CCJC News Bulletin 4*, 15 March 1945, CCJC-MAC, folder 10.

77 JCCD, Minutes, 21 December 1945, 31 January 1946, LAC, MG 28 V7, vol. 1, file 7; *Nisei*

Affairs 1, 6 (19 January 1946); Nunoda, "A Community in Transition," 249-50; Fowke, *They Made Democracy Work,* 19-20, LAC, MG 28, series 6, vol. 2, file 13. The Southern Alberta Youth Council, a group of young Nisei in the Lethbridge area, donated $201.81 to the CCJC to help with court costs. Southern Alberta Youth Council, Minutes, 24 March 1946, LAC, MG 31 F8, Minoru Takada Papers.

78 *New Canadian,* 19 July, 8 August, 18 August, and 19 September 1945. Order-in-Council P.C. 946 transferred the administration of the incarceration camps to the Department of Labour on 5 February 1943.

79 JCCD executive, Minutes, 26 February 1946, LAC, MG 28 V7, microfilm reel C12818, file 1-7.

80 Quoted in Kitagawa, *This Is My Own,* 260.

81 JCCD Annual Secretariat Report, 1 November 1946, LAC, MG 28 V7, microfilm reel C12818, file 1-8. As of 2 April, the Issei were allowed to join the JCCD; as of the date of this report, 150 had done so. JCCD, Minutes of the Organizational Conference, 30 August-2 September 1946, LAC, MG 28 V7, vol. 1, file 8; Singh, "Wartime Toronto and Japanese Canadians," 244; Nunoda, "A Community in Transition," 300-315.

82 Toru Matsumoto, Committee on Resettlement of Japanese Americans, "To the Delegates," 7 December 1945, Mudd Library, ACLU Papers, vol. 2664.

83 Japanese American Evacuation Claims Act, 50 U.S.C. App. s. 1981 *et seq.,* s. 1981(a).

84 United States, Commission on Wartime Relocation and Internment of Civilians, *Personal Justice Denied: Report of the Commission on Wartime Relocation and Internment of Civilians,* rev. ed. (Seattle: University of Washington Press, 1997), 118; Roger Daniels, *Prisoners without Trial: Japanese Americans in World War II* (1993; rev. ed., New York: Hill and Wang, 2004), 88-90.

85 United States, *Personal Justice Denied,* 118-19.

86 The solicitors involved in claims settlement were R.J. McMaster (British Columbia); W.E. Huckvale and L.S. Turcotte (Alberta); Morris Shumiatcher (Saskatchewan), a prominent provincial human rights activist and drafter of the Saskatchewan Bill of Rights; Messrs Cherniack and Cherniack (Manitoba), of whom J.A. Cherniack was a member of the Jewish Labour Committee; Mr. F.A. Brewin, Mr. R.A. Best (Ontario); and Roger Ouimet (Quebec), a member of the Montreal CLU. CCJC to Japanese Canadian claimants, "Claims Commission, 1947-1951," n.d., LAC, MG 28, series 1, 14, vol. 2, file 11.

87 CCJC, "Report of the Sub-committee on Restrictions and Property Losses," 26 October 1946, LAC, MG 28, series 1, vol. 1, file 1, pt. 2 of 2; JCCD, Executive Committee Minutes, 10 November 1946, LAC, MG 28 V7, vol. 1, file 7; CCJC, Minutes, 6 November 1946, CCJC-MAC, folder 5; "JCCD Reports," n.d., CCJC-MAC, folder 12; "Statement to Claimants Re: Origin, Nature and Work of the Co-operative Committee on Japanese Canadians, April 1950," 3-15, CCJC-MAC, folder 13; F.A. Brewin, "A Review of Property Claims," *New Canadian,* 20 October 1948, LAC, RG 36/27, vol. 34, file 2202; Donalda MacMillan to Thelma Perry Scambler, 2 May 1947, LAC, MG 30 C160, Grace Thompson Papers; Tanaka to Scambler, 18 July 1947, LAC, MG 30 C160; Brewin to Scambler, 2 October 1947, LAC, MG 30 C160; JCCD to Winnipeg CCJC, 14 April 1948, LAC, MG 30 C160; JCCD to the Scamblers, 15 April 1948, LAC, MG 30 C160. Thelma Scambler and her husband, Charles, were fixtures in the Winnipeg branch of the CCJC. F. Andrew Brewin and fellow lawyers A.B. Mortimer, J.B. Allen, and A. Best produced a draft document outlining their hopes for the kind of claims commission that could be established in Canada. Their brief was patterned after the US act of Congress to apply to Canadian conditions. As noted above, however, the government did not establish a commission reflective of the broadened terms of reference that characterized the American Evacuation Claims Commission. "Draft re: Terms of Reference to Japanese Canadian Property Claims," n.d. (1947?), CCJC-MAC, folder 11.

88 "Statement to Claimants Re: Origin, Nature and Work of the Co-operative Committee on Japanese Canadians, April 1950," 3-15, CCJC-MAC, folder 13; F.A. Brewin, "A Review of Property Claims," *New Canadian,* 20 October 1948, LAC, RG 36/27, vol. 34, file 2202; "Report of P.S. Ross and Sons, Auditor," 31 May 1950, LAC, MG 32 C26, vol. 1, F. Andrew

Brewin Papers; G. Tanaka to "Claimants," 28 February 1950, LAC, MG 28 V7, reel C12818. The Japanese Canadian community was by no means automatically unanimous regarding CCJC and NJCCA handling of the claims. A group known as the Toronto Claimants Committee was especially vocal in its disapproval. For more on the dissent, see Nunoda, "A Community in Transition," chap. 9, and Ad Hoc Committee, *Japanese Canadian Redress*.

89 Editorial, "A Wrong Redressed in Part," *Toronto Globe and Mail*, 15 June 1950.
90 G. Tanaka to Louis St. Laurent, 23 September 1950, LAC, MG 28 V7, microfilm reel C12818; St. Laurent quoted in Sunahara, *The Politics of Racism*, 159-60. Not all Japanese Canadians were satisfied with the outcome of the Bird Commission, or with their partnership with the CCJC. See Miki, *Redress*, chap. 5, and Nunoda, "A Community in Transition." In addition, in 1968, nearly twenty years after the Bird Commission, Mr. Torazo Iwasaki sued the Canadian government for the return of property confiscated during the war. In his Exchequer Court case, Iwasaki maintained, among other issues, that the Orders-in-Council authorizing the seizure of property were void for uncertainty on the basis of "race." However, the Exchequer Court, and subsequently the Supreme Court of Canada, rejected Iwasaki's claim because the Supreme Court and the Privy Council had upheld the orders in the court challenges detailed above. *Iwasaki v. The Queen* (1968), 2 D.L.R. (3d) 241; *Iwasaki v. The Queen* (1970), S.C.R. 437.
91 Quoted in Cheryl Greenberg, "Black and Jewish Responses to Japanese Internment," *Journal of American Ethnic History* 14 (Winter 1995): 4-5.
92 *Crisis* 49 (January 1942): 7 (emphasis in original); Harry Paxton Howard, "Americans in Concentration Camps," *Crisis* 49 (September 1942): 281-84, 301-2.
93 Thomas to John Haynes Holmes, 14 November 1942, Firestone Library, NT Papers, microfilm reel 56, file II:B:1; Daniels, *Concentration Camps, North America*, 78-79; Girdner and Loftis, *The Great Betrayal*, 126; Greenberg, "Black and Jewish Responses," 13-15; Cheryl Greenberg, *Troubling the Waters: Black-Jewish Relations in the American Century* (Princeton, NJ: Princeton University Press, 2006), 86-87.
94 Thomas to John Haynes Holmes, 11 March 1942, Firestone Library, Norman Thomas (NT) Papers; Holmes to Thomas, 12 March 1942, Firestone Library, NT Papers.
95 Editorial, "Negro and Evacuation," *Pacific Affairs* 16, 11 (18 March 1943); "Civil Liberties in Wartime," *Pacific Affairs* 17, 25 (25 December 1943); Thomas Borstelman, *The Cold War and the Color Line* (Cambridge, MA, and London: Harvard University Press, 2001), 39.
96 Princeton University, Mudd Manuscript Library (PUL), Undergrad Alumni Records, Norman Thomas, Class of 1905, folder 3, Norman Thomas, *Democracy and Japanese Americans* (New York: Post War World Council, 2 January 1942), 33; Besig to Baldwin, 12 April 1942, PUL, ACLU Papers, vol. 2396; Julia Chung quoted in *Pacific Affairs* 16, 6 (11 February 1943); Chinese American grad student quoted in 17, 5 (7 August 1943); 18, 10 (11 March 1944); 19, 16 (21 October 1944); Daniels, *Concentration Camps, North America*, 162-64.
97 Peter S. Li, *The Chinese in Canada*, 2nd ed. (Toronto: Oxford University Press, 1998), 90-91; Jin Tan and Patricia E. Roy, *The Chinese in Canada*, Canada's Ethnic Groups History Booklet 9 (Ottawa: Canadian Historical Association, 1985), 14-15; Carole F. Lee, "The Road to Enfranchisement: Chinese and Japanese in British Columbia," *BC Studies* 30 (Summer 1976): 44-76; Stephanie D. Bangarth, "'We Are Not Asking You to Open Wide the Gates for Chinese Immigration': The Committee for the Repeal of the Chinese Immigration Act and Early Human Rights Activism in Canada," *Canadian Historical Review* 84, 3 (September 2003): 395-422.
98 Interview, Fujiwara by Shellard; Singh, "Wartime Toronto and Japanese Canadians," 200; Greg Robinson, "'Two Other Solitudes': Historical Encounters between Japanese Canadians and French Canadians," 2005, http://www.discovernikkei.org/wiki/index.php/Robinson_Two_Solitudes; Sunahara, *The Politics of Racism*, 86-87. On ethnic cooperation in the US, see, for example, Jitsuo Morikawa, "Japanese Americans," address at annual meeting, Home Missions Council of North America, stenographic notes, 8 January 1946, Presbyterian Historical Society, RG 26, National Council of Churches Papers, box 8, folder 18.

99 "Organizations Co-operating with or Interested in the Work of the Co-operative Committee for Japanese Canadians," n.d., LAC, MG 28 V7, microfilm reel C12818; JCCD General Meeting, 21 March 1947, LAC, MG 28 V7, microfilm reel C12818.
100 Lee, "The Road to Enfranchisement," 58-59, 72-73.
101 James W. St. G. Walker, *"Race," Rights and the Law in the Supreme Court of Canada: Historical Case Studies* (Waterloo, ON: Wilfrid Laurier University Press, 1997), 192-99; Ross Lambertson, *Repression and Resistance: Canadian Human Rights Activists, 1930-1960* (Toronto: University of Toronto Press, 2005), chap. 5; Irving Abella, "Jews, Human Rights, and the Making of a New Canada," *Journal of the Canadian Historical Association* 11 (2000): 3-16; Carmela Patrias and Ruth A. Frager, "'This Is Our Country, These Are Our Rights': Minorities and the Origins of Ontario's Human Rights Campaigns," *Canadian Historical Review* 82, 1 (March 2001): 1-35.
102 "Rabbi Raps Fascist Tendencies in Treatment of Japanese Canadians," *New Canadian*, 8 December 1945; Abraham L. Feinberg, *Storm the Gates of Jericho* (Toronto and Montreal: McClelland and Stewart, 1964), 62-73, 112-15, 144-47.
103 Greenberg, "Black and Jewish Responses," 15.
104 Quoted in ibid.
105 Quoted in ibid., 15-16.
106 Schuyler cited in WRA, *Japanese-Americans* (n.p.: 1944?), 17-18, CCJC-MAC, folder 22: Japanese-Americans. More information about African American opposition to incarceration can be gleaned from C.K. Doreski, "'Kin in Some Way': The *Chicago Defender* Reads the Japanese Internment, 1942-1945," in Todd Vogel, ed., *The Black Press* (New Brunswick, NJ: Rutgers University Press, 2001), 161-87.
107 George Schuyler, letter to the editor, *Pacific Citizen* 17, 28 (15 January 1944).
108 "Negro Attorney Upholds Rights of Nisei at West L.A. Forum," *Pacific Citizen* 16, 13 (1 April 1943); Greg Robinson, "Norman Thomas and the Struggle against Internment," *Prospects* 28 (2003): 4.
109 "National JACL to File Briefs in Evacuation Test Cases before U.S. Supreme Court," *Pacific Citizen* 16, 17 (29 April 1943).
110 Doreski, "'Kin in Some Way,'" 161-82.
111 Quoted in "The Japanese Americans," *Race Relations: A Monthly Summary of Events and Trends* (Negro Universities Press, New York) 2, 7 (February 1945): 197-98. See also "Japanese-Americans," *Race Relations* 2, 12 (July 1945): 361-62. My gratitude goes to Heather Mackenzie, who collected relevant articles from this publication for the period between 1944 and 1945. See also "Returning Evacuees Suffer Legion Prejudice on Coast," *Call*, 2 May 1945, Mudd Library, ACLU Papers, vol. 2659; "Interracial Tension Fails to Develop," *Social Question Bulletin*, January 1946, Mudd Library, ACLU Papers, vol. 2730.
112 Daniels, *Concentration Camps, North America*, 158.
113 *New Canadian*, 14 August 1945.
114 A. Philip Randolph was a pioneering labour leader and activist. His March on Washington Movement in 1941 was essential to the formation of the first Fair Employment Practices Committee and the integration of the armed forces. See Paula F. Pfeiffer, *A. Philip Randolph, Pioneer of the Civil Rights Movement* (Baton Rouge: Louisiana State University Press, 1990).
115 *Pacific Citizen*, "Negro and Evacuation," 16, 11 (18 March 1943); 17, 18 (28 August 1943); 18, 11 (18 September 1943); "Minorities and the Nisei," 18, 16 (18 March 1944); 18, 17 (20 May 1944); 20, 7 (17 February 1945).
116 Mike Masaoka, "Statement for the Standing Subcommittee on Immigration and Naturalization of the Committee on the Judiciary," House of Representatives, US Congress, 19 March 1947, Mudd Library, ACLU Papers, series 3, box 1055, folder 7.

Chapter 5: "The War Is Over. Long Live the War!"
1 ACLU, "Memorandum on the Court Cases Contesting the Evacuation of American Citizens of Japanese Ancestry," January 1943, Princeton University, Seeley G. Mudd Manuscript Library [Mudd Library], MC 005, Roger N. Baldwin Papers, box 18, folder 9.

2 On Hirabayashi's personal reasons for resistance, see chap. 4. Peter Irons, *Justice at War: The Story of the Japanese American Internment Cases* (Berkeley: University of California Press, 1983), 87-93. Farquharson quoted in ibid., 92.

3 Farquharson to Baldwin, 14 May 1942, Mudd Library, American Civil Liberties Union [ACLU] Papers, vol. 2470; Baldwin to Farquharson, Mudd Library, ACLU Papers, vol. 2470; ACLU, Minutes, 18 May 1942, Mudd Library, ACLU Papers, vol. 2396.

4 Forster to Besig, 1 June 1942, Mudd Library, ACLU Papers, vol. 2465; Irons, *Justice at War*, 114.

5 Baldwin to Besig, 8 June 1942, Mudd Library, ACLU Papers, vol. 2397; Besig to Baldwin, 2 July 1942, Mudd Library, ACLU Papers, vol. 2397; ACLU, "Memorandum on the Court Cases Contesting the Evacuation of American Citizens of Japanese Ancestry," January 1943, Mudd Library, MC 005, box 18, folder 9.

6 NC-ACLU, Minutes, 4 June 1942, Mudd Library, ACLU Papers, vol. 2463; ACLU, Minutes, 8 June 1942, Mudd Library, ACLU Papers, vol. 2363.

7 ACLU, "Memorandum on the Court Cases Contesting the Evacuation of American Citizens of Japanese Ancestry," January 1943, Mudd Library, MC 005, box 18, folder 9; Irons, *Justice at War*, 115-16.

8 For more details on the ACLU schism, see Chapter 2.

9 ACLU memorandum, "To the Active Members of the Corporation," 22 May 1942, Mudd Library, ACLU Papers, vol. 2444; "Resolution concerning Removals from Military Areas, Adopted by the ACLU June 22, 1942," Mudd Library, ACLU Papers, vol. 2444.

10 "Resolution concerning Removals from Military Areas, Adopted by the ACLU June 22, 1942," Mudd Library, ACLU Papers, vol. 2444; "Report of Lawyers Committee to Study Evacuation Cases," 25 June 1942, Mudd Library, ACLU Papers, vol. 2444; "Supplementary Report on Lawyers Committee to Study Evacuation Cases," 29 June 1942, Mudd Library, ACLU Papers, vol. 2444.

11 "Resolution concerning Removals from Military Areas, Adopted by the ACLU June 22, 1942," Mudd Library, ACLU Papers, vol. 2444; Baldwin to Wirin, Besig, and Farquharson, 24 June 1942, Mudd Library, ACLU Papers, vol. 2397.

12 See Chapter 4 for details on the Wakayama case. Wirin to Baldwin, 27 June 1942, Mudd Library, ACLU Papers, vol. 2398.

13 ACLU, Minutes, 6 July 1942, Mudd Library, ACLU Papers, vol. 2395; Farquharson to Baldwin, 29 June 1942, Mudd Library, ACLU Papers, vol. 2740; Farquharson to Thomas, 13 July 1942, Princeton University, Firestone Library, Norman Thomas Papers. Farquharson notes in the latter letter that, due to poor organization at the S-ACLU, she had already undertaken to establish a citizens' committee to raise money and otherwise concern itself with *Hirabayashi* even before the national ACLU took its decision.

14 Besig to Baldwin, 2 July 1942, Mudd Library, ACLU Papers, vol. 2397.

15 Irons, *Justice at War*, 130-35; Samuel Walker, *In Defense of American Liberties: A History of the ACLU* (New York: Oxford University Press, 1990), 140-42.

16 Quoted in Irons, *Justice at War*, 140-43.

17 Quoted in ibid., 143-45. The *Milligan* case was decided following the cessation of the Civil War. This precedent-setting litigation arose from President Abraham Lincoln's suspension of the writ of habeas corpus, which allowed military authorities to arrest allegedly disloyal citizens and send them, without trial, over the Confederate lines into the South. Due to the suspension, army officials refused to obey civil court orders, even in areas not under martial law. In *Milligan*, the Supreme Court established the principle that trial by a military court was unconstitutional in any region where the civil courts were functioning and that such constitutional rights as those to habeas corpus or to trial by jury in a civil court could not be suspended in time of war. Baldwin, "Evacuations and the Constitution," n.d., Mudd Library, MC 005, box 22, folder 1.

18 Besig to Baldwin, 2 July 1942, Mudd Library, ACLU Papers, vol. 2397.

19 ACLU, Minutes, 20 July 1942, Mudd Library, ACLU Papers, vol. 2397; Fraenkel to Forster, 17 June 1942, Mudd Library, ACLU Papers, vol. 2470; Irons, *Justice at War*, 151.

20 Irons, *Justice at War*, 154-55.

21 A writ of certiorari enables a superior court to call up the records of an inferior court so as to review its judgment for legal error, or to move a case there pending to the higher court. Certiorari is most commonly used by the US Supreme Court. A party who wishes to appeal a decision to the Supreme Court must first petition it for a writ of certiorari. The writ is granted only at the court's discretion *and* when at least three of its members believe the case involves an issue of significance to the public interest. When the Supreme Court denies a writ, it is thereby accepting the lower court's decision.

22 See, all in Mudd Library, ACLU Papers, Alexander Meiklejohn to Baldwin, 5 October 1942, vol. 2638; Baldwin to Meiklejohn, 8 October 1942, vol. 2638; Besig to Baldwin, 8 October 1942, vol. 2397; Baldwin to Besig, 13 October 1942, vol. 2397; Besig to Baldwin, 16 October 1942, vol. 2397; Baldwin to Besig, 20 October 1942, vol. 2397; Besig to Baldwin, 22 October 1942, vol. 2397; Baldwin to Besig, 26 October 1942, vol. 2397; Besig to Baldwin, 29 October 1942, vol. 2397; Walter Frank to Bishop Parsons, 9 November 1942, vol. 2397; Parsons to Frank, 11 November 1942, vol. 2397; Parsons to John Haynes Holmes, 12 December 1942, vol. 2397; Besig to Baldwin, 14 December 1942, vol. 2397; Baldwin to Besig, 22 December 1942, vol. 2397; Norman Thomas to Baldwin, 10 November 1942, vol. 2397, box 10, folder 4. See also Osmond K. Fraenkel diary, 2, 16 November 1942, Mudd Library, MC 192, Osmond K. Fraenkel Diary Excerpts, 1933-1969; Irons, *Justice at War,* 168-69.

23 This position was in stark contrast to the ACLU's First World War defence of the First Amendment, with respect to Espionage Act cases and, later, to its position on the "Red Scare." ACLU, "Resolution Adopted by Board of Directors on October 19, 1942," Mudd Library, ACLU Papers, vol. 2466; Osmond K. Fraenkel diary, 12, 26, 30 October 1943, 18, 20, 23, 30 November 1943, 2, 3, 21 December 1943, Mudd Library, MC 192, box 1, folder 1.

24 Besig to Baldwin, 4 February 1943, Mudd Library, ACLU Papers, vol. 2468; Baldwin to Besig, 8 February 1943, Mudd Library, ACLU Papers, vol. 2468; Forster to Besig, 17 February 1943, Mudd Library, ACLU Papers, vol. 2468; Osmond K. Fraenkel diary, 4, 5 January 1943, Mudd Library, MC 192, box 1, folder 1.

25 A.L. Wirin to Forster, 10 February 1943, Mudd Library, ACLU Papers, box 10, folder 3; Forster to Wirin, 13 February 1943, Mudd Library, ACLU Papers, vol. 2463; Wirin to Forster, 29 February 1943, Mudd Library, ACLU Papers, vol. 2463.

26 The JACL *Hirabayashi* brief is discussed at length in the preceding chapter.

27 See, all in Mudd Library, ACLU Papers, Farquharson to Baldwin, 11 March 1943, vol. 2470; Baldwin to Farquharson, 20 April 1943, vol. 2470; Farquharson to Baldwin, 29 April 1943, vol. 2470; Baldwin to Farquharson, 30 April 1943, vol. 2470; Wirin to Forster, 29 March 1943, vol. 2470; Wirin to Baldwin, 17 April 1943, vol. 2468; Forster to Wirin, 21 April 1943, vol. 2468.

28 *Hirabayashi v. United States,* 320 U.S. 81 (1943); Fraenkel quoted in "Memorandum on the Court Cases Contesting the Evacuation of American Citizens of Japanese Ancestry," January 1943, Mudd Library, MC 005, box 18, folder 9.

29 *Hirabayashi,* 320 U.S. 81 (1943), Brief Amicus Curiae for the Northern California Civil Liberties Unition, 58-59.

30 See, all in Mudd Library, ACLU Papers, vol. 2466, ACLU, Minutes, 8 March, 16 April, 10 May 1943; Besig to Holmes, 9 April 1943; Baldwin to Parsons, 14 April 1943; Besig to Holmes, 20 April 1943; Parsons to Holmes, 1 May 1943; Parsons to Holmes, 18 May 1943; Parsons to Baldwin, 12 May 1943; Holmes to Parsons, 13 May 1943; "Memo for the Meeting with Bishop Parsons – Friday, June 4, 1943," 3 June 1943; Baldwin to Parsons, 22 June 1943; Baldwin to Parsons, 31 August 1943. Letters also continued to flow well into December and 1944. The national board's threat of disaffiliation was not unique in ACLU history. In fact, the board went so far as to expel its Chicago branch for offering legal support to alleged pro-German seditionists, contrary to the 19 October Seymour Resolution.

31 US Circuit Court of Appeals, *John T. Regan vs. Cameron King, as Registrar of Voters in the City and County of San Francisco, State of California,* No. 10,299, Brief for Japanese American Citizens League, amicus curiae, 16 February 1943, Mudd Library, MC 072, Arthur

Garfield Hays Papers, box 24, folder 2; *Hirabayashi v. United States,* 320 U.S. 81 (1943), Brief, Japanese American Citizens League, amicus curiae; "JACL Brief in Evacuation Raised Cases Opposes Race Issue by Government Attorney," *Pacific Citizen* 16, 19 (13 May 1943); Irons, *Justice at War,* 192-93.

32 Walker, *In Defense of American Liberties,* 145-46; Irons, *Justice at War,* 194-95, 227.

33 The *Hirabayashi* and *Yasui* decisions will be detailed later in this chapter. Wirin to Forster, 26 June 1943, Mudd Library, ACLU Papers, vol. 2476; Forster to Wirin, 1 July 1943, Mudd Library, ACLU Papers, vol. 2476.

34 Forster to Wirin, 1 September 1943, Mudd Library, ACLU Papers, vol. 2588; Baldwin to Fraenkel, 31 May 1944, Mudd Library, ACLU Papers, vol. 2588; Baldwin to Besig, 2 June 1944, Mudd Library, ACLU Papers, vol. 2585; Columbia University, Butler Library, Oral History Collection, Alan F. Westin interview with Roger Nash Baldwin, 18 December 1874. For further information on the cooperative manoeuvres between the ACLU and the Department of Justice, see Irons, *Justice at War,* chap. 10.

35 *Korematsu v. United States,* 323 U.S. 214 (1944); Irons, *Justice at War,* 302-3.

36 *Korematsu,* 323 U.S. 214 (1944); Wirin to Baldwin, 24 April 1944, Mudd Library, ACLU Papers, vol. 2587; Forster to Kido, 9 May 1944, Mudd Library, ACLU Papers, vol. 2587; Baldwin to Besig, 2 June 1944, Mudd Library, ACLU Papers, vol. 2585; Horsky to Baldwin, 15 June 1944, Mudd Library, ACLU Papers, vol. 2588; Quoted in Irons, *Justice at War,* 303.

37 *Korematsu,* 323 U.S. 214 (1944), Brief, Japanese American Citizens League, amicus curiae, p. 80.

38 *Ex Parte Endo,* 323 U.S. 283 (1944), note 76, Brief for Petitioner, p. 36.

39 Quoted in Irons, *Justice at War,* 309.

40 *Ex Parte Endo,* Brief of the American Civil Liberties Union, amicus curiae, pp. 6-7.

41 Seymour to Baldwin, 23 August 1944, Mudd Library, ACLU Papers, vol. 2466.

42 *Hirabayashi,* 320 U.S. 81 (1943). This discussion of the Japanese American cases is informed by the summary of Eugene V. Rostow, "The Japanese-American Cases – A Disaster," *Yale Law Journal* 54 (June 1945): 489-533. It should be noted that the unanimous decision was an orchestrated one, hence the publication of three concurring opinions that condemned Stone's association of race with guilt. For an excellent treatment of the process by which Chief Justice Stone manipulated the justices to a unanimous opinion, see Irons, *Justice at War,* 228-52.

43 Quoted in Rostow, "The Japanese-American Cases," 489-533.

44 As pointed out in note 42 and elsewhere in this chapter, the decision was not emotionally unanimous. Some twenty years later, Douglas expressed his deep regret – "grave doubts," as he put it – in a May 1962 interview with Princeton professor Walter F. Murphy. Transcriptions of Conversations between Justice William O. Douglas and Professor Walter F. Murphy, 23 May 1962, cassette 8, http://infoshare1.princeton.edu/libraries/firestone/rbsc/finding_aids/douglas/douglas8.html.

45 Ibid.

46 Ibid.

47 Ibid. Under pressure from his colleagues on the bench, particularly Justice Felix Frankfurter, Murphy changed his dissent to a reluctant concurrence. Sidney Fine, "Mr. Justice Murphy and the Hirabayashi Case," *Pacific Historical Review* 33, 2 (May 1964): 195-209; Irons, *Justice at War,* 242-50. According to Irons, Murphy was especially sensitive to racial issues and had dealt sympathetically with racial and ethnic minorities throughout his career. Due to his Irish Catholic background, he also identified with minority persecution. In *Schneiderman,* a case decided on the same day as *Hirabayashi,* Murphy's majority opinion referred to his belief in the United States as a melting pot. He commented that Americans "are a heterogeneous people. In some of our larger cities a majority of the schoolchildren are the offspring of parents only one generation, if that far, removed from the steerage of the immigrant ship." *Schneiderman v. United States,* 320 U.S. 118 at 120 (1943). Irons, *Justice at War,* 242-43.

48 *Hirabayashi,* 320 U.S. 81 at 111 (1943).

49 This characterization of the US Supreme Court is from Jerry Kang, "Denying Prejudice: Internment, Redress, and Denial," *UCLA Law Review* 51, 4 (2004): 933-1013.

50 The discussion of segmentation is informed by Kang, "Denying Prejudice," and Patrick O. Gudridge, "Remember Endo?" *Harvard Law Review* 116 (2003): 1947-49. However, Kang and Gudridge differ as to how *Endo* should be remembered. Gudridge perceives *Endo* as a positive foil for the negative *Korematsu* decision. More specifically, *Endo* serves as an example in which the Supreme Court checks the excesses of the executive branch in time of war, whereas *Korematsu* affirms the constitutionality of forcible evacuation. By contrast, Kang maintains that the two cases were "hand and glove, part of a broader strategy of denial." Although Gudridge denies that segmentation played a role in *Endo*, Kang disagrees, asserting that it was part of the administrative law dodge in that case. According to him, "decoupling" the two components – evacuation and detention – enabled the court to accept military authorization to evacuate and to reject WRA authority over indefinite detention. Had it considered both segments together, the court would have had difficulty explaining how the executive branch and Congress could authorize one aspect of the program but not another.

51 JACC brief quoted in Irons, *Justice at War*, 231, 234; Kang, "Denying Prejudice," 943-48.

52 *Yasui v. United States*, 320 U.S. 115 at 117 (1943). When the case returned to Judge Fee, he cooperated with the Supreme Court's dictum and struck down the ruling regarding Yasui's citizenship. Roger Daniels, *Concentration Camps, North America: Japanese in the United States and Canada during World War II* (Malabar, FL: R.E. Krieger, 1981), 136n8.

53 *Korematsu*, 323 U.S. 214, Brief of the American Civil Liberties Union, amicus curiae, p. 11.

54 *Korematsu*, 323 U.S. 214 at 219.

55 For the justification, see *Hirabayashi*, 320 U.S. 81 at 95; Brief of the States of California, Oregon, and Washington, amicus curiae, *Hirabayashi*, 320 U.S. 81 at para. 11; *Korematsu*, 323 U.S. 214 at 222. As Kang notes, Public Proclamation No. 5, issued on 30 March 1942, allowed exemptions from curfew or evacuation orders for German and Italian aliens. Likewise, Public Proclamation No. 13, issued on 19 October 1942, exempted all Italian aliens from military curfew and travel regulations. Kang, "Denying Prejudice," 958n137.

56 *Korematsu*, 323 U.S. 214 at 223. This discussion of the *Korematsu* case is informed by Nanette Dembitz, "Racial Discrimination and the Military Judgment: The Supreme Court's Korematsu and Endo Decisions," *Columbia Law Review* 45 (March 1945): 175-239.

57 *Korematsu*, 323 U.S. 214 at 226.

58 Ibid. at 232.

59 Ibid. at 240.

60 Ibid. at 242.

61 Ibid. at 246.

62 Ibid. at 243-44.

63 John Q. Barrett, "A Commander's Power, a Civilian's Reason: Justice Jackson's *Korematsu* Dissent," *Law and Contemporary Problems* 68 (Spring 2005): 57-79.

64 Quoted in Kang, "Denying Prejudice," 949-55 (emphasis added).

65 *Hirabayashi*, 320 U.S. 81 at 100.

66 *Korematsu*, 323 U.S. 214 at 216 (emphasis added).

67 See Chapter 6 for historical and contemporary applications of "strict scrutiny" based on the Japanese American cases.

68 *Ex Parte Endo*, 323 U.S. 283 at 297.

69 Ibid. at 300-301. See also Kang, "Denying Prejudice," 959-60, and Gudridge, "Remember Endo?" 1947-49.

70 *Ex Parte Endo*, 323 U.S. 283 at 303 (emphasis added); Kang, "Denying Prejudice," 960-61; Gudridge, "Remember Endo?" 1952-53.

71 Much has been made of Roosevelt's favourable statements concerning Japanese Americans, in particular his 1 February 1943 remark that "Americanism is a matter of the mind and heart; Americanism is not, and never was, a matter of race or ancestry." Greg Robinson discusses this in light of Roosevelt's overarching anti-Japanese sentiments, in *By Order*

of the President: FDR and the Internment of Japanese Americans (Cambridge, MA: Harvard University Press, 2001), 170-73.

72 *Ex Parte Endo,* 323 U.S. 283, at 309 and 310.

73 Transcript of Conversations. Douglas also stated that *Korematsu* and *Endo* were delayed in the court for some time because Frankfurter, who desired the delay, hoped that the "thing would solve itself ... and we wouldn't have to reach the question [of constitutionality]." When the case could be delayed no longer and the court had reached but not yet published its decision, Frankfurter allegedly tipped off the War Department regarding its nature. Consequently, on the day before *Endo* was issued, 18 December 1944, a Sunday no less, the War Department rescinded its orders. That the court's operative principle regarding incarceration was a spurious form of delay is also supported by the fact that it reached its verdict *after* Roosevelt's November re-election. Robinson, *By Order of the President,* 221-27, 230; Irons, *Justice at War,* 345, 405n82. Irons' evidence for Frankfurter's leak is based on an interview with Roger Daniels.

74 "Regarding Japanese Canadians," *CCJC Bulletin 2,* 24 January 1946, McMaster University Archives, Co-operative Committee on Japanese Canadians Papers [CCJC-MAC], folder 10; CCJC, Minutes, 21 December 1945, Library and Archives Canada [LAC], MG 28, CCJC Papers, series 1, vol. 1, file 1, pt. 2 of 2; CCJC, Minutes, 8 January 1946, LAC, MG 28, series 1, vol. 1, file 1, pt. 2 of 2; Edith Fowke, *They Made Democracy Work: The Story of the Cooperative Committee on Japanese Canadians* (Toronto: Cooperative Committee on Japanese Canadians, 1951), 18-19.

75 "A Record of the Work of the Cooperative Committee on Japanese Canadians, June 1943 to September 1947," 9-10, CCJC-MAC, folder 12.

76 "Canadian-Japanese Charge Government with Coercion," *Winnipeg Free Press,* 11 January 1946.

77 As R.L. Gabrielle Nishiguchi notes, five boats had already sailed for Japan between 31 May and 24 December 1946. In total, 3,964 people were transported to Japan; over 65 percent of them were either Canadian-born or naturalized citizens of Canada. Nishiguchi, "'Reducing the Numbers': The 'Transportation' of the Canadian Japanese (1941-1947)" (MA thesis, Carleton University, 1993), 3-4.

78 Fowke, *They Made Democracy Work,* 19; "Delegation Asks Ottawa Consider Japs in Canada," *Toronto Daily Star,* 4 January 1946; CCJC memorandum, "The Concern of the Canadian People for Christian and Democratic Treatment of Japanese Canadians," 4 January 1946, LAC, MG 32 C26, F. Andrew Brewin Papers, vol. 3; "Regarding Japanese Canadians," *CCJC News Bulletin 2,* 24 January 1946, CCJC-MAC, folder 10.

79 Fowke, *They Made Democracy Work,* 19; F.P. Varcoe to Norman Robertson, "Memorandum," 4 January 1946, LAC, MG 26 J4, William Lyon Mackenzie King Papers, vol. 283, file 2965 "A Record of the Work of the Cooperative Committee on Japanese Canadians, June 1943 to September 1947," 10, CCJC-MAC, file 12.

80 "Ledger on Activities in January 1946," n.d., LAC, MG 32 C26, vol. 1; J.W. Corman, attorney general of Saskatchewan, to Brewin, 15 January 1946, LAC, MG 32 C26, vol. 1; R.J. McMaster to Brewin, 16 January 1946, LAC, MG 32 C26, vol. 1. Saskatchewan was the only province to support the CCJC. Brewin to Corman, 28 January 1946, LAC, MG 32 C26, vol. 1.

81 *In the Matter of a Reference as to the Validity of Orders in Council of the 15th Day of December, 1945 (P.C. 7355, 7356 and 7357), in Relation to Persons of the Japanese Race* (1946), S.C.R. 248 *[In the Matter of a Reference].*

82 McMaster would be central to the nationwide efforts to secure compensation for Japanese Canadians who lost property as a result of their relocation. "Ledger on Activities in January 1946," n.d., LAC, MG 32 C26, vol. 1; R.J. McMaster to Brewin, 31 December 1945, LAC, MG 32 C26, vol. 3; Brewin to McMaster, 3 January 1946, LAC, MG 32 C26, vol. 3; Cartwright to Brewin, 3 January 1946, LAC, MG 32 C26, vol. 3; Brewin to Arnold Campbell, 5 January 1946, LAC, MG 32 C26, vol. 3.

83 "Ledger on Activities in January 1946," n.d., LAC, MG 32 C26, vol. 1; Brewin to Dillon Myer, WRA, 12 January 1946, LAC, MG 32 C26, vol. 1.

84 "Case for the Appellant, in the matter of a reference as to the validity of Orders-in-Council of the 15th day of December 1945 (P.C. 7355, 7356, 7357) in relation to persons of the Japanese Race, 1946," LAC, MG 32 C26, vol. 3.
85 Brewin, Notes re: maintaining powers of the National Emergency Transitional Powers Act, n.d., LAC, MG 32 C26, vol. 3.
86 *In the Matter of a Reference,* (1946) S.C.R. 248; Brewin to Campbell, 5 January 1946, LAC, MG 32 C26, vol. 1; "Appendix 'B': Standard Texts on 'Japanese Race,'" n.d., LAC, MG 32 C26, vol. 1.
87 "Appendix 'B': Standard Texts on 'Japanese Race,'" n.d., LAC, MG 32 C26, vol. 1.
88 "Case for the Appellant, in the matter of a reference as to the validity of Orders-in-Council of the 15th day of December 1945 (P.C. 7355, 7356, 7357) in relation to persons of the Japanese Race, 1946," LAC, MG 32 C26, vol. 3.
89 Fowke, *They Made Democracy Work,* 20-21; "A Record of the Work of the Cooperative Committee on Japanese Canadians, June 1943 to September 1947," 12, CCJC-MAC, file 12.
90 CCJC, Minutes, 5 April 1946, LAC, MG 28, series 1, vol. 1, file 1, pt. 2 of 2.; Fowke, *They Made Democracy Work,* 21.
91 *In the Matter of a Reference* (1946), S.C.R. 248.
92 Ibid.; "Summary of Effect of the Supreme Court Judgement re: Japanese Orders," n.d., LAC, MG 26 J4, vol. 283, file 2965.
93 *In the Matter of a Reference* (1946), S.C.R. 248.
94 Ibid.
95 Fowke, *They Made Democracy Work,* 23; CCJC memo to Consultative Groups, 16 August 1946, CCJC-MAC, file 7; "A Record of the Work of the Cooperative Committee on Japanese Canadians, June 1943 to September 1947," 12-13, CCJC-MAC, folder 12; *CCJC News Bulletin 5,* 30 March 1946, CCJC-MAC, folder 10; CCJC, "Memorandum for the Members of the House of Commons and Senate of Canada," April 1946, CCJC-MAC, folder 13.
96 It should be remembered that, when a Privy Council decision was declared, a branch of the council relayed it to the sovereign in the form of advice. According to Cabinet rule, no minority or dissenting views could be announced in these instances. In this, Privy Council practice differed from that of the Supreme Courts of Canada and the United States, and even from that of the House of Lords (Britain's highest court of appeal), where dissenting judgments were often delivered. Brewin, "Memorandum for Co-operative Committee on Japanese Canadians on the Judgment of the Judicial Committee of the Privy Council," 22 December 1946, CCJC-MAC, folder 13.
97 *Co-operative Committee on Japanese Canadians et al. v. Attorney-General of Canada et al.* (1947), A.C. 87, 1 DLR. 577 at 586.
98 Ibid., 589, 593.
99 Lord Simon quoted in Fowke, *They Made Democracy Work,* 23; Brewin, "Memorandum for Co-operative Committee on Japanese Canadians on the Judgment of the Judicial Committee of the Privy Council," 22 December 1946, CCJC-MAC, folder 13. Interestingly, Sir Lyman Duff, one of the Judicial Committee members who heard the case against the deportation orders, was a former chief justice of the Supreme Court of Canada. Patricia E. Roy et al., eds., *Mutual Hostages: Canadians and Japanese during the Second World War* (Toronto: University of Toronto Press, 1990), 180, and David R. Williams, *Duff: A Life in the Law* (Vancouver: UBC Press, 1984). For more on the Canadian campaign for a bill of rights, see Christopher MacLennan, *Toward the Charter: Canadians and the Demand for a National Bill of Rights, 1929-1960* (Kingston and Montreal: McGill-Queen's University Press, 2003), especially chaps. 4, 5, and 6.
100 Fraenkel, "The War, Civil Liberties and the Supreme Court," n.d., Mudd Library, ACLU Papers, box 33, folder 4.
101 *Duncan v. Kahanamoku,* 327 U.S. 304 (1946).
102 Claire L'Heureux-Dubé, "Realizing Equality in the Twentieth Century: The Role of the Supreme Court of Canada in Comparative Perspective," *International Journal of Constitutional Law* 1, 1 (2003): 35.

Conclusion: "They Made Democracy Work"
The title of this chapter comes from Edith Fowke, *They Made Democracy Work: The Story of the Co-operative Committee on Japanese Canadians* (Toronto: Co-operative Committee on Japanese Canadians, 1951).

1 Tanaka quoted in "Report of 2nd National JCCA Conference," n.d. (1947?), Library and Archives Canada [LAC], MG 31 F8, Minoru Takada Papers.

2 George Tanaka, "For the Protection of Human Rights," 26 January 1950, LAC, MG 28 V7, National Japanese Canadian Citizens Association Papers, microfilm reel C12830 *Nisei Affairs* 2, 1 (January 1947); *Nisei Affairs* 2, 3 (April 1947); *Nisei Affairs* 2, 4 (June 1947); Muriel Kitagawa, *This Is My Own: Letters to Wes and Other Writings on Japanese Canadians, 1941-1948,* ed. Roy Miki (Vancouver: Talonbooks, 1985), 236-41; Ross Lambertson, *Repression and Resistance: Canadian Human Rights Activists, 1930-1960* (Toronto: University of Toronto Press, 2005), chaps. 5 and 8; James W. St. G. Walker, "The 'Jewish' Phase in the Movement for Racial Equality in Canada," *Canadian Ethnic Studies* 34, 1 (2002): 1-24.

3 Quoted in "New JACL Policy," *Pacific Citizen* 19, 3 (9 December 1944).

4 Japanese American Citizens League, Anti-discrimination Committee, "National Legislative Program-1949," Princeton University, Seeley G. Mudd Manuscript Library [Mudd Library], MC 005, Roger N. Baldwin Papers, box 1056.

5 Ibid.; Mike Masaoka, Statement for the Standing Subcommittee on Immigration and Naturalization of the Committee on the Judiciary, House of Representatives, US Congress, 19 March 1947, Mudd Library, American Civil Liberties Union [ACLU] Papers, series 3, box 1055, folder 7; Masaoka to Baldwin, 29 July 1947, Mudd Library, ACLU Papers, vol. 42; Cheryl Greenberg, "Black and Jewish Responses to Japanese Internment," *Journal of American Ethnic History* 14 (Winter 1995): 27-28.

6 "JACL Establishes Defense Fund for Civil Rights Cases," *Pacific Citizen* 28, 22 (7 December 1946).

7 See Chapter 2 for *Oyama v. California,* the challenge to the California Alien Land Law.

8 For more on this discussion, see Greg Robinson and Toni Robinson, "*Korematsu* and Beyond: Japanese Americans and the Origins of Strict Scrutiny," *Law and Contemporary Problems* 68, 29 (September 2005): 29-49.

9 *Plessy v. Ferguson,* 163 U.S. 537 (1896).

10 *McLaurin v. Oklahoma,* 339 U.S. 637 at 3, JACL brief amicus curiae (1950). The *McLaurin* case involved an African American who was admitted to the University of Oklahoma's School of Education but was forced to sit in a separate area of the classroom and restricted to specified areas in the cafeteria and library. The other case of note, *Sweatt v. Painter,* 339 U.S. 629 (1950), revolved around Heman Marion Sweatt, who endured similar treatment at the University of Texas Law School. Robinson and Robinson, "*Korematsu* and Beyond," 50.

11 Robinson and Robinson, "*Korematsu* and Beyond," 50-52.

12 *Brown v. Board of Education of Topeka, Kansas,* 347 U.S. 483 (1954).

13 *Bolling v. Sharpe,* 347 U.S. 497 (1954).

14 *Brown,* 347 U.S. 483 at 495.

15 *Bolling,* 347 U.S. 497 at 500; see also 499n3.

16 Robinson and Robinson, "*Korematsu* and Beyond," 53-55.

17 Joy Kogawa, *Obasan* (Toronto: Penguin, 1983), 187.

18 ACLU, Minutes, 17 August 1942, Mudd Library, ACLU Papers, vol. 2395.

19 Samuel Walker, *In Defense of American Liberties: A History of the ACLU* (New York: Oxford University Press, 1990), 42-50, 72-76.

20 This term paraphrases the title of Peter J. Kellogg's "Civil Rights Consciousness in the 1940s," *Historian* 42, 1 (1979): 18-41.

21 Mary Ann Glendon, *Rights Talk: The Impoverishment of Political Discourse* (New York: Free Press, 1991), 12-30.

22 Michael Hemmings, "The Church and the Japanese in Canada, 1941-1946: Ambulance Wagon to Embattled Army?" (M. Theol., Vancouver School of Theology, 1990), 136-37.

23 Alan Davies and Marilyn F. Nefsky, *How Silent Were the Churches? Canadian Protestantism and the Jewish Plight during the Nazi Era* (Waterloo: Wilfrid Laurier University Press, 1998), 127-31. For the allegation that the churches were largely silent on the issue of Jewish refugees from the Third Reich, see Irving Abella and Harold Troper, *None Is Too Many: Canada and the Jews of Europe 1933-1948* (Toronto: Lester and Orpen Dennys, 1983), 51. For the views of a United Church missionary who likens the situation of the Japanese Canadians to that of the Jewish minority in Germany, see Dr. G.E. Bott to Arnup, 4 May 1943, United Church of Canada, Central Archives [UCC], Board of World Missions, Japan Mission, 1880-1971, box 6, file 138.

24 *CCJC News Bulletin 8,* 10 February 1947, CCJC-MAC, folder 10.

25 Patricia E. Roy, "Lessons in Citizenship, 1945-1949: The Delayed Return of the Japanese to Canada's Pacific Coast," *Pacific Northwest Quarterly* 93, 2 (Spring 2002): 69-80.

Afterword

1 For more on redress, see Roger Daniels, "Redress Achieved," in Roger Daniels et al., eds., *Japanese Americans: From Relocation to Redress* (Salt Lake City: University of Utah Press, 1986), 219-23; Leslie T. Hatamiya, *Righting a Wrong: Japanese Americans and the Passage of the Civil Liberties Act of 1988* (Stanford: Stanford University Press, 1993); Roy Miki and Cassandra Kobayashi, *Justice in Our Time: The Japanese Canadian Redress Settlement* (Vancouver: Talonbooks, 1991); and Roy Miki, *Redress: Inside the Japanese Canadian Call for Justice* (Vancouver: Raincoast Books, 2004).

2 Miki, *Redress,* chap. 6.

3 *Hansard* (29 June 1984), 5307.

4 Bush quoted in Daniels, "Redress Achieved," 222 (emphasis added).

5 Quoted in Miki, *Redress,* 317-19.

6 Peter Power, "An Apology 94 Years in the Making," *Toronto Star,* 22 June 2006.

7 Daniels, "Redress Achieved," 200-201. On the stigma of incarceration and the effect on the Sansei generation, see Tetsuden Kashima, *Judgment without Trial: Japanese American Imprisonment during World War II* (Seattle: University of Washington Press, 2003), chap. 10. On the findings of the CWRIC, see United States, Commission on Wartime Relocation and Internment of Civilians, *Personal Justice Denied: Report of the Commission on Wartime Relocation and Internment of Civilians,* rev. ed. (Seattle: University of Washington Press, 1997).

8 Aiko Herzig-Yoshinaga is a fascinating example of an "ordinary person" who had a tremendous impact on a justice campaign. Her story also underscores the lack of awareness of contributions made by those behind the scenes, particularly women, who serve in a "team" environment for those who attract more attention. I am indebted to Greg Robinson for drawing my attention to Herzig-Yoshinaga and, by extension, to Thomas Y. Fujita-Rony, who wrote about her. See Thomas Y. Fujita-Rony, "'Destructive Force': Aiko Herzig-Yoshinaga's Gendered Labor in the Japanese American Redress Movement," *Frontiers: A Journal of Women Studies* 24, 1 (2003): 38-60.

9 Fred Korematsu continued to speak out against injustice until his death on 30 March 2005. Gordon Hirabayashi now lives in Edmonton, Alberta, where he is professor emeritus of sociology at the University of Alberta. Minoru Yasui became a civil rights lawyer but died in 1986, before all his claims within his writ of error *coram nobis* were overturned. Mitsuye Endo (Tsutsumi) died in May 2006. Although she remained very private, she continued her role as quiet activist in Chicago as assistant to the city's Human Rights Commission.

10 See, for example, Jerry Kang, "Watching the Watchers: Enemy Combatants in the Internment's Shadow," *Law and Contemporary Problems* 68 (2005), http://ssrn.com/abstract= 627401; Roger Daniels, "*Korematsu v. United States* Revisited: 1944 and 1983," in Annette Gordon-Reed, ed., *Race on Trial: Law and Justice in American History* (Oxford and New York: Oxford University Press, 2002), 139-59; Roger Daniels, "Incarceration of the Japanese Americans: A Sixty-Year Perspective," *History Teacher* 35, 3 (May 2002): 297-310,

http://www.historycooperative.org/journals/ht/35.3/daniels.html; and Cass R. Sunstein, *Radicals in Robes: Why Extreme Right-Wing Courts Are Wrong for America* (Cambridge, MA: Basic Books, 2005).

11 David Cole, "Manzanar Redux?" *Los Angeles Times*, 16 June 2006; "Amicus Brief Ties Internment to 9/11 Cases," *Rafu Shimpo Online*, 9 April 2007, www.rafu.com/amicus.html; Lydia Lin, "Following in their fathers' footsteps," *Pacific Citizen*, 20 April 2007.

12 Kirk Makin, "Security Trumps All, Crown Tells Top Court," *Toronto Globe and Mail*, 15 June 2006; Editorial, "Anti-terror Laws Are Tough Enough," *Toronto Star*, 15 June 2006; Don Butler, "Sacrifice Civil Liberties for Security, Canadians Say," *Ottawa Citizen*, 24 June 2006. On the Supreme Court's unanimous ruling, see CTV.ca News Staff, "SCC Rules against Federal Security Certificates," *sympatico.MSN.ca News*, 23 February 2007, http://www.ctv.ca/servlet/ArticleNews/story/CTVNews/20070223/security_certificates_070223?s_name=&no_ads=. Currently, it is impossible to determine if any part of the Japanese Canadian reference case was included in the materials presented to the Supreme Court regarding the security certificates issue. I would like to thank two legal eagles, David Wright and Daniel S.J. Bangarth, for their opinions on this matter.

13 Columnist Rod Mickleburgh covered the Save Joy Kogawa House campaign in the *Toronto Globe and Mail* ("Donations needed to save a landmark," 21 April, and "Firm helps buy B.C. landmark," 1 June), as did Camille Bains in "Kogawa's childhood home to be saved," 29 April.

14 Val Ross, "War museum faces a second offensive," *Globe and Mail*, 19 July 2007, p. R1-2. For more information on Nisei enlistment, see Patricia E. Roy, "The Soldiers Canada Didn't Want: Her Chinese and Japanese Citizens," *Canadian Historical Review* 59, 2 (1978): 341-58, and Roy Ito, *We Went to War: The Story of the Japanese Canadians Who Served during the First and Second World Wars*, 2nd ed. (Stittsville, ON: Canada's Wings, 1992).

15 Edith Fowke, *They Made Democracy Work: The Story of the Co-operative Committee on Japanese Canadians* (Toronto: Co-operative Committee on Japanese Canadians, 1951).

Bibliography

Manuscripts and Official Records
Anglican Church of Canada. General Synod Archives, Toronto. GS75-103. Missionary Society of the Church in Canada. Series 1. Board of Management and Executive Committee, 1884-1968.
–. General Synod Archives. GS75-103. Missionary Society of the Church in Canada. Series 3-3. Leonard A. Dixon Files.
British Columbia Security Commission. *Report on the Removal of Japanese from Protected Areas, March 4, 1942 to October 31, 1942*. 1942, Vancouver, BC.
Canada. Department of Labour. *Two Reports on Japanese Canadians in World War II, 1944/1947*. New York: Arno Press, 1978.
–. House of Commons. *Debates*. Ottawa: Queen's Printer, 1935-50.
–. Senate. *Journals of the Senate of Canada*. Ottawa: Queen's Printer, 1948.
–. Senate. *Official Report of Debates*. Ottawa: Queen's Printer, 1947-48.
Columbia University. Butler Library, New York. Department of Rare Books and Manuscripts. Institute of Pacific Relations Collection.
–. Butler Library. Oral History Collection. Alan F. Westin interview with Roger Nash Baldwin, 18 December 1974.
–. Butler Library. Oral History Collection. Corliss Lamont Interview.
–. Butler Library. Oral History Collection. Reminiscences of Ben W. Huebsch.
–. Butler Library. Oral History Collection. Reminiscences of Osmond K. Fraenkel.
–. Butler Library. Oral History Collection. Reminiscences of Roger Nash Baldwin. Dr. Harlan Phillips, Nov.-Dec. 1953, January 1954.
Library and Archives Canada, Ottawa. MG 26 J1-J4. William Lyon Mackenzie King Papers.
–. MG 26 J13. William Lyon Mackenzie King Diary.
–. MG 28 V1-3. Co-operative Committee on Japanese Canadians Papers.
–. MG 28 V7. National Japanese Canadian Citizens Association Papers.
–. MG 30 C69. Margaret Foster Papers.
–. MG 30 C160. Grace Thompson Papers.
–. MG 30 D200. Grace Tucker Papers.
–. MG 30 D211. Francis Reginald Scott Papers.
–. MG 30 E151. Laurent Beaudry Papers.
–. MG 30 E266. Saul M. Cherniack Papers.
–. MG 31 E26. Muriel Kitagawa Papers.
–. MG 31 E87. R.G. Robertson Papers.
–. MG 31 F8. Minoru Takada Papers.
–. MG 31 I1. Edith Ellen Holtom Papers.
–. MG 32 C12. Grace MacInnis Papers.
–. MG 32 C13. H.W. Herridge Papers.
–. MG 32 C26. F. Andrew Brewin Papers.

–. MG 55/28, #12. Canadian Civil Liberties Union Papers.
–. MG 55/28, #17. United Churches – Japanese.
–. RG 2. Privy Council Office Records.
–. RG 14 D2, volume 559, Sessional Paper 185A. *Report by Justice Henry I. Bird on Royal Commission to Investigate Property Losses by Japanese Canadians during the Second World War.* 13 June 1950.
–. RG 18. R.C.M.P. Papers.
–. RG 25. Department of External Affairs Records.
–. RG 27. Department of Labour, Japanese Division.
–. RG 33/60, Volume 2. "Report of His Honour Judge J.C.A. Cameron on Royal Commission to Investigate Activities of the Black Dragon Society in British Columbia at Vancouver, BC. 19 December 1942.
–. RG 36/27. Boards, Offices and Commissions, Series 27: British Columbia Security Commission, 1942-1948.
McMaster University Archives, Hamilton, ON. Co-operative Committee on Japanese Canadians Papers.
Presbyterian Historical Society, Philadelphia, PA. NCC RG 18. Federal Council of the Churches of Christ in America Records, 1894-1952.
–. RG 26. National Council of Churches Papers.
–. RG 301.7. Board of National Missions. Series 2: Department of City, Immigrant and Industrial Work. Subseries 2: Jacob A. Long, Superintendent Files, 1910-57.
Princeton University. Firestone Library, Princeton, NJ. Norman Thomas Papers.
–. Seeley G. Mudd Manuscript Library. American Civil Liberties Union Microfilm Collection.
–. Seeley G. Mudd Manuscript Library. American Civil Liberties Union Papers.
–. Seeley G. Mudd Manuscript Library. General Manuscripts. Norman Thomas Papers.
–. Seeley G. Mudd Manuscript Library. MC 005. Roger N. Baldwin Papers.
–. Seeley G. Mudd Manuscript Library. MC 072. Arthur Garfield Hays Papers.
–. Seeley G. Mudd Manuscript Library. MC 082. Peggy Lamson Collection on Roger Baldwin.
–. Seeley G. Mudd Manuscript Library. MC 192. Osmond K. Fraenkel Diary Excerpts, 1933-1969.
–. Seeley G. Mudd Manuscript Library. Undergraduate Alumni Records. Norman Thomas, Class of 1905.
United Church of Canada. Central Archives. Victoria University, Toronto. Board of Overseas Missions. Minutes and General Correspondence.
–. Central Archives. Victoria University, Toronto. Board of World Missions. Japan Mission, 1880-1971.
–. Central Archives. Victoria University, Toronto. Esther Ryan Papers.
–. Central Archives. Victoria University, Toronto. Fellowship for a Christian Social Order Papers.
–. Central Archives. Victoria University, Toronto. General Council Committees Section. Commission on the Church, Nation and World Order. Records, 1941-1944.
–. Central Archives. Victoria University, Toronto. Women's Missionary Society. Home Missions. Oriental Work, 1927-1962.
United States of America. Congress. House Select Committee Investigating National Defense Migration, *Hearings before the Select Committee Investigating National Defense Migration, Part 29.* 77th Cong., 2nd Sess. Washington, DC: Government Printing Office, 1942.
–. Congress. House Select Committee Investigating National Defense Migration. *Problems of Evacuation of Enemy Aliens and Others from Prohibited Military Zones, Part 30.* 77th Cong., 2nd Sess. Washington, DC: Government Printing Office, 1942.
–. *Congressional Record.* 78th Cong., 1st Sess. 1943.
–. House of Representatives. Report of the Select Committee Investigating National Defense Migration. *Preliminary Report and Recommendations on Problems of Evacuation of Citizens and Aliens from Military Areas.* (H.R. No. 1911) 77th Cong., 2nd Sess. Washington, DC: Government Printing, 19 March 1942.
–. War Department, Chief of Staff. *Final Report: Japanese Evacuation from the West Coast, 1942.* Washington, DC: Government Printing, 1943.

Newspapers and Journals
Call
Canadian Forum
Christian Century
Christian Social Action
Common Sense
Commonweal
DenverPost.com
Maclean's
Montreal Star
Nation
New Canadian
New Republic
Nisei Affairs
Ottawa Citizen
Ottawa Journal
Pacific Citizen
Race Relations: A Monthly Summary of Events and Trends. New York: Negro Universities
　　Press, February 1945.
Rafu Shimpo Online
Saturday Night
Toronto Daily Star
Toronto Globe and Mail
Vancouver Daily Province
Vancouver Sun
Varsity
Washington Post
Winnipeg Free Press

Jurisprudence
Bolling v. Sharpe, 347 U.S. 497 (1954).
Brown v. Board of Education of Topeka, Kansas, 347 U.S. 483 (1954).
Co-operative Committee on Japanese Canadians et al. v. Attorney-General of Canada et al.
　　(1947), A.C. 87, 1 D.L.R. 577.
Duncan v. Kahanamoku, 327 U.S. 304 (1946).
Ex Parte Endo, 323 U.S. 283 (1944).
Hirabayashi v. United States, 320 U.S. 81 (1943).
In the Matter of a Reference as to the Validity of Orders in Council of the 15th Day of Decem-
　　ber, 1945 (P.C. 7355, 7356 and 7357), in Relation to Persons of the Japanese Race (1946),
　　S.C.R. 248.
Iwasaki v. The Queen (1968), 2 D.L.R. (3d) 241.
Iwasaki v. The Queen (1970), S.C.R. 437.
Korematsu v. United States, 323 U.S. 214 (1944).
McLaurin v. Oklahoma, 339 U.S. 637 (1950).
Oyama v. California, 332 U.S. 633 (1948).
Plessy v. Ferguson, 163 U.S. 537 (1896).
Schneiderman v. United States, 320 U.S. 118 (1943).
Takahashi v. Fish Commission, 334 U.S. 410 (1948).
Toyosaburo Korematsu v. United States, 140 F. 2d 289, 300-304 (9th Cir. 1943).
Yasui v. United States, 320 U.S. 115 (1943).

Published Works
Abella, Irving. "Jews, Human Rights, and the Making of a New Canada." Presidential
　　Address. *Journal of the Canadian Historical Association* 11 (2000): 3-16.
–, and Harold Troper. *None Is Too Many: Canada and the Jews of Europe 1933-1948.* Toronto:
　　Lester and Orpen Dennys, 1983.

Ad Hoc Committee for "Japanese Canadian Redress: The Toronto Story." *Japanese Canadian Redress: The Toronto Story.* Toronto: Hpf Press, 2000.

Adachi, Ken. *The Enemy That Never Was: A History of the Japanese Canadians.* Rev. ed. Toronto: McClelland and Stewart, 1991.

Allen, Richard. *The Social Passion: Religion and Social Reform in Canada, 1914-1928.* Toronto: University of Toronto Press, 1971.

Anderson, Carol. "Bleached Souls and Red Negroes: The NAACP and Black Communists in the Early Cold War, 1948-1952." In Brenda Gayle Plummer, ed., *Window on Freedom: Race, Civil Rights, and Foreign Affairs, 1945-1988,* 93-113. Chapel Hill: University of North Carolina Press, 2003.

–. *Eyes off the Prize: The United Nations and the African American Struggle for Human Rights, 1944-1955.* Cambridge: Oxford University Press, 2003.

Anderson, Kay J. *Vancouver's Chinatown: Racial Discourse in Canada, 1875-1980.* Montreal and Kingston: McGill-Queen's University Press, 1991.

Austin, Allan. *From Concentration Camp to Campus: Japanese American Students and World War II.* Urbana: University of Illinois Press, 2004.

Bangarth, Stephanie D. "The Co-operative Committee on Japanese Canadians and the American Civil Liberties Union: Engaging Debate, 1942-1949." *Princeton University Library Chronicle* 63, 3 (Spring 2002): 496-533.

–. "The Long, Wet Summer of 1942: The Ontario Farm Service Force, Small-Town Ontario and the Nisei." *Canadian Ethnic Studies* 37, 1 (2005): 40-62.

–. "Mackenzie King and Japanese Canadians." In John English, Kenneth McLaughlin, and P. Whitney Lackenbauer, eds., *Mackenzie King: Citizenship and Community,* 99-123. Toronto: Robin Brass Studio Press, 2002.

–. "Religious Organizations and the 'Relocation' of Persons of Japanese Ancestry in North America: Evaluating Advocacy." *American Review of Canadian Studies* 34, 3 (Fall 2004): 511-40.

–. "'We Are Not Asking You to Open Wide the Gates for Chinese Immigration': The Committee for the Repeal of the Chinese Immigration Act and Early Human Rights Activism in Canada." *Canadian Historical Review* 84, 3 (September 2003): 395-422.

Barrett, John Q. "A Commander's Power, a Civilian's Reason: Justice Jackson's *Korematsu* Dissent." *Law and Contemporary Problems* 68 (Spring 2005): 57-79.

Benedict, Ruth. *Race: Science and Politics.* New York: Modern Age Books, 1940.

Berger, Thomas R. *Fragile Freedoms: Human Rights and Dissent in Canada.* Rev. ed. Toronto: Irwin, 1982.

Bernard, Elaine. "A University at War: Japanese Canadians at UBC during World War II." *BC Studies* 35 (Autumn 1977): 36-55.

Borgwardt, Elizabeth. *A New Deal for the World: America's Vision for Human Rights.* Cambridge, MA, and London: Belknap Press of Harvard University Press, 2005.

Borovoy, Alan A. "Fair Accommodation Practices Act: The 'Dresden Affair.'" *University of Toronto Faculty of Law Review* 14 (January 1956): 13-23.

Borstelman, Thomas. *The Cold War and the Color Line: American Race Relations in the Global Arena.* Cambridge, MA, and London: Harvard University Press, 2001.

Bosworth, Allan. *America's Concentration Camps.* New York: W.W. Norton, 1967.

Boyer, Paul S., Clifford E. Clark Jr., Joseph F. Kett, Thomas Purvis, Harvard Sitkoff, and Nancy Woloch. *The Enduring Vision: A History of the American People.* Lexington, MA: D.C. Heath, 1990.

Broadfoot, Barry. *Years of Sorrow, Years of Shame: The Story of the Japanese Canadians in World War II.* Toronto: Doubleday Canada, 1977.

Brogan, Hugh. *The Pelican History of the United States of America.* London: Longman Group, 1985.

Bruner, Arnold. "The Genesis of Ontario's Human Rights Legislation: A Study in Law Reform." *University of Toronto Faculty of Law Review* 37, 236 (1979): 236-53.

Bundy, Edgar C. *Collectivism in the Churches: A Documented Account of the Political Activities of the Federal, National and World Council of Churches.* Wheaton, IL: Church League of America, 1958.

Chang, Gordon. "'Superman Is About to Visit the Relocation Centers' and the Limits of Wartime Liberalism." *Amerasia Journal* 19, 1 (1993): 37-59.

Christgau, John. "Collins versus the World: The Fight to Restore Citizenship to Japanese American Renunciants of World War II." *Pacific Historical Review* 54, 1 (1985): 1-32.

Chuman, Frank. *Bamboo People*. Del Mar, CA: Japanese American Citizens, 1976.

Cohn, Werner. "The Persecution of Japanese Canadians and the Political Left in British Columbia, December 1941-March 1942." *BC Studies* 68 (Winter 1985-86): 3-22.

Collins, Donald E. *Native American Aliens: Disloyalty and the Renunciation of Citizenship by Japanese Americans during World War II*. Westport, CT: Greenwood Press, 1985.

Columbo, John Robert. *The Dictionary of Canadian Quotations*. Toronto: Stoddart, 1991.

Cook, Ramsay. "Canadian Freedom in Wartime, 1939-1945." In W.H. Heick and Roger Graham, eds., *His Own Man: Essays in Honour of Arthur Reginald Lower*, 37-53. Montreal and Kingston: McGill-Queen's University Press, 1974.

Dahlberg, Gunnar. *Race, Reason and Rubbish*. London: G. Allen and Unwin, 1942.

Daniels, Roger. *Asian America: Chinese and Japanese in the United States since 1850*. Seattle: University of Washington Press, 1989.

–. *Concentration Camps, North America: Japanese in the United States and Canada during World War II*. Malabar, FL: R.E. Krieger, 1981.

–. *Concentration Camps USA: Japanese Americans and World War II*. New York: Holt Rinehart and Winston, 1972.

–. "The Decision to Relocate the North American Japanese: Another Look." *Pacific Historical Review* 51 (February 1982): 71-77.

–. "Incarceration of the Japanese Americans: A Sixty-Year Perspective." *History Teacher* 35, 3 (May 2002): 297-310. http://www.historycooperative.org/journals/ht/35.3/daniels.html.

–. "Incarceration, Redress, Reconsiderations: Reviewing the Story of the Japanese-Americans." *Immigration and Ethnic History Newsletter* 37, 2 (November 2005): 1, 8.

–. "The Japanese Experience in North America: An Essay in Comparative Racism." *Canadian Ethnic Studies* 9, 2 (1977): 91-100.

–. *The Politics of Prejudice: The Anti-Japanese Movement in California and the Struggle for Japanese Exclusion*. 2nd ed. Berkeley and Los Angeles: University of California Press, 1977.

–. *Prisoners without Trial: Japanese Americans in World War II*. 1993. Rev. ed., New York: Hill and Wang, 2004.

–, Leonard J. Arrington, Harry H.L. Kitano, and Sandra C. Taylor, eds. *Japanese Americans: From Relocation to Redress*. Salt Lake City: University of Utah Press, 1986.

Davies, Alan, and Marilyn F. Nefsky. *How Silent Were the Churches? Canadian Protestantism and the Jewish Plight during the Nazi Era*. Waterloo, ON: Wilfrid Laurier University Press, 1998.

Dembitz, Nanette. "Racial Discrimination and the Military Judgement: The Supreme Court's *Korematsu* and *Endo* Decisions." *Columbia Law Journal* 45 (March 1945): 175-239.

Donohue, William A. *The Politics of the American Civil Liberties Union*. New Brunswick, NJ: Transaction Books, 1985.

Doreski, C.K. "'Kin in Some Way': The *Chicago Defender* Reads the Japanese Internment, 1942-1945." In Todd Vogel, ed., *The Black Press*, 161-87. New Brunswick, NJ: Rutgers University Press, 2001.

Downey, Jean Miyake. "Healing Japanese Canadian Diasporan History: Multicultural Noh Play *The Gull* Premieres in Vancouver." *Kyoto Journal* 62 (2006). http://www.kyoto journal.org/10,000things/043.html.

Draper, Paula Jean. "Fragmented Loyalties: Canadian Jewry, the King Government and the Refugee Dilemma." In Norman Hillmer, Bohdan Kordan, and Lubomyr Luciuk, eds., *On Guard for Thee: War, Ethnicity and the Canadian State, 1939-1945*, 151-77. Kingston, ON: Canadian Committee for the History of the Second World War, 1988.

Dreisziger, N.F. "7 December 1941: A Turning Point in Canadian Wartime Policy toward Enemy Ethnic Groups?" *Journal of Canadian Studies* 32, 1 (Spring 1997): 93-111.

Drinnon, Richard. *Keeper of Concentration Camps: Dillon S. Myer and American Racism*. Berkeley and Los Angeles: University of California Press, 1987.

Egerton, George. "Entering the Age of Human Rights: Religion, Politics, and Canadian Liberalism." *Canadian Historical Review* 85, 3 (September 2004): 451-79.

Eisenberg, Ellen. "'As Truly American as Your Son': Voicing Opposition to Internment in Three West Coast Cities." *Oregon History Quarterly* 104, 4 (Winter 2003): 542-65.

Eisenhower, Milton S. *The President Is Calling.* Garden City, NY: Doubleday Press, 1974.

Elfendahl, Gerald. "Remembering Walter Woodward (1910-2001)." *People's History Library* n.d. http://www.historylink.org/essays/output.cfm?file_id=3111.

Feinberg, Abraham L. *Storm the Gates of Jericho.* Toronto and Montreal: McClelland and Stewart, 1964.

Fine, Sidney. "Mr. Justice Murphy and the Hirabayashi Case." *Pacific Historical Review* 33, 2 (May 1964): 195-209.

Fingard, Judith. "From Sea to Rail: Black Transportation Workers and Their Families in Halifax, c. 1870-1916." *Acadiensis* 24, 2 (Spring 1995): 49-64.

Fiset, Louis, and Gail M. Nomura, eds. *Nikkei in the Pacific Northwest: Japanese Americans and Japanese Canadians in the Twentieth Century.* Seattle and London: University of Washington Press, 2005.

Foner, Philip S. *Organized Labor and the Black Worker, 1916-1973.* New York: Praeger, 1974.

Fowke, Edith. *They Made Democracy Work: The Story of the Co-operative Committee on Japanese Canadians.* Toronto: Co-operative Committee on Japanese Canadians, 1951.

Frey, Sylvia. *Water from the Rock: Black Resistance in a Revolutionary Age.* Princeton, NJ: Princeton University Press, 1991.

Fujita-Rony, Thomas Y. "'Destructive Force': Aiko Herzig-Yoshinaga's Gendered Labor in the Japanese American Redress Movement." *Frontiers: A Journal of Women Studies* 24, 1 (2003): 38-60.

Garey, Diane. *Defending Everybody: A History of the American Civil Liberties Union.* New York: TV Books, 1998.

Geiger-Adams, Andrea. "Pioneer Issei: Tomekichi Homma's Fight for the Franchise." *Nikkei Images* 8, 1 (Spring 2003): 1-5.

Girdner, Audrie, and Anne Loftis. *The Great Betrayal.* New York: Macmillan Press, 1969.

Gleason, Philip. *Speaking of Diversity: Language and Ethnicity in Twentieth-Century America.* Baltimore: Johns Hopkins University Press, 1992.

Glen, A. "Methods and Theories in Community Practice." In H. Butcher, A. Glen, P. Henderson, and J. Smith, eds., *Community and Public Policy.* London: Pluto Press, 1993.

Glendon, Mary Ann. *Rights Talk: The Impoverishment of Political Discourse.* New York: Free Press, 1991.

Goa, David J. "Redeeming the War on the Home Front: Alberta's Japanese Community during the Second World War and After." In K.W. Tingley, ed., *For King and Country: Alberta in the Second World War,* 313-326. Edmonton: Provincial Museum of Alberta, 1995.

Gordon-Reed, Annette, ed. *Race on Trial: Law and Justice in American History.* Oxford and New York: Oxford University Press, 2002.

Government of Canada. *Wayfarers: Canadian Achievers.* Canada Heirloom Series, vol. 5. s.v. "Samuel I. Hayakawa," by Mel James. http://collections.ic.gc.ca/.

Granatstein, J.L., and Gregory A. Johnson. "The Evacuation of the Japanese Canadians, 1942: A Realist Critique of the Received Version." In Norman Hillmer, Bohdan Kordan, and Lubomyr Luciuk, eds., *On Guard for Thee: War, Ethnicity and the Canadian State, 1939-1945,* 101-29. Kingston, ON: Canadian Committee for the History of the Second World War, 1988.

Greenberg, Cheryl. "Black and Jewish Responses to Japanese Internment." *Journal of American Ethnic History* 14 (Winter 1995): 3-37.

-. *Troubling the Waters: Black-Jewish Relations in the American Century.* Princeton, NJ: Princeton University Press, 2006.

Grodzins, Morton. *Americans Betrayed: Politics and the Japanese Evacuation.* Chicago: University of Chicago Press, 1949.

Gudridge, Patrick O. "Remember Endo?" *Harvard Law Review* 116 (2003): 1933-70.

Guterson, David. *Snow Falling on Cedars.* New York: Vintage Books, 1995.

Hannant, Laurence. *The Infernal Machine: Investigating the Loyalty of Canada's Citizens.* Toronto: University of Toronto Press, 1995.

Harvey, Robert. *Amache: The Story of Japanese American Internment in Colorado During World War.* New York: Roberts Reinhart, 2003.

Hatamiya, Leslie T. *Righting a Wrong: Japanese Americans and the Passage of the Civil Liberties Act of 1988.* Stanford, CA: Stanford University Press, 1993.

Hayashi, Brian Masaru. *Democratizing the Enemy: The Japanese American Internment.* Princeton, NJ, and Oxford: Princeton University Press, 2004.

Hays, Arthur Garfield. *City Lawyer: The Autobiography of a Law Practice.* New York: Simon and Schuster, 1942.

Henkin, Louis. *The Age of Rights.* New York: Columbia University Press, 1990.

Hillmer, Norman, and J.L. Granatstein. *Empire to Umpire: Canada and the World to the 1990s.* Toronto: Copp Clark Longman, 1994.

Hogg, Peter W. *Constitutional Law of Canada.* 2nd ed. Toronto: Carswell, 1985.

Hohri, William Minoru. *Repairing America: An Account of the Movement for Japanese-American Redress.* Pullman: Washington State University Press, 1988.

Horn, Michiel. "'Free Speech within the Law': The Letter of the Sixty-Eight Toronto Professors, 1931." *Ontario History* 72, 1 (March 1980): 27-48.

–. *The League for Social Reconstruction: Intellectual Origins of the Democratic Left in Canada 1930-1942.* Toronto: University of Toronto Press, 1980.

Howe, R. Brian. "The Evolution of Human Rights Policy in Ontario." *Canadian Journal of Political Science* 24, 4 (December 1991): 783-802.

–. "Incrementalism and Human Rights Reform." *Journal of Canadian Studies* 28, 3 (Autumn 1993): 29-44.

Hughes, David R., and Evelyn Kallen. *The Anatomy of Racism: Canadian Dimensions.* Montreal: Harvest Books, 1974.

Iacovetta, Franca. "'A Respectable Feminist': The Political Career of Senator Cairine Wilson, 1921-1962." In Linda Kealey and Joan Sangster, eds., *Beyond the Vote: Canadian Women and Politics,* 63-85. Toronto: University of Toronto Press, 1989.

Irons, Peter. *The Courage of Their Convictions.* New York: Free Press, 1988.

–. *Justice at War: The Story of the Japanese American Internment Cases.* Berkeley: University of California Press, 1983.

Ito, Roy. *We Went to War: The Story of the Japanese Canadians Who Served during the First and Second World Wars.* 2nd ed. Stittsville, ON: Canada's Wings, 1992.

Iwaasa, David. "Canadian Japanese in Southern Alberta, 1905-1945." In Roger Daniels, ed., *Two Monographs on Japanese Canadians,* 99-155. New York: Arno Press, 1979.

Kang, Jerry. "Denying Prejudice: Internment, Redress, and Denial." *UCLA Law Review* 51, 4 (2004): 933-1013.

–. "Watching the Watchers: Enemy Combatants in the Internment's Shadow." *Law and Contemporary Problems* 68 (2005). http://ssrn.com/abstract=627401.

Kashima, Tetsuden. *Judgment without Trial: Japanese American Imprisonment during World War II.* Seattle: University of Washington Press, 2003.

Kellogg, Peter J. "Civil Rights Consciousness in the 1940s." *Historian* 42, 1 (1979): 18-41.

Kessler, Lauren. *Stubborn Twig: Three Generations in the Life of a Japanese American Family.* New York: Penguin Books, 1994.

Kitagawa, Muriel. *This Is My Own: Letters to Wes and Other Writings on Japanese Canadians, 1941-1948.* Edited by Roy Miki. Vancouver: Talonbooks, 1985.

Kogawa, Joy. *Obasan.* Toronto: Penguin, 1983.

Kraut, Benny. "Towards the Establishment of the National Conference of Christians and Jews: The Tenuous Road to Religious Goodwill in the 1920s." *American Jewish History* 77 (March 1988): 388-412.

Lambertson, Ross. "'The Dresden Story': Racism, Human Rights, and the Jewish Labour Committee of Canada." *Labour/Le Travail* 47 (Spring 2001): 43-82.

–. *Repression and Resistance: Canadian Human Rights Activists, 1930-1960.* Toronto: University of Toronto Press, 2005.

Lamson, Peggy. *Roger Baldwin: Founder of the American Civil Liberties Union: A Portrait.* Boston: Houghton Mifflin, 1976.

LaViolette, Forrest E. *The Canadian Japanese and World War II: A Sociological and Psychological Account.* Toronto: University of Toronto Press, 1948.

Lee, Carole F. "The Road to Enfranchisement: Chinese and Japanese in British Columbia." *BC Studies* 30 (Summer 1976): 44-76.

L'Heureux-Dubé, Claire. "Realizing Equality in the Twentieth Century: The Role of the Supreme Court of Canada in Comparative Perspective." *International Journal of Constitutional Law* 1, 1 (2003): 35-57.

Li, Peter S. *The Chinese in Canada.* 2nd ed. Toronto: Oxford University Press, 1998.

Lin, Elbert. "*Korematsu* Continued." *Yale Law Journal* 112 (2003): 1911-18.

MacLennan, Christopher. *Toward the Charter: Canadians and the Demand for a National Bill of Rights, 1929-1960.* Kingston and Montreal: McGill-Queen's University Press, 2003.

Magosci, Paul Robert, ed. *Encyclopedia of Canada's Peoples.* Toronto: University of Toronto Press, 1999. http://www.multiculturalcanada.ca/mcc/ecp/.

Markmann, Charles Lam. *The Noblest Cry.* New York: St. Martin's Press, 1965.

Matsumoto, Toru. *Beyond Prejudice.* New York: Friendship Press, 1946.

Matthews, Robert O., and Cranford Pratt, eds. *Human Rights in Canadian Foreign Policy.* Kingston and Montreal: McGill-Queen's University Press, 1988.

McNaught, J.K. *A Prophet in Politics: A Biography of J.S. Woodsworth.* Toronto: University of Toronto Press, 1959.

Meehan, John D. *The Dominion of the Rising Sun: Canada Encounters Japan.* Vancouver: UBC Press, 2004.

Miki, Roy. *Redress: Inside the Japanese Canadian Call for Justice.* Vancouver: Raincoast Books, 2004.

–, and Cassandra Kobayashi. *Justice in Our Time: The Japanese Canadian Redress Settlement.* Vancouver: Talonbooks, 1991.

Montagu, Ashley. *Man's Most Dangerous Myth: The Fallacy of Race.* 4th ed. Cleveland: World Publishing, 1964.

Moody, Kim. *An Injury to All: The Decline of American Unionism.* London: Verso/New Left Books, 1988.

Murray, Alice Yang, and Roger Daniels. *What Did the Internment of Japanese Americans Mean? Historians at Work.* Boston, MA: Bedford/St. Martin's Press, 2000.

Myer, Dillon. *Uprooted Americans: The Japanese Americans and the War Relocation Authority during World War II.* Tucson: University of Arizona Press, 1971.

Myrdal, Gunnar. *An American Dilemma.* New York: Harper and Row, 1944.

Nishiguchi, Gabrielle. "Innocence Lost: The Wartime Experience of Japanese-Canadian Children." *Archivist* 121 (2003): 9-13.

Nishimoto, Richard. *Inside an American Concentration Camp: Japanese American Resistance at Poston, Arizona.* Tucson: University of Arizona Press, 1995.

Norton, Mary Beth, David M. Katzman, and David W. Blight. *A People and a Nation: A History of the United States.* 4th ed. Boston: Houghton Mifflin, 1994.

O'Brien, Robert W. *The College Nisei.* Palo Alto, CA: Pacific Books, 1949.

Oiwa, Keibo. "The Structure of Dispersal: The Japanese-Canadian Community of Montreal 1942-52." *Canadian Ethnic Studies* 18, 2 (1986): 20-37.

–, ed. *Stone Voices: Wartime Writings of Japanese Canadian Issei.* Montreal: Vehicule Press, 1991.

Okihiro, Gary Y. *Cane Fires: The Anti-Japanese Movement in Hawaii, 1865-1945.* Philadelphia: Temple University Press, 1991.

–. "Japanese Resistance in America's Concentration Camps: A Re-evaluation." *Amerasia Journal* 2 (Fall 1973): 20-34.

–. "Tule Lake under Martial Law: A Study in Japanese Resistance." *Journal of Ethnic Studies* 5, 3 (Fall 1977): 71-85.

Omatsu, Maryka. *Bittersweet Passage: Redress and the Japanese Canadian Experience.* Toronto: Between the Lines, 1992.

O'Neill, William L. *A Better World. The Great Schism: Stalinism and the American Intellectuals.* New York: Simon and Schuster, 1983.

Orend, Brian. *Human Rights: Concept and Context.* Peterborough, ON: Broadview Press, 2002.

Patrias, Carmela. "Socialists, Jews, and the 1947 Saskatchewan Bill of Rights." *Canadian Historical Review* 87, 2 (June 2006): 265-92.

–, and Ruth Frager. "'This Is Our Country, These Are Our Rights': Minorities and the Origins of Ontario's Human Rights Campaigns." *Canadian Historical Review* 82, 1 (March 2001): 1-35.

Petryshyn, J. "Class Conflict and Civil Liberties: The Origins and Activities of the Canadian Labour Defense League, 1925-1940." *Labour/Le Travail* 10 (Autumn 1982): 39-63.

Pfeiffer, Paula F. *A. Philip Randolph, Pioneer of the Civil Rights Movement.* Baton Rouge: Louisiana State University Press, 1990.

Popeo, Daniel J. *Not OUR America: The ACLU Exposed!* Washington, DC: Washington Legal Foundation, 1989.

Robertson, Gordon. *Memoirs of a Very Civil Servant: Mackenzie King to Pierre Trudeau.* Toronto: University of Toronto Press, 2000.

Robinson, Greg. *By Order of the President: FDR and the Internment of Japanese Americans.* Cambridge, MA: Harvard University Press, 2001.

–. "Nisei in Gotham: The JACD and Japanese Americans in 1940s New York." *Prospects* 30 (2006): 1-15.

–. "Norman Thomas and the Struggle against Internment." *Prospects* 28 (2003): 1-15.

–. "'Two Other Solitudes': Historical Encounters between Japanese Canadians and French Canadians." 2005. http://www.discovernikkei.org/wiki/index.php/Robinson_Two_ Solitudes.

–, and Toni Robinson. "*Korematsu* and Beyond: Japanese Americans and the Origins of Strict Scrutiny." *Law and Contemporary Problems* 68, 29 (September 2005): 29-55.

Rostow, Eugene V. "The Japanese-American Cases – A Disaster." *Yale Law Journal* 54 (June 1945): 489-533.

Roy, Patricia E. "British Columbia's Fear of Asians: 1900-1950." *Histoire Sociale/Social History* 13, 25 (May 1980): 161-72.

–. "The Christian Churches and the Japanese-Canadians during and after World War II." In Ludgard De Decker, ed., *Toward a Just Society: The Interplay of Power and Influence.* Victoria, BC: Centre for Studies in Religion and Society, University of Victoria, 1998.

–. "Citizens without Votes: East Asians in British Columbia, 1872-1947." In Jorgen Dahlie and Tissa Fernando, eds., *Ethnicity, Power, and Politics in Canada,* 151-71. Toronto: Methuen Press, 1981.

–. "Lessons in Citizenship, 1945-1949: The Delayed Return of the Japanese to Canada's Pacific Coast." *Pacific Northwest Quarterly* 93, 2 (Spring 2002): 69-80.

–. *The Oriental Question: Consolidating a White Man's Province, 1914-41.* Vancouver: UBC Press, 2003.

–. "The Soldiers Canada Didn't Want: Her Chinese and Japanese Citizens." *Canadian Historical Review* 59, 3 (September 1978): 341-58.

–. *A White Man's Province: British Columbia Politicians and Chinese and Japanese Immigrants, 1858-1914.* Vancouver, BC: UBC Press, 1989.

–, J.L. Granatstein, Masako Iino, and Hiroko Takamura, eds. *Mutual Hostages: Canadians and Japanese during the Second World War.* Toronto: University of Toronto Press, 1990.

Sakamoto, Kerri. *The Electrical Field.* Toronto: Alfred A. Knopf, 1998.

Schmeiser, Douglas A. *Civil Liberties in Canada.* London: Oxford University Press, 1964.

Schwartz, Mildred A. "Citizenship in Canada and the United States." *Transactions of the Royal Society of Canada,* 4th ser., 14 (1976): 83-95.

Seidler, Murray B. *Norman Thomas: Respectable Rebel.* 2nd ed. Syracuse: Syracuse University Press, 1967.

Shaffer, Robert. "Cracks in the Consensus: Defending the Rights of Japanese Americans during World War II." *Radical History Review* 72 (1998): 84-120.

Shimizu, Yon. *The Exiles: An Archival History of the World War II Japanese Road Camps in*

British Columbia and Ontario. Wallaceburg, ON: Shimizu Consulting and Publishing, 1993.

Singh, Jarnail. "Wartime Toronto and Japanese Canadians." *Polyphony* 6, 1 (Summer 1984): 199-200.

Sittser, Gerald. *A Cautious Patriotism: The American Churches and the Second World War.* Chapel Hill: University of North Carolina Press, 1997.

Spickard, Paul R. "The Nisei Assume Power: The Japanese American Citizens League, 1941-1942." *Pacific Historical Review* 52, 2 (May 1983): 147-74.

Sunahara, Ann Gomer. "Deportation: The Final Solution to Canada's 'Japanese Problem.'" In Jorgen Dahlie and Tissa Fernando, eds., *Ethnicity, Power and Politics in Canada,* 254-78. Toronto: Methuen Press, 1981.

–. "The Japanese American and Japanese Canadian Relocation in World War II: Historical Records and Comparisons." *Canadian Ethnic Studies* 10, 31 (1978): 126-28.

–. *The Politics of Racism: The Uprooting of Japanese Canadians during the Second World War.* Toronto: James Lorimer, 1981.

Sunstein, Cass R. *Radicals in Robes: Why Extreme Right-Wing Courts Are Wrong for America.* Cambridge, MA: Basic Books, 2005.

Suzuki, Lester E. *Ministry in the Assembly and Relocation Centers of World War II.* Berkeley: Yardbird, 1979.

Svonkin, Stuart. *Jews against Prejudice: American Jews and the Fight for Civil Liberties.* New York: Columbia University Press, 1997.

Swanberg, W.A. *Norman Thomas: The Last Idealist.* New York: Charles Scribner's Sons, 1976.

Takaki, Ronald. *Strangers from a Different Shore: A History of Asian Americans.* Rev. ed. Boston: Back Bay Books, 1998.

Tan, Jin, and Patricia E. Roy. *The Chinese in Canada.* Canada's Ethnic Groups History Booklet 9. Ottawa: Canadian Historical Association, 1985.

Tarnopolsky, Walter S. *The Canadian Bill of Rights.* 2nd ed. Toronto: McClelland and Stewart, 1978.

Taylor, Sandra C. *Advocate of Understanding: Sidney Gulick and the Search for Peace with Japan.* Kent, OH: Kent State University Press, 1984.

–. "'Fellow-Feelers with the Afflicted': The Christian Churches and the Relocation of the Japanese during World War II." In Roger Daniels, Leonard J. Arrington, Harry H.L. Kitano, and Sandra C. Taylor, eds. *Japanese Americans: From Relocation to Redress,* 123-29. Salt Lake City: University of Utah Press, 1986.

–. *Jewel of the Desert: Japanese American Internment at Topaz.* Berkeley: University of California Press, 1993.

ten Broek, Jacobus, Edward N. Barnhart, and Floyd W. Matson. *Prejudice, War, and the Constitution.* Berkeley: University of California Press, 1958.

Thomas, Dorothy S., and Richard S. Nishimoto. *The Spoilage.* Berkeley and Los Angeles: University of California Press, 1946.

Thompson, R.S. *Empires of the Pacific.* New York: Basic Books, 2001.

United States. Commission on Wartime Relocation and Internment of Civilians. *Personal Justice Denied: Report of the Commission on Wartime Relocation and Internment of Civilians.* Rev. ed. Seattle: University of Washington Press, 1997.

Valverde, Marianna. *The Age of Soap, Light, and Water: Moral Reform in English Canada, 1885-1925.* Toronto: McClelland and Stewart, 1991.

Walker, James W. St. G. "Allegories and Orientations in African-Canadian Historiography." *Dalhousie Review* 77, 2 (1997): 154-77.

–. "The Fall and Rise of Africville." *Literary Review of Canada* 2 (July 1993): 3-5.

–. "The 'Jewish Phase' in the Movement for Racial Equality in Canada." *Canadian Ethnic Studies* 34, 1 (2002): 1-24.

–. *"Race," Rights and the Law in the Supreme Court of Canada: Historical Case Studies.* Waterloo and Toronto: Osgoode Society for Canadian Legal History and Wilfred Laurier University Press, 1997.

Walker, Samuel. *In Defense of American Liberties: A History of the ACLU.* New York: Oxford University Press, 1990.

Ward, W. Peter. "British Columbia and the Japanese Evacuation." *Canadian Historical Review* 57, 3 (September 1976): 289-309.
–. "The Oriental Immigrant and Canada's Protestant Clergy, 1855-1925." *BC Studies* 22 (Summer 1974): 40-55.
–. *White Canada Forever: Popular Attitudes and Public Policy toward Orientals in British Columbia.* 2nd ed. Montreal and Kingston: McGill-Queen's University Press, 1990.
Weglyn, Michi Nishiura. *Years of Infamy: The Untold Story of America's Concentration Camps.* Rev. ed. Seattle: University of Washington Press, 1996.
Weinrib, Lorraine E. "Terrorism's Challenge to the Constitutional Order." In Ronald Daniels, Patrick Macklem, and Kent Roach, eds., *The Security of Freedom: Essays on Canada's Anti-terrorism Bill,* 97-108. Toronto: University of Toronto Press, 2001.
Williams, David R. *Duff: A Life in the Law.* Vancouver, BC: UBC Press, 1984.
Xing, Jun. "Governor Ralph Carr: An American and Colorado Hero." *CASAE News* (Center for Applied Studies in American Ethnicity) 4 (November-December 1996): 4
Young, Charles H., and Helen R.Y. Reid. *The Japanese Canadians.* Toronto: University of Toronto Press, 1939.

Unpublished Works
Bagnall, John Charles. "The Ontario Conservatives and the Development of Anti-discrimination Policy, 1944 to 1962." PhD diss., Queen's University, 1984.
Bean, Barton. "Pressure for Freedom: The American Civil Liberties Union." PhD diss., Cornell University, 1955.
Brewin, John F. "'He Who Would Valiant Be': The Makings of a Canadian Anglican Christian Socialist." M. Theol. thesis, Vancouver School of Theology, 1999.
Cherniak, Saul M. "Canada and the Japanese Canadians." Paper presented before the Jewish Historical Society of Western Canada, Winnipeg, Manitoba, 1 December 1998.
Cook, Ramsay. "Canadian Liberalism in Wartime: A Study of the Defence of Canada Regulations and Some Canadian Attitudes to Civil Liberties in Wartime 1939-1945." MA thesis, Queen's University, 1955.
Grenon, Jeffrey T. "OFFENSIVE HISTORY and the GOOD WAR: The Internment of Japanese Canadians and Japanese Americans in World War II." MA thesis, Queen's University, 2001.
Harrison, M. "The Social Influence of the United Church of Canada in British Columbia, 1930-1948." MA thesis, University of British Columbia, 1975.
Hemmings, Michael. "The Church and the Japanese in Canada, 1941-1946: Ambulance Wagon to Embattled Army?" M.Theol., Vancouver School of Theology, 1990.
Holman, Andrew C. "'A Quietly Excellent Piece of International Goodwill': The Canadian-American Women's Committee, *Popular Diplomacy,* and Canadian-American Relations, 1941-69." Paper presented at the ACSUS Biennial Conference, St. Louis, Missouri, 16-21 November 2005.
Howe, R. Brian. "Human Rights Policy in Ontario: The Tension between Positive and Negative State Values." PhD diss., University of Toronto, 1988.
Lambertson, Ross. "Activists in the Age of Rights: The Struggle for Human Rights in Canada – 1945-1960." PhD diss., University of Victoria, 1997.
–. "Aroused by Injustice: The Canadian Human Rights Policy Community, 1945-1955." Paper presented at the Canadian Ethnic Studies Conference, Toronto, 24-26 March 2000.
Lord, Charles R. "The Response of the Historic Peace Churches to the Internment of the Japanese Americans during World War II." MA thesis, Associated Mennonite Biblical Seminaries, 1981.
McDaid, Thomas. "The Response of the American Civil Liberties Union to the Japanese American Internment." MA thesis, Columbia University, 1969.
Nishiguchi, R.L. Gabrielle. "'Reducing the Numbers': The 'Transportation' of the Canadian Japanese (1941-1947)." MA thesis, Carleton University, 1993.
Nunoda, Peter Takaji. "A Community in Transition and Conflict: The Japanese Canadians, 1935-1951." PhD diss., University of Manitoba, 1991.

Olyan, Sidney. "Democracy in Action: A Study of the Co-operative Committee on Japanese Canadians." MA thesis, University of Toronto School of Social Work, 1951.

Skebo, Suzanne. "Liberty and Authority: Civil Liberties in Toronto, 1929-1935." MA thesis, University of British Columbia, 1968.

Sohn, Herbert A. "Human Rights Legislation in Ontario: A Case Study." PhD diss., University of Toronto, 1975.

Sunahara, Ann Gomer. "The Wartime Experience of North American Japanese: Some Canadian and American Comparisons." Paper presented at the Canadian Historical Association annual meeting, Montreal, June 1980.

Wright, Claudia Frances Ayres. "Legitimation by the Supreme Courts of Canada and the United States: A Case Study of Japanese Exclusion." PhD diss., Claremont Graduate School, Claremont, CA, 1973.

Videos

"Of Civil Wrongs and Rights: The Fred Korematsu Story." *P.O.V.*, PBS, 11 July 2001.

"Throwaway Citizens." *The Fifth Estate*, CBC, 24 October 1995.

Interviews

Dr. Wes Fujiwara by Ms. Gayle Shellard. 1989.

Mr. George Tanaka by Mr. Gerry Shikatani. Multicultural History Society of Ontario Archives. 17 May 1978.

Transcriptions of Conversations between Justice William O. Douglas and Professor Walter F. Murphy, Cassette 8. 23 May 1962. http://infoshare1.princeton.edu/libraries/firestone/rbsc/finding_aids/douglas/douglas8.html.

Index

Note: Page numbers in italic type indicate illustrations.

Aboriginal peoples, 150
academic groups, 89-92
ACLU. *See* American Civil Liberties Union
Act Respecting Communistic Propaganda (1937), 35
advocacy, Nikkei. *See* opposition to Nikkei policies
AFL. *See* American Federation of Labor
African Americans: ACLU and, 190; CIO and, 93-94; equality for, 186, 253n10; as historical agents, 207n9; *Korematsu* case and, 185; Nikkei relations with, 150, 152-53; and racism, 36, 100, 135; responses of, to Nikkei policies, 6, 55, 70, 114, 146-47, 151-53; rights groups of, 146-47; and unions, 94
African Canadians, 150
Alberta Contact Committee, 119
Alien Land Act (California). *See* California Alien Land Act
Allen, J.B., 242n87
Allen, Richard, 79
American Civil Liberties Union (ACLU), 3, 6, 108; advocacy by, 38; and African Americans, 190; California branches of, 49, 56-58, 124, 138, 158, 161-63, 218n33; CIO and, 93; and citizenship renunciation, 33-34; civil liberties groups and, 94, 97; and compulsory civilian service, 56-57; and deportation, 67; and disaffiliation, 163, 246n30; effects of, 42; and human rights, 188; and incarceration, 58; influence of, 69; internal politics of, 49-50, 52-58, 148, 157-58, 161; and international Nikkei, 67, 221n89; JACL and, 114, 124, 135,

137; membership of, 50-52, 187; mission of, 50, 55; motivations of, 42; and Nikkei policies, 41-42, 49, 52-59, 66-69; origins of, 50; and other advocacy groups, 8, 12, 38, 40, 49, 57, 66; public relations activities of, 49, 55; and religious groups, 42, 51, 87-88; and resettlement, 87; and restitution claims, 144; and Roosevelt, 53-57, 190, 219n52, 219n58; Seattle branch of, 57-58; and social issues advocacy, 69, 186; strategies of, 188-89; tactics of, 57, 59; and test cases, 58-59, 99, 113-14, 124, 135, 137-41, 154-74, 180-82, 238n25
American Committee for Protection of Foreign Born, 93
An American Dilemma (Myrdal), 165
American Ethical Union, 186
American Federation of Labor (AFL), 93, 228n58
American Friend (journal), 75
American Friends Service Committee (AFSC), 52, 70, 71, 73, 75, 77, 139, 156. *See also* Society of Friends
American Jewish Committee, 186
American Jewish Congress, 50, 185
American Jewish Congress Women's Division, 147
amicus curiae, 58-59
Anglican Church, 72, 74, 76, 77, 80, 81, 225n32
Anti-Defamation League, 50, 186, 217n22
Arab Americans, 198-99
Armstrong, A.E., 30, 80
Armstrong (Anglican minister), 74
arrests, 121

dispersal policy, 3, 27-28, 34, 43, 46, 60, 72, 77, 82, 92, 213n27, 216n5
Dominion Franchise Act, 116
Dominion Franchise Amendment, 79
Douglas, T.C., 110
Douglas, William O., 168, 173-74
A Dream of Riches (exhibition), 195
Drew, George A., 63
Drinnon, Richard, 6
Duff, Lyman, 250n99
Duncan v. Kahanamoku (1946), 182

education: equality in, 186, 253n10; Nikkei students, 89-90, 230n92; student responses to Nikkei policies, 89-92
egalitarian rights, 9, 35
Eighth Amendment of US Constitution, 165
Eisenberg, Ellen, 6
Eisenhower, Dwight D., 230n90
Eisenhower, Milton S., 89-90, 123
Emergencies Act (1988), 195
Emergency Committee for Civil Rights, 97
employment discrimination, 141, 183, 184, 193
Endo, Mitsuye, 113, 138, 141, 154, 155, 159-60, 198, 252n9
Endo case (1944), 28, 59, 138, 141, 155-56, 159-60, 164, 166-67, 173-74, 181, 248n50
Ennis, Edward, 164
Episcopalian Church, 72
equal protection of the law, 9, 19, 159-61, 171-73
equality, struggles for, 186
Ernst, Morton, 53
Estey, J.W., 178
ethnic profiling, 198-99
ethnic studies, methodologies in, 4-5
evacuation, 10
Evans, Harold, 162
Ex Parte Endo (1944). See *Endo* case (1944)
Ex Parte Milligan (1866), 160, 245n17
exclusion, map of zones for, 15
Executive Order 9066: ACLU and, 52-57, 147-48, 162; cancellation of, 154; effects of, 22-23; legal challenges to, 154, 157-60, 173; responses to, 34, 52, 70, 72, 74, 86, 107-8; revocation of, 1
Executive Order 9102, 26, 173
expatriation: by Canada, 21; definition of, 11. *See also* deportation; repatriation

faculty, 89, 92
fair employment practices, 183, 184, 193

Fair Employment Practices Committee, 244n114
fair play, 4, 72, 76, 95, 99, 114, 115, 118, 127, 129
families, separation of: deportation policy on, 178; relocation policy on, 27, 52, 117-19
Farquharson, Mary, 57, 139, 156-59
FBI. *See* Federal Bureau of Investigation
FCSO. *See* Fellowship for a Christian Social Order
Federal Bureau of Investigation (FBI), 33, 73, 121, 199
Federal Council of Churches, 73, 77, 88, 223n9
Federal Council of the Churches of Christ (FCCC), 75
Federationist (newspaper), 109
Fee, James Alger, 159, 161, 169, 248n52
Feinberg, Abraham, 7, 63, 150-51, 220n78
Fellowship for a Christian Social Order (FCSO), 79-80
Fellowship of Reconciliation (FOR), 43, 51, 79, 81, 84, 139
Fifth Amendment to US Constitution, 160-61, 163, 171
Filipinos, 153, 185
financing of advocacy activities. *See* fundraising
Finerty, John, 51
Finlay, James, 47, 63, 146
Fisher, Galen, 94-95, 125-26, 223n12, 231n110, 232n111
fishing boats, impounding of, 20
Flynn, Elizabeth Gurley, 50, 218n25
Ford, Gerald R., 1
Foreign Missions Conference, Presbyterian Church of North America, 8, 72
Forsey, Eugene, 35, 48
Forster, Clifford, 59, 126, 139, 157, 162, 164
Fortune (magazine), 100
442nd Regimental Combat Team, 3, 28
Fourteenth Amendment to US Constitution, 9, 18, 161, 211n33
Fowke, Edith, 102, 201; *They Made Democracy Work*, 102-3
Fowler, J.H., 47
Fraenkel, Osmond, 160, 162-64, 166, 181
Frager, Ruth, 7
franchise. *See* voting rights
Franco, Don, 47, 91
Frankfurter, Felix, 174, 247n47, 249n73
Fraser Valley, 21